SMART SURVl

Over the last decade, law enforcement agencies ⸺ged in increasingly intrusive surveillance methods, from location tracking on cell phones to reading metadata off of e-mails. As a result, many believe we are heading towards an omniscient surveillance state and irrevocable damage to our privacy rights. In *Smart Surveillance*, Ric Simmons challenges this conventional wisdom by taking a broader look at the effect of new technologies and privacy, arguing that advances in technology can enhance our privacy and our security at the same time. Rather than focusing exclusively on the rise of invasive surveillance technologies, Simmons proposes a fundamentally new method of evaluating government searches – based on quantification, transparency, and efficiency – resulting in a legal regime that can adapt as technology and society change.

RIC SIMMONS is the Chief Justice Thomas J. Moyer Professor for the Administration of Justice and Rule of Law at the Moritz College of Law at The Ohio State University. He is the coauthor of four textbooks on evidence and criminal procedure, and he has published over two dozen scholarly articles in law journals. His scholarship focuses on the Fourth Amendment and how courts and legislatures should react to the impact of new technologies in regulating surveillance.

Smart Surveillance

HOW TO INTERPRET THE FOURTH AMENDMENT IN THE TWENTY-FIRST CENTURY

RIC SIMMONS

Ohio State University Moritz College of Law

CAMBRIDGE
UNIVERSITY PRESS

CAMBRIDGE
UNIVERSITY PRESS

University Printing House, Cambridge CB2 8BS, United Kingdom

One Liberty Plaza, 20th Floor, New York, NY 10006, USA

477 Williamstown Road, Port Melbourne, VIC 3207, Australia

314–321, 3rd Floor, Plot 3, Splendor Forum, Jasola District Centre, New Delhi – 110025, India

79 Anson Road, #06–04/06, Singapore 079906

Cambridge University Press is part of the University of Cambridge.

It furthers the University's mission by disseminating knowledge in the pursuit of
education, learning, and research at the highest international levels of excellence.

www.cambridge.org
Information on this title: www.cambridge.org/9781108483605
DOI: 10.1017/9781108692939

First published 2019

Printed in the United Kingdom by TJ International Ltd. Padstow Cornwall

A catalogue record for this publication is available from the British Library.

ISBN 978-1-108-48360-5 Hardback
ISBN 978-1-108-72896-6 Paperback

Contents

Acknowledgments

For their feedback on earlier incarnations of this work, I would like to thank Kiel Brennan-Marquez, Carin Ciano, Bryan Choi, Peggy Davis, Kris Franklin, David Gray, Mike Hintze, Dennis Hirsch, Renée Hutchins, Mary Leary, Rebecca Lipman, Michael Mannheimer, Lawrence Rosenthal, Laurent A. Sacharoff, Andrew Selbst, Christopher Slobogin, Stephen Smith, and Natalie Venatta. I also want to thank the participants in the 2012 South East American Law School Conference, the 2016 Privacy Law Scholars Conference, the 2017 Big Data and Criminal Law Round-table, and the 2018 CrimFest conference. Further thanks to Daniel Colston Courtney Cook, Justine Daniels, Erin Hassett, Joe Jakubowski, Kelsey Kornblut, Paige Weinstein, and Amanda Wood for their research assistance. Above all, and as always, thanks to Angie Lloyd for constant support and invaluable feedback.

Portions of the following articles appear in substantially reworked form in this book: *From Katz to Kyllo: A Blueprint for Adapting the Fourth Amendment to Twenty-First Century Technologies*, 53 HASTINGS L.J. 1303 (2002); *Can Winston Save Us from Big Brother? The Need for Judicial Consistency in Regulating Hyper-Intrusive Searches*, 55 RUTGERS L. REV. 547 (2003); *Technology-Enhanced Surveillance by Law Enforcement Officials*, 60 N. Y. U. ANN. SURV. AM. L. 711 (2005); *Why 2007 Is Not Like 1984: A Broader Perspective on Technology's Effect on Privacy and Fourth Amendment Jurisprudence*, 97 J. L. & CRIMINOLOGY 531 (2007); *Ending the Zero-Sum Game: How to Increase the Productivity of the Fourth Amendment*, 36 HARV. J. L. & PUB. POL'Y 549 (2013); *Quantifying Criminal Procedure: How to Unlock the Potential of Big Data in Our Criminal Justice System*, 2016 MICH. ST. L. REV. 947 (2016).

Introduction

The Myth of the Surveillance Panopticon

The telescreen received and transmitted simultaneously. Any sound that Winston made, above the level of a very low whisper, would be picked up by it; moreover, so long as he remained within the field of vision which the metal plaque commanded, he could be seen as well as heard. There was of course no way of knowing whether you were being watched at any given moment. How often, or on what system, the Thought Police plugged in on any individual wire was guesswork. It was even conceivable that they watched everybody all the time. But at any rate they could plug in your wire whenever they wanted to. You had to live – did live, from habit that became instinct – in the assumption that every sound you made was overheard, and, except in darkness, every movement scrutinized.[1]

George Orwell, 1984

George Orwell's chilling vision of the future showed how a totalitarian state could use new technologies to destroy privacy and freedom. Orwell wrote the novel in 1948,[2] when computers filled entire rooms, processing data at a snail's pace. Television was in its infancy, and devices like thermal imagers and particle detectors existed only in science fiction.[3] At the dawn of this technological revolution, Orwell presented a clear message: new technologies would allow the state to dramatically increase its power over the individual, enabling totalitarian states to control every aspect of its citizens' lives.[4]

Many people today have come to believe that our world is starting to resemble Orwell's dystopia. They read about law enforcement agents using powerful new surveillance technologies and react with trepidation.[5] Over the last century, the government has tapped our phones;[6] installed video cameras and hidden microphones in our offices, homes, and hotel rooms;[7] intercepted our e-mails;[8] scanned crowds for images of our faces;[9] monitored our web browsing;[10] seized and copied our hard drives;[11] and even looked through the walls of our houses.[12] The National Security Agency runs secret programs using third party companies that collect our e-mails, browsing history, telephone calls, social media, and stored data. Law

1

enforcement agencies use devices known colloquially as "Stingrays" which can mimic cell phone towers and intercept our telephone calls.[13] Video cameras watch us from fixed locations throughout the city, satellites monitor us from space, and soon drones will fill the skies to monitor our movements.

Politicians,[14] judges,[15] Fourth Amendment scholars,[16] and lay people[17] from across the political spectrum have reacted with anxiety and alarm, calling for greater regulation from courts or legislatures to protect our privacy rights. The message is nearly unanimous: modern technology poses a grave threat to our privacy, and we must act quickly to reign in the overbearing surveillance state.

This book challenges the conventional wisdom and argues that new surveillance technologies are perfectly compatible with strong privacy protections. To achieve this compatibility, modern surveillance techniques require different methods of evaluation and regulation based on a new paradigm that measures the efficiency of the new technology and then compares the efficiency with existing surveillance techniques. Under this new paradigm, we will find many contexts in which new surveillance technology can increase privacy when compared to traditional surveillance techniques. In other contexts, new surveillance methods can provide more security without any significant loss in privacy. But to maximize the efficiency of these technologies, we must adopt a fresh perspective on regulating government surveillance. We must move away from the Orwellian paradigm that views technology as the enemy of privacy rights and find ways to make technology, including surveillance technology, enhance our privacy.

UNPRECEDENTED CHALLENGES TO FOURTH AMENDMENT LAW

Law enforcement surveillance in the United States is regulated primarily by the Fourth Amendment, as interpreted by the courts. Like most constitutional provisions, the Fourth Amendment uses broad language, prohibiting "unreasonable searches and seizures" and requiring a warrant to be supported by "probable cause." The most specific language in the Fourth Amendment states that people should be secure in their "houses, papers, and effects."[18]

The Fourth Amendment arose out of a series of eighteenth-century abuses involving government agents. In two famous British cases from the 1760s, royal agents investigating "seditious libel" against the King entered the homes of pamphleteers and seized all of their papers.[19] Meanwhile, in the colonies, British customs inspectors obtained broad search warrants that allowed them to search any private residence or business for contraband, a practice that led to a number of lawsuits and standoffs between colonists and British authorities.[20] In responding to these abuses, it is logical that the drafters of the Fourth Amendment were concerned specifically with protecting houses and papers.

For over a century after the Fourth Amendment was ratified in 1791, government surveillance was a straightforward affair: there were no actual "police" as we currently understand the term (the first metropolitan police force was not created until 1844,[21] and the Federal Bureau of Investigation was not founded until 1908).[22] Government agents conducting surveillance were still mostly customs agents looking for contraband. Neither their methods of surveillance nor the places and things they were surveilling changed in any significant way from colonial times. The Fourth Amendment was rarely invoked but worked fairly well when it was, prohibiting government agents from entering a person's home or going through his or her papers without a warrant. The warrants needed to be supported by probable cause – defined as "a reasonable ground of suspicion"[23] that the defendant was guilty.

In the early twentieth century, new technologies began to change surveillance methods. The invention of the telephone allowed individuals to communicate privately with each other from long distances, enabling conspirators to manage their criminal enterprises without leaving their homes. Government agents responded with a new surveillance technique: wiretapping telephones to listen in on these private conversations.

In its initial attempt to apply the Fourth Amendment's eighteenth century language to new technology, the United States Supreme Court failed miserably. The government had wiretapped the telephone of Roy Olmstead, whom they suspected of running a large bootlegging operation. Olmstead argued that the wiretap violated his Fourth Amendment rights. In a 1928 decision, the Court examined the language of the Fourth Amendment and concluded that no search occurred because the government agents had not entered Olmstead's home.[24] According to the Court, "[t]he reasonable view is that one who installs a telephone instrument with connecting wires intends to project his voice to those quite outside, and that the wires beyond his house, and the messages passing over them, are not within the protection of the Fourth Amendment."[25]

Over the next few decades, the Supreme Court struggled to apply the Fourth Amendment to other new technologies. The advent of the automobile allowed criminals to transport contraband quickly and secretly. Law enforcement responded by stopping and searching cars – and all the containers inside the car – without obtaining a warrant. The Court faced a choice: permit this practice and reduce the privacy of everyone in an automobile, or prohibit the practice and allow criminals to freely move contraband out of reach while the police went to a judge for a warrant. Since its first automobile search case in 1925, the Court has struggled with how to apply the Fourth Amendment in this context: it has decided over a dozen cases involving searches of automobiles and their contents,[26] and has overruled its own precedent six times.[27]

As the twentieth century progressed, technological advances began to change surveillance tools as well. Police officers traced suspects with small mobile tracking devices; they employed informants wearing miniature recording devices; they used drug-sniffing dogs; they installed devices that obtained outgoing phone numbers; they flew airplanes and helicopters over homes and businesses, using telescopic cameras to photograph details on the ground and in backyards; and they conducted mandatory urine testing for drugs on state employees.[28] The Supreme Court had to judge the legality of these searches by applying Fourth Amendment language that was meant to prohibit customs inspectors and British soldiers from ransacking homes. These cases pushed the traditional method of interpreting the Fourth Amendment to the breaking point – and all of these examples are over thirty years old.

The last thirty years have only exacerbated this problem. Technological innovations have given us new ways to communicate and store information and have also given the police new methods of obtaining that information. Private citizens own smart phones, encryption software, and other devices that allow us to convey information in ways unfathomable two centuries ago. We use computers which can hold the equivalent of millions of pages of information, and we store even greater amounts of information in the cloud. We spend hours each day on the Internet, while leaving data trails for others to follow. Law enforcement officials gather information with Internet sniffers, drone-mounted cameras, DNA sequencing, and thermal imagers. Meanwhile, we give private companies billions of pieces of data, which the companies then provide to the government, who process the information with big data algorithms.

The Supreme Court has taken important steps to adapt to these innovations. In the early years of Fourth Amendment jurisprudence, the Court evaluated government surveillance with a formalist binary test. If the government surveillance intruded on the defendant's property rights, the court deemed the surveillance a "search" and the defendant received full Fourth Amendment protections; if the surveillance did not infringe on property rights, it was not a search and was completely unregulated by the Fourth Amendment. In the late 1960s, the Court adopted two revolutionary changes to this doctrine. First, in 1967, the Court adopted a new test for whether a surveillance constituted a "search" by focusing on whether the surveillance violated the defendant's reasonable expectation of privacy.[29] One year later, the Court abandoned its binary "search-or-no-search" rule and created a new legal standard of "reasonable suspicion" for less intrusive methods of surveillance[30] thus creating different tiers of surveillance with different legal standards to govern each tier.

These doctrinal shifts helped the Court navigate the evolving technologies of the late twentieth century, but they are insufficient to address modern surveillance techniques. This book proposes that it is now time for the Court to create a new doctrinal framework, analogous to the bold changes the Court made in the late 1960s. First, the Supreme Court needs to realign its "reasonable expectations of privacy" analysis so that it is more precise and more reflective of what society actually believes is intrusive. Second, the Court must adjust its legal standards to incorporate new quantitative tools that are more and more commonplace in law enforcement investigations, such as big data algorithms that can predict criminal behavior. Finally, the Court must expand the number of legal standards applicable to surveillance so that each standard more precisely matches the level of intrusiveness of the surveillance. These changes will require the Court to move away from the zero-sum game approach[31] that currently dominates its jurisprudence and evaluate new surveillance methods through a new lens: the cost–benefit analysis theory.

THE ZERO-SUM GAME MENTALITY

Over the past few decades, the Court has generally followed a specific doctrine known as the "equilibrium adjustment theory" when applying the Fourth Amendment to new technologies.[32] The equilibrium adjustment theory is based on a fundamental truism of criminal procedure: that the goal of policymakers is to strike the appropriate balance between liberty and security. The underlying assumption is that there is, and always will be, a trade-off between liberty and security, and the only way to get more security is to forfeit some liberty. The job of the courts is to mediate that struggle, to be referees in the "game" of cat-and-mouse between the police officer and the criminal. Before the Fourth Amendment was written, the parameters of the game were well-established by Benjamin Franklin, who declared: "[t]hey who can give up essential liberty to obtain a little temporary safety, deserve neither liberty nor safety."[33]

Judges frequently refer to criminal investigations as a competitive enterprise, in which the job of the courts is to maintain the equilibrium between both sides. The Supreme Court has repeatedly stated that the purpose of the Fourth Amendment is to act as a safeguard against the law enforcement officer "engaged in the often competitive enterprise of ferreting out crime."[34] In a seminal article in the *Harvard Law Review* setting out the equilibrium adjustment theory,[35] Professor Orin Kerr argued that "the basic dynamic of Fourth Amendment law resembles a zero-sum game,"[36] and asserted that the fundamental principle driving Fourth Amendment jurisprudence over the past hundred years has been the courts' desire to maintain an "equilibrium" between police power and civil liberties.[37] As new technologies are developed and put into use by criminals or by law enforcement officials, the equilibrium is disrupted, and the law must adjust to restore the appropriate balance.

This zero-sum model can be represented by a one-dimensional graph, with privacy on one end of the spectrum and security on the other end of the spectrum. The first step requires the society to decide where it wants to set the original balance:

Privacy ---------**X**----------------------**X**----------------------**X**----------------------**X**------- **Security**
　　　　　　　Anarchy　　　　　　Libertarian　　　　　Law and order　　　Totalitarian
　　　　　　　　　　　　　　　　ideology　　　　　　　ideology　　　　　　state

FIGURE 1

Professor Kerr sets the balance by imagining a "Year Zero," an imaginary time when police investigated crime without any special investigatory tools, and when criminals committed crime without any special technologies to aid them.[38] The goal of the equilibrium adjustment doctrine is to ensure that the balance between security and privacy remains. Assume the balance between privacy and security at Year Zero fell somewhere close to the middle, perhaps leaning somewhat towards privacy rights:

FIGURE 2

Assume that a technological innovation arises that increases privacy, such as the automobile.[39] When compared to Year Zero, individuals can now transport themselves and their cargo quickly and in relative secrecy, which increases privacy. Criminals also get the benefit of this technology, making it easier for them to avoid detection, which decreases security. Now, in situations where suspects use automobiles, the balance has shifted towards privacy rights, and away from security. This disrupts the equilibrium:

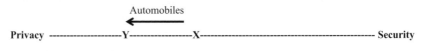

FIGURE 3

The law then reacts – in this case, by loosening the rules on surveillance to allow police to search cars without a warrant.[40] This change restores the equilibrium to (roughly) the level it was at Year Zero:

FIGURE 4

This equilibrium adjustment process occurs with every type of new technological innovation that individuals (and criminals) use to increase their privacy, such as telephones[41] or personal computers. It also applies to new technological innovations that increase the government's surveillance power. For example, assume the government begins to use thermal imagers to detect the heat patterns emanating from a home.[42] These devices increase security by helping police detect the presence of heat lamps, which criminals can use to secretly grow marijuana indoors. But they also reveal some intimate details about the home that police could not have known in Year Zero without entering the home.[43] Thus, the courts will intervene with a new legal rule: the police may not use a thermal imager unless they first obtain the warrant. This warrant requirement means that the interior of the home has as much privacy as it did in Year Zero. It also neutralizes the security benefits of the new surveillance technology: we are at exactly the same level of privacy and security as we were before this new surveillance technology was invented. This demonstrates how the equilibrium adjustment theory always provides a zero-sum result; we can never improve our security nor lose any privacy when applying this theory.

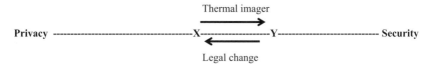

FIGURE 5

A NEW PARADIGM

The equilibrium adjustment theory is relatively simple to apply and it appeals to our sense of fairness; after all, what could be more fair than to maintain the balance that we have lived with for decades? But as societal and technological changes become more pronounced, certain flaws in the equilibrium adjustment theory become apparent.

The first problem is the absence of any normative proof that the balance of "Year Zero" is the right balance. Professor Kerr envisions Year Zero as a time before criminals or police were able to use tools to commit or investigate crime. The Supreme Court appears to have set Year Zero as the date when the Fourth Amendment was adopted; in a recent case, the Court stated that "we must assure [] preservation of that degree of privacy against government that existed when the Fourth Amendment was adopted."[44] Either way, the goal of the equilibrium adjustment theory is to return us to the balance that existed between privacy and security in an era over two hundred years ago.

There is no reason, however, to believe the balance of that era was the optimal balance for society. [45] Even if Year Zero did feature the ideal balance between privacy and security at the time, that ideal balance may have evolved as society changed. In Year Zero, for example, it may have been sensible to create a rule that an individual surrenders all Fourth Amendment rights in information that shared with third parties. If you write a letter to your friend detailing your plans to kill your neighbor, and the friend then decides to share the letter with the police, it would make no sense for you to claim that the government was violating your Fourth Amendment rights by reading the letter. But in modern society, we unavoidably reveal vast amounts of information to hundreds of private corporations, and many of us believe that this information deserves some privacy protections. Thus, changes in technology and in society will alter the optimal balance between privacy and security. The equilibrium adjustment theory has no way of accommodating that changing standard; it will always assume that Year Zero's balance for third-party information is optimal.

Similarly, changes in society or technological advances may result in an *increased* need for security in certain areas. For example, at Year Zero, it was illegal to search a suspect without some evidence specific to the suspect that he was committing a crime. Courts have generally adhered to this rule, known as the individualized suspicion requirement. But after a series of airplane hijackings in the late 1960s, the federal government in 1970 instituted mandatory searches of all individuals who were about to board an airplane, with no individualized suspicion requirement.[46] If courts had blindly followed the equilibrium adjustment theory, they would have struck down these searches to restore the balance from Year Zero. But in evaluating these cases, courts refused to follow the equilibrium adjustment model and instead recognized that the new danger posed by hijackers required a change in the balance between privacy and security in this context. These courts have permitted suspicionless airport searches even though they do not neatly fit into Fourth Amendment doctrine.

The second and more fundamental problem with the equilibrium adjustment theory is that it adopts the traditional zero-sum paradigm involving privacy and security. But there is not always a one-for-one trade-off between privacy and security. It is possible, in other words, to increase privacy without affecting security; or, conversely, to increase security without affecting privacy. To illustrate, we need to stop thinking about privacy and security as opposite poles of a single axis, but instead as two independent variables on a two-dimensional graph. This two-dimensional graph will still contain our initial line showing the trade-off that usually occurs between privacy and security, as in our automobile example.

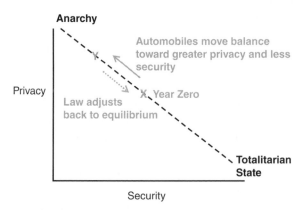

FIGURE 6

In the automobile example, the balance between privacy and security remains on the zero-sum line, reflecting that in this situation there can be no gain to privacy without a loss to security. But this new, two-dimensional representation allows us to contemplate situations in which there is not a one-for-one trade-off between security and privacy; situations in which one value can increase while the other stays constant, creating a positive-sum game.

A positive-sum change can occur because of a technological advance. For example, assume that law enforcement agents searching for firearms can use metal detectors instead of subjecting individuals to a pat-down. The metal detectors are just as accurate in detecting firearms, so there is no loss in security, but the privacy intrusion is much lower, so individuals experience an increase in privacy.

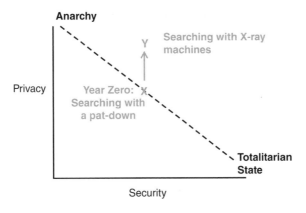

FIGURE 7

Another example involves so-called Internet sniffers. These are software programs that can search through immense amounts of data looking for specific key words and images. Imagine that a law enforcement agent believes that a suspect is guilty of distributing child pornography through e-mail. The agent could look through all the suspect's e-mails for the next few months to see if there are any child pornography attachments. This would be an effective method of detecting criminal activity, but it would come at a very high price to the suspect's privacy. Whether the suspect is guilty or innocent, the agent will have inspected a large amount of private communications.

Now assume that the agent instead installs an Internet sniffer on the suspect's email account and programs the sniffer to only alert the agent if the sniffer finds a child pornography image. The level of security will be the same: if the suspect transmits child pornography, the agent will know about it. But the privacy intrusion will be much less, since the agent will learn nothing else about the suspect's e-mails (and if the suspect is in fact innocent, the agent will learn nothing at all about the suspect's e-mails).

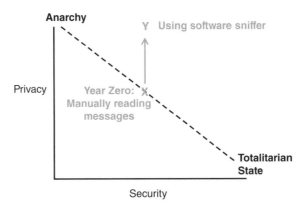

FIGURE 8

Other technological changes, from big data algorithms to gun detectors to continuous GPS monitoring, have created the possibility of similar positive-sum changes.

But they also raise important and challenging questions about how best to regulate these new technologies, such as whether to consider the economic cost of the surveillance method or the severity of the crime being investigated.

In order to improve on the equilibrium adjustment theory, our new paradigm must be dynamic, in the sense that it needs to respond to changing expectations of privacy or new security needs. In order to achieve that flexibility, it needs to be able to measure both the level of intrusion posed by different types of surveillance and the security benefits that the surveillance provides. Finally, the paradigm needs to acknowledge that the trade-off between privacy and security is not a zero-sum game, and it ought to encourage surveillance methods that allow for a positive-sum change. The cost–benefit analysis theory proposed in this book meets all of these criteria. It represents a fundamental rethinking of how courts approach this problem, but the proposed changes are no more radical than the changes the Supreme Court made in the late 1960s when it adopted the *Katz* "reasonable expectation of privacy" test and created different tiers of surveillance in *Terry* v. *Ohio*.[47] In fact, many facets of the cost–benefit analysis theory are updates to these earlier changes: the theory requires us to measure reasonable expectation of privacy (and other levels of intrusiveness) with greater precision and creates more tiers of surveillance to reflect the realities of modern surveillance.

MOVING FORWARD

The first section of the book will describe the cost–benefit theory. Chapter 1 introduces the theory by examining how to measure the costs of different types of surveillance, particularly the cost to our privacy. Currently the Supreme Court determines these costs, but the Court is poorly situated to make these determinations. Under the current regime, the Court usually only rules on whether the intrusiveness of a particular surveillance exceeds a certain threshold of intrusiveness – that is, whether the surveillance is a "search." But the cost–benefit theory requires a more precise calculation of the level of intrusiveness; it requires a measurement of the degree to which the surveillance infringes on our privacy. Furthermore, the Supreme Court decides only one or two cases a year on this issue, which is insufficient to keep up with the multitude of new types of surveillance that occur in modern investigations.

Chapter 2 focuses on the benefits side of the equation and notes that the rise of big data's predictive algorithms allows law enforcement to measure the likely success rate of surveillance with far greater precision than previously possible. These predictive algorithms have the potential to revolutionize criminal investigations in many ways, making them cheaper, more accurate, and less biased. However, surveillance technologies must be designed in ways to ensure that they meet the Fourth Amendment's requirement of particularized suspicion and to ensure that they do not rely on tainted data.

In Chapter 3 the book addresses another challenge of applying the cost–benefit analysis theory: how to incorporate quantified costs and benefits into a legal system that currently uses broad, descriptive standards to evaluate searches. We will see that descriptive standards are inconsistently applied in their current form, and thus provide inadequate guidance for police attempting to follow them. The chapter also points out the dissonance between the manner in which judges apply the current standards and the way in which lay people believe the standards should be applied. Quantifying the applicable legal standards will make the standards more transparent and allow judges to apply a greater range of standards. Quantification will also allow judges to use the results of predictive algorithms as formal factors when evaluating the legality of particular forms of surveillance.

The next section of the book applies the cost–benefit analysis theory to various methods of technology-enhanced surveillance. The book divides these surveillance methods into four broad categories: reactive surveillance, in which the government adopts new surveillance technologies in order to keep up with privacy-enhancing technology; binary searches, which collect information without infringing on legitimate privacy rights; mosaic searches, which collect and process massive amounts of publicly available information; and hyper-intrusive searches, which allow the government to detect our most private, intimate information.

Chapter 4 begins by examining reactive surveillance, such as thermal imagers, decryption tools, and devices that reveal the phone numbers that are being dialed on a telephone. These are tools which the government needs in order to respond to privacy-enhancing technology used by private citizens. Although reactive surveillance tools can be very intrusive, in most contexts they are only being used to learn information that would ordinarily be public but has been hidden by new forms of privacy-enhancing technology, such as heat lamps, cell phones, and encryption tools. In evaluating reactive surveillance, we need to consider both the level of criminal activity that is potentially masked by the privacy-enhancing technology, and how the privacy-enhancing technology has affected society's expectations of privacy. In the context of encryption, we need to assist law enforcement even further, by creating a key escrow system which will give law enforcement the ability to decrypt any piece of data upon obtaining the proper legal authority.

Chapter 5 describes a uniquely productive type of surveillance known as a binary search. Binary searches reveal no information other than the absence or presence of illegal activity. The Supreme Court has determined that a binary search does not implicate the Fourth Amendment, since an individual does not have a legitimate expectation of privacy in illegal conduct. The cost–benefit analysis theory encourages binary searches, because they are the archetypal example of positive sum surveillance: if designed properly, they can increase the level of crime detection without increasing the level of privacy infringement. Soon facial recognition technology and advances in crime recognition software will allow law enforcement to achieve nearly 100% enforcement for certain crimes. Such a development, though theoretically desirable, has potentially negative side effects, especially in the current environment of overcriminalization.

Chapter 6 examines mosaic searches, and discusses the potential and challenges created by big data surveillance. Recent developments in surveillance technology allow police to engage in various methods of widespread, low-cost surveillance, from tracking a person's location through her cell phone to predicting behavior based on a person's telephone records, credit card purchases, and other publicly available details. Data points will only become more numerous in the future, as camera-mounted drones and self-driving cars become common. Courts and legislatures have been wary of these widespread surveillance techniques, and in fact have sought to restrict them because their financial cost is so low that they allow law enforcement to engage in nearly indiscriminate surveillance. But the cost–benefit analysis theory shows that courts should adopt the opposite approach: all other factors being equal, a surveillance method that is less expensive should be encouraged, not restricted. Furthermore, encouraging low-cost widespread surveillance will help to even out the massive inequities we now see in government surveillance, where the poor and people of color bear a much greater cost than more enfranchised and less surveilled citizens. Finally, applying the cost–benefit analysis theory will require the government to demonstrate the benefits of indiscriminate surveillance, which will encourage the government to develop and utilize more productive (and less intrusive) methods of surveillance.

Chapter 7 explores a specific aspect of mosaic searches: information that individuals turn over to private companies. Under the controversial third-party doctrine, individuals surrender all Fourth Amendment rights when they share information with a third party. In modern society, we routinely share vast amounts of private information with a variety of companies and organizations; this trend will accelerate with the emerging technology of smart devices and the "Internet of Things." These developments have led most legal scholars to criticize the third-party doctrine as anachronistic and a significant threat to privacy. This chapter will argue that the conventional wisdom is wrong for two reasons. First, modern information sharing enhances our privacy; thus, some aspects of the third-party doctrine can be classified as reactive surveillance. But more importantly, the cost–benefit analysis theory reveals that this massive private collection could result in a positive-sum shift in surveillance. On the privacy side, corporations themselves can assert their own Fourth Amendment rights to keep this information secret – a phenomenon we are already seeing in many technology companies that store and transfer our data.[48] On the security side, millions of companies are constantly collecting billions of pieces of data, all of which can be available to help solve crimes when the government can meet the appropriate standard to overcome the companies' Fourth Amendment rights.

Chapter 8 discusses the final category of technology enhanced surveillance: hyper-intrusive searches. These searches occur when law enforcement agents use surveillance technology to see and hear private, intimate information that would otherwise be undetectable. This category includes video monitoring of private places and real-time interception of oral or digital communication. This type of surveillance unquestionably needs greater regulation; the question is what form that regulation will take. This chapter reviews the variety of different tools that courts have at their disposal to regulate hyper-intrusive searches and examines which of these tools will make these searches more productive.

The primary theme of this book is that we should not regard new technology as an enemy to privacy, even when the government is wielding it as a surveillance tool to investigate crime. Our own use of technology has already enhanced our privacy considerably and will continue to do so, and with the appropriate regulatory paradigm, the government's new surveillance tools can dramatically enhance our security with minimal effect on our privacy. The first step in developing this regulatory regime is to move away from the zero-sum game that currently dominates the Court's analysis. Therefore, we will begin our discussion by proposing the cost–benefit analysis theory as the fundamental basis for regulating government surveillance.

1

The Cost–Benefit Analysis Theory

When you get the dragon out of his cave on to the plain and in the daylight, you can count his teeth and claws, and see just what is his strength. But to get him out is only the first step. The next is either to kill him, or to tame him and make him a useful animal. For the rational study of the law the blackletter man may be the man of the present, but the man of the future is the man of statistics and the master of economics.

Oliver Wendell Holmes, *The Path of the Law* (1897)

INTRODUCTION

Our first step in breaking out of the zero-sum mentality is to see the criminal justice system not as a *competition* between police and criminals, but instead as an *industry* with inputs (costs) and outputs (benefits); that is, to apply the basic principles of economics to the field of criminal procedure. Although the Law and Economics movement has been around for nearly sixty years,[1] there has been surprisingly little application of economic principles to criminal procedure.[2] Judge Richard Posner's foundational textbook *Economic Analysis of the Law* for example, devotes only five of its 716 pages to criminal procedure.[3] Perhaps this is because criminal procedure, unlike tort law or contract law, deals with fundamental rights, which are less amenable to cost–benefit analysis.[4] But the mere fact that the Fourth Amendment protects fundamental rights does not mean that we cannot apply economic principles to evaluate it. If the goal of applying the Fourth Amendment is to achieve the proper balance between privacy rights and the needs of law enforcement, economic principles can inform that analysis.[5]

The goal in applying these economic principles to Fourth Amendment law is to increase the efficiency of the criminal justice system – that is, to maximize output while minimizing costs. This focus on efficiency does not mean that we are indifferent to the constitutional rights of our citizens. To the contrary, the potential infringement of these rights is one of the costs that we are seeking to minimize. Another more quantifiable cost is the tangible monetary cost incurred by law enforcement organizations (and thus ultimately by society) to undertake a given type of surveillance.[6] The output that we are seeking is crime control, or more specifically in the Fourth Amendment context, the identification of those who are guilty of a crime and collection of evidence which can be used to demonstrate their guilt.[7] As the zero-sum equilibrium adjustment model predicts, there generally is a positive correlation between our inputs (the money we spend and the degree to which we infringe on our own freedom) and our output (identifying the guilty and recovering incriminating evidence). In other words, it is generally true that the more we "spend" – either by giving up privacy or expending resources – the more we receive in benefits.

But this is not always the case. And herein lies the primary advantage of applying the cost–benefit analysis theory to evaluate law enforcement surveillance: once we use economic analysis to measure the costs and benefits of different surveillance methods, we can see that there are two ways in which Fourth Amendment doctrine could in fact be a positive-sum game. First, advances in surveillance technology can increase the effectiveness of catching criminals without reducing the privacy rights of ordinary citizens – that is, it is possible to increase the output without increasing the cost.[8] And second, changing norms and attitudes may decrease the value of certain kinds of privacy to individuals, causing the cost of certain types of surveillance to decrease. Unfortunately, this means that Fourth Amendment doctrine can also be a negative-sum game. Criminals can also take advantage of technological advances, which will decrease the benefits of the system as costs are held constant. Likewise, evolving societal norms could make certain types of privacy more valuable, thus increasing the cost of certain kinds of surveillance with no increase in benefits. But by using the cost–benefit analysis theory, we can identify the surveillance methods that create positive-sum changes and those that create negative-sum changes.

Another advantage is that the cost–benefit analysis theory helps identify potential trade-offs in the system between different costs. For example, more money spent on training police could result in less infringement on constitutional rights while maintaining the same level of output (that is, detecting the same amount of evidence of criminal activity). More controversially, we may be able to keep the same level of output by adopting newer types of surveillance that are less expensive but result in greater infringement on our privacy rights. It may well be that this latter trade-off is one that many people will never want to undertake, as even a savings of millions of dollars is not worth even a slight loss of privacy rights. But an economic analysis of the question at least makes that choice more transparent.

Once we have identified the productivity of different forms of surveillance, we can take steps to encourage more productive types of surveillance and discourage the less productive ones. This can be done in several ways. First, courts could adjust the legal standard of suspicion that law enforcement must show before engaging in different methods of surveillance. If a certain surveillance method is very product-ive – that is, if it produces a high level of output with a low cost in terms of resources and infringements on our privacy – then courts could encourage law enforcement agents to use this surveillance method by lowering the level of suspicion necessary before the government is allowed to engage in the surveillance.[9] Second, law enforcement officers could be given more or less freedom to act before obtaining approval from courts or other authorities. For more productive searches, the police would be permitted to engage in the search as long as they had the requisite level of suspicion without the requirement of obtaining a warrant or a court order from a magistrate. Finally, less productive searches could be discouraged by adding other requirements besides requiring a certain level of suspicion, such as requiring the police to prove that the search is the least restrictive means of obtaining the infor-mation, or that the search be conducted in such a way as to minimize the amount of non-criminal information that is obtained. All of these methods are currently used to different degrees to regulate government surveillance in different contexts; the cost–benefit analysis theory seeks to harmonize these different restrictions into a more cohesive organization.

APPLYING ECONOMIC ANALYSIS TO FOURTH AMENDMENT DOCTRINE

The first step is to create a formula that takes all of the relevant costs and benefits into account. We should note at the outset that this formula is not meant to be literally applied; as of now, the technology does not exist to accurately quantify the cost and benefits of every type of surveillance. Instead, we will use this formula as a tool to re-conceptualize the way we think about the relationship between surveil-lance, privacy, and security.

Until recently, scholars had done little to apply economic principles to questions of criminal procedure.[10] Those that did tended to focus on the post-arrest aspects of criminal procedure – for example, how to regulate plea bargaining or prosecutorial discretion to produce an optimal result.[11] In 2003, Professor Craig Lerner provided the first serious attempt to apply economic principles to the Fourth Amendment when he proposed a formula for determining whether probable cause exists in a certain case.[12] Professor Lerner chose as his starting point the famous Learned Hand formula from tort law, which is used to calculate whether a party has been negligent. Under Hand's formula, a party is negligent if the burden, or cost, of taking precau-tions to prevent an accident (B) is less than the probability of the accident occurring (P) times the social loss of the accident (L). In mathematical terms, if $B < P * L$, then the defendant was negligent.[13]

Professor Lerner adapts the formula to the criminal procedure context by propos-ing that a search would be reasonable if the social cost of the search in terms of the intrusion on privacy (C) is less than the social benefit (B) of the search multiplied by the probability of the search being successful (P).[14] In mathematical terms: If $C < P * B$, then the search is reasonable and probable cause exists.[15] Professor Lerner fine-tunes his formula with a few more variables,[16] but this basic principle remains the foundation of his argument.

Professor Lerner intentionally deviates from established Fourth Amendment doctrine in one very significant way: he considers both the likelihood of success of the surveillance and the severity of the crime being investigated as factors in determining whether probable cause exists.[17] In other words, the social benefit "B" in his formula is not a constant, but a variable – it will be higher if the police are investigating a rape or a murder, and lower if they are investigating a petty larceny or a simple assault. It will also be higher if the search is very likely to uncover evidence of a crime, and lower if it is a mere fishing expedition that has a low likelihood of producing useful evidence. Consequently, under Professor Lerner's formula, a court may find probable cause to support an intrusive search (with a high "C") if the police are investigating a particularly severe crime or had a good chance of uncovering evidence. On the other hand, under this formula, a court would conclude that there was no probable cause to support the same search if the alleged crime were less severe or the likelihood of success was low.[18] This approach is consistent with Professor Lerner's economic analysis methodology: to weigh the costs and benefits of a particular course of action, it is important to have a realistic – as opposed to a formalistic – evaluation of the likely benefits. Professor Lerner also argues that this approach is supported both by common sense and by the "reasonableness" language of the Fourth Amendment.[19] Indeed, a number of other scholars have proposed that courts should take into account the severity of the crime at hand in assessing Fourth Amendment "reasonability,"[20] though this approach has gained very little traction with the courts.[21]

We will use Professor Lerner's formula as the starting point for our analysis. The principle is simple: every type of surveillance has a cost and an expected benefit. Professor Lerner uses this formula to determine whether probable cause exists in a particular case. If the expected benefit exceeds the expected cost, there is probable cause, and a search should be permitted.[22] Our focus, however, is somewhat different. We are not attempting to create a minimum standard for when a type of surveillance should be permitted; instead, we are attempting to measure the efficiency, or productivity, of any given type of surveillance. Once we determine which type of searches are the most efficient, we can devise legal rules which encourage more efficient searches and discourage the less efficient ones.[23]

Therefore, our formula should take the form of an equation, in which the resources and costs (C) are the inputs to the system and the benefits (B) are the output.[24] To make the equation balance, we will add a variable X to the left side of the equation to act as the conversion rate between the costs and the benefit. In economic terms, X is the "productivity" of the system – if X is high, we receive a large amount of output in exchange for a small amount of input. If X is low, we receive a small amount of output in exchange for a large amount of input.[25] Our equation thus begins simply:

$$(C * X) = B$$

For example, when the police enter someone's home to conduct a search, the cost "C" is very high; when they conduct a brief frisk of a suspect, C is somewhat lower. If the search is extremely likely to turn up strong evidence of a serious crime, such as a 75% chance that the police will recover a bloody knife with the perpetrator's fingerprints on it, then the benefit "B" is very high. On the other hand, if the search only has a 10% chance of recovering evidence of a minor shoplifting crime, B is very low.

The productivity, X, will vary depending on the type of surveillance that is used. If the productivity is high (lots of benefits at a very low cost), we should encourage the surveillance and set a very low legal standard for police who want to engage in the surveillance. If the productivity is low (very little benefit and very high cost), we want to set a very high legal standard. Thus, to determine the productivity for each type of surveillance, we must first define the costs and benefits of the equation.

As noted above, we are not seeking to fill in actual numbers for these variables; in most cases, it will be difficult, if not impossible, to calculate precise values for these factors. The point of creating the equation is fivefold. First, it increases the transparency of the system, so that we can better understand the advantages and disadvantages of each type of surveillance. Second, it forces judges and other policymakers to consider the impact of surveillance more holistically by examining all the costs and benefits of a given type of surveillance. Third, the equation gives us a tool for comparing different surveillance methods, enabling us to design laws and regulatory regimes that encourage higher productivity searches and discourage lower productivity searches. Fourth, it encourages those who carry out the surveillance and those who evaluate the surveillance to seek out empirical evidence to measure the costs and benefits, even if the measurements cannot be exactly precise. Finally, the equation provides a guide to developing flexible and scalable legal standards and restrictions for those searches; as we will see in Chapter 3, courts and legislatures have already developed a tiered approach in creating standards for searches, and calculating the productivity for each surveillance type will assist us in determining what tier the surveillance belongs in.

COSTS OF SURVEILLANCE

The cost of a given type of surveillance can be divided into two categories: (1) the amount of resources (money, time, and equipment) that are used in conducting the surveillance; and (2) the degree to which the surveillance violates privacy interests. The expenses of the first category, known as "administrative costs," are borne directly by law enforcement.[26] Thus, they are already internalized by the police and need not be considered when calculating the cost of the surveillance. If a certain type of surveillance is very inexpensive relative to comparably effective surveillance, law enforcement agencies will already face the appropriate incentives to switch to the less expensive surveillance. For example, if a CCTV camera offers the same surveillance benefits as a police officer stationed at a guard post, law enforcement agencies will tend to switch to the camera to lower their administrative costs. Since the point of determining the productivity of the search is to provide police with the proper incentive structure in developing or employing certain types of surveillance, there is no need to include costs which are already internalized by the police. Nevertheless, before we move forward with the formula, it is worth examining the ways in which new technologies have changed the administrative costs of surveillance.

First, we must acknowledge that many new technologies available to the general population have *increased* the administrative cost of surveillance by making it harder for law enforcement to detect criminal activity. The best example of this is the invention of telephone in 1876. The telephone has probably done more to decrease the productivity of law enforcement surveillance than any other single device in history. Ever since the telephone became ubiquitous – and ever since Congress decided to prohibit warrantless surveillance of telephonic communications in 1934[27] – criminals have been able to use the telephone to shield their communications. They use it to plan with co-conspirators, transfer funds from place to place, or facilitate interactions with customers for drug sales, prostitution, and gambling activities. Before the advent of the telephone, all these communications either had to take place in person, requiring meetings in public places or travelling on public streets, or by writing (a much less efficient method which leaves a permanent record of the illicit transactions). Once these communications could take place indoors, safe from the eyes of investigating officers, the cost of surveillance for many crimes increased substantially even as its success rate dropped significantly.

Over the past thirty years, the widespread use of computers and Internet communications has once again dramatically lowered the productivity of law enforcement surveillance. Courts (and Congress) are still working through the extent to which these activities implicate the Fourth Amendment,[28] but the ability of criminals to store, transfer, and encrypt data has certainly made surveillance of their activities more expensive and less successful. We will explore these types of technological changes, and the new surveillance techniques that law enforcement officers have used to counter them, in Chapter 4.

Other forms of new technology have decreased the administrative cost of surveillance by providing law enforcement officers with new tools to conduct their investigations. Many of these new technologies provide the same success rate as the traditional surveillance that they replace, but they represent an unambiguous improvement in Fourth Amendment productivity because they provide that identical benefit more cheaply than before. For example, computerized recordkeeping and modern data search techniques allow police officers to investigate many crimes instantaneously from the dashboard computer of their cars. If they suspect that a car they see on the road might be stolen, police officers can enter the license plate number into their computer and quickly connect to a database of stolen cars. If they suspect that an individual whom they have pulled over has an outstanding warrant or a suspended driver's license, they can check local, state, and federal records within a matter of minutes.[29] Similar technology allows police to check the fingerprints of suspects to see if they have committed other crimes, or have outstanding warrants under different names.[30]

The other category of surveillance costs is the privacy cost. In contrast to administrative costs, the privacy costs of surveillance are external – that is, they are borne not by the actor conducting the surveillance, but by those who are the subjects of the surveillance.[31] Thus, the privacy cost needs to be included in the formula when calculating the productivity of the surveillance. The privacy cost of a specific type of surveillance encompasses many different factors, including the level of physical intrusion onto the suspect, the loss of dignity to the subject of the search, the number of people affected by the search, the amount of time the search takes, how private the information obtained may be, and whether the search was conducted in public or in private.

Quantifying the value of an invasion of privacy is a challenging exercise. Lack of privacy creates at least two types of tangible economic costs, as well as a significant intangible cost. The two tangible costs can be categorized as avoidance costs and defensive costs.[32] Avoidance costs are the losses that occur when a lack of privacy causes individuals to refrain from socially useful (but perhaps embarrassing) activities, such as buying condoms or visiting a therapist.[33] Defensive costs are the money people spend to protect their privacy when they feel their privacy is at risk – such as encoding e-mails, building high fences over their yards, or driving to meet someone in person rather than speak to her over the telephone.[34]

Surveillance also has an intangible cost because privacy has its own intrinsic value. Privacy allows us to engage in many activities which may not have economic value, but which create utility for those who engage in them, such as sunbathing naked in the backyard or saying intimate things to a spouse over the telephone. Privacy is also critical to our political system, because more privacy fosters communication and interaction among those who hold political views which may be unpopular.

Calculating the intangible value of a privacy interest is further complicated by the fact that our conception of privacy is a moving target that evolves over time. The Supreme Court has held that the Fourth Amendment's privacy interest is triggered in one of two ways: first, if the government surveillance commits a physical intrusion or trespass onto the subject's property interest;[35] or second, if the government surveillance infringes on the suspect's reasonable expectation of privacy.[36] The first type of privacy is unlikely to change much with time, but society's reasonable expectation of privacy can shift as new technologies become more prevalent and as cultural norms evolve.[37] Like other factors we will consider, this shift can work both ways: some aspects of life that we originally considered public we may now reasonably expect to be private, whereas other aspects of life that we originally considered to be private can now be thought of as public. The cost–benefit calculation needs to take these changes into account and discourage the use of surveillance methods whose heightened privacy cost has now made them less productive, while encouraging law enforcement officials to take advantage of lower privacy expectations in other contexts.

Two hundred years ago, citizens had a very different conception of privacy than we do today.[38] In certain aspects, modern citizens experience – and therefore expect – greater privacy than citizens did in the past. A couple of centuries ago, most Americans worked in the open fields, traveled from one place to another by walking or riding on horseback while exposed to the world, and engaged in private conversations only when visiting each other in their homes. Today, many Americans have a private workspace, most travel insulated in a private car, and almost everyone expects to be able to have a private conversation with anyone else in the country at any time or place that they choose. In other ways, our expectation of privacy is lower today than in the past. For example, given the ubiquitous nature of electric light, we no longer expect the night-time darkness to hide our activities. We also know that, at any time, planes and satellites (whether used by the government or a private company like Google) can see and record the exterior of our homes and private land, and even our own movements. We expect to see surveillance cameras in private businesses and even in public spaces.[39] In still other contexts, we are struggling to understand what level of privacy we expect to have. New concepts such as social media, Internet search engines, and cloud storage are changing our perceptions about what information should be kept private and what information is fair game for public exposure.

Frequently, this shift in what we reasonably expect to be private is caused not by the *invention* of the new technology, but by its subsequent widespread use throughout society. It was not the invention of the airplane in the nineteenth century, but rather its ubiquitous use in the mid-twentieth century that led the Court to hold in *California* v. *Ciraolo*, that an individual had no reasonable expectation of privacy in what could be seen from the air.[40] The Court acknowledged the potential of new technologies to change expectations of privacy in *United States* v. *Kyllo*, stating that using a thermal imager to gather information previously unknowable without physical intrusion by using "a device that is not in general public use."[41] If, in the near future, we all carry thermal imagers on our smart phones and routinely point them at houses to see where heat is emanating, the occupants of those houses would presumably lose their reasonable expectation of privacy in that information, and law enforcement agents could freely use thermal imagers without a warrant. As the

Court stated in *Kyllo*, "[i]t would be foolish to contend that the degree of privacy secured to citizens by the Fourth Amendment has been entirely unaffected by the advance of technology."[42]

Widespread use of new technologies can also *increase* society's reasonable expectation of privacy. In 1986, when the internet was young and unknown to the general population, Congress passed the Electronic Communication and Privacy Act (ECPA), which set rules for monitoring voice and electronic communication. Under the ECPA, voice communication received robust protection, and the ECPA provided a suppression remedy, mandating that all evidence obtained in violation of the ECPA be excluded from court.[43] But electronic communication did not receive the same level of protection.[44] Law enforcement officers did not need to meet the same standards to receive a warrant to intercept e-mails or access stored e-mails,[45] and if they did violate those rules, the ECPA did not require suppression.[46] At the time, legislators believed that the internet was developing into a tool for commerce, which deserved less protection than the sometimes intimate conversations that occurred using the telephone.[47] Furthermore, e-mails easily could be intercepted by the government because they were transferred and stored by third-party internet service providers. Thus, Congress reasoned, most people using the internet would not expect the same level of privacy as they would when speaking on the telephone.[48]

These assumptions may have been true in 1986 when the ECPA was passed. But as the technology of electronic communication has become widespread – indeed, as it has become the primary method of interpersonal communication for a large number of Americans[49] – our reasonable expectation of privacy in electronic communications has shifted. Courts are now properly recognizing this shift and extending full Fourth Amendment protection to electronic communications, thereby overruling the ECPA's anachronistic judgment on the degree of privacy that should be afforded to this medium. In 2010, the Sixth Circuit held in *United States* v. *Warshak* that e-mails deserved the same protection as telephone conversations, arguing that "the Fourth Amendment must keep pace with the inexorable march of technological progress, or its guarantees will wither and perish."[50]

Thus, in our formula, C_p (the privacy cost) is not constant for any given form of surveillance. It will increase or decrease as certain types of technology become more widespread (as with airplanes and perhaps, someday, thermal imagers), or as technology is used in different ways (as with the Internet).

But new uses of technologies are not the only way that reasonable expectations of privacy can change: cultural and economic shifts can also change what we consider to be private. Today, we are in the midst of a significant cultural shift regarding our expectation of privacy for the information we share online and the information we share with private companies. Many younger Americans have grown up with the expectation that information about themselves will be shared through social media sites, public blogging, or smart phone applications that reveal where they are at all

times. Some scholars call this generation "digital natives,"[51] and surveys have shown
that they consistently display less concern about keeping information about themselves private than the "digital immigrants" who did not grow up amid the ubiquity
of information-sharing technology.[52] Other surveys have shown that digital natives
are indeed concerned with privacy, but that they are less concerned about the type
of information that is shared and more concerned about who has control of their
information.[53] This generation has grown up in the era of massive corporate data
collection, in which private companies like Google and Facebook and even retail
stores collect information about customer preferences and then use it to target
advertising or sell it to others.[54]

Eventually, these digital natives will become a majority of the population, and
they will likely maintain their different – and in some ways, more relaxed – attitudes
about data privacy as they get older.[55] Thus, society's reasonable expectation of
privacy will diminish, at least with regard to the personal and commercial data that
digital natives are accustomed to sharing.[56] This inexorable shift has caused some
scholars concern. For example, Professor Teri Baxter argues that the shift will
"erode" Fourth Amendment protection.[57] Professor Baxter proposes legislative fixes
or altering the "reasonable expectation of privacy" test itself.[58]

But Professor Baxter and others who propose solutions to this supposed problem
fail to demonstrate why this shift in our reasonable expectation of privacy – and the
resultant loosening of Fourth Amendment restrictions – is a problem to be solved in
the first place. This is another example of the zero-sum mentality: the implicit
assumption that the amount of privacy that we now enjoy from government searches
is the optimal (or at least the minimum sufficient) amount; thus, any technological
or societal change which lowers this amount of privacy is a negative development.
Thus, the reflexive response is to change the law to return to the pre-existing levels of
privacy.

This response is short-sighted. The "reasonable expectations" standard is meant to
be a flexible one; it ought to adjust as the amount of privacy that we expect evolves.
If as a society we become more willing to tolerate certain invasions of our privacy,
the C_p, or privacy cost, of certain types of surveillance decreases, thus making those
types of surveillance more productive. The level of intrusiveness of a surveillance
method is not measured against a fixed scale, but against the subjective belief of the
individual and the reasonable belief of society. In other words, the changing
expectations of privacy is not a problem to be solved, but an opportunity to use
certain surveillance methods more frequently because these methods are no longer
perceived to be as intrusive as they used to be.

As an example, consider the surveillance of text messages by employers, as
described in the 2010 Supreme Court case *City of Ontario* v. *Quon*.[59] In *Quon*, a
city employer issued pagers to all of its workers, but notified its workers that it had
the right to monitor the content of those texts at any time.[60] Later, the employer read
through the plaintiff's texts and noticed that some of the texts were sexually

explicit.[61] The plaintiff then sued the city employer, alleging that when the city read his texts, it violated his reasonable expectation of privacy.[62]

The trial court and appellate court both found that the plaintiff had a reasonable expectation of privacy in the content of the texts that he sent using the government pager.[63] The legal question was a tricky one, requiring courts to interpret the fractured Supreme Court decision of *O'Connor* v. *Ortega*, where a state-run hospital conducted a search of the office and files of one of its employees.[64]

In *Quon*, the Supreme Court avoided the question of whether the plaintiff had a reasonable expectation of privacy in the context of his text messages. The Court explained that the *Katz* standard must remain a flexible one:

> Rapid changes in the dynamics of communication and information transmission are evident not just in the technology itself but in what society accepts as proper behavior. As one *amici* brief notes, many employers expect or at least tolerate personal use of such equipment by employees because it often increases worker efficiency. Another *amicus* points out that the law is beginning to respond to these developments, as some States have recently passed statutes requiring employers to notify employees when monitoring their electronic communications. At present, it is uncertain how workplace norms, and the law's treatment of them, will evolve.
>
> Even if the Court were certain that the *O'Connor* plurality's approach were the right one, the Court would have difficulty predicting how employees' privacy expectations will be shaped by those changes or the degree to which society will be prepared to recognize those expectations as reasonable. Cell phone and text message communications are so pervasive that some persons may consider them to be essential means or necessary instruments for self-expression, even self-identification. That might strengthen the case for an expectation of privacy. On the other hand, the ubiquity of those devices has made them generally affordable, so one could counter that employees who need cell phones or similar devices for personal matters can purchase and pay for their own. And employer policies concerning communications will of course shape the reasonable expectations of their employees, especially to the extent that such policies are clearly communicated.[65]

The Court re-affirmed this position in *United States* v. *Jones* in 2012:

> Dramatic technological change may lead to periods in which popular expectations are in flux and may ultimately produce significant changes in popular attitudes. New technology may provide increased convenience or security at the expense of privacy, and many people may find the tradeoff worthwhile. And even if the public does not welcome the diminution of privacy that new technology entails, they may eventually reconcile themselves to this development as inevitable.[66]

In other words, as technology and societal norms change, the C_p for a given type of surveillance also changes. Professor Baxter correctly points out that for many new technologies, this will result in a lowering of our expectation of privacy as the younger generation begins to replace the digital immigrant generation:

Youth and young adults may believe that any expectation of privacy when using many forms of technology is unreasonable. This may reflect their greater understanding of the technology and the risks involved in using almost any technology. They may be familiar with successful attempts to hack into or access codes or accounts, and understand that few if any sites or accounts are truly secure. Consequently, they may consider any subjective expectation of privacy to be unreasonable.[67]

Professor Baxter means this to be a warning – as a dire consequence which must be avoided – and she proposes new tests to prevent this legal shift from occurring.[68] But nowhere is it written in stone that the contents of text messages on government-issued pagers must be protected by the Fourth Amendment. Indeed, the entire point of a flexible *Katz* test is that *nothing* about what the government is or is not allowed to search is written in stone. If in fifty years society no longer considers the content of text messages to be private, there is no reason to limit government surveillance of those messages.

In short, the failure to acknowledge the evolution of society's reasonable expectation of privacy is another weakness of the zero-sum equilibrium adjustment model.[69] Should we really base society's current expectation of privacy on what law enforcement could accomplish back in the 1970s? Is it the job of the courts to freeze our expectation of privacy at a certain point in time, and keep it at that level regardless of what the vast majority of individuals may come to believe is publicly available information? If so, what era should we look to when we determine what the "proper" level of privacy is? Should it be 1967, when the *Katz* case was decided? Or, should it be 1791, when the Fourth Amendment was ratified? At any rate, the Court has made it clear in *Ciraolo* and *Kyllo* that the *Katz* test was *not* meant to freeze a certain expectation of privacy in place; instead, the standard was meant to adjust to new technological and societal changes.

Of course, society's reasonable expectation of privacy can shift both ways, as we saw with the ECPA and e-mail contents. Our paradigm for surveillance regulation needs to keep up with how this expectation shifts in either direction over time. Otherwise we run the risk of either overregulating certain surveillance methods based on outdated conceptions of what people wish to keep private, or under-regulating other surveillance methods based on a misunderstanding of how intrusive people actually believe the surveillance to be.

CALCULATING THE PRIVACY COST

Given the constantly evolving technology and ever-changing societal values, it may seem impossible to determine the privacy cost of any given type of surveillance. The challenge is amplified by the fact that our system's current method of determining the privacy cost for different types of surveillance is imperfect, to say the least. Under the current system, this task falls primarily to the Supreme Court, as it evaluates the constitutionality of different types of surveillance in cases that come before it. There are several problems with this method. First, the Court's decisions are imprecise. The Court has effectively created four categories of surveillance. At the lowest level is surveillance which is completely unregulated by the Fourth Amendment, such as following someone on a public street. The next level is surveillance that is classified as a "search," but which law enforcement is allowed to engage in if they have reasonable suspicion, such as stopping a person on the street and asking them questions. The third level is surveillance that is classified as a search – looking through a car or a home – which requires probable cause, and usually a warrant. At the highest level, are the "hyper-intrusive searches," such as no-knock search warrants and bodily intrusions, which require law enforcement to meet a higher standard than probable cause.[70] But in the vast majority of cases, the Court classifies surveillance into the first or third category. Only one type of surveillance – the stop and frisk – has been placed into the second category, and only four or five have been placed into the fourth category. Thus, in the vast majority of cases, the Court only tells us whether the surveillance does or does not infringe on our reasonable expectation of privacy, not the *degree* to which the surveillance intrudes on our privacy.

Second, using the Supreme Court to determine the privacy cost of various types of surveillance is a very slow process. The Court only hears a handful of Fourth Amendment cases each year, and only some of these rule on whether a type of surveillance is a search.[71] Since the Court adopted the "reasonable expectation of privacy" test in 1967, it has ruled on fewer than forty different types of government surveillance – an average of less than one per year. Given the wide diversity of surveillance methods, the rapid advance of technology (which is both giving the government new surveillance tools and creating new types of devices that the government needs to search), and our own constantly evolving expectations of privacy, there is no way the Court can provide enough guidance to police or to lower courts at that deliberative pace.

Most importantly, however, the Court's vision of what does and does not constitute a search often does not match up well with society's conception of privacy. Consider a partial list of what does and does not violate our "reasonable expectation of privacy," according to the Supreme Court:

"Unreasonable Search" – Violates Our Reasonable Expectation of Privacy

Wiretapping a conversation on a public telephone
Stopping and frisking a suspect on the street
Using a tracking device to track an item on private property
Reaching inside a vehicle and moving papers to see the VIN number
Moving stereo equipment to read a serial number
Thermal imaging of a home
Taking a cheek swab for DNA sample
Conducting breath and blood tests for alcohol[72]

Not an "Unreasonable Search" – Does Not Violate Our Reasonable Expectation of Privacy

Police informant wears an electronic listening device during a conversation with suspect
Obtaining customer records from banks
Searching a car that the passengers and drivers did not own
Obtaining phone numbers that were dialed from a certain phone line
Using a tracking device to follow a car for one trip on a public road
Drug-sniffing dogs sniffing unopened luggage in a public space
Trespassing onto private property some distance from the home
Looking through garbage left out for collection
Observing private property from a helicopter hovering at four hundred feet
Drug-sniffing dog smelling the exterior of a car during a traffic stop[73]

Many of these decisions cut against our own intuitions of what violates our reasonable expectation of privacy. Most people would be surprised to learn that a police officer reading a stereo's serial number or a car's vehicle identification number infringes on the owner's reasonable expectation of privacy.[74] And as we shall see below, a substantial number of people believe their reasonable expectation of privacy is being infringed upon when police officers trespass onto their property, or sift through their garbage, or fly a helicopter overhead to look down on their greenhouse. As Justice Scalia once noted, the definition of "reasonable expectation of privacy" "bear[s] an uncanny resemblance to those expectations of privacy that [the Supreme] Court considers reasonable."[75] Often the Court arrives at the wrong answer.

The Court's ability to provide legal guidance about whether surveillance infringes on our privacy interest will be further hampered by its ill-advised decision in the 2012 case of *United States* v. *Jones*.[76] In *Jones*, the Court supplemented its reasonable expectation of privacy test with the "trespass" doctrine, holding that the government conducts a Fourth Amendment search when it invades an individual's property interest.[77] Although this doctrine has sound historical roots,[78] it provides very little guidance to lower courts, law enforcement, or the general population as to what actions intrude on our privacy interests in today's digital age. It also focuses on the wrong question: when evaluating whether a government action implicates our Fourth Amendment rights, most people would not care about whether the action intrudes on our property rights, but rather whether (or, more importantly, to what degree) the action invades our privacy. Consider the three cases in which the Court has applied the *Jones* physical trespass doctrine. In *Jones* itself, the government placed a small object underneath the defendant's car in a way that was not visible to anyone and which did not harm the car's operation in any way.[79] In *Florida* v. *Jardines*, the police walked onto the defendant's front porch with a drug-sniffing dog.[80] And in *Grady* v. *North Carolina*, the government forced the defendant to wear an ankle bracelet to monitor his location.[81] In all of these cases, the Court applied the trespass doctrine and determined that a Fourth Amendment search occurred. But in each of these cases, the government action that would be most objectionable was not the trivial intrusion onto property rights, but rather the information that was gathered by means of that intrusion – that is, the privacy intrusion.[82] For example, assume the government had merely placed an inert box underneath Jones' car; or had walked onto Jardines' porch with a dog that had no drug-sniffing abilities; or had required Grady to wear a piece of plastic around his ankle. None of these actions would appear to violate the Fourth Amendment; at best they are a nuisance, not an infringement onto our constitutionally protected rights. Thus, the Court's detour into the physical trespass doctrine makes it even less useful as an arbiter for when our privacy rights have been implicated.

Fortunately, there are other sources for determining the degree of privacy intrusion of each of these surveillance methods. Some empirical work has already been done: in a seminal 1994 article,[83] Professors Christopher Slobogin and Joseph E. Schumacher surveyed over 200 individuals and developed an "Intrusiveness Rating Score" for fifty types of government surveillance. Respondents were asked to measure, on a scale of 0 to 100, the extent to which the surveillance was an "invasion of privacy or autonomy." The surveillance methods ranged from relatively nonintrusive (such as going through foliage in a park or looking down a dark alley with a flashlight) to relatively intrusive (such as reading a personal diary or monitoring a phone for thirty days).

Unlike the Supreme Court's decisions, the results of the Intrusiveness Rating Scores seem far more intuitively correct. As the authors noted, although the survey results were consistent with some Supreme Court jurisprudence,[84] they diverged in many significant areas. For example, law enforcement trespassing on private fields or using a dog to sniff for narcotics are both considered not to be searches by the Supreme Court, but they ranked relatively equal to a pat down, which the Court has held is a search.[85]

Professor Slobogin has repeated this research many times, adding on new types of surveillance with each survey.[86] As he and his original co-author acknowledge, these findings are subject to a number of potential criticisms,[87] but at the very least they provide an excellent starting point if we are ranking the level of intrusiveness of various forms of government surveillance. And recently other scholars have conducted their own surveys on a variety of different types of surveillance, including monitoring locations through cell phones and tracking online purchase history.[88] Nearly every empirical study has noted a wide gap between the Supreme Court case law and the opinions of the general population as to which types of surveillance violate society's reasonable expectation of privacy.[89]

Some modern Fourth Amendment scholars have begun advocating for expanding the use of this kind of empirical work in determining the intrusiveness of different surveillance methods.[90] But there are also other potential methods of evaluating the intrusiveness of a given type of surveillance. For example, Santa Clara County in

California requires law enforcement agencies to prepare an "Anticipated Surveillance Impact Report" before it purchases any new surveillance tool, describing both the fiscal cost and the "potential impact on civil liberties and privacy" of the new device. These documents must describe "[t]he potential impact(s) on civil liberties and privacy, and a description of whether there is a plan to address the impact(s)."[91] Professor Michael Gentithes favors using a "sensitivity index" in certain contexts to determine how much protection information should have, and he proposes that parties and amici could guide the courts by presenting arguments as to where information falls along the sensitivity index.[92]

Once these intrusiveness costs are calculated, there needs to be a mechanism for integrating them into the law. This integration could happen informally, as courts begin to pay attention to the relevant empirical research and even cite the results of these studies in their opinions. This would still be a very slow process, however, and there would be no way of ensuring uniformity as to what type of empirical evidence the court would use. Furthermore, courts have been reluctant to rely on empirical evidence in determining the intrusiveness of a search, preferring instead to rely on their own intuition. A more radical solution would be to have a separate institutional entity measure and set these numbers. Legislatures could do the methods fact-finding and then pass laws that classify surveillance types into different categories based on their intrusiveness levels. Or the legislature could delegate the task to an administrative agency, which would conduct its own research and then categorize surveillance types.

The Controlled Substance Act (CSA) could act as a model for this mechanism. When Congress passed the CSA in 1971, it set up five different schedules of drugs, described the characteristics that would lead a specific drug to be categorized in each schedule, and then categorized every significant drug into one of the five schedules. It then delegated to the Drug Enforcement Agency and the Federal Drug Administration the authority to review these categorizations and recategorize any existing controlled substance as appropriate, as well as the authority to categorize any new controlled substances not covered by the original law. This process was necessary because new types of drugs were appearing with regular frequency, and Congress would be unable to keep up if it tried to categorize them on its own.

A similar process could work to establish the intrusiveness of surveillance methods. Congress could set up a scheduling scheme with five or six categories, from Schedule I for the most intrusive searches (such as wiretapping or in-home video surveillance) to Schedule VI for the least intrusive (such as a subpoena for business documents). The agency could use surveys, hearings, and other research to determine which surveillance types belong in each category, and the agency could regularly update the schedule, moving surveillance methods up or down the ladder as societal expectations of privacy change. Courts could then use these schedules as evidence of the level of intrusiveness involved with each type of surveillance under review.

Another possible way to force police to internalize the privacy cost of the surveillance would be to combine the administrative cost with the privacy cost. Professor Miriam H. Baer has proposed an innovative system for accomplishing this goal.[93] She would force law enforcement agencies to internalize the privacy cost of their actions by creating a tax on surveillance methods based on the intrusiveness of the technique. For example, a police department could be charged $5 for every stop-and-frisk it carried out, $4 for every consent search, and $2 for every automobile search. (Searches carried out with a warrant would be free, since the police obtained pre-clearance for those searches). Thus, if a city engaged in 1,000 frisks on a given year, it would have to pay $5,000. If the police recovered a high number of guns and other weapons from these frisks, it would determine that the extra money was worth the benefits, and it would continue its frisks at that rate, and perhaps even increase them. If the hit rate for its frisks was low, however, it might choose to shift to a less intrusive strategy – say, installing more cameras in public places (which are not subject to the intrusiveness tax) or seeking to engage in consensual searches, which are cheaper.[94]

Professor Baer's proposal is elegant, though she acknowledges it may have practical problems, such as whether the federal government would have the authority to tax municipal police departments[95] and the disparate income effect it would have on poorer cities.[96] It would also be difficult to translate the privacy costs of each type of surveillance into a monetary amount. Professor Baer proposes an administrative agency to calculate the privacy cost of each type of surveillance and translate the privacy cost into a monetary cost. Under the cost–benefit analysis theory, legislatures or administrative agencies would calculate the privacy costs, and then courts or legislatures would adjust the legal rules required to engage in the surveillance based on those costs.[97]

BENEFITS OF SURVEILLANCE

The benefit of a search is a function of two factors: the chance that the surveillance will be successful multiplied by the societal value of a successful surveillance.[98] Both of these factors require more explanation. First, there are two different ways that a search can be successful: gathering evidence which helps police identify the perpetrator of a crime, and gathering evidence that can be used to help convict the perpetrator in court. A given type of surveillance might provide either or both of these results, and may be successful in either category to a different degree. For example, anonymous informants may help law enforcement agents learn the identity of the perpetrator, and may provide probable cause to arrest him, but would not help to convict the perpetrator in court. Conversely, once a suspect has been identified and is in custody, law enforcement officers may conduct a number of searches of the defendant's home, car, computer, or office in order to gain more evidence to use against him.

For the purposes of our analysis, there is no reason to distinguish between the two different types of successful surveillance. Rather, what we care about is the probability that the surveillance will be helpful in convicting the correct person in court. Thus, we can gauge the success of a surveillance on a scale of zero to one – "zero" meaning that the surveillance has absolutely no chance of providing any useful information leading to the conviction of the perpetrator, and "one" meaning that the search will, with absolute certainty, reveal information that will be sure to convict the correct perpetrator. Although in the real world there will be no method of surveillance that can reach this ideal level, there are some that come close. Dashboard cameras on police cruisers that are activated during drunk driving arrests, for example, have a very strong chance of providing nearly incontrovertible evidence that a particular defendant committed the crime: there will be video evidence of erratic driving, video evidence of the defendant emerging from the driver's seat, and video evidence of his performance on the field sobriety tests.[99] On a more Orwellian level, covert video cameras in every home would be almost certain to succeed in identifying and gathering incontrovertible evidence of many crimes, from domestic violence to illicit drug use. Of course, the extraordinary cost of such surveillance – both in terms of the administrative costs and the infringement on privacy – makes this method of surveillance extremely low in productivity.

Historically, it has been nearly impossible to gauge the success rate of a given type of surveillance. Individual police departments might keep statistics on specific initiatives, such as a more aggressive stop and frisk program or the increased presence of security cameras on the streets, but it was difficult to draw broad conclusiveness about the effectiveness of different surveillance methods. With the advent of big data analysis and predictive algorithms, all of that is changing, and soon police officers will be able to input facts into a computer and receive the precise odds that they will uncover evidence of criminal activity if they engage in a frisk or a search. We will discuss the potential of this new wave of quantification in the next chapter.

The benefits of surveillance are also dependent upon the severity of the crime being investigated.[100] The more severe the crime that is being investigated, the greater the societal benefit of the surveillance. For example, we would be more willing to bear a high-cost surveillance to gather evidence in a terrorism investigation than we would to gather evidence in a shoplifting investigation.

Determining the severity of the crime being investigated is one of the easiest aspects of our project, because the criminal justice system already provides us with an unambiguous ranking of each crime on the books. Thus, we can use the length of the potential sentence as a proxy for the severity of the crime: the higher the expected sentence, the greater the societal benefit in a successful search.

So far, the Supreme Court has soundly rejected the idea that the severity of the crime should affect the evaluation of the surveillance, generally holding that one standard should apply across the board to every criminal investigation.[101] However, some commentators have argued that quantifying the probable cause standard would enable courts to adopt a sliding scale based on the severity of the crime being investigated.[102] As Professor Lerner has pointed out, lower courts have dropped some hints that the probable cause standard should be lower for police investigating a mass shooting or a kidnapped child than they would be for a low-level drug possession case.[103] Judge Richard Posner, writing an *en banc* decision for the Seventh Circuit, held that probable cause should be "a function of the gravity of the crime" in the context of exigent circumstances.[104]

Given this definition of "benefits," we can now rewrite our formula as follows:

$$C_P * X = E * S$$

In this formula, "C_P" is the privacy cost of a search. (Since the administrative cost is already internalized by the law enforcement agency, it need not be included in the formula). "E" is the percentage chance that the surveillance results in success-fully providing information that will lead to the conviction of the perpetrator (whether by correctly identifying him or by gathering admissible evidence against him), and "S" is the multiplier based on the seriousness of the crime for which the evidence is being gathered.

APPLYING THE MODEL

Now that we have a rough formula in place, we can begin to search for areas where we can achieve an increase of productivity. These increases occur when we can decrease the variables on the left side of the equation while holding the right side of the equation constant, or when we increase the variables on the right side of the equation while holding the left side of the equation constant.

One way to increase productivity is to develop surveillance techniques that provide the same level of output but cost less in terms of privacy costs. The best example of this type of surveillance is what is known as "binary surveillance." Binary surveillance refers to a surveillance method that only produces one of two results: positive (meaning that illegal activity has been detected) or negative (meaning that illegal activity has not been detected).[105] The surveillance provides no other infor-mation about the person or area being monitored, and so represents an insignificant intrusion on the target's privacy. In fact, the Supreme Court has held that binary surveillance does not even count as a "search" under the Fourth Amendment because it does not infringe on an expectation of privacy that society is prepared to recognize as legitimate.[106]

A simple example of a binary surveillance technique is a field test for narcotics. If a law enforcement officer reasonably believes that a certain substance may be narcotics, she can legally seize a very small amount of the substance and mix it with certain chemicals.[107] If the substance tests positive for narcotics, the law enforcement officer knows that the substance is contraband and that a crime has occurred. If the substance tests negative, the officer knows nothing about the substance other than the fact that it is not an illegal drug. Therefore, because the suspect has no legitimate interest in possessing contraband, assuming other procedural prerequisites are satisfied, the surveillance does not implicate the Fourth Amendment[108] – the officer either learns nothing at all about the defendant or learns that the defendant is engaging in illegal activity. We will consider the potential of binary searches in Chapter 5.

Case Study: Surveillance at Airport Security Checkpoints

Airport security checkpoints provide a relatively easy example to apply our cost–benefit analysis. Up until recently, law enforcement officials had essentially two different options at airport security checkpoints. They could conduct a brief physical search of every passenger, or they could use a magnetometer to scan every passenger for metal, and then conduct a more thorough physical search if metal was detected. By applying our formula, we can see that magnetometer surveillance has the higher productivity of the two options.

First consider the brief physical search. On the cost side of our equation, we can see that frisks carry a high cost in terms of intrusiveness – they involve physical touching and squeezing of the body, and they last over a minute on average.[109] On the Slobogin/Schumacher survey, frisks received an average score of 54.76, just below searches of newspaper offices.[110] On the other side of the equation, the success rate of frisks is substantial, but it is somewhat dependent on the level of intrusiveness of the frisk: the longer and more comprehensive the search, the more likely it is to uncover a weapon. Thus, it is hard to make productivity gains with this method because costs will inevitably rise as the expected benefits rise.

On the other hand, magnetometers carry a much lower privacy cost because they do not involve any physical touching of the suspect and they reveal no private information other than the absence or presence of metal.[142] Under the Slobogin/Schumacher survey, walking through a metal detector received a very low average "intrusiveness" score of 13.5, just above searching through foliage in a public park.[111] Magnetometers do have a significant false positive rate, in that they will frequently alert to the presence of innocuous metal as opposed to the presence of a dangerous weapon, and in these cases the suspect may be subjected to a physical frisk. But the majority of those searched will avoid a physical search, resulting in a low overall cost to privacy.[112]

The success rate for magnetometers has varied over time as both law enforcement and criminals have been able to take advantage of new technologies. As soon as the technology of metal detection advanced to the point where widespread use of these machines became economically feasible, the productivity of surveillance at airport checkpoints increased substantially because magnetometers allowed for faster, less intrusive searches than frisks and they nearly always detected the presence of weapons. However, as the technology for weapons evolved, criminals began to use weapons that are undetectable to metal detectors, such as ceramic knives or plastic explosives.[113] This in turn made the magnetometers less productive, either because of a lower success rate; or a more frequent need to resort to more intrusive physical searches.[114] Thus, law enforcement officers have now turned to a new type of surveillance: full-body scanners that use a magnetic imaging system which display an image of the person with black silhouettes of any object that the person is carrying inside their clothing.[115] These scanners involve a greater privacy intrusion than magnetometers, since magnetometers merely report the presence or absence of metal, while the full body scanners show the outline of any item the individual is carrying. (A later survey conducted by Professor Slobogin indicated that the average level of intrusiveness given to full body scanners was 67, nearly identical to a pat down of outer clothing).[116]

On the other hand, full body scanners have a higher hit rate than magnetometers, since they can detect many different types of weapons, not merely metal weapons; thus, they will detect more criminal activity. In deciding between magnetometers and full body scanners, we will have to consider the increased and privacy cost of full body scanners compared to the increased level of detection and deterrence they provide.

The Next Steps: Calculating Benefits and Quantifying Legal Restrictions

So far, we have only used the cost–benefit analysis to compare the productivity of two (or more) different surveillance options in a given context. In our airport security case study, we held a number of variables constant, such as the severity of the crime we are trying to prevent, and the context in which law enforcement is conducting the surveillance. We also took it as a given that we needed *some* type of surveillance in this context. Given these narrow circumstances, determining the most productive of the available options was relatively simple. But this is usually not the question we are trying to answer. Usually, we are addressing two far more complicated questions: should the surveillance be allowed at all, and if so, what legal rules should we impose on law enforcement before it is allowed to conduct the surveillance?

Luckily the cost–benefit analysis theory can answer these questions as well. One of the advantages of using this theory is that it can consider every relevant variable, including the severity of the crime and evolving societal expectations of privacy in different contexts. For example, society has demonstrated a rapidly diminishing reasonable expectation of privacy at airport checkpoints over the past few decades. After a wave of hijackings in the late 1960s, passengers on airplanes were willing to accept more intrusive searches in exchange for safer air travel.[117] The result was that the privacy cost of all airport searches dropped. After the terrorist attacks of September 11, 2001, a further shift in public attitudes occurred, and the general population became willing to accept even more intrusive surveillance methods at airport checkpoints. Thus, although certain types of searches (taking off shoes and belts, walking through metal detectors, submitting to a pat-down, allowing law enforcement officers to see silhouettes of items inside your clothing), may carry a high privacy cost in other contexts, the privacy cost for the identical method of surveillance at airport checkpoints is relatively small, which lowers the cost side of the equation. Furthermore, the severity of the crime being detected – an act of terrorism involving an airplane – is extremely high, which raises the benefits side of the equation.

Another advantage of the cost–benefit analysis theory is that it provides us with a value for the productivity of the search. So far we have only used this value as a point of comparison – if we have two different surveillance options, and one has a higher productivity, we should prefer the more productive search over the less productive one. But our productivity value can also be used to determine whether the surveillance should be allowed at all, and if so, what type of legal rules law enforcement officers should have to meet before being able to conduct the surveillance. For example, we could decide that some types of surveillance – government surveillance cameras watching every room of our homes, or police monitoring every e-mail and telephone call that a person makes – are so low in productivity that we should never allow them, since the benefits simply do not outweigh the enormous costs. On the other hand, other types of surveillance – using red light cameras or monitoring public twitter feeds – are so productive that the government should be allowed to engage in them without restriction, since they cost so little and bring significant benefits.

But the most interesting questions involve the surveillance methods that fall in between these two extremes. For these types of surveillance, we must determine what conditions must be present before the government can undertake these actions. This in turn requires us to measure with greater precision the benefits of the surveillance that is being proposed. Chapter 2 will explore the emerging use of big data's predictive algorithms in the criminal justice system and show how they can provide not just greater accuracy and fairness, but also the increased precision that is necessary for the cost–benefit analysis theory.

Chapter 3 will then turn to the method that we use to regulate surveillance: the legal rules that determine whether a surveillance method will be allowed. Under our legal system, these conditions are usually set out as degrees of certainty that criminal activity is present. The Supreme Court has created at least two levels of certainty: reasonable suspicion and probable cause. Legislators and lower courts have created more categories, such as the relevance standard and the "probable cause plus" standard. In order to move forward with our analysis, we need to move beyond these descriptive categories and set quantitative legal standards for different types of surveillance.

2

Measuring the Benefits of Surveillance

Whether you stand still or move, drive above, below, or at the speed limit, you will be described by the police as acting suspiciously should they wish to stop or arrest you. Such subjective, promiscuous appeals to an ineffable intuition should not be credited.

United States v. *Broomfield* (7th Cir. 2005)[1]

INTRODUCTION

The previous chapter introduced the cost–benefit analysis theory and derived a formula that would determine the productivity of any given type of surveillance. On the left side of the formula are the costs of the surveillance – both the administrative costs and the privacy costs. On the right side of the equation is the benefit of the surveillance: the chance that the surveillance will uncover evidence of criminal activity. The ratio of benefit to cost is the productivity of the search.

This chapter focuses on the benefit side of the equation. Specifically, it examines how law enforcement agencies can use big data's algorithms to predict the success rates of their surveillance with extremely high levels of precision. This precision will allow courts to make better informed decisions as to the productivity of the surveillance. Not incidentally, big data algorithms can also make the results of the surveillance more accurate in predicting criminal behavior and less biased against poor and minority communities.

But despite this potential, two significant obstacles potentially bar the effective incorporation of big data tools into criminal investigations. First, there is the danger that these predictive algorithms may be hard-wired to produce discriminatory results. If the predictive algorithms consider race or religion as a factor, then using these algorithms to predict behavior is unacceptable (and illegal) no matter how much they may increase accuracy.

Second, Fourth Amendment law mandates that decisions to stop or search a suspect be based at least in part on individualized suspicion. Because big data involves processing large amounts of information, its algorithms frequently generate predictions based on broad generalizations rather than specific conduct. Thus, in their current form, many of these algorithms cannot on their own form the basis for the legal standards of reasonable suspicion or probable cause.

These obstacles are not insurmountable barriers. Big data algorithms can be structured so that they are truly race neutral and account for individualized conduct when making their calculations. But to ensure that they meet these requirements, the factors they apply must be transparent to judges. In other words, it is not sufficient for reviewing courts to know that these algorithms are working; the courts must also understand how the algorithms work to ensure that they meet the appropriate legal standards.[2]

If those who design the big data tools can ensure the transparency of their algorithms and databases, not only will these tools become more acceptable to the courts, but the transparency of these calculations will simultaneously improve the transparency of the criminal justice system. Moreover, if courts embrace the use of numerically quantifiable data, not only will we achieve greater accuracy in the administration of justice, but we will also achieve greater clarity of the process. This increased accuracy and clarity is essential if we institute a cost–benefit analysis, since it is necessary to calculate the exact benefits of specific surveillance methods and assist in matching legal standards of review to each of those methods.

THE PROMISE OF BIG DATA: INCREASED ACCURACY

"Big data" is the practice of accumulating extraordinarily large amounts of information from a variety of different sources and then processing that information using statistical analysis.[3] The results of these analyses are termed "mechanical predictions" in contrast with subjective "clinical judgments," which are based on the individual decision-maker's past experience and knowledge.

Private companies have been using big data for over a decade to predict consumer behavior. Retailers use it to determine and change shopping habits.[4] Insurance companies rely on big data to try to identify the safest drivers and healthiest people in their customer pool.[5] Banks and credit agencies use big data to determine the likelihood that a potential borrower is a credit risk.[6] And all sorts of companies buy and sell this data to each other, seeking to mine it for information about their customers that they can use for economic advantage.[7]

In the criminal law context, mechanical predictions can be used to assist decision-makers in making the judgment calls that are integral to the criminal justice system. They are used to provide more effective allocation of police resources;[8] to notify police of potentially dangerous individuals at specific locations;[9] to identify potential criminals based on their social media posts;[10] to guide efforts to intervene with individuals before they engage in criminal activity;[11] to advise judges making decisions about pretrial detention;[12] and to provide guidance to judges at sentencing.[13]

The extraordinary promise of applying big data to the criminal justice system is based on two aspects of these mechanical predictions. First, the underlying data is usually gathered from public sources, and therefore, the use of such data does not constitute a "search" under the Fourth Amendment.[14] Thus, law enforcement officers have a significant amount of freedom in acquiring this information, which means that they can obtain the predictions from big data without needing to meet any legal standard such as reasonable suspicion or probable cause. Essentially, big data algorithms are force multipliers, allowing police to generate more predictive power from the same public information that has always been available to them. We will explore this practice in more detail in Chapter 6.

The second enticing aspect of big data's mechanical predictions is that they are more accurate than clinical judgments. Studies have shown that big data's mechanical predictions are, on average, 10 percent more accurate than clinical judgments.[15] These methods have increased the accuracy of many different aspects of criminal justice, from predicting where crime is likely to occur to determining which defendants are most likely to succeed if released on parole.[16] The increased accuracy offered by big data can also lead to both greater efficiency and fairness. The criminal justice system will be more efficient because police and courts will be able to focus their finite resources more effectively. It will be fairer because fewer innocent people will be stopped, frisked, searched, or arrested if big data can successfully narrow the field of legitimate suspects.

Big data's predictive algorithms have enormous potential to impact the criminal justice system. Law enforcement officers already use these tools to determine where crime is likely to occur and to allocate their resources accordingly. And the results from these predictive algorithms can probably influence police officers when they make their informal clinical judgments about whether reasonable suspicion or probable cause exists. But predictive algorithms could go much further than this kind of informal influence. In the future, police could formally cite the results from predictive algorithms in court when justifying their stops or searches or when applying for a search warrant. And ultimately, the results from big data's predictive algorithms could be outcome determinative, meaning that a police officer or a judge who is determining whether reasonable suspicion or probable cause exists would only consider the algorithm's output and ignore all other evidence. We are a long way from this point in the context of reasonable suspicion or probable cause, but some courts are coming close to allowing mechanical predictions to be outcome determinative for bail, sentencing, and parole decisions.[17]

PREDICTIVE ALGORITHMS AND POLICING

Police have a long history of using massive amounts of data to help decide where to allocate resources.[18] In the 1990s, law enforcement use of data compilation gained national attention with the New York Police Department's COMPSTAT program.[19]

Crime mapping algorithms quickly spread to other cities and became a staple of big-city policing.[20] Today, more advanced software has made crime-predicting capabilities available in smaller jurisdictions, and the National Institute of Justice is funding research into the efficacy of these programs.[21]

These crime prediction software systems vary in their sophistication. One program known as PredPol (short for "predictive policing") only looks at past reports of criminal activity and then highlights areas of the precinct in which crime has been most prevalent during specific time periods.[22] The police department then assigns more officers to the high-crime areas to detect or deter crime more effectively. Police officers using the software in a suburb of Los Angeles saw their crime rate decrease by 13 percent over the course of four months, while it rose by 0.4 percent in surrounding areas.[23] A more sophisticated program called HunchLab also uses reports of past criminal activity, but adds in additional factors.[24] Some of these extra factors, such as the proximity to subway stations or bars, or the current weather conditions, have an obvious correlation to particular types of criminal activity. Other factors seem unrelated, such as the decrease in aggravated assaults on windy days, or the increase in car thefts near schools.[25]

The Fresno Police Department uses crime prediction software in a somewhat different way, employing a software system called Beware to warn police officers of the threat level for the location of a 911 call.[26] As law enforcement officers are on their way to the location, workers in police headquarters plug the address into the Beware program, which quickly analyzes countless pieces of data, including "arrest reports, . . . commercial databases, deep Web searches and . . . social media postings" that are associated with that address.[27] The program then offers a rating for the location: green for safe, yellow for caution, and red for dangerous.[28] Police officers who arrive at the scene can take appropriate precautions based on that rating.

Chicago takes this process one step further, using predictive software to determine which individuals are most likely to be involved in a crime.[29] Using a special algorithm designed by an engineer at the Illinois Institute of Technology, the Chicago Police Department created a "heat list" of 400 people who are "most likely to be involved in a shooting or homicide."[30] Police will then deploy resources to monitor these individuals more closely than other individuals[31] in an attempt to deter their criminal behavior by letting them know they are under increased surveillance, or to swiftly apprehend them if they do commit crimes.[32]

Using predictive software to determine how to allocate scarce law enforcement resources is not limited to investigations of street crime. The Internal Revenue Service (IRS) uses a secret algorithm to determine which of the over one hundred million tax returns should be audited each year. The IRS algorithm scans through every tax return, looking for outlying levels of deductions or other factors that indicate a higher chance of fraud, and then it assigns a risk level to each return.[33] Those returns with high risk factors are then personally reviewed by IRS agents to see if an audit is appropriate.[34]

Some critics of adapting big data to our criminal justice system argue that it does not, in fact, make more accurate predictions. Professor Bernard Harcourt has argued that predictive policing may actually reduce the efficiency of stops and searches, because when police focus their resources on certain portions of the population, they necessarily withdraw resources from other portions of the population.[35] According to his model, crime will decrease among those who are targeted, but it will increase among those who are not targeted. Thus, whether the overall crime rate decreases actually depends on the comparative elasticity of the crime rate in each of the two groups; that is, whether the effect on the crime rate is greater for those who are targeted than for those who are not.[36] This critique is persuasive if the police are using a very basic predictive policing model that focuses on one specific neighborhood or (as in Harcourt's example) one specific race. But the critique becomes weaker if the police are using a multi-factor algorithm to direct resources, and it becomes weaker still if it is merely used to determine whether reasonable suspicion or probable cause exist. However, Harcourt's objection does highlight the need to ensure that the data used by the predictive algorithm remains current; that is, if there is a feedback effect that makes certain factors less likely to indicate criminal activity, the algorithm should be adjusted to ensure that those factors are given less weight or eliminated entirely. It also highlights a legitimate concern about relying on data which itself may be tainted by past discrimination or inaccurate decisions, a topic we will address in this chapter.

PREDICTIVE ALGORITHMS AS BACKGROUND DATA

PredPol, Hunchlab, Beware, Chicago's "heat list," and the IRS algorithm represent what we could call the first stage of crime prediction algorithms – algorithms used to help police decide where and how to deploy their resources, but not used (at least formally) to make any specific legal determination.[37] But as the amount of data about individuals grows and becomes more accessible, police will use big data at later stages of the criminal justice system. It is likely that police already informally use these tools as background information in making their determination as to whether reasonable suspicion or probable cause exists.

Assume a police officer observes marginally suspicious activity – say, a suspect walking slowly down the street at night, peering into windows, and constantly looking over his shoulder. If the officer is using crime prediction software, and the software informs her that she is currently in a low crime neighborhood with few burglaries, she may simply assume that the suspect is engaged in innocent conduct and merely watch the suspect for a few minutes until he leaves the area. But if the software informs her that there are many burglaries that occur in this neighborhood at this time of night, that extra factor could be enough to change her response and lead her to conduct a brief stop and frisk of the suspect. Or consider a police officer who uses risk assessment software and shows up at a home in response to a 911 call to find two individuals in a heated argument, one with a bruise on his cheek. The injured individual refuses to tell the police officer whether he has been assaulted. If the risk assessment software flashes a peaceful green, the responding officer might simply give a warning to the two individuals or ask one of them to take a walk to cool down. But if the software presented a red light, indicating the presence of a violent individual at the location, the officer might decide that she has probable cause to arrest the noninjured individual and charge him with assault.

The same calculus would occur – consciously or unconsciously – when an officer is investigating a potential crime and a member of a heat list is a suspect, or when an IRS agent is reviewing a return that has already been flagged by the software. Other police officers have mobile applications that can display the location of individuals suspected of gang activity, registered sex offenders, or those who have outstanding warrants, thus allowing a police officer to quickly generate reasonable suspicion or probable cause.[38] Indeed, presence in a "high crime area" is a factor that is frequently cited by police officers who are explaining why they believed that reasonable suspicion existed,[39] and the fact that a suspect is a known violent felon could also be used by an officer in deciding whether to make an arrest.[40] Many law enforcement agents (and many lay people) would say that it would be foolish to ignore these signals when deciding on the appropriate course of action.

Although police probably use these results as background information in making their determination, so far no law enforcement agent or prosecutor has formally used the results of crime prediction software in court as a factor to support reasonable suspicion or probable cause.[41] Instead, courts rely on the testimony of the law enforcement officers to establish the necessary factors, even in situations where big data could provide more accurate information.[42]

PREDICTIVE ALGORITHMS AS FORMAL FACTORS

The increasing pervasiveness of predictive algorithms in policing means that police officers will soon be using these predictions as part of their arguments justifying reasonable suspicion or probable cause. Moreover, as police officers use these factors more often, judges will begin to expect this kind of hard data and may begin to reject the current subjective, experiential, or anecdotal evidence that officers currently rely upon.[43] This will almost certainly result in more accurate determinations overall. To see why, we need to take a closer look at the current system that is used to determine reasonable suspicion or probable cause.

For example, consider the "high crime area" determination that is frequently cited by police officers as a factor supporting reasonable suspicion or probable cause. The opinion of a police officer about how much crime occurs in a certain area is likely to be based on a small sample of cases; it may be based on an outdated reputation of a neighborhood; and it is possibly tainted by many different kinds of bias.[44] Even if accurate, it is inappropriately comparative. If the neighborhood in question has three times the number of drug arrests per week than all of the surrounding neighborhoods, that fact in itself is irrelevant to a reasonable suspicion argument.[45] Instead, the police officer and the judge should consider the absolute number of criminal activity – does the neighborhood in question have two drug arrests per week, or ten drug arrests per week, or fifty drug arrests per week?[46]

Another example is the legal authority to conduct a frisk. Under *Terry* v. *Ohio*, an officer is only allowed to frisk a suspect during a stop if the officer has a reason to believe the suspect is armed. Up until now, that "reason to believe" – like the reasonable suspicion underlying the stop itself – has been based on the opinion and past experience of the police officer and evaluated based on the intuition of the reviewing court. Police officers routinely testify, for example, that individuals suspected of engaging in narcotics transactions are more likely to have weapons on their person. In practice, judges have credited this testimony, regularly approving *Terry* frisks when the police officer had reasonable grounds to believe a suspect was engaged in narcotics trafficking.[47] But what is the actual link between selling narcotics and weapons possession? If the former actually does make the latter more likely, what is the degree of increase in probability? Is it the same for every city, and every neighborhood of every city, and every type of narcotic? Clinical judgments can answer none of these questions – nor can they answer these questions for any other factor relied upon by police when justifying a *Terry* frisk. Thus, the "reason to believe" standard has become a legal term of art, defined not by actual probability but by years of precedents in which certain fact patterns have been approved by courts based solely on the experience, expertise, and intuition of police officers.

In fact, the Bureau of Justice review of over 200,000 criminals who were convicted in state court shows that only 8.6 percent of those who were convicted of drug dealing carried a firearm at the time of the arrest, and only 7.8 percent of those convicted of drug possession carried a firearm at the time of the arrest.[48] Does an 8.6 percent chance give officers a "reason to believe?" Judges have never answered this question, preferring instead to rely on the self-reported intuition and experience of the very police officers who are trying to justify their own actions. But under the cost–benefit analysis theory, judges would know the degree to which each factor affected the likelihood that the frisk would reveal a weapon, and could then make their own independent evaluation of whether the likelihood of success met the legal standard for reasonable suspicion. And as we will see in the next chapter, judges will need to quantify these broad descriptive legal standards to make these determinations.

Other factors used for clinical judgments also may comport with the intuition of police officers (and with the intuition of the judges who review the police officers' actions) but may be empirically false. For example, flight from police has long been held to be a significant factor in determining reasonable suspicion,[49] but studies have shown that the facts are far more nuanced than the simple intuition used by judges. For example, in 1999 the New York city police made one arrest for every nine *Terry* stops that they undertook – a hit rate of around 11 percent. Whether an

11 percent likelihood of finding contraband constitutes reasonable suspicion is a question we will discuss at length in Chapter 3. For our current purposes, the interesting question is which factors increase or decrease this hit rate. For example, if the police stop was based merely on the fact that the suspect fled the crime scene, the ratio of stops to arrests falls to 26:1, an extremely low hit rate of under 4 percent – indicating that this factor alone is very unlikely to constitute reasonable suspicion. However, if the stop was based on the fact that the flight was motivated by the presence of a police officer, the hit rate increases to a respectable 6.3 percent, showing that the relevant factor is not just flight but also the fact that the suspect was fleeing from the police. Even more interesting is the hit rate for stops that are based on the combination of flight from a police officer in a high crime neighborhood. When these two factors are combined, the hit rate for stops drops to 2.2 percent[50]. At first this is a counter-intuitive finding: if flight from a police officer increases the chances that the individual is committing a crime, and if we assume (as nearly very court does) that hit rates are higher in high crime neighborhoods, why does the hit rate drop precipitously when these two factors are combined? One feasible answer is that the relationship between the police and residents in high-crime neighborhoods is so fraught that a high percentage of residents – including innocent residents – will run from the police because they fear harassment or abuse.[51] But for our purposes we do not need to determine the reasons behind the data – all that matters is the data itself. And it turns out that in this case the courts' intuition is completely backward: flight from the police in a high crime area does not create anything like reasonable suspicion; in fact, it is not at all a reliable indicator of criminal activity.

Courts have long been criticized for deferring to the various factors police officers use in determining that they have the authority to make a *Terry* stop. In his dissent in *United States* v. *Sokolow*, Justice Thurgood Marshall listed dozens of cases in which different circuit courts had approved of contradictory factors offered to show that a suspect fit a "drug courier profile" at an airport: first to deplane, last to deplane, de-planed in the middle, one way ticket, round-trip ticket, nonstop flight, changed planes, gym bag, new suitcase, traveled alone, traveled with companion, acted nervously, acted too calmly.[52] As one pair of commentators noted, "Apparently almost any human trait can be a basis for suspicion, and nearly everybody exhibits several potentially suspicious … factors at any given time."[53]

In the 2013 case of *Floyd* v. *City of New York*,[54] a class action suit challenging the stop-and-frisk policies of the New York Police Department, the trial judge criticized the often used police factors such as "furtive movements," "high crime area," and "suspicious bulge" as overly vague.[55] During testimony in the case, two police officers testified as to what they understood "furtive movements" to mean:

One [officer] explained that "furtive movement is a very broad concept," and could include a person "changing direction," "walking in a certain way," "[a]cting a little suspicious," "making a movement that is not regular," being "very fidgety," "going in and out of his pocket," "going in and out of a location," "looking back and forth constantly," "looking over their shoulder," "adjusting their hip or their belt," "moving in and out of a car too quickly," "[t]urning a part of their body away from you," "[g]rabbing at a certain pocket or something at their waist," "getting a little nervous, maybe shaking," and "stutter[ing]." Another officer explained that "usually" a furtive movement is someone "hanging out in front of [a] building, sitting on the benches or something like that" and then making a "quick movement," such as "bending down and quickly standing back up," "going inside the lobby ... and then quickly coming back out," or "all of a sudden becom[ing] very nervous, very aware."[56]

In the statistics from the *Floyd* case, police officers cited "furtive movements" as a factor in 42 percent of their stops.[57]

Not only are many of the clinical judgment factors overly vague, their supposed link to criminal activity is based on a very limited data set. Factors offered by law enforcement officers are frequently supported only by the officer's own prior experience, and in approving (or disapproving)[58] of these factors as probative of criminal activity, courts either cite the expertise of the officers or use their own intuition to evaluate the probability that a crime will occur.

Unsurprisingly, the result of these vague standards and limited data sets is a troublingly low hit rate for police officers conducting stop and frisks. The recent expansion of *Terry* stops in New York City resulted in a regime in which only 12 percent of all *Terry* stops in New York City resulted in an arrest or a summons.[59] During that same period, only 1.5 percent of the *Terry* frisks produced evidence of a weapon.[60] In other words, in the absence of big data's predictive algorithms, the intuitions and the experiences of individual police officers have the potential to be wildly inaccurate.

The aggressive policing at issue in *Floyd* is not an outlier: courts are notoriously imprecise when evaluating *Terry* stop and frisks. One factor commonly cited by the police when justifying a frisk is the type of crime the person is suspected of having committed. Courts have consistently held that some crimes, such as robbery,[61] narcotics trafficking,[62] growing large amounts of marijuana,[63] rape,[64] or burglary,[65] all involve a high risk of the suspect carrying a weapon and are thus a legitimate factor in determining whether the suspect is armed.[66] But is the nature of the crime enough on its own to create reasonable suspicion? Is it enough when combined with one other observation by the police officer, such as a "furtive move" or a "suspicious bulge"?

Generally, courts will find that if the officer reasonably believes that the suspect is guilty of one of these "weapons likely" crimes, then that belief is sufficient to create reasonable suspicion that a suspect is armed.[67] But surely the risk of a suspect carrying a weapon is not identical for all five of those crimes – so in theory, courts should require some corroboration in the case of certain suspected crimes and less (or none) in the case of others. This is not what happens: courts merely state that the suspected crime is "likely to involve the use of weapons"[68] and then generally find that the frisk was justified. Meanwhile, other suspected crimes, such as passing counterfeit money[69] or possession of illegal drugs,[70] are held to not be a legitimate factor – that is, an individual suspected of these crimes has absolutely no greater likelihood than anyone else to be carrying a weapon. In reaching these conclusions, courts generally rely on their intuition rather than any actual evidence that indicates the prevalence (or dearth) of weapons on suspects who commit these crimes. And in the absence of empirical evidence, courts create a false binary categorization: suspicion of certain crimes generates reasonable suspicion on its own, while suspicion of other crimes does not add to the probability of a weapon being present.

Occasionally, courts do venture into the realm of data when deciding whether reasonable suspicion or probable cause exist, with decidedly mixed results. In a recent case, the Ninth Circuit attempted to determine if suspicion of domestic violence was a legitimate factor in determining whether the individual was armed.[71] The majority held that suspicion of domestic violence did not increase the likelihood of the suspect possessing a weapon. To support its conclusion, the court cited studies that concluded that "domestic violence calls for service account for a relatively small proportion of the overall rate of police officers murders" and that 36.7 percent of domestic violence victims had at some point in their lives been threatened or harmed by a weapon during a domestic violence incident.[72] The dissent cited FBI studies demonstrating that 33 percent of assaults on police officers in a recent year were committed while police were responding to "disturbance calls," which is "a category which includes domestic violence calls," and that over a ten year period, three times more police officers were killed responding to domestic violence calls than those responding to burglary calls.[73] None of these studies establish any quantitative probability that perpetrators of domestic violence use or carry weapons; they merely establish the undeniable fact that perpetrators of domestic violence sometimes carry weapons and sometimes pose a risk to police officers.[74]

The court did cite one seemingly useful study: a Bureau of Justice report covering seven years, which concluded that 15 percent of domestic violence attacks involved a weapon.[75] But this statistic is almost certainly too crude to be useful. Like "burglary" or "narcotics trafficking," the crime of domestic violence encompasses many different kinds of behavior – some of them probably linked to a high likelihood of weapons possession, and some linked to a relatively low likelihood.[76] In order to effectively use statistics, courts will need more sophisticated and detailed data, which can be applied to the facts of the specific case. For example, courts may want to know whether the alleged domestic violence occurred at home or in a public place. Or what percentage of individuals living in the neighborhood possess firearms. Or whether the police are responding at night or during the daytime. This type of detailed data needs to be developed so that courts can use it to review specific cases. Without specific data, courts may identify these factors as relevant, but then apply their own flawed intuition to how each factor affects the ultimate question of reasonable suspicion.

Thus, there is a growing dissonance between the objective, data-driven tools used by police officers to guide their conduct, and the intuitive arguments and subjective experience used by police officers to justify that conduct in court. Given the success of the data-driven tools in everyday police work, it seems inevitable that they will soon be formally used by police officers in assessing whether reasonable suspicion or probable cause exists.[77] Data-driven predictive algorithms represent an opportunity to dramatically increase the accuracy of these decisions, thus ensuring that fewer innocent citizens are searched or detained while increasing the efficiency of our law enforcement resources.[78]

CHALLENGES TO USING PREDICTIVE ALGORITHMS

As noted in the last section, crime prediction software could soon be used by police officers on the street and by judges in criminal courts to help show reasonable suspicion or probable cause. This development could result in more accurate and consistent determinations of whether these standards have been met; but only if certain obstacles can be overcome. First, there is a concern that predictive algorithms would use factors that are illegal for courts to consider, such as the race of the subject.[79] Similarly, the underlying data that the algorithms use may be itself biased; thus, using these algorithms would not actually increase accuracy, but merely reinforce decades of discriminatory policing. Also, the law requires police officers and judges to act on facts that are specific to the case at hand, and general probability factors used by big data may not be able to provide for this specificity requirement.

All of these obstacles are surmountable, but only if the algorithms and databases used by the big data analyses are made more transparent so that courts can evaluate the underlying processes and the standards being used, and only if courts are willing to accept the quantified world of predictive software.

To the extent that human beings have a hand in creating the algorithms and compiling the data that the algorithms use, human biases will infect the results. Although it is impossible to eliminate these biases altogether, there are ways to minimize the problems they create.

DIRECT AND INDIRECT USE OF FORBIDDEN FACTORS

Mechanical predictions are not necessarily race-blind. If an individual's race is a significant factor in determining whether a certain outcome is likely to occur, then the individuals who are designing (and using) the algorithm may be tempted to use race as one of the inputs in to achieve more accurate results. In some cases outside the context of criminal procedure, this may be relatively harmless. For example, when companies use big data to decide where to market certain products, or when political campaigns use big data to decide which voters to contact with a certain kind of outreach. In other cases, race-based factors can be harmful (and illegal); such as when a company is evaluating a customer's credit risk for a home loan[80] or hiring job applicants.[81] In the context of criminal procedure, race-based factors are especially problematic, both on legal and moral grounds.

For the purposes of this discussion, let's assume that a private company has developed an algorithm that can predict with great accuracy whether drugs will be found inside a certain house. The algorithm requires the user to enter six different inputs, such as the neighborhood where the house is located, the prior criminal convictions of the house's owner, and observations made by police officers about activity outside the house. One of these inputs is the race of the owner of the home. Assume, further, that without using the race factor, the algorithm can predict the presence of drugs with 40 percent accuracy, but with the race factor, the algorithm can predict the presence of drugs with 55 percent accuracy. The police have purchased this algorithm and are using it in their warrant application. Should they input the race factor to enhance the algorithm's accuracy? In other words, would it be illegal for the state to use race as a factor in determining probable cause or reasonable suspicion if it could be definitively proven that using race made the prediction more accurate?

Surprisingly, Fourth Amendment jurisprudence has little to say about whether race can be used as a factor in determining reasonable suspicion or probable cause. Courts are unanimous in holding that race alone can never be the basis for a stop or a search, for the obvious reason that a person's race alone can never create probable cause or even reasonable suspicion that criminal activity is occurring.[82] However, some courts have approved cases in which race was one of many factors in deciding whether reasonable suspicion or probable cause existed; for example, when searching for illegal immigrants near the Mexican border.[83] Other courts have disagreed, arguing that a person's race is "of such little probative value [in the reasonable suspicion analysis] that it may not be considered as a relevant factor."[84]

As these cases make clear, the only problem with using race under Fourth Amendment jurisprudence is that in the vast majority of cases, the race of a subject is not a relevant indicator as to whether the suspect is more or less likely to engage in criminal activity.[85] Therefore, any law enforcement official who does consider race is almost certainly doing so because of an irrational bias against that particular race. But this objection is not entirely valid in every circumstance. As noted earlier in the chapter, if the law enforcement officer is looking for illegal immigrants near the Mexican border, for example, the suspect's race could be one factor in trying to predict whether the suspect was illegally in the country. Likewise, if a person seems "out of place" due to her race (for example, a white person in a predominantly black neighborhood), her race could be one factor that would lead to reasonable suspicion that she was engaging in criminal activity.[86]

Given this jurisprudence, there is no valid Fourth Amendment objection to using race as a factor in a mechanical prediction algorithm for reasonable suspicion or probable cause. Assuming we have a properly designed algorithm,[87] race would only be used as a factor if it actually was a useful predictor of individualized suspicion; in other words, there would be empirical statistical proof that in the given context, race did help determine whether or not an individual was guilty of a crime.[88] In our hypothetical case, in which the use of race increased the accuracy of the prediction from 40 percent to 55 percent, using the race-based factor would not be prohibited under the Fourth Amendment.

The Equal Protection Clause is another matter, however. Under the Equal Protection Clause, race can only be used as a factor in state actions if the use of race is necessary and if it is narrowly tailored to achieve a compelling state interest.[89] This is a difficult, if not impossible, burden for law enforcement to meet in the stop-and-search context. Some courts have held that the use of race as a factor does not require exclusion as long as there were a sufficient number of other factors to justify the stop or search,[90] while others have noted that law enforcement officers violate the Equal Protection Clause if they incorporate race routinely as a factor in their drug courier profile.[91] Neither of these principles bodes well for using race as a factor in mechanical prediction algorithms, regardless of how accurate they might be. As further evidence that racial factors are forbidden by the Equal Protection Clause, nearly all civil suits alleging racial profiling result in consent decrees that forbid the use of race as a factor.[92]

Outside the Fourth Amendment context, the seminal case on racial bias in the criminal justice system is *McCleskey* v. *Kemp*, in which a black defendant argued that the state of Georgia engaged in racial discrimination when administering the death penalty.[93] The defendant relied on a study that showed that defendants who killed white victims were far more likely to be sentenced to death than those who killed black victims.[94] The study also showed that black defendants were more likely to get the death penalty than white defendants.[95] The Supreme Court rejected the defendant's arguments, holding that in order to prevail on an equal protection claim, the defendant had to demonstrate that the decision-makers in the process acted with a "discriminatory purpose."[96] The Justices were concerned with interfering with the discretion that is given to prosecutors, judges, and juries, and thus said it required "exceptionally clear proof before [the Court] would infer that the discretion has been abused."[97]

Based on this jurisprudence, it is hard to see our hypothetical algorithm passing constitutional muster. Even assuming that drug prevention is a compelling state interest, law enforcement would be hard pressed to argue that using the race-based factor was necessary and narrowly tailored to accomplish that purpose. The use of the algorithm would probably be considered nothing more than a sophisticated method of racial profiling – an institutionalization of using race as a factor in determining probable cause.

The only plausible defense for the state would be to argue that although race is clearly a factor in the decision made by the algorithm, the decision is not made with a "discriminatory purpose" as forbidden by *McCleskey*. In other words, those who design and use the algorithm are (arguably) not acting with racial animus or out of any intent to treat the members of one race differently than another. This narrower definition of "discriminatory purpose" is consistent with *McCleskey's* language, which held that "'[d]iscriminatory purpose' ... implies more than intent as volition or intent as awareness of consequences. It implies that the decisionmaker ... selected or reaffirmed a particular course of action at least in part 'because of,' not merely 'in spite of,' its adverse effects upon an identifiable group."[98] This does not really fit the state's motivation in using the algorithm – the police are not choosing to use the algorithm (or, more specifically, the race factor) "because of" its adverse effects on a particular race; they are using it to increase the accuracy of their predictions.

However, the narrow definition of "discriminatory purpose" is not borne out in other areas of criminal procedure. For example, in the context of jury selection, the Court held that if a defendant established a pattern of racial discrimination in peremptory jury challenges, the prosecutor could only prevail if she could provide a racially neutral reason for making those challenges.[99] The Court further noted that "the prosecutor may not rebut the defendant's prima facie case of discrimination by stating merely that he challenged jurors of the defendant's race on the assumption – or his intuitive judgment – that they would be partial to the defendant because of their shared race."[100] This would be analogous to a prosecutor arguing that explicit discrimination should be allowed in the probable cause algorithm because it increases the accuracy of the prediction.

Thus, our hypothetical algorithm could not legally use race as a factor, even if that factor was demonstrated to increase the accuracy of the predictions. This legal conclusion is consistent with most individuals' intuitive moral sense, and (relatedly) to the political feasibility of using predictive algorithms. In the past, the media has harshly criticized racial profiling,[101] and it is unlikely that the public would support a system that regularly and explicitly used race as a significant factor to determine whether to stop a person or search his home.

But explicit use of race is not the only potential problem in the context of predictive algorithms, and this is where the need for transparency becomes even more important. It would be easy for courts to enforce a rule that prohibits the police from using the defendant's race directly as a factor in predictive algorithms, but this may not prevent the algorithm from relying on factors that are strongly correlated to race. Assume we change our hypothetical algorithm and remove the race factor altogether, but still use the location of the house as one of the factors. As has been established by decades of redlining neighborhoods,[102] location can be an effective proxy for race in the context of providing insurance, banking services, health care, or many other types of services.[103] As we saw earlier, current software used by police to predict crime patterns is highly location-specific, and it is plausible to imagine a scenario in which higher-crime areas track the racial make-up of specific

neighborhoods. We can call this "indirect discrimination" as opposed to the unconstitutional direct discrimination that occurs when race is officially used as a factor.[104]
Nearly every predictive program that is currently in use has given rise to concerns
about indirect discrimination.[105] Thus, before law enforcement agents and judges
officially use these programs to formally help them make their decisions, we need to
determine whether it is legally or ethically permissible to use these nonracial
elements that are correlated with race.

One way of answering this question is to note that proxies for race are already used
in determinations of reasonable suspicion or probable cause. Police officers routinely testify that they made their observations in a "high crime area" as a factor that
led to their reasonable suspicion or probable cause.[106] In many instances, higher
crime neighborhoods will tend to be inner city neighborhoods with higher propor-
tions of certain minority groups[107] (or at least this will be the perspective of many
police officers and judges).[108]

And this formal use of proxies for race under the current system is only the tip of
the iceberg. The unconscious (or conscious) racial biases of police officers and
judges permeate every aspect of the front end of the criminal justice system.[109]
Under the current system, police officers disproportionately stop and frisk black and
Latino suspects, and they are more likely to engage in violent and even lethal
conduct when interacting with these suspects.[110] The findings from the class action
lawsuit challenging the expanded police stop and frisks in New York City[111] found
that over an eight and half year period, 52 percent of all the citizens subjected to
Terry stops were black, even though black citizens made up only 23 percent of the
population.[112] Studies have shown similar numbers in Philadelphia,[113] Los
Angeles,[114] Boston,[115] and on the New Jersey turnpike.[116] Unlike the formal factors
which can (at least in theory) be proven to be proxies for race, the use and effect of
these informal decisions are difficult to detect and even more difficult to prove in
court. These implicit biases on the part of police officers are also difficult to cure,
even in the long run, since they exist in almost every individual, even those who
harbor no conscious prejudices.[117]

In other words, the current system relies on personal, subjective clinical
judgments that are based on some known factors (which are explicitly described
by the police officer or judge when requesting a warrant or justifying their decision)
and some unknown factors (such as unconscious biases). Even for the known
factors, the decision-makers do not (and most likely could not) quantify the degree
to which they relied on each individual factor.

For example, assume a police officer is driving through a neighborhood and
notices a young black man standing on the street corner. The young man is dressed
in a way that is common in the neighborhood, but which is also consistent with gang
affiliation. The man then looks over at the officer, immediately places something in
his pocket, and then walks briskly away from the officer. Assume at this point the
officer honestly believes that there is a reasonable suspicion that the man is engaging

in criminal activity (that is, the officer is not out to hassle the young man and is not simply stopping people indiscriminately in the hope of finding contraband). The officer then gets out of her car and orders the man to stop.

Later on, the officer is required to justify her stop by explaining why she had reasonable suspicion to believe criminal activity was afoot. She lists the following factors:

(1) the action took place in a high crime neighborhood;
(2) the suspect hid an item after noticing a police officer;
(3) the suspect attempted to leave the scene after noticing a police officer.

The police officer does not list (and may not even be consciously aware of) other factors that led her to believe the suspect may have been engaged in criminal activity:

(1) the suspect's race (the officer subconsciously believes that black men are more likely to possess guns or drugs than white men);
(2) the suspect's age (the officer believes that men in their twenties are more likely to be engaged in criminal activity than children or men over forty);
(3) the suspect's gender (the officer believes that men are more likely to carry drugs or weapons than women);
(4) the suspect's clothing (which is common to the neighborhood, but which the police officer subconsciously associates with criminals);
(5) the way the suspect looked at the police officer, which the officer could not describe in testimony, but which she associated with hostility to authority and to police specifically.

Racial bias played a role in the officer's determination that the defendant was likely engaged in criminal activity, but it is impossible to know to what degree. Of the formal elements, the fact that the encounter took place in a "high crime neighborhood" is correlated to race, but neither the officer nor the judge reviewing her conduct are able to explain exactly how important that factor was out of the three that were listed. And the fact that the suspect's race led the officer to focus on this individual (as opposed to the young white man she observed standing on a different street corner two minutes before this interaction) may have played a significant role in her decision or a very minor role. Likewise, the suspect's clothing (another proxy for race) may have been a strong motivator for her to act, or it may have been relatively insignificant. There is simply no way to measure, much less prove, the degree to which race, or proxies for race, influenced her decision to detain the suspect. Over the course of many years and tens of thousands of stops, a clear pattern will probably emerge that shows that this police department disproportionately stops people of color, but effective remedies at that point are hard to come by.

It is against this current state of affairs that we must evaluate any future use of predictive software. Unlike clinical judgments, predictive software will only base its results on the formal factors that are coded into its system. Thus, there will be no unconscious or hidden human biases that affect its decision. Furthermore, we can precisely quantify the degree to which each of the formal factors affects the result, so a judge (or a policymaker) can make an informed judgment as to whether certain factors that are proxies for race are dominating the calculation. In other words, under the current system of clinical judgments, the only way to infer indirect discrimination is by reviewing the aggregate results after many months or years have passed. Under a system of mechanical predictions, the level of indirect discrimination can be assessed even before a stop or a search occurs by examining the algorithm the police intend to use. Thus, the mechanical predictive algorithms can be designed to ignore (or at least minimize) improper factors such as race – something that may be impossible to do if we leave these determinations to the subjective determinations of police officers.

All of this, however, depends on a high level of transparency in the algorithm itself, so that judges, policymakers, and police departments can review the factors, their correlation (if any) to race, and the strength of any specific factor in reaching the result. We will examine the challenges of achieving this transparency level at the end of this chapter.

PREEXISTING BIASES IN THE UNDERLYING DATA

A related concern about using mechanical predictions involves the underlying data that is used by the predictive algorithms. Put simply, if the underlying data is discriminatory, then the results that are based on that data will be discriminatory, and the supposedly race-blind algorithms will be doing nothing more than reinforcing the existing racial bias in the criminal justice system. In the civil context, commentators are beginning to pay close attention to these potential problems, noting that "[i]f a sample includes a disproportionate representation of a particular class ... the results of an analysis of that sample may skew in favor of or against the over- or underrepresented class."[118]

As an example, assume that for the past twenty years a metropolitan police department has been disproportionately stopping, searching, and arresting black and Latino citizens. This disproportionate treatment does not stem from the fact that citizens from these groups are more likely to commit crimes, but from inherent racial biases in the criminal justice system, such as the tendency of police to engage with minorities more than with whites and the increased level of policing in minority neighborhoods.[119] Assume also that these stops, searches, and arrests result in a higher conviction rate than stops, searches, and arrests of white citizens – again, not because the police are better at predicting crime for the minority citizens, but because of downstream biases in the criminal justice system. Black and Latino defendants tend to be poorer,[120] so they are less likely to be able to afford private lawyers and less likely to be able to afford bail; and because of conscious or subconscious prejudice on the part of prosecutors and judges, black and Latino defendants are more likely to be over-charged[121] (leading to higher rates of conviction at the plea bargaining stage) and more likely to be convicted by a jury if the case goes to trial.[122]

These discriminatory stops, searches, arrests, and convictions will become the underlying data for the city's predictive algorithms, and they create two problems for mechanical predictions. The first is related to the disproportionately high rate of encounters between the police and members of the minority community – the so-called "hassle" rate.[123] This will create large amounts of data about certain individuals or areas of a city and disproportionately small amounts of data about other individuals or areas. Thus, when an algorithm determines whether a neighborhood is a "high crime area," it will have a skewed interpretation of the frequency of crimes in different areas. This in turn will lead to more frequent searches of individuals in the "high crime areas," which will create a self-fulfilling prophecy as more individuals are stopped, searched, arrested, and thus convicted in those areas. Likewise, if an individual is determined to be at "high risk" for committing a crime, it could merely be reflecting the prejudices of police officers who have had previous encounters with the individual.[124] Professor Bernard Harcourt refers to this as the "ratchet effect": if certain factors are already perceived as leading to higher levels of criminal activity, a predictive algorithm will lead police and judges to conduct and authorize more searches on suspects who meet these factors, leading to more arrests that are linked to those factors.[125]

The second problem relates to the disproportionately high ratio of convictions to arrests for minority populations – what is referred to as the "hit" rate.[126] The primary way to know whether a stop, search, or arrest is successful (is a "hit") is by examining conviction rates. Thus, even if the police do find contraband at the same rate for every ethnic group that is searched, if certain minority groups are convicted at a higher rate after the contraband is discovered, the statistics will indicate a higher hit rate for those minority groups than for others. In other words, because these citizens are unfairly convicted at a higher rate, the stops and searches against them will seem more effective.[127]

As with the decision-making process itself, this problem is not new to mechanical predictions. The "data" that are used by police officers and judges today – their own subjective experiences – is similarly flawed.[128] The danger in moving towards a big data analysis in this context is not that a new problem will be created, but that the old problems will persist despite big data's promise of color blind objectivity. Even worse, these old problems will become institutionalized, and thus will be even harder to successfully challenge and expose because they are presented as part of the "hard science" of big data.

These problems with underlying data are not insoluble. The issue is common to many uses of big data, and it arises when statistics that are kept for one purpose are used for another.[129] Stop-and-frisk statistics and criminal conviction numbers are not recorded for the purposes of sophisticated statistical study; thus, those who collect them generally make no effort to correct for any biases inherent in the process.[130] Part of the solution thus involves correcting the data – that is, estimating the rate of over-representation of minorities in the hassle rates and hit rates and then adjusting the numbers accordingly.[131] Another solution would be to use data from different sources, not just from information that results from police–citizen encounters. For example, algorithms could draw their underlying data from the Bureau of Justice Statistics' National Crime Victimization Survey,[132] which tracks crimes based on victim reports, as opposed to the more traditional method of tracking crime through police reports.[133]

Once again, these solutions require real transparency in the data being used. Courts and policymakers need to demand to see the source of the data used by the predictive algorithms and need the tools to evaluate whether the data is representative of reality or the product of discriminatory decisions or unfair processes from the past.

ENSURING THE COMPUTER LOOKS FOR INDIVIDUALIZED SUSPICION

Individualized suspicion is a bedrock requirement of almost any police action that implicates the Fourth Amendment.[134] If police officers knew that 60 percent of everyone living in a certain building were guilty of possessing drugs, they would not be allowed to arrest everyone in the building, even though they would have probable cause to believe that each person is guilty.[135] The Fourth Amendment demands particularity; that is, not merely a statistical likelihood that a suspect is guilty based on his membership in a certain group, but a reference to particular characteristics or actions by the suspect that shows that he specifically is likely to be guilty.[136]

One objection to using mechanical predictions is that they will dilute or even eliminate the individualization requirement by focusing on broad categories instead of the individual's particularized conduct.[137] Even if big data's mechanical predictions could lead to more accurate results, it would be legally and morally wrong to punish a person based on membership in a specific group (such as economic class or age) instead of focusing on the person's individual actions.[138]

In order to address this concern, we first have to define what we mean when we say that suspicion must be individualized.[139] In general, we mean that police officers must look at the specific characteristics and actions of the suspect himself, and not determine reasonable suspicion or probable cause merely because the suspect is a member of a certain group. However, individualized suspicion does not preclude inferring facts about an individual based on his membership in a certain group; it simply requires the presence of additional factors that are specific to the suspect. Even in the analog world of clinical judgments, police officers and judges routinely rely on assumptions about an individual based in part on the characteristics of their group. For example, police officers will give some weight to a suspect's known gang affiliation, while magistrates making bail determinations will consider whether a defendant is unemployed or has a criminal record.

However, it would be inappropriate to stop, search, or arrest an individual solely based on his membership in a specific group.[140] This would be saying that the group characteristics of the individual are so suspicious that at any given moment there is reason to believe that he is likely to be engaging in criminal activity. To avoid this problem, courts have held that the police officer must observe conduct that gives her some reason to believe that the suspect is currently engaging in criminal activity.[141] These actions may be legal (but suspicious) conduct, such as running from the police, exiting a location where drugs are known to be sold while sticking something in a pocket, or wearing a heavy coat on a summer day. Or they may be legal and innocuous conduct, such as buying a one-way ticket or traveling without luggage. But the reasonable suspicion or probable cause cannot be based only on who the person is; it must also be based on what the person does.[142]

The Supreme Court has repeatedly reminded us of the need to consider the specific actions of the individual in a search. In *Ybarra* v. *Illinois*, law enforcement officers with a warrant to search a tavern stopped and frisked every individual inside the tavern, under the theory that mere presence in a tavern where drugs were sold generated reasonable suspicion that any of these people possessed drugs.[143] The Supreme Court rejected this argument, explaining that "the *Terry* exception does not permit a frisk for weapons on less than reasonable belief or suspicion directed at the person to be frisked."[144]

A mechanical prediction that is used to demonstrate reasonable suspicion or probable cause must meet these same criteria.[145] Law school hypotheticals aside, it is hard to imagine a situation in the real world where group characteristics alone rise to the level of reasonable suspicion, but it is theoretically possible that a mechanical prediction would arrive at that result. Thus, any predictive software used to calculate whether reasonable suspicion or probable cause exists must require the observing officer to input the specific actions of the suspect as well as his general characteristics. The software would thus use these specific actions as part of its analysis, and it would be designed so that it could not find reasonable suspicion or probable cause – regardless of the percentage chance of criminal activity occurring – unless the specific actions were a significant factor in the determination.[146]

Thus, to create a system where police officers and judges use data-centric mechanical predictions in making their decisions, these algorithms must become more transparent. This transparency will allow judges to ensure that the algorithm is not relying upon unconstitutional factors, either directly or indirectly, in reaching its conclusions. Transparency is also required so that judges can ensure that at least some of the factors leading to this number are specific to each suspect. And as we will see, transparency is also necessary so that judges can add additional factors to these algorithms in order to adjust their results to the facts of a specific case.

TRANSPARENT ALGORITHMS AND DATA SETS

The first step is to convince companies who make these algorithms to share the details of their operation – if not the source code, at least the factors that their predictive models consider and the weight that the models assign to each factor. The transparency requirement is necessary not only for the algorithm itself but also for the underlying data sets, in order to avoid the ratchet effect discussed earlier.[147] Courts need to be able to examine the underlying evidence the algorithm is using in order to ensure that they are not already tainted by race or by proxies for race – and if they are, the data sets need to be adjusted to remove the taint. Greater transparency for the data sets will also help with another growing problem with our increasing reliance on big data: erroneous information in the government and private databases upon which these algorithms rely.[148] As we have seen earlier, police are already relying on these predictive algorithms to direct resources and place certain people under suspicion, so cleansing the algorithms of discriminatory factors and purging inaccurate information is already long overdue.

Another reason to mandate transparency is to ensure that the individualized suspicion requirement is met. As noted earlier,[149] some predictive algorithms may base their conclusions solely on group membership and external factors, thus violating the legal requirement that reasonable suspicion or probable cause be based on individualized suspicion. If the inputs used by the algorithm are open for the judge to examine, then she can ensure that the conclusion is based on the required level of individual activity. And if there are no inputs based on individualized suspicion, the judge must demand additional facts from the law enforcement officer to establish individualized suspicion – she will be forced to switch from an "outcome determinative" use of predictive algorithms to a "formal factor" model.

Unfortunately, up until now, companies have been extremely secretive about the details of their predictive algorithms, because they consider these details to be valuable proprietary information.[150] The company that provides the Beware software to police departments does not even allow the police departments to know the details of the algorithm.[151] Recently, the American Civil Liberties Union (ACLU) had to make a public records request to the Fresno Police, seeking information about the factors used by its predictive software, but the results still did not provide anything like the kind of transparency needed to evaluate the constitutionality of the program.[152] This secrecy is not limited to private corporations; even private individuals who design these algorithms refuse to disclose exactly how they work.[153]

Thus far, this secrecy has not posed significant legal problems, since predictive algorithms are only being used to direct police resources. But this will probably change soon, regardless of whether police and courts begin to use predictive algorithms to establish legal cause to stop or search. There is growing concern that using mechanical predictions is just a sophisticated form of racial profiling,[154] and if police want to continue to use algorithms, they will need to reveal (or require their algorithm creator to reveal) the details of these algorithms. Sufficient transparency will not only reassure the public (and the courts) that the determinative factors used by the algorithm are not related to race, it will also lay the groundwork for formally adopting these algorithms into the legal system. And, not incidentally, it may reveal that some algorithms are relying on forbidden factors in reaching their conclusions, which would require the algorithm to be redesigned with the offending factors removed. The ACLU's recent public records request, for example, revealed that one of the Fresno Police Department's predictive software algorithms used the social media hashtag #BlackLivesMatter as a risk factor for "police hate crimes."[155]

But requiring the software engineers and statisticians who design mechanical predictions to reveal the factors being used and the weights assigned to each factor is only the first step. Modern day predictive software is not static; the more sophisticated algorithms will adjust the factors as they go, learning from experience. As the algorithm makes thousands or millions of predictions, it will learn which of those predictions were correct, and it will change the weight assigned to each of its factors accordingly to improve its accuracy. This process, known as machine learning,[156] ensures that the algorithm's mechanical predictions improve with feedback, but it makes it even more difficult for the courts to evaluate the degree to which each factor is relevant to the machine's conclusions.[157] As Professor Richard Berk has noted, "forecasting becomes a distinct activity that differs from explanation.... .What matters most is forecasting accuracy. Combining explanation with forecasting can compromise both."[158] In other words, the most accurate algorithms – those that use machine learning to sift through millions of different data points – may be the least transparent.[159]

However, as we have seen in other contexts in the criminal justice system, it is possible to overcome these obstacles. A judge does not need an intricate understanding of the underlying code of the algorithm; she only needs to know (1) the factors that the algorithm used and (2) the historical accuracy of the algorithm's results.[160] Although the experts who design the algorithm need to consider hundreds or thousands of data points to determine which factors are the most predictive, for practical reasons, the algorithm will probably only use eight or nine factors, just like the sentencing risk assessment tools.[161] Thus, the first piece of information should be easy for law enforcement to provide, since presumably it is law enforcement officers who input the data. And the accuracy of the results should be available, since an integral part of developing big data's algorithms is to calculate (and then improve on) the accuracy of the predictions that are made.

Once the judge obtains this information, she would then need to evaluate (1) whether the specific inputs are proxies for a forbidden factor, such as race, and (2) whether they contain sufficient particularity to justify the stop, search, or arrest. In other words, the judge does not need to know exactly how the algorithm arrived at its results, only which factors it considered in doing so. The judge would also have to determine whether the accuracy of the algorithm is sufficient to meet the required legal standard, a question we turn to in the next section.

And if a judge wanted to understand the way the algorithm processed the inputs, she would not have to decipher the meaning of the underlying source code, much less understand the evolution of the data in a machine learning environment. Just as judges hear from experts in a *Daubert* hearing when they are called upon to determine the reliability of a new and complex scientific process, a judge who is called upon to evaluate the methodology and reliability of a predictive algorithm could also listen to experts testifying from both sides.[162]

This transparency requirement is not a weakness of adopting mechanical predictions, but one of its strengths. Courts currently rely on a combination of their own intuition (an internal, subjective algorithm) and experience (an internal, limited database) when reviewing the decisions of a police officer (decisions based on a combination of the police officer's intuition and experience). It has already been conclusively demonstrated that these intuitions are subject to significant levels of racial bias,[163] but it is difficult for a judge to know if (or to what degree) her own intuition may be suffering from this problem. Likewise, the judge's personal experiences are probably partially based on problematic data. These hidden biases are difficult to remove from a person's decision-making process.[164] With the proper transparency requirements, however, these biases can be detected in mechanical predictions.

HOW TO USE THE QUANTIFIED FACTORS

Once we use the predictive algorithms in determining if the legal standard is met for the surveillance, the next step is to decide whether the results from the predictive algorithms should determine the outcome, or whether they will just be one of several factors used by officers and judges. As an example, take Professor Andrew Ferguson's modern-day re-creation of Detective McFadden observing John Terry on the streets of Cleveland:

> [McFadden] observes John Terry and, using facial recognition technology, identifies him and begins to investigate using big data. Detective McFadden learns through a database search that Terry has a prior criminal record, including a couple of convictions and a number of arrests. McFadden learns, through pattern-matching links, that Terry is an associate (a "hanger on") of a notorious, violent local gangster – Billy Cox – who had been charged with several murders. McFadden also learns that Terry has a substance abuse problem and is addicted to drugs.[165]

Now assume that the detective plugs all of John Terry's background information into a predictive algorithm, which tells him that John Terry has a 1 percent chance of involvement in criminal activity at any moment during the day. This result would not be sufficient to create reasonable suspicion. Then our modern Detective McFadden could do some more quick research through the police database and add in some other factors; for example, the criminal history database reveals that

Terry has multiple convictions for armed robbery of businesses, and license plate data connects Terry to other unsolved robberies in this area.[166] This, combined with the earlier information about Terry, tells the detective that Terry has a 5 percent chance of possessing an illegal weapon at any given time. We still probably do not have reasonable suspicion. Indeed, it is unlikely that only background information on a suspect could ever meet the reasonable suspicion standard – this is akin to saying there are people who are so suspicious that there is always reasonable grounds to believe they are engaging in criminal activity anytime they are seen in public.[167]

Regardless of how much the prediction is based on background information alone, Detective McFadden cannot legally have reasonable suspicion at this point because he has not yet considered any individualized conduct on Terry. So Detective McFadden must incorporate Terry's individualized conduct into the calculus. As it turns out, the detective sees Terry pacing back and forth outside a business multiple times, looking in the window, and then conferring with another individual.[168] Now the modern-day Detective McFadden has two options. He can take the 5 percent chance that Terry is carrying an illegal weapon and then incorporate that into his own subjective calculation, combining that factor with his own observations of Terry pacing, looking, and conferring.[169] Or he can simply input these observations into the algorithm, which would then automatically combine these observations along with other data to give a percentage chance that the suspect was involved in criminal activity. The first is an example of using the predictive algorithm as a factor; the second is an example of the "outcome determinative" model.

From this basic example, we can see that the "outcome determinative" option has a number of advantages. First, it will be simpler for officers and judges to apply, since it will not require individual officers and judges to process numerical probabilities; the algorithm does all the processing itself and gives the decision-maker an exact number. The predictive algorithm will (presumably) use statistics from thousands of previous cases to establish whether the relevant facts create the level of suspicion necessary to reach reasonable suspicion or probable cause. These results (and thus the algorithm itself) can be periodically tested every few months to ensure they are still reliable – and as part of that testing, the algorithm can be adjusted to give different weights to different types of data or even to add or remove certain types of data altogether. Second, the outcome determinative model will minimize the biased factors that human decision-makers apply in making these determinations. Both reasonable suspicion and probable cause require the officer to show specific, objective facts to support their conclusion,[170] and forcing police officers to input these specific facts into the algorithm will make it harder for them to consciously or subconsciously use factors based on race.

The outcome determinative model could even work in cases where the police officers and judges need to evaluate an informant's reliability to make a probable cause determination. For example, assume there is a reliable algorithm that predicts the chance that drugs will be found at a certain location. It requires five different variables to produce a result, and three of these data points are particular to the suspect's observed behavior. None of these data points are related, either directly or indirectly, to race, religion, or any other protected class. Assume that a police officer has personal knowledge of all these factors and inputs them into the software, which predicts a 75 percent chance that drugs will be found at the location. Given these facts, a court will almost certainly find that probable cause exists, and a search warrant should be issued.

How would the model work if the police officer does not have any personal knowledge about the case, and instead her affidavit quotes an informant who provides the information about all five variables? Once again, all five variables are entered into the software, and the algorithm predicts a 75 percent chance that drugs will be found at the location, assuming that the information is correct. How can the algorithm (and thus the judge) account for the inevitable reliability questions that accompany the use of informants? To preserve the outcome determinative model, the software must be designed so that the credibility of the informant is accounted for as part of the algorithm. In many cases, this would be feasible. Generally, search warrant applications only have a few different categories of informants: known informants who have provided accurate information in the past, known informants who have never provided information before, anonymous informants, etc. Thus, these specific categories could be inputs into the software, so that after each relevant factor is entered, the algorithm would ask about the source of the fact – did it come from personal observation by the affiant police officer, or from an informant; and if from an informant, how much is known about the informant and his prior track record?[171] These categories would be as specific as the descriptions currently used by police officers in search warrant affidavits.

Any outcome determinative model in this context will require a far more sophisticated algorithm, with many more inputs for the different behaviors that might be observed. And in designing these algorithms, the programmers will need to stay away from the vague factors that currently cause unreliability and are open to abuse, such as "furtive movements" or "acting suspiciously."[172] Other inputs, such as "suspicious bulge" or "nervous behavior," which could conceivably refer to specific facts that indicate the presence of criminal activity, may need to be defined with more specific language. And the inputs need to allow for exculpatory information to ensure that the algorithm complies with the "totality of the circumstances" requirement of the probable cause determination.[173]

Given these practical problems, it is unlikely that any predictive algorithm could ever be designed that accounts for every possible type of specific behavior that a police officer might use in making a reasonable suspicion or probable cause determination. Some predictive algorithms could be designed in certain basic, often-repeated scenarios (observations made of individuals exiting buildings where drugs are sold, observations made during routine traffic stops, etc.),[174] but the potential range of observed activity is simply too broad to conceive of a world in which every possible relevant factor is accounted for in the algorithm. And in some cases, the police officer or judge may have her own opinion about the reliability of an informant that is not adequately accounted for by the five or six traditional categories of the algorithm's inputs. Furthermore, it may be politically unacceptable to take human beings completely out of the loop, since this would require police officers and judges to ignore information (whether inculpatory or exculpatory) that is probative to the reasonable suspicion/probable cause determination.

Thus, there will be some situations in which the predictive algorithm is merely one of the factors that the judge considers. In these cases, the judge will need to incorporate the conclusions of the predictive algorithm alongside other factors. We will call these "independent" factors to show that they are above and beyond the factors used by the algorithm. For example, assume that the algorithm uses five different inputs and predicts a 25 percent likelihood that drugs will be found at a given location. The judge also knows about three independent factors that on their own do not quite rise to the level of probable cause. The judge will know that the software predicted a 25 percent likelihood. If the predictive algorithm is meant to be one of the many factors that she considers, she would then need to combine the 25 percent chance from the algorithm and the unquantified "almost-but-not-quite" factors from her own judgment. How does she balance the specific number from the algorithm with her own intuitive conclusion? Does she have to quantify her "almost-but-not-quite" conclusion? Assume she can do this (and with time, judges would get better at this task with practice), and she quantifies her subjective conclusion at a 30 percent likelihood. How much weight does she give to her 30 percent compared to the 25 percent from the algorithm?

To accurately combine the results from the predictive algorithm with other factors, we need to take two steps. First, to avoid double counting, we need to separate the factors that have already been considered by the algorithm from the factors that have not.[175] The transparency that we already require from these algorithms should make this task easier; the decision-maker will be able to review the factors used by the algorithm and then remove those from her own independent analysis.

Second, the decision-maker must use the predictive algorithm as the starting point and then adjust the percentage chance up or down as she adds in the independent factors. One method of doing this is to apply Bayes theorem, which is a process of combining known probabilities with new evidence to create a new, updated probability.[176] The predictive algorithm would provide the decision-maker with a base rate or prior probability that criminal activity is present, and then the decision-maker would apply the probability of criminal activity based on the relevant evidence that was not considered by the predictive algorithm (known as the "current probability").[177] This extra evidence could include personal observations by the police officer (assuming those observations are not accounted for by the algorithm already) or extra information about the reliability of the informant that was not accounted for by the algorithm.

For example, let's return to the modern-day version of Detective McFadden and John Terry.[178] We know from our algorithm (based only on background information about John Terry) that there is a 5 percent chance that Terry is carrying an illegal weapon at any given time. Detective McFadden then observes him pacing, looking, and conferring and realizes this is the kind of behavior that he would expect a potential robber to engage in before committing the crime.[179] Thus, Detective McFadden estimates that a person who is planning a robbery is 90 percent likely to engage in the kind of behavior that Terry is currently engaging in. And although the detective realizes that there are some innocent explanations for this behavior (perhaps Terry is window shopping, and then conferring with his friend about what to buy), because Terry has repeated this behavior multiple times means that the odds of him not planning a robbery are only about 10 percent. Given these estimates, the detective can complete a Bayesian calculation (or, more likely, input these estimates into a simple calculator that will then conduct the Bayesian calculation) and determine that the chances that Terry is engaged in criminal activity are 32.1 percent.[180] We would then compare that probability to the quantified legal standard for reasonable suspicion to see whether the stop and frisk is justified.

In contrast, assume that our modern Detective McFadden, like the real-life Detective McFadden, did not have any information about John Terry's background. Instead, he merely observed Terry's suspicious behavior. Under Bayes' theorem, our base rate would be much lower. Perhaps we recognize that this is a high crime neighborhood, so we know that 1 percent of the population is carrying an illegal weapon at any given time. If Detective McFadden makes the same observations as before and he calculates the same odds of criminal activity based on those observations, the chances that Terry is engaged in criminal activity drops to only 8.3 percent.[181] In other words, the lower base rate from the lack of a big data algorithm makes the detective's prediction of criminal activity much less accurate.

Thus, even if predictive algorithms are not outcome determinative, using a more statistical approach to determine reasonable suspicion or probable cause will allow police officers and judges to incorporate more reliable base rates into their calculations. Predictive algorithms will also help these decision-makers avoid a common problem when making predictions: ignoring or undervaluing the base rate. As evident from our example, a very low base rate or prior probability for potential criminal activity means that even very suspicious independent factors might not result in a very high resulting probability. In fact, studies have shown that individuals who make predictions frequently undervalue or ignore base rates and instead give too much weight to the independent factors that they observe.[182] Forcing police officers and judges to incorporate a more accurate base rate in making their calculations would be another benefit of using a quantified system of criminal procedure.

Of course, the more we allow the decision-makers to use independent factors, the more we lose the benefits of predictive algorithms, such as the increased accuracy and the mitigation of subjective and biased human input. For example, when Detective McFadden enters in his own probability estimates into the Bayes calculation, he may underestimate the chance that Terry has an innocent explanation for his conduct because Terry is African-American, and the detective has an irrational implicit bias against African-Americans. This would result in a higher prediction of criminal activity for Terry than it would for a white person with the same background engaging in the same activity. Thus, we should design our algorithms to avoid the need for independent factors as much as possible, since the biases in the algorithms can be detected and minimized.

CONCLUSION

Big data's predictive algorithms have the potential to revolutionize the way police investigate crime and the way the courts regulate the police. For centuries, courts have been crafting legal standards for police officers who were making clinical judgments based on experience and intuition. The imprecision and subjectivity of these legal standards were a necessary evil – they were required given the subjective factors that were used by the police, but their accuracy could not be tested, they made the system less transparent, and they opened the door to inconsistent and frequently discriminatory results. With the rise of big data's predictive algorithms, we have an opportunity to increase the accuracy and the transparency of the way we apply the standards and of the standards themselves, making the system more efficient, more fair, and more open.

To reap these benefits, we need to ensure that the predictive algorithms are race neutral and that they take into account individual suspicion. This may require new types of algorithms that are specifically designed for determining reasonable suspicion and probable cause. It will certainly require that the algorithms are transparent, so that reviewing courts can understand what factors the algorithm is using.

To be sure, a system of mechanical predictive algorithms and quantified legal standards will not be perfect. It will probably be impossible to scrub all residue of racial discrimination from the existing databases, and police officers and judges will make mistakes when trying to use the predictive algorithms as base rates and then adding their own independent observations. And the predictive algorithms themselves will still make mistakes, and thus will not always be as accurate as we prefer. But the current system relies too much on the implicit and sometimes, explicit biases of police officers and judges; vague standards that can be manipulated by police officers, which are more or less incomprehensible to lay people; and accuracy rates (when they can be measured) that vary wildly from jurisdiction to jurisdiction. The time has come for courts to embrace the enhanced precision and transparency that big data algorithms can offer.

But all this extra precision will be of little use if the courts cannot apply the results of predictive algorithms to the appropriate legal standards. In the next chapter, we will examine the legal standards that regulate government surveillance and consider the advantages and disadvantages of quantifying these standards. We will then apply the cost–benefit analysis theory by linking the quantified legal standard to the productivity of the surveillance.

3

Quantifying Criminal Procedure

The process does not deal with hard certainties, but with probabilities. Long before the law of probabilities was articulated as such, practical people formulated certain common sense conclusions about human behavior; jurors as factfinders are permitted to do the same – and so are law enforcement officers.

United States v. *Cortez* (1981)[1]

INTRODUCTION

The previous two chapters introduced an equation to measure the productivity of surveillance, with privacy costs and benefits on one side and the benefits to law enforcement on the other. The chapters examined both the cost and the benefit side of the equation, calling for more empirical work in determining the privacy cost of surveillance and noting that the widespread adoption of predictive algorithms by the police will result in greater precision in determining the likely benefits of a given surveillance. But all of this improved data on costs and benefits will be of little use without a quantitative legal standard to judge it against. Assume that a court reviewing a *Terry* frisk had access to an extremely accurate database that took into account five different race-neutral factors, including specific acts by the suspect, and the database reported that of all the suspects who met these twelve factors in the past five years, 19.2 percent of them were armed. Would that constitute reasonable suspicion that this particular suspect was armed and therefore allow the police to conduct a frisk when they confronted the suspect? If not, how close is it – close enough that a suspicious movement by the suspect is enough to put the risk across the line?[2] Without a quantified definition of reasonable suspicion, judges are unable to answer these questions, and so instead rely on their own intuition – the "common sense intuition" that Chief Justice Burger was referring to in the introductory quotation. But as we have seen, this common sense intuition is frequently wildly inaccurate and often based on implicit or explicit bias.

In this chapter, we will focus on the legal standard that courts should set for each method of surveillance. Setting this legal standard is far more complicated now than it was a few decades ago. Before 1968, there was effectively only one legal standard: probable cause. Thus, there was only one question that a court had to determine: was the surveillance a "search" under the Fourth Amendment? If it was, the government had to establish probable cause before engaging in the surveillance; if it was not, the surveillance was completely unregulated.

This basic paradigm was shattered by *Terry* v. *Ohio*, in which the Supreme Court held that "a rigid all-or-nothing model of justification and regulation under the [Fourth] Amendment" was inadequate.[3] *Terry* created a new legal standard of "reasonable suspicion" to apply to a less intrusive type of search. The Court later expanded this spectrum of legal standards and created higher standards for more intrusive searches, such as no-knock search warrants[4] and bodily intrusions.[5] At the same time, Congress has added a number of new levels to this spectrum, from "certified relevance," when law enforcement is seeking "address" information, such as the phone numbers that were dialed on a telephone;[6] to "specific and articulable facts," when law enforcement is seeking stored e-mail which has not yet been opened by its recipient;[7] to the strict Title III standards that apply to wiretapping and intercepting electronic communications in transit.[8]

This spectrum of legal standards opens the door to our cost–benefit analysis theory. Almost all of the legal standards correspond to a likelihood that the law enforcement officer will find evidence of criminal activity: certified relevance means that law enforcement need only show a small chance that evidence will be found, while probable cause requires a much higher likelihood. In other words, these standards are about *predictions*: trying to determine the odds that a proposed surveillance will be successful. This corresponds to the benefits side of our equation: all other things being equal, the more likely it is that a surveillance will find evidence, the more productive the surveillance will be. If the surveillance method is very intrusive and/or very expensive, we will want to require a very high level of certainty (such as probable cause) before allowing the search; if the surveillance method is not at all intrusive and/or not very expensive, we need only require a very low level of certainty (such as certified relevance).[9] In every case, we are asking the law enforcement officer to make a prediction to a certain level of certainty that the surveillance will be successful, and we are then asking the court to decide whether that level of certainty is sufficient given the costs of the search.

Since the inception of our criminal justice system, law enforcement officers and judges have relied primarily on experience, training, intuition, and common sense in making their predictions.[10] In response, courts have crafted broad standards to accommodate these subjective judgments and allow for flexibility in application.

The broad, flexible nature of these standards is no accident: they have been intentionally left imprecise by generations of courts. One reason is the nearly infinite number of different facts that could arise in any criminal case, which make hard and fast rules rather impractical.[11] But the main reason these rules have been kept ambiguous is that police and courts have historically lacked the necessary tools to evaluate the accuracy of their predictions with any precision. Thus, state actors have been forced to rely on their own subjective beliefs and anecdotal evidence in making their predictions.[12]

As we saw in the last chapter, all of that is now changing. Big data analysis is providing police and judges with tools that can predict future behavior with greater precision than ever before. These tools hold out the promise of increased fairness and greater objectivity at many of the critical decision points in our criminal justice system. They also will be able to quantify the benefits of various forms of surveillance, allowing us to predict with much greater precision the success rate for each of these methods. We saw in the last chapter how law enforcement officers can use big data's algorithms to derive a relatively precise prediction of the likelihood of finding evidence. But these quantified predictions will be of no use unless we reform the broad, ambiguous legal standards that courts now use to evaluate surveillance. The current legal standards that govern police officers and judges are imprecise and subjective. Courts have deliberately created them to be imprecise and seem to have every intention of keeping them that way. Unfortunately, these nebulous standards are a poor fit for big data's highly precise tools and for the cost–benefit analysis that we are proposing. This chapter argues in favor of adopting precise legal standards for different levels of surveillance in order to harmonize the analytical world of big data with the legal world of criminal justice.

Note that requiring a certain standard of certainty is not the only way to regulate government surveillance. As noted in Chapter 1, courts or other policymakers can create other legal restrictions in order to discourage low-productivity searches, such as requiring preclearance from a court, a prosecutor, or a high-ranking law enforcement official; imposing standards to minimize the amount of innocent information that is collected; or mandating a showing that the surveillance is the least restrictive means of obtaining the information.[13] Chapter 8 discusses these options in greater detail; this chapter will focus on setting a standard of certainty as the primary way of regulating surveillance.

This chapter provides a roadmap for a transition from intuitive descriptive standards to empirically tested quantitative standards. It first explains why a move to quantified legal standards is an improvement over the descriptive standards now used by courts. It then examines the current set of descriptive standards and attempts to determine what level of certainty courts are applying when they use these standards – in other words, it seeks to translate the current standards of reasonable suspicion and probable cause into quantitative terms. Finally, the chapter proposes that these descriptive standards be jettisoned altogether in favor of a fully quantified system that could adjust more precisely to the productivity of different types of surveillance.

DESCRIPTIVE STANDARDS VS. QUANTIFIED STANDARDS

The current legal regime provides for different legal standards for different surveillance methods, some set by courts and some set by statutes. Many types of surveillance require no showing of suspicion at all on the part of law enforcement.[14] Some require a showing of "certified relevance" – little more than a ministerial approval by the courts.[15] Some require reasonable suspicion[16] or probable cause,[17] but allow the police officer to make that judgment on the spot, to be reviewed later by a neutral magistrate. Others require law enforcement to prove probable cause to a neutral magistrate before conducting the surveillance.[18]

Simply stated, the quantitative results from mechanical predictions are incompatible with these broad, flexible standards used by police and judges in the current world of criminal procedure.[19] Reasonable suspicion and probable cause are standards that have been intentionally kept vague by the courts. The Supreme Court has long resisted setting specific probabilities for the flexible concepts of reasonable suspicion or probable cause,[20] explaining that it is a "practical, nontechnical conception" which is "incapable of precise definition or quantification into percentages."[21] The Court explains to us that the concepts are not "readily, or even usefully, reduced to a neat set of legal rules"[22] and then follows through on this promise by providing a multitude of messy rules for police and lower courts to follow. Probable cause is defined as evidence that would "warrant a man of prudence and caution in believing that the offense has been committed," "a fair probability that contraband or evidence of a crime will be found,"[23] or a "reasonable ground to believe that the accused [is] guilty."[24] Reasonable suspicion is defined as "obviously less demanding than ... probable cause,"[25] requiring merely "some minimal level of objective justification."[26] The closest the Supreme Court has come to quantifying either of these standards is when it explained that reasonable suspicion "is considerably less than proof of wrongdoing by a preponderance of the evidence."[27]

These definitions are rather unhelpful in providing guidance or clarity as to when a stop or a search is appropriate. No lay person would possibly know what these terms mean in the real world; police officers and law students must study dozens of fact patterns from case law to get a sense of what kinds of factors will create reasonable suspicion or probable cause.

This imprecision has its costs: it creates inconsistency from jurisdiction to jurisdiction and even from judge to judge, and it makes it harder for police to know whether their actions are legal at the time they take those actions. It forces magistrates and judges to rely on the subjective descriptions and personal judgments of the police officers. The vague standards breed vague descriptions to meet those standards, such as "high crime neighborhood," "acting nervous," and "suspicious hand movements." Police officers who testify to these factors are usually not acting in bad faith; they are merely trying to find ways to satisfy the ambiguous legal standard. Perhaps worst of all, the imprecise standards make it difficult to evaluate the constitutionality of law enforcement actions on a larger scale. Assume that a study of all probable-cause-based automobile searches in a jurisdiction demonstrated that 32 percent of the time, police officers who conducted these searches found contraband. Does this mean that the police in this jurisdiction are meeting the probable cause standard? Without any quantification of the standard, it is impossible to tell.

In the past, the imprecision of these terms was a necessary evil. If the Supreme Court had instructed police that they needed to be at least 20 percent certain of an individual's guilt before conducting a *Terry* stop, the precise quantification would not have helped individual officers in making their on-the-spot decisions. It makes more sense for officers to be given some broad guidelines (e.g., "more than a mere hunch" or "some level of objective justification required") and then teach them through training and trial and error what courts will approve and what they will not (e.g., observing a suspect leave a known crack house and then run from a uniformed police officer constitutes reasonable suspicion; observing a suspect leave a known crack house with no other suspicious behavior does not). Similarly, telling a magistrate that she should only issue the warrant if there is a 45 percent chance of finding contraband would be unlikely to help her make the decision in a world of clinical judgments. The magistrate must consider a myriad of subjective factors from the police officer's affidavit: the credibility of an informant, the reports of unusual but not blatantly illegal activity, and so on. Given the messiness of the evidence confronted by police and judges, a messy standard makes the most sense. Such a standard allows the decision-makers to follow their intuition and make a subjective judgment about whether "something seems not right about this situation" (reasonable suspicion) or "I believe there is a good chance that a crime has been committed" (probable cause).

But as we saw in Chapter 2, in today's data-driven world, evidence is becoming less messy and more quantifiable. Police and courts can analyze the results of hundreds of thousands of past frisks and searches to see which factors are likely to lead to the discovery of weapons or contraband. In today's world, a magistrate might be able to plug in the facts set out in a search warrant application and come up with a very close approximation as to the percentage chance of finding contraband. Even if the police are relying on the credibility of an informant, there will be some data regarding the reliability of that informant's past information – or, if the informant has no past track record, there will be some historical data about the reliability of new informants in this jurisdiction who share certain relative characteristics with the informant in this case.

It is true that historically, judges themselves are very reluctant to adopt quantitative legal standards.[28] In a survey of 400 trial court judges from the late 1960s, judges were asked whether they would approve of using specific percentages or probabilities in determining standards of proof, and "[t]he judges were almost unanimous in their rejection of the proposal for both criminal and civil trials."[29] Furthermore, there is evidence that decision makers who are untrained in statistics (like most judges) will be unable to accurately use quantitative predictions.[30]

Numerous scholars have also objected to creating specific quantifiable standards. For example, Professor Orin Kerr argues that quantification of probable cause would lead to less accurate probable cause determinations because warrant applications only provide a limited amount of information, and under the current system, judges are able to use their intuition to account for the missing facts.[31] Professor Kerr argues that when a judge gets a warrant application, she only sees the selective facts that the police want her to see: investigative techniques that successfully found evidence to build towards probable cause.[32] The application will not describe any investigative techniques that were used that failed to find evidence, nor will it describe any possible investigative techniques that could have been used that were not used.[33] In the current non-quantified world, Professor Kerr argues, judges can use their intuition about what might be missing from the warrant application, and judges will instinctively (and perhaps subconsciously) factor that into their decision.[34] If the probable cause standard became quantified, at, say, 40 percent, judges would merely calculate the odds (incorrectly) based on the selective facts in the affidavit and would suppress their natural intuition to be suspicious about the facts that might not have been included.

Although Professor Kerr claims his argument is based on the value of judicial intuition, it is really about the need for particularized suspicion. He uses an example of law enforcement who have a well-documented study that 60 percent of all Harvard dorm rooms contain illegal drugs, and he posits that police officers attempt to use that study to get a warrant to search a specific dorm room.[35] A judge would rightfully be suspicious of this request, he argues, because the judge's intuition would make her wonder why the police have chosen this room in particular – thus leading to the conclusion that she is not getting the full story from the police.[36] But this is merely a restatement of the requirement that suspicion be particularized – that the affidavit must contain some information that links this specific suspect to the illicit activity. And as noted in Chapter 2, this is an important consideration in designing big data's algorithms for criminal law application – we need to either ensure that the inputs contained some reference to the individual actions or behavior of the suspect himself, or allow for police and judges to add in their own observations of individual activity.[37]

A more troubling critique of using predictive algorithms is the Supreme Court's requirement that the decision-maker use a "totality of the circumstances" test in determining whether reasonable suspicion or probable cause exist.[38] Professor Michael Rich argues that a predictive algorithm can never determine probable cause on its own because the algorithm is by definition limited in the factors that it considers in making its determination.[39] A predictive algorithm might be programmed to consider only a handful of factors, or it might be programmed to consider hundreds of factors, but it can never consider every factor that could possibly be relevant to a probable cause analysis.[40] A human being at least has the potential to incorporate new observations, but a predictive algorithm is limited by its previous programming.[41]

One response to this critique is that it somewhat misrepresents what the Court means by "totality of the circumstances." This requirement does not mean that the decision-maker must consider every possible factor – that would be impossible for a human being or for a computer. Indeed, courts have noted that once a police officer has established that probable cause exists, the officer is under no further duty to investigate or gather exculpatory data.[42]

Instead, "totality of the circumstances" means that two requirements need to be satisfied. First, it means that courts should reject a formalistic checklist of factors (such as the pre-*Gates* "two pronged" test)[43] and be willing to consider many different factors in deciding whether probable cause exists.[44] Certainly a predictive algorithm can be designed to consider hundreds of different factors, far more than the average police officer observing the scene and far more than are typically included in an affidavit in a warrant application.[45] It is true that no predictive algorithm will ever be able to consider every relevant factor, whether inculpatory or exculpatory. But of course this is also true for police officers and judges. In fact, predictive algorithms could conceivably process thousands of different factors, many more than a human being could.

In other words, although it is easy to come up with examples of cases in which a police officer makes an observation that is not programmed into the predictive algorithm and which dramatically increases (or decreases) the level of suspicion in a situation, it is just as easy to think of examples in which a predictive algorithm considers relevant factors that an average police officer would never consider. Many of the factors that human police officers consider to be relevant may in fact be irrelevant, or may be given insufficient weight or too much weight. And, as many commentators have pointed out, some of the "intuitions" of police officers and even judges are grounded in implicit racial bias, making their conclusions not just inaccurate but also discriminatory.[46]

The second aspect of the "totality of the circumstances" requirement, is that the police and courts must consider potential exculpatory evidence as part of the totality of the circumstances, since certain observations or background facts may actually lower the level of suspicion.[47] Predictive algorithms can – and should – be pro-grammed to consider possible exculpatory evidence as well, and to weigh that evidence in reaching their conclusions.

In short, quantifying these standards will allow police and judges to use predictive algorithms, bringing a number of benefits: the opportunity to reduce discriminatory bias in the system; greater accountability for police actions; and a higher level of accuracy (that is, fewer searches of those who are innocent and more searches of those who are in fact engaged in criminal activity). There is nothing inherent about these tests that would forbid courts from adopting quantitative standards, but courts have been extremely reluctant to do so.[48] In the next section, we will talk about the feasibility of such a shift.

MAKING PREDICTIVE ALGORITHMS WORK IN THE CRIMINAL
JUSTICE SYSTEM

The next step is to assign quantified levels of certainty to each of the current descriptive standards. This will give judges a baseline from which to build out more precise quantitative standards if courts decide to move away from the descriptive standards altogether. Even if removing the descriptive standards altogether ends up being too radical a change, providing a numerical equivalent for the descriptive standards is necessary if courts are going to use predictive algorithms in evaluating surveillance.

Under current law, a police officer seeking a search warrant states that she believes there is probable cause to believe that contraband will be found in the suspect's house, and a judge appraises that assertion by reviewing and evaluating the facts that the police officer places in her affidavit, including the credibility of any informants (and of the police officer herself). The judge then reaches her own conclusion about whether a person of reasonable caution would believe that contraband is present at the location.

In a world of predictive algorithms that keeps the descriptive standards, the police officer will instead present the magistrate with the output of a computer program which states that, given the facts known to the police officer, there is a 40 percent chance that contraband will be found in the suspect's house. The judge will then examine the algorithm that was used to ensure that it meets the appropriate legal standards, and will then make a ruling as to whether the 40 percent level of certainty meets the probable cause standard. Depending on the circumstances, the judge may make a decision based solely on the output of the algorithm (the "outcome determinative" model), or she may consider the output of the algorithm as one factor to combine with other relevant facts (the "formal factor" model).

As discussed in Chapter 2, under either model the predictive algorithm would need to be sufficiently transparent for the judge to be able to confirm that the computer is not using discriminatory factors or data and that at least some of the factors used by the computer are specific to this particular suspect. (If the algorithm has no factors that are based on individualized suspicion, a judge needs to combine the 40 percent result with specific facts about this particular suspect in order to arrive at her own percentage.) Assuming these factors are met, the judge then needs to decide whether the 40 percent chance of finding contraband meets the legal standard that has been set for this particular type of surveillance. This means that courts must overcome their resistance to quantifying these legal standards. As part of overcoming that reluctance, in some cases judges must also become comfortable with manipulating these probabilities and combining them with other factors in order to reach their own independent conclusions.[49]

In one sense, the use of predictive algorithms to establish reasonable suspicion or probable cause is not so revolutionary. The Supreme Court has not been averse to using statistical data in other Fourth Amendment contexts. For example, when the Court was determining whether a drunk driving checkpoint was "reasonable" under the special needs doctrine, it noted that the checkpoint resulted in a 1.6 percent hit rate for drunk drivers,[50] and also that similar checkpoints around the country had a 1 percent hit rate.[51] And as we will see later, lower courts already routinely evaluate the reliability of certain tools, such as breathalyzers or drug dogs, that are used to demonstrate probable cause.[52] The need for courts to use success rates to evaluate probable cause will only increase as sophisticated investigative technologies such as facial recognition software or gun detectors become more widely used. In a sense, predictive algorithms will be doctrinally no different from these other tools that are already being used to establish probable cause.

CALCULATING BASELINE NUMBERS

Our first task is to determine what quantitative percentages are currently associated with these two legal standards. Once we have those numbers as a baseline, we can see how they may need to be adjusted to fit into our cost–benefit analysis. There are two ways to determine what percentages judges are actually using in practice. The first is through reverse engineering, by examining the stops and searches that have been approved under the current law and seeing how often they are successful. The second is more straightforward: simply ask the judges what percentage they use when applying these standards.

We will first use the reverse engineering approach. If we measure the hit rates for stops and searches that courts have approved using the traditional standards, we should get a number that is at least above the minimum level of suspicion that is required. For example, if across the country, courts approve of 100,000 probable cause searches and police find contraband in 45,000 of those searches, we can know that generally a prediction which is 45 percent accurate is at least high enough to satisfy the probable cause standard.

Information like this is sparse, but there are some useful data points. For example, a review of police tactics in Philadelphia concluded that only 3 percent of the *Terry* stops resulted in recovery of contraband; the review also concluded that reasonable suspicion was lacking for somewhere between 35 percent and 50 percent of these stops. [53] This implies that for these judges reasonable suspicion means more than a 3 percent likelihood. And as we saw in the last chapter, a 1999 study of stops and frisks in New York City showed a hit rate of 11 percent for the year. This rate seems to have held constant; the district court in the *Floyd* case held that the Terry stops in New York City in the early 2000s were often conducted without reasonable suspicion. These stops had a 12 percent hit rate; thus, the *Floyd* judge believed that a 12 percent rate was too low to constitute reasonable suspicion.[54] In contrast, we know that before the New York Police Department Street Crime Unit began its aggressive stop-and-frisk policy, its hit rate for *Terry* stops was a more respectable 21 percent.[55]

Reviewing probable cause searches of automobiles provides some real-world data as to the percentage chance necessary to establish probable cause. An independent review of the San Antonio police showed that their probable cause automobile searches resulted in a hit rate of 35.1 percent.[56] As part of a settlement of a federal civil rights action in 1995, Maryland State Troopers were required to report every stop and search of a car on their highways,[57] which showed a 52.5 percent hit rate for probable cause searches.[58] And a review of the Florida State Police showed a 38.2 percent success rate for such searches.[59]

Another way to estimate the number is to look at cases involving alerts by drug-sniffing dogs, which can constitute probable cause as long as the dog's reliability has been established.[60] Thus, when a court needs to determine whether a positive alert by a drug dog is sufficient to establish probable cause, the Supreme Court has instructed the reviewing judge to consider the training and past performance of the drug dog in controlled testing environments.[61] Lower courts have already (albeit grudgingly) approved specific numerical success rates for drug dogs as sufficient to establish that the dog's positive alert creates probable cause, holding that accuracy rates of 50 percent,[62] 55 percent,[63] 58 percent,[64] and 60 percent[65] were all sufficient to satisfy the probable cause standard.[66]

On the other hand, Professor Max Minzner points out that the success rate for search warrants, which allegedly use the same probable cause standard as automobile searches are somewhere between 84 percent and 97 percent.[67] Although this dramatic disparity between different applications of the probable cause standard makes it more challenging to determine the "correct" number through reverse engineering, it provides yet another compelling reason to quantify the standard. Are courts being too lenient in reviewing probable cause for warrantless searches, or are they requiring too high a showing for warrant applications? Or perhaps we want two different standards, one for the on-the-spot decisions made by police officers, and one for the greater legitimacy and presumed legality of search warrants? None of these questions can be truly addressed until the probable cause standard is quantified.

Putting the search warrant data aside for the moment, the small amount of data we have from reverse engineering these decisions gives us an estimate for reasonable suspicion at around 20 percent and probable cause somewhere between 40 percent and 50 percent.

The second method we can use to determine the level of certainty that judges use when applying these legal standards is to ask the judges what numbers they are using when they make their determination. Unsurprisingly, there is very little data on this question as well. In fact, up until now there has been only one known survey of judges, which took place nearly forty years ago. In 1982, a law professor surveyed all active and retired federal judges to ask them to quantify the concepts of reasonable suspicion and probable cause.[68] One hundred sixty-six responded with a numerical answer.[69] The results for probable cause were spread over a wide range (from 10 percent to 90 percent), but the vast majority of judges were between the 30 percent range and the 60 percent range:

Percentages assigned to probable cause:

1982 Federal Judge Survey

(%)	Result
10	2
20	5
30	27
40	44
50	52
60	25
70	8
80	2
90	1

This results in a mean average of 44.5 percent and a median average of 50 percent.[70]

The results for reasonable suspicion were also spread out over a wide range (with three judges inexplicably responding with either 0 percent or 100 percent), and showed less agreement among the respondents:[71]

Percentages assigned to reasonable suspicion:

1982 Federal Judge Survey

(%)	Result
10	24
20	33
30	49
40	21
50	23
60	9
70	2
80	0
90	0
100	1

This results in a mean average of 31.3 percent and a median average of 30 percent.

Given the age of this survey – and the lack of any other data on this question – I conducted my own survey in 2018 of federal magistrates. Every federal magistrate was sent a survey[72] asking what level of certainty they require in five different scenarios: reasonable suspicion for a *Terry* stop, "reason to believe" a suspect is armed for a *Terry* frisk; probable cause for a warrantless arrest; probable cause for a warrantless search (under circumstances when probable cause will authorize a search, such as an automobile search); and probable cause for a search warrant. The survey also asked whether their level of certainty for probable cause changes depending on the circumstances (such as the severity of the crime or the location being searched), and it allowed the respondents to make any comments at the end.

Forty-six magistrates filled out the survey with numerical values.[73]

2018 Federal Magistrate Survey Results

Legal Standard	Median Average (%)	Mean Average (%)	Std. Dev.
Reasonable suspicion (for *Terry* stop)	33	35.4	15.7
Reason to believe (for *Terry* frisks)	33	36.9	16.8
Probable cause (for automobile exception)	51	52.1	12.1
Probable cause (for warrant)	51	52.4	11.64
Probable cause (for arrest)	51	53.4	12.8

In addition, 28 percent of the magistrates responded that their standard of probable cause would vary depending on the circumstances. Many of these respondents stated that a more severe crime would lower their probable cause standard, though not to a very great degree.

As with the 1982 survey, this survey reveals a wide variation in the responses among the magistrates. Fourteen percent of the respondents indicated that they would find probable cause for a warrantless search with a likelihood of 40 percent or less, while another 19 percent would require a degree of certainty of 60 percent or higher. Likewise, over a quarter of the magistrates set the standard for "reasonable suspicion" at 20 percent or lower, while another quarter of the magistrates set it at 50 percent or higher. This inconsistency confirms the need for a more quantified approach; as of now, the terms "reasonable suspicion" and "probable cause" can mean dramatically different things to different magistrates.

When we compare the numbers we get from reverse engineering actual cases and the numbers we get from the judicial surveys, we also see a slight discrepancy. In practice, we see some courts allowing stops and frisks with only a 21 percent average success rate, yet when asked what level of certainty they believe is required, the average comes out at over 30 percent. And in practice many courts are allowing probable cause searches at a rate of 35–38 percent, while the average level of certainty from the surveys is around 50 percent. This implies that courts believe they are setting a certain level of certainty as the standard, but in fact they are allowing stops, frisks, and searches to go forward with a lower level of certainty. Again, this dissonance argues in favor of more effective recordkeeping and some level of quantification, so that courts can at least see the hit rates that result from the stops, frisks, and searches they are approving.

Before we leave the question of setting a baseline number, we should look at one more set of data: the degree of certainty that lay people believe should be used for these types of surveillance. We know that the legal standard should depend in part on the intrusiveness of the surveillance, and we saw in Chapter 1 that courts may not always correctly measure how intrusive the surveillance actually is. Just as we used the Slobogin/Schumacher surveys of lay people as a reality check on the intrusiveness determinations of the Supreme Court, we should learn what level of certainty lay people believe should apply to these searches. Furthermore, one of the purposes of making these standards more transparent is so that we can review them and see if they are consistent with the public's view of where the standards should be.

To get an idea of where lay people would set this standard, I conducted a survey of over 630 individuals.[74] Unlike the magistrates from the previous survey, the lay people were not likely to be familiar with the terms "reasonable suspicion" and "probable cause." Thus, the survey described the context for each type of surveillance and then asked the respondent the level of certainty they would require before law enforcement was permitted to engage in the surveillance.

2018 Lay person survey results

Surveillance type	Legal standard	Median average (%)	Mean average (%)	Std. dev.
Level of certainty that an individual is involved in criminal activity that should be required before an officer can briefly stop the individual and ask questions (n = 635)	Reasonable suspicion (for *Terry* stop)	69	64.2	23.4
Level of certainty that an individual is armed that should be required before an officer can frisk a suspect that he has legally stopped (n = 633)	Reason to believe (for *Terry* frisks)	69	63.3	27.2
Level of certainty that contraband will be found that should be required before a police officer can search a car after it has been legally pulled over (n = 625)	Probable cause (for automobile exception)	75	70.2	22.1
Level of certainty that contraband will be found that should be required before a judge should issue a search warrant for someone's home (n = 657)	Probable cause (for warrant)	75	72.7	18.8
Level of certainty that a suspect is guilty that should be required before a police officer can arrest the suspect (n = 627)	Probable cause (for arrest)	86	80.7	18.9
Level of certainty that incriminating evidence will be discovered that should be required before the police can wiretap a telephone (n = 628)	Title III standard (probable cause plus minimization and least intrusive means)	84	79.7	18.5

These numbers are consistent with the intrusiveness surveys conducted by Professors Slobogin and Schumacher, which found that the average intrusiveness of a frisk was 71.5, while the average intrusiveness for the search of a car was 74.6, and that of a bedroom search was 81.2.[75] In other words, although judges see a substantial difference in the intrusiveness of a frisk and the search of a home, and have crafted their legal standards accordingly; lay people do not see such a significant difference in intrusiveness and so would set the legal standard at similar level.

But what is even more startling is the vast difference between the level of certainty defined by the magistrates and judges – both in their actual decisions and in the surveys – and the level of certainty defined by lay people. Here are the results side by side:

	1982 survey of federal judges (Median/Mean %)	2018 survey of federal magistrates (Median/Mean %)	2018 survey of lay people (Median/Mean %)
Reasonable suspicion (engage in *Terry* stop)	30 / 31.3	33/ 35.4	69 / 64.2
Reason to believe (frisk during *Terry* stop)	N/A	33 / 36.96	69 / 69.3
Probable cause (car search)	50 / 44.5*	51 / 52.1	75 / 70.2
Probable cause (warrant)	50 / 44.5*	51 / 52.4	75 / 72.7
Probable cause (arrest)	50 / 44.5*	51 / 53.4	86 / 80.7

* Survey did not specify the context of the probable cause determination

This discrepancy does not mean that the judges are "wrong" to permit stops and searches with a relatively low level of certainty – after all, the judges are the experts and probably have a sophisticated sense of where to strike the balance. But the discrepancy does strongly show that we need to be having a more comprehensive debate about what these numbers should be. The lay people may lack expertise, but they are the ones who are being subjected to these stops and searches, and they should be made aware that the level of certainty used by courts is significantly lower than the level of certainty that lay people believe is appropriate. But we cannot have the debate when the courts' decisions are shrouded in impenetrable legalese such as "whether a man of prudence and caution believes that the offense has been committed."[76]

MOVING BEYOND THE DESCRIPTIVE STANDARDS

Determining the baseline numbers for reasonable suspicion and probable cause is just the first step. Courts and legislatures have created many more legal standards for a wide array of surveillance methods, such as "certified relevance" and "specific and articulable facts." But one of the purposes of quantifying these standards is that we no longer need to rely on any of this descriptive terminology: we can instead set a specific percentage of certainty that is required for any given type of surveillance. We will also no longer be limited by a certain number of categories. For the sake of administrative simplicity, we probably do not want to have a unique standard for every single type of search, but by using numbers instead of descriptive terms, we can assign any number we want to a given type of surveillance. We can also be far more precise as to the level of certainty that we seek, and we can easily adjust the numbers as the costs of the search increase or decrease.

For example, courts currently apply a "probable cause" standard for a wide variety of searches, including searching a car (without a warrant), or a workplace or home (with a warrant). If courts adopted a quantified standard, they could state that searching a car requires a 20 percent level of certainty, searching a workplace requires a 40 percent level of certainty, and searching a home requires a 60 percent level of certainty. Some of the magistrates in the survey noted that they in fact subtly adjust their probable cause standard depending on the location being searched; we also know that lay people believe that searching different locations results in different levels of intrusiveness.

Similarly, the current probable cause standard is meant to be constant regardless of the crime being investigated. But our cost–benefit analysis theory suggests that perhaps police searching a car for a murder weapon should have to meet a lower level of certainty than police who are searching a car for drugs.

One objection to this model is that it complicates the process of reviewing the legality of a search, since we are no longer applying one uniform standard for a given category of searches. After all, in theory it is much easier to simply know that any search requires a showing of probable cause, regardless of the location being searched or the severity of the crime. But as noted earlier, the current system employs at least six different legal standards for different situations, so judges already have a large number of gradations to keep track of. It is true that the vast majority of cases call for only one of two different standards – "reasonable suspicion" or "probable cause" – but as we have just seen, these terms imply a uniformity that does not in fact exist. In reality, each judge and magistrate has her own concept of what these standards mean. The 1982 judge survey and the 2018 magistrate survey confirm this – a significant percentage of judges and magistrates set the probable cause level at 30 percent, while a similar percentage set the standard at 60 percent. Similarly, "reasonable suspicion" got significant responses at the 10 percent range all the way through the 50 percent range. In other words, the current system also lacks uniformity for different searches, but it is a random, unpredictable inconsistency based on the magistrate or judge who happens to be hearing the case. Assigning a number to different types of searches would ensure that the legal standards would differ based on intrusiveness or level of crime, rather than the specific judge that is reviewing the case.

Professor Slobogin provides a model for this type of quantification. In his book *Privacy at Risk*, he proposes four tiers of legal standards: a "relevance" standard for very brief and non-intrusive searches and seizures, such as roadblocks, casual questioning, and searches of businesses; "reasonable suspicion" for stop-and-frisks; "probable cause" for standard searches; and "clear and convincing" for extremely severe intrusions such as bodily intrusions, reading a private diary, or prolonged undercover operations.[77] He offers quantifications for each of these terms: 5 percent likelihood for "relevance"; 30 percent likelihood for "reasonable suspicion"; 51 percent likelihood for "probable cause"; and 75 percent likelihood for "clear and convincing.[78] Writing just over a decade ago, Professor Slobogin conceded that these percentages "may seem artificial and even misleading," and that they would be difficult to "translat[e] percentages into anything police and magistrates can use on the street."[79] But with the increased use of predictive algorithms by police officers and judges, this argument can now be turned on its head. As police officers and judges rely more and more on predictive algorithms and their quantitative results, it will become harder to translate the percentages that police use on the street into the broad legal standards that judges have historically used to evaluate police conduct. Thus, the criminal justice system will be forced to move away from their broad descriptive legal standards and adopt specific numerical values instead.

Thus, contrary to what Professor Slobogin suggested in the pre-algorithmic era, it is likely that in modern times quantifying these standards will lead to decisions which are *more* accurate and *more* consistent. At the very least, there is evidence that quantifying these types of legal concepts will make the concepts more meaningful and useful to police officers and judges. It is true that if a police officer is told that probable cause is the equivalent of 40 percent certainty, she will not be able to apply that exact number when she is deciding whether to make an arrest. But studies have shown that decision makers are at least responsive to quantified standards, and that they are more useful to decision makers than mere verbal descriptions of those standards. For example, in a 1985 study of jurors, researchers found that mock jurors were unable to meaningfully distinguish between the terms "preponderance of the evidence, "clear and convincing evidence," and "beyond a reasonable doubt," even when given the typical jury instructions describing each standard.[80] In other words, when given the same set of facts, jurors convicted the defendant at approximately the same rate regardless of which legal standard they were given. (There was in fact a small difference between the standards, but it was the opposite of what the standards should have led them to: jurors convicted the defendant at a 43 percent rate under the "beyond a reasonable doubt" standard, but convicted them at a 38 percent rate for a "clear and convincing" standard and a 31 percent rate for a "preponderance of the evidence standard).[81]

Another group of mock jurors were given the same standards, but instead of using typical jury instructions to describe the standards, they were given quantified numbers. "Preponderance" was defined as at least 51 percent; "clear and convincing" was defined as at least 71 percent, and "beyond a reasonable doubt" was defined as at least 91 percent.[82] Providing jurors with these numerical guides succeeded in creating a significant difference in the rate of conviction for the different standards of proof: jurors convicted the defendant only 31 percent of the time under a "beyond a reasonable doubt" standard; 52 percent of the time under a "clear and convincing" standard, and 66 percent of the time under a "preponderance" standard.[83] There is no way of knowing whether the jurors accurately applied the percentage certainty that they were given for each standard, but it appears that they came closer to the meaning of the standard when given numerical definitions rather than descriptive definitions. Thus, shifting from an intuitive "feel" for what constitutes reasonable suspicion or probable cause to a quantified number may be easier than it first sounds.

Even so, the transition from descriptive standards to quantitative standards will be challenging. Police and judges are familiar with the current descriptive standards, and they have an intuition as to what types of fact patterns meet these standards. If police and judges are not using predictive algorithms, it will be hard for them to distinguish between a 20 percent likelihood and a 40 percent likelihood, especially if they are uncomfortable with statistics and numerical probabilities. Initially there will likely be inaccurate estimations by judges and inconsistencies between different judges as they attempt to estimate these percentages, especially for cases in which predictive algorithms have not been used. But removing the intuition from the process is a critical aspect of the shift from descriptive standards to numerical standards. The intuitions of police officers and judges are highly inaccurate and are subject to biases and prejudice. We can see from the surveys and the case law that the current system also has inaccurate estimations and inconsistencies between judges; the vague descriptive legal standards currently in use are masking these inaccuracies and inconsistencies. The advantage of using quantitative standards is that the decisions can ultimately be reviewed using statistical data.

This potential for review will be especially useful for situations in which similar or identical fact patterns are repeatedly brought before the courts. Consider the following hypothetical. Assume the standard for a *Terry* stop to investigate drug possession is set at 20 percent. Police routinely stop suspects based on the following fact pattern: the suspect entered a building were drugs are known to be sold and emerged from the building five minutes later. Courts routinely approve of these stops. However, after thousands of stops are made based on these two factors, courts review the data and learn that only 10 percent of these individuals actually have drugs on them. Courts will now know that these two factors alone do not meet the legal standard, and they will no longer approve stops when only these two factors are present. Instead, judges will require the presence of at least one more factor: such as the fact that the encounter occurred at night, or the suspect attempted to flee when he saw the presence of a police officer. Once the third factor is added to the analysis, the data show that 25 percent of the stops reveal the presence of drugs on the suspect;

thus, the courts can confirm that *Terry* stops under these circumstances are valid. This type of self-correction is nearly impossible with descriptive standards, since judges have different opinions as to when "criminal activity is afoot," and there is no way to establish which judges are applying the standards correctly.

Not only will quantifying these standards will help to ensure uniformity among judges, it will also provide a chance for meaningful debate in close cases. Consider *Navarette* v. *California*, a seminal Supreme Court case involving the definition of reasonable suspicion.[84] In *Navarette*, an anonymous 911 caller claimed that a pickup truck had driven her off of the highway, and provided police with the truck's license number. The police quickly located the truck and followed it for five minutes, but observed no suspicious activity. The police then pulled the truck over based only on the information from the anonymous tip, and ultimately recovered marijuana from the bed of the truck. The truck driver was convicted of marijuana possession, and he appealed the case, arguing that the anonymous tip did not provide police with reasonable suspicion that the truck driver was engaged in illegal activity.

The *Navarette* case divided the Supreme Court. Five Justices held that the anonymous tip was sufficient to establish reasonable suspicion of drunk driving, which justified the stop. Justice Scalia wrote a scathing dissent, labelling the holding as a "freedom destroying cocktail," arguing that anonymous reports of traffic violations are not reliable, and that even if they were, a single instance of reckless driving does not support reasonable suspicion of drunk driving.[85] Both sides referenced a precedent, *Florida* v. *J.L.*, in which the police got an anonymous tip that a young man in a plaid shirt standing at a bus stop was carrying a gun, and the Supreme Court held that the anonymous tip did not constitute reasonable suspicion.[86] According to the *Navarette* majority, the tip about the truck driver's reckless driving was more reliable than the tip about the gun in *J.L.* and thus satisfied the reasonable suspicion requirement; according to the dissent, the *Navaratte* tip was less reliable than the *J.L.* tip and thus fell short of reasonable suspicion.

Both the majority opinion and the dissent in *Navarette* made doctrinal and intuitive arguments about the reliability of the tip, but neither side used nor even mentioned any empirical evidence about how often anonymous tips prove to be accurate, and thus the Justices ended up talking past one another. But cases like *J.L.* and *Navarette* could easily be resolved if courts were willing to quantify the legal standards and then refer to empirical evidence. Courts could set reasonable suspicion as a certain percentage chance – say 33 percent – that criminal activity is afoot. They could then consider empirical evidence to see whether specific types of anonymous tips meet that standard. Perhaps anonymous 911 calls reporting reckless driving accurately identify drunk drivers 50 percent of the time, or perhaps only 5 percent of the time. For all their arguments about the traceability of 911 calls and the typical actions of drunk drivers, not one of the *Navarette* Justices actually knew the likelihood that the driver was drunk based on the evidence of the anonymous call. (Of course, the same could be said about the *J.L.* case – it may be true that anonymous 911 calls reporting that individuals have guns are correct 45 percent of the time, or perhaps they are correct only 10 percent of the time. In truth, the *J.L.* Court had no idea how reliable such tips were. And the *Navarette* Court had no idea whether their tip was more or less reliable than the *J.L.* tip). These numbers would not be difficult to collect and process, especially given today's data processing technology.

Even better, quantifying these standards and then referring to empirical evidence would mean that these cases would rarely need to be litigated at all. Police officers themselves would know the quantified standard and would have access to the empirical evidence. When they received a tip, anonymous or otherwise, they could consult the data and see how often tips with those characteristics end up being accurate. If the reliability crossed the legal threshold, they could proceed with their *Terry* stop; if not, they would know that they had to collect more information through observation and other investigation before they could proceed.

LINKING THE LEGAL STANDARD TO THE PRODUCTIVITY OF THE SURVEILLANCE

Once we have calculated the productivity of each type of search, we should attach the most lenient legal standards to the most productive searches and the strictest legal standards to the least productive searches. Luckily, we need not worry about incorporating the administrative cost into the legal standard, since that cost is already internalized by law enforcement. But courts do need to consider the severity of the crime being investigated. This will ensure that the legal standard for each surveillance method is roughly aligned to its productivity. This standard can then be changed as the productivity of the surveillance changes, based on new technologies or evolving expectations of privacy.

The first three chapters described all of the components of the cost–benefit analysis theory. Subsequent chapters will demonstrate how conducting a cost–benefit analysis provides new insights into the ways in which we should regulate different types of technology-enhanced surveillance. In the next chapter we will consider the case of "reactive" surveillance, in which the government appears to be using an extremely intrusive method of surveillance but is actually just responding to the widespread use of privacy-enhancing technology. In evaluating these "reactive" searches, we need to consider both the level of criminal activity that is potentially being masked by the privacy-enhancing technology, and how the privacy-enhancing technology has affected society's expectations of privacy.

4

Reactive Surveillance

So yes, every software release we do, we get more and more secure. And we've been doing it for years. That path, the path toward more security and more privacy is a path we've been on for a long time.

Apple CEO Tim Cook[1]

INTRODUCTION

The use of technology to enhance government surveillance is nothing new; police have been deploying new technologies to investigate crime since the advent of flashlights and fingerprints in the early twentieth century. But over the past fifty years, both the development and use of surveillance technology has multiplied exponentially, allowing law enforcement to eavesdrop on our private communications and monitor us in nearly every facet of our lives. Legal scholars have also reacted with alarm, decrying the loss of privacy and individual rights brought on by new surveillance technologies.[2]

But the truth is somewhat more complicated. In reality, modern technology's effect on our privacy has been ambivalent. In many ways, modern technology has turned out to be the totalitarian state's worst enemy. Video cameras are indeed everywhere in public, but they are also embedded into cell phones and wielded by millions of individual citizens – and as a result we are watching the government agents as carefully as they are watching us.[3] These videos can be posted instantaneously to the internet to reach what is literally a limitless audience on platforms that are nearly impossible to censor. And these same cell phones can communicate information to every corner of the globe, defying government censors.[4] Meanwhile the internet has exponentially increased the flow of personal, commercial, and political information to and from individuals, in ways that are largely beyond state control. Private companies and law enforcement agencies do in fact use powerful computers to sift through billions of pieces of data and learn information about us. But powerful computers also sit on all of the desks and in the pockets of almost every American, allowing each of us to create, store, manipulate, and process vast amounts and types of data in ways that were inconceivable forty years ago.[5] New technologies have indeed dramatically altered the balance of power between state control and individual autonomy – but the direction of that shift varies depending on the context.

The reason for this variation is that the impact of new surveillance technologies is only one aspect of the story of how technology has affected privacy in modern society. Over the past century, millions of individuals – both innocent and culpable – have begun using everyday technology to increase their privacy. Fourth Amendment scholars misunderstand the implications of new technologies by focusing only on its use by government agents, all but ignoring the ways in which technology has enabled average citizens and criminals to keep their activities hidden from law enforcement.[6]

There is no doubt that some types of new surveillance technologies pose an unequivocal threat to our privacy. Those are the surveillance methods that most closely resemble the frightening law enforcement tools from Orwell's *1984*, such as installing video cameras inside our homes or intercepting our private telephone calls and e-mail messages. These surveillance methods represent a severe increase in the privacy cost of surveillance far beyond the increased security that it provides. These surveillance methods, which I call hyper-intrusive searches, must be strictly regulated with the highest legal standard. But most types of technology-enhanced surveillance do not fall into this most extreme category, and instead require a more nuanced approach to regulation.

This book divides technology-enhanced surveillance into four categories. In this chapter we examine reactive searches, in which the government adopts new surveillance technology in order to keep up with new privacy-enhancing technologies. Chapter 5 discusses binary searches, which collect information without infringing on legitimate privacy rights at all and represent the most productive type of surveillance that exist. Chapters 6 and 7 examine mosaic searches, which involve collecting and processing massive amounts of publicly available information. Chapter 8 then addresses all of the technology-enhanced surveillance methods that are left over: the hyper-intrusive searches which deserve the highest level of regulation. By applying the cost–benefit analysis theory to each of these categories, we can determine what amount of regulation is appropriate for each type of surveillance.

REACTIVE SEARCHES

The conventional wisdom regarding new surveillance technology consists of two assertions, one factual and one normative. The factual assertion is that the effect of new technologies has been to alter the balance between individual privacy and the state's power to investigate crimes, thereby decreasing individual privacy and increasing the ability of government agents to learn private information about us.[7] This assertion is incorrect – or, more accurately, it is incomplete – and therefore too simplistic, because it does not take into account the wide variety of ways in which our own use of technology has increased our individual privacy and decreased the government's investigatory power. The normative assertion is that this shift is a negative development, and therefore it is necessary to restore the original balance – either by creating more regulations or statutes to limit government power, or perhaps by changing the way the Fourth Amendment is interpreted by the courts in cases involving new technologies.[8] This is a classic example of the equilibrium adjustment theory: it assumes that law enforcement and criminals are engaged in a zero-sum game, and that the job of the court is to ensure that the competitors in the game remain equally matched.

In order to understand the true impact of technology on privacy – and, more specifically, in order to accurately gauge the effect of new surveillance technology on the balance between individual privacy and government investigatory power – the first step is to evaluate how technology has changed the amount of privacy in society for everyday citizens. As in any context in which we are examining the effects of technology on society, the changes tend to be subtle and incremental in the short term, but dramatic and momentous in the long run. In the field of medicine, for example, each new drug or surgical technique might have a small influence on the way a certain disease is treated – but the cumulative effect of all of these advances has increased life expectancy in this country from around forty-seven to seventy-eight over the past one hundred years.[9]

Likewise, the effect of new technologies on our privacy in everyday life is easy to overlook, since we quickly adapt to the small gains that are made and fail to notice how fundamentally our lives are changing. By taking a broader perspective, however, we can see how new technology has dramatically increased the amount of privacy each of us now enjoys in our lives.

To better visualize this broad perspective, let us engage in a time-travel thought experiment. Assume that Sally and Harry, two residents of early nineteenth century America, wish to have a private communication with each other. Their options are limited. Sally could invite Harry to her home – though of course anyone could see Harry entering and leaving Sally's home, so the fact that they were conversing would be information readily available to the public. Sally could write Harry a letter, but again the name of the person she was communicating with would be open to the world. More troubling would be the fact that, assuming there was no legal impediment, any government agent wishing to know the content of Sally's communication could intercept and read the mail before it got to its destination.

Now assume that Sally and Harry live in 1950. The technological advance of the telephone[10] has greatly increased their chances of having a private conversation. Casual observers of their affairs will have no idea that the two of them are talking, much less what they are talking about. But although the telephone is an improvement, it is not foolproof. You can only use the telephone at certain locations – your home, your office, perhaps a quasi-public phone booth. Furthermore, the local telephone operator might be listening in on your conversation.[11] And once again (assuming no legal restrictions exist), government agents could obtain phone records from the telephone company to determine whom Sally is calling, or set up a device to tap Sally's phone.[12] It should be noted, however, that these actions by the government require substantially more effort and technical expertise than simply looking at Sally's outgoing and incoming mail.[13]

Finally, assume that Sally and Harry live in the modern world. Now they can communicate with each other from almost any spot in the country using cell phones, with no chance of a human operator casually eavesdropping on their conversation. They can also send e-mails or instant messages to each other from their computers. And if they are very worried about privacy, they can easily take measures to make their conversation even more secure. A cell phone can be bought and used for a day and then discarded, making the calls much more difficult to trace.[14] E-mail can be sent and received to and from anonymous accounts, or the two individuals could purchase an inexpensive encryption program which would shield their e-mail communications from even the most sophisticated government code breakers.[15]

Of course, the government has been able to find ways to intercept electronic communication, but this in itself does not mean that the new technology has led to a decrease in privacy. A modern-day Sally and Harry still have all the old ways of communicating with each other – they can still visit each other's houses, send each other mail, or call each other on land-based phone lines. In other words, technology has given them *more* ways to communicate, by giving them more options to choose from in deciding which method of communicating is the most secure.

And the economic effects of new technologies must be factored in, since in discussing the effect of technology on privacy, we should not look at the amount of privacy a person has in theory, but the amount they have (or used to have) in practice. In 1800, a face-to-face visit was extremely difficult to set up – most people lived in rural areas that were great distances apart, and travel between residences took considerably longer than it does today. Those who lived in urban areas could more easily travel to see each other – but nineteenth century cities were difficult places to find privacy, as most individuals lived in apartments or tenements which were shared with many other family members. As has been true throughout history, the very rich – enjoying private residences and easy access to transportation – could engage in private conversations without a problem, but for the vast majority of citizens, private communications were difficult to come by.

The telephone was invented in 1876,[16] but in the early twentieth century, it was still a rare device, used only by those wealthy enough to afford them.[17] By the 1950s, the telephone was more commonplace, but almost no home had more than one phone line, and many residences still had no telephone.[18] Today, 92 percent of Americans have their own personal telephone which they carry with them everywhere[19] – cellular phones are so inexpensive that they are prevalent among every economic class[20] – and those that do not have a cell phone almost certainly have access to a traditional telephone. In short, advancing technology has not only given us devices which dramatically increase our privacy, but has also made these devices affordable to almost everyone.

The same analysis can be applied to most other categories of privacy. Take data storage: a nineteenth century diary writer would have very limited options as to how to secretly record and store his writings. In modern times, the diary could be written on a laptop computer, accessible only by someone with the password – or stored on a hard drive the size of a pen and hidden almost anywhere. More broadly, the rise of the personal computer and the internet has allowed individuals to stay in the privacy of their own home to conduct many activities which formerly had to be done in public An individual today can browse and shop for any item he or she might want, from clothing to cooking utensils to pornography;[21] she can access and download almost any kind of picture, political treatise, song, or book;[22] she can even "develop" her own digital pictures, insert them into a pamphlet she is writing, and print multiple copies of the pamphlet for distribution later.[23] A generation ago, almost any of these tasks would require the average person to leave her home and personally visit any number of other businesses: it was impossible to browse through and purchase a book without leaving your home, for example, while developing your own pictures and printing your own pamphlet at home was possible only with expensive and unwieldy equipment.

Thus, one of the primary effects of technology on society over the past two hundred years has been to *increase* the amount of privacy in our everyday lives. Individuals can now conduct many more activities secretly, particularly activities which involve communicating, storing, or processing information. Unfortunately, what has been good for individual privacy has also been good for criminals. Sally and Harry may not be sending love letters but instead may be planning to blow up a government building; the diary writer might also be trying to hide illicit financial information in order to cheat on her taxes; the computer user may not simply be shopping for a book or printing up a pamphlet, but could also be trying to hack into secure databases, send child pornography, or print counterfeit checks. So as technology has enabled individuals to live more private and secret lives, law enforcement agents have been forced to turn to new surveillance technologies which enable them to investigate individuals using privacy-enhancing technology to commit crimes.

This broader perspective reveals that much of the new surveillance technologies used by the government over the past century shows the state constantly playing catch-up, trying to find new ways to overcome the increased use of privacy-enhancing technology by those conducting criminal activity. This reactive surveillance includes many of the more sophisticated surveillance technologies that are intended to track communications – tracing telephone calls, examining web browser history, and collecting metadata for e-mails. This category also includes searches of more sophisticated storage techniques – such as creating and sifting through a bitstream copy of a suspect's hard drive. And it could conceivably include more aggressive surveillance measures that government agents employ in order to combat the wider and more dangerous array of criminal activity that might be taking place inside a home.

One example of these more aggressive measures is the recent case of *Kyllo* v. *United States,* in which government agents used a thermal imager to detect marijuana-growing heat lamps inside a suspect's home.[24] If Danny Lee Kyllo had sought to grow marijuana 100 years ago, he would be forced to do so outdoors in a field, where it could be seen by others. Even if Kyllo had attempted to hide the marijuana by locating the plants far inside his property,[25] concealed by trees or other crops, the Fourth Amendment did not prevent a law enforcement agent from venturing onto the property – even if he were trespassing – to view the marijuana.[26] Thus, the *Kyllo* case is an example of a defendant using technology – high-powered heat lamps – in order to better conceal his illegal actions, and the government then using another new technology – thermal imagers – in an attempt to counter the defendant's concealment.[27]

As the *Kyllo* example indicates, it is sometimes difficult to distinguish between reactive surveillance technology and hyper-intrusive searches. Certainly, without modern technology, law enforcement officers could not listen in on our phone conversations, track our e-mails, search our hard drives, or measure the amount of heat emerging from our homes. But without modern technology to enable these activities in the first place, much of the suspects' conduct could be monitored using traditional surveillance methods.

Courts have struggled to regulate reactive searches. Frequently they engage in the intuitive but ultimately misguided strategy of trying to find the proper analogy between the new surveillance technology and a more traditional form of surveillance. In theory, this strategy simplifies the analysis: if using a thermal imager on a home is analogous to entering a home, then it is self-evident that the Fourth Amendment prohibits using law a thermal imager without a warrant. But this strategy has two significant flaws: first, courts often choose an inappropriate analogy; and second, both the privacy-enhancing technology and the reactive surveillance technology may change the level of intrusiveness of the surveillance in important ways.

Most analogies between new surveillance technologies and traditional surveillance methods are too tenuous to be useful, and occasionally the analogy chosen by courts is disastrously inappropriate. This is because it is not clear at first how society itself views the privacy-enhancing technology – what degree of privacy do we expect when we use a new type of technology to communicate, store data, or conduct

certain activities in our home? We have already discussed the most infamous
example of a court's failure to understand the true nature of privacy-enhancing
technology surveillance technology: when the Supreme Court considered the
constitutionality of wiretapping telephones in *Olmstead* v. *United States*.[28] Here
was a classic case of reactive government surveillance: the telephone had been
around for over fifty years, and it was by then commonly used by individuals to
communicate private messages from the sanctuary of their own homes. Unsurprisingly, criminals such as Olmstead were also able to use this new technology to hide
their activities from government investigators more effectively.[29] In response, law
enforcement agents began using their own kind of new technology – an instrument
that could be connected to the telephone wires outside a person's home and allow
the user to eavesdrop on the conversation.

The Court, in evaluating this reactive technology, had no obvious pre-technology
analogy to fall back on. The Court first considered analogizing the telephone
conversation with sending a sealed letter from your house, which would have given
the phone conversation full Fourth Amendment protection, but it ultimately
rejected that analogy, since "papers" are specifically protected by the Fourth
Amendment, while oral conversations are not.[30] The Court then considered
whether intercepting the phone call was akin to entering the house and eavesdropping on a conversation between two people inside the house, but rejected that
because there was no actual physical invasion of the defendant's property.[31] Thus,
the only analogy left was that of the individual broadcasting his telephone communication to the world with no expectation of privacy, as though the defendant were
standing at his window and shouting words to the outside world.

Congress eventually stepped in to protect telephone conversations from unregulated government wiretapping,[32] but the damage done by the Court's poor choice of
analogy continued. The focus on property rights that laid the foundation for
Olmstead muddled the Court's analysis in later cases involving first-category surveillance technology such as electronic eavesdropping devices.[33] This doctrinal error
was not fixed until the 1967 case of *Katz* v. *United States*, in which the court finally
set out a coherent doctrine for dealing with surveillance technology and the Fourth
Amendment.[34]

But even in the post-*Katz* era, reactive surveillance technologies continue to give
the Court problems. In 1979, the Court decided *Smith* v. *Maryland*,[35] another case
in which the Court faced government use of reactive surveillance to counteract a
criminal's use of privacy-enhancing technology. On March 5, 1976, Michael Smith
robbed Patricia McDonough in Baltimore.[36] After the robbery, Smith began calling
McDonough at her home, threatening her and using obscene language.[37]

Like the defendant in *Olmstead*, Michael Smith was using privacy-enhancing
technology to conceal his crimes from the police[38] – if he had lived 100 years earlier
and decided to threaten and verbally abuse his victim in her own home, he would
have had to go to her house in person, an action that would greatly increase his

chances of being apprehended. But because Smith used a telephone, the police were forced to respond with their own new technology – in this case, they asked the phone company to install a pen register device on Smith's phone, which allowed them to track the phone numbers of all outgoing telephone calls.[39]

As in the *Olmstead* case, the Court in *Smith* searched for an analogy for the phone numbers of outgoing calls in order to determine whether law enforcement officers invaded a "legitimate expectation of privacy" when they used the pen register to obtain this information.[40] One obvious analogy to the phone numbers would be to the content of telephone calls themselves, which Congress deemed private information.[41] But the Court rejected this analogy, stating that "a pen register differs significantly from the listening device employed in *Katz*, for pen registers do not acquire the *contents* of communications."[42] Instead, the Court reasoned that the phone numbers Smith dialed were akin to any other information that an individual turns over to a third party.[43] Smith could certainly not have any subjective expectation of privacy in these numbers, because "[a]ll telephone users realize that they must 'convey' phone numbers to the telephone company, since it is through telephone company switching equipment that their calls are completed."[44] And society would not recognize any such expectation of privacy as "reasonable," because "a person has no legitimate expectation of privacy in information he voluntarily turns over to third parties."[45] The Court then analogized the phone numbers dialed by Smith – information which he "voluntarily" gave to the telephone company – to financial information that a bank depositor gives to bank employees.[46] The Court also cited cases of giving financial information to an accountant[47] and giving information to an undercover government informant.[48] Based on these analogies, the Court determined that the information was not protected by the "because the defendant had knowingly turned it over to a third party.

It did not take long for this analogy – and the reasoning behind it – to prove to be dangerously short-sighted. In modern society, we share many different types of data with third parties. Some of this data is innocuous, and some is extremely private. Everyone who sends an e-mail from anywhere in the world is "voluntarily" sending its contents to a number of internet service providers as part of the communication process. Thus, under the *Smith* rationale, the Fourth Amendment does not protect the contents of e-mail communication.[49] In modern digital communication networks, information is usually to numerous third-party locations before it finally reaches its destination,[50] and it is now obvious that the transfer of that required information is different from giving financial information to a bank or revealing information to a confidential informant. But this was not obvious to the Supreme Court in 1979, and as a result the Court chose a poor analogy to decide the case. Once again, Congress has been forced to intervene to ensure that the content of an e-mail message deserve the same level of privacy as a telephone call.[51] We will discuss the third party doctrine in greater detail in Chapter 7.

The wide diversity of privacy-enhancing technologies ensures a never-ending stream of reactive surveillance for courts to deal with. What level of protection should we give to information posted on a semi-public website or a statement made in a password-protected chat room? What level of protection does information stored on network hard drives or cloud servers deserve? Even personal hard drives pose real challenges for courts. Is information on a hard drive analogous to information stored in a file cabinet? If so, is it a "seizure" if the government merely copies the contents of the hard drive without taking it away? Is it a "search" if the government merely retains a copy of the contents without looking at them?[52]

Even if the courts are able to find an accurate analogy to a traditional surveillance method, the search for analogous pre-technology surveillance ignores the degree to which the privacy-enhancing technology decreases security. If the privacy-enhancing technology makes criminal activity far easier, we need to set a lower standard for reactive surveillance, but if the technology increases privacy with no measurable effect on security, there is little justification for employing reactive surveillance. The argument-by-analogy method also ignores the possibility that societal or technological changes may have altered the degree to which the surveillance infringes on a person's privacy.

Applying the cost–benefit analysis theory to reactive surveillance allows us to consider these questions. First, we need to estimate the decrease in security that occurred as a result of the privacy-enhancing technology. This will affect the level of benefit that we receive from the reactive surveillance. If the privacy-enhancing technology does very little to decrease security, then any new form of surveillance used to defeat the privacy-enhancing technology will only provide a very small benefit. For example, the ability to stream movies directly into one's home increases a person's privacy, since the individual no longer has to travel in public to watch the movie in the theater (as would be the case before the 1980s) nor travel to a video rental store in public to rent the movie (as would be the case before the 2010s). There are many reasons why a person may want to keep his viewing preferences private: he may want to watch pornography, or a documentary that espouses an unpopular political opinion, or a genre of movie that he thinks his friends would disapprove of. By ordering a movie online and downloading it directly to a television set or computer, the viewer need never expose his or her viewing preferences to the public. The information is revealed to the private company that provides the movie, of course, but that was also true when the individual went to a video store to rent movies. We will consider the issue of question sharing information with private companies in Chapter 7.

This privacy-enhancing technology does almost nothing to decrease security, however, since there is no crime against watching any kind of movie. (The exception is child pornography, which can be easily detected through binary searches, as we will see in the next chapter). Thus, a new surveillance technique that revealed all of the movies a person was streaming into their home would provide almost no benefit and would therefore be a very unproductive form of reactive surveillance. In contrast, a new surveillance technique that allowed law enforcement to track the location or outgoing phone calls of pre-paid burner cell phones would potentially have far greater benefit, since those privacy-enhancing devices are much more likely than streaming video technology to assist and conceal criminal activity. The actual level of benefit would have to be measured by examining the degree to which the use of a burner cell phone increases the chances of criminal activity being present, but there is a good chance we would see a significant benefit, and thus a high level of productivity, for reactive surveillance that could track and trace burner cell phones.

The second step in applying the cost–benefit theory is to determine the amount of privacy society believes should be accorded the information that would be obtained by the reactive technology. Standards of privacy have significantly changed in the twenty-first century, partly in response to new technologies, and partly in response to shifting societal norms.

Individuals use technology to place an unprecedented amount of private information into the public arena – both intentionally and unintentionally. Many individuals choose to use what we have termed "privacy-enhancing technology" in precisely the opposite way – to make their private lives more public. Diaries and scrapbooks which were once kept on bookshelves or hidden in drawers are now posted on blogs and social media along with personal pictures and messages from friends. Telephone conversations that used to occur in homes or private phone booths are now carried out on the street and in malls, stores, and other public areas.

As noted in Chapter 1, the widespread adoption of new technologies can change society's reasonable expectation of privacy. And the widespread use of surveillance technology itself can change society's expectation of privacy. As advances in technology have made more intrusive surveillance possible, individuals' expectations of privacy have incrementally diminished. The Supreme Court acknowledged this phenomenon as well in *Kyllo*, when it held that the use of intrusive surveillance technology was a Fourth Amendment search only "if the government uses a device that is not in general public use."[53] In other words, if a technology becomes so widespread that it changes societal expectations of privacy, it will alter the cost–benefit analysis and lower the legal standard required for its use as a surveillance tool. This does not mean that the government can automatically lower our expectation of privacy (and thus the legal standards that the government must meet to conduct surveillance) merely by using certain surveillance tools more frequently. As the Court recognized, societal expectations of privacy are much more likely to be affected when the general population adopts the technology for themselves. Private individuals have adopted the use of flashlights, binoculars, and airplanes to the extent that these surveillance tools have undoubtedly affected society's expectation of privacy in their actions. Other types of surveillance tools, such as wiretapping equipment, thermal imagers, or electronic eavesdropping devices, have never been widely used by the public and so are unlikely to change society's expectations of privacy.

Of course, much of the loss of privacy in our society is not due to our own personal choice. Because of the ease of information transfer in modern life, records that used to be public only in theory are now public in practice – from how much you paid for your house to how much money you gave to your Congressman's campaign fund.[54] Criminal records have traditionally been kept confidential, but now individuals who have been convicted of a sex offense have their names posted on public websites, along with their address and details of their crime.[55] Information that used to be buried in a file cabinet in a remote county courthouse is now posted on the web for anyone to access. Meanwhile, companies buy and sell lists of consumer purchases and preferences, maintaining this commercial yet personal information on vast computer databases.[56] These actions almost certainly diminish consumers' expectation of privacy in commercial information.[57] And as employers monitor employees' telephone and e-mail use in the workplace, they diminish society's expectation of privacy at work.

All of these uses of technology – both by private citizens and private companies – change the cost variable in our equation in ways that may be difficult to predict. Under the cost–benefit analysis theory, we need to measure these changes in order to determine the proper standard for reactive surveillance. When making these measurements, we need to focus on the type of information that is being discovered by the surveillance, not on the type of pre-technology search that is the best analogy to the new technology. For example, in evaluating the privacy cost of the thermal imager in *Kyllo*, we should not ask "Is a thermal imager analogous to entering a home or analogous to placing a hand on the walls of a home to feel heat?" Instead, we should ask how much privacy people expect to have in the patterns of heat that emerge from the home. The likely answer is some, but not much – although again, the degree of privacy intrusion needs to be determined by experts in an administrative agency or scientifically measured through a representative survey, not guessed by a majority of non-representative Supreme Court Justices. In *Kyllo* itself, the Court was engaged in a simplistic "search-or-no-search" analysis, and so the only question it answered is that the use of the thermal imager violated society's reasonable expectation of privacy, not the *degree* to which it violated that right). On the other side of the equation, we need to acknowledge that the security gain of using a thermal imager is significant, since the privacy-enhancing technology of heat lamps has made growing marijuana virtually undetectable otherwise.

Another advantage of using the cost–benefit analysis is that it can identify ways to make the use of surveillance technology more productive. For example, a law enforcement officer using a thermal imager only needs to know whether the home under surveillance is producing a certain threshold of heat, or heat in a telltale pattern, not every detail about the heat. Thus, a less sensitive thermal imager would actually be a more productive surveillance tool – it would tell the police less about the details of what was going on in the home but would still be sensitive enough to detect the amount of heat produced by heat lamps. A cost–benefit analysis would result in a lower legal standard for using a less precise thermal imager, and thus would encourage the police to develop and use those devices, resulting in a positive-sum gain: a lower privacy cost with an equal level of security.

ENCRYPTION: THE ULTIMATE PRIVACY-ENHANCING TECHNOLOGY

In December of 2015, two ISIS-inspired terrorists entered a non-profit organization that provided benefits to people with developmental disabilities and shot thirty-six people, killing fourteen of them. The victims were mostly government employees working for the San Bernardino Department of Public Health. The shooters were killed after they exchanged gunfire with the police shortly after the event, but law enforcement officers were concerned that others may have helped them plan the attack. The FBI also wanted to know the identities of any ISIS members overseas that had been in communication with the shooters. During the course of their investigation, the FBI recovered an iPhone that had been issued to one of the shooters by his employer, and they had strong reason to believe that the phone contained evidence of the shooters' plans and contacts. The police had clear legal authority to search the iPhone: they had the consent from the phone's owner, and at any rate they had probable cause to support a warrant application for the search. There was one complication: the iPhone was encrypted, and thus the FBI was unable to access the information inside.[58]

Encryption provides us with an extreme example of privacy-enhancing technology. Encryption technology has become so advanced that the government's attempts to catch up have proven futile – that is, there is no type of reactive surveillance technology which can be used to counteract the greater privacy enjoyed by individuals (including criminals) who make a serious effort to encrypt their communications.[59]

The technological advantage the encoder holds over the codebreaker is based on the fact that sophisticated codes are only decipherable with the encryption key. This key is a series of binary numbers – generally hundreds of binary numbers strung together. In order to decipher the code, the codebreaker must try every single possible key one at a time. This is not so difficult for a key which is 4 or 8 binary numbers long (since there are only 16 or 256 possible keys, respectively). But every time the encoder adds another digit to the string of numbers, she doubles the number of potential keys that have to be tested by the codebreaker – thus easily reaching a number of potential keys which is beyond even the fastest supercomputer to attempt in any reasonable amount of time.[60] Whenever the government designs a computer that processes information twice as fast, the encoder need only add another digit to the key in order to stay ahead of the decryption technology. [61] Thus, for the sophisticated criminal, private data storage and private communications are all but guaranteed, regardless of what methods the government uses to try to obtain the information and regardless of the legal standard the government is able to meet in seeking to obtain the information.

The tension between encrypted data and law enforcement needs has grown significantly in recent years. Most technology companies have adopted a strategy of "full-disk encryption," in which an entire digital device is locked unless the user knows the passcode, and they have also designed the system so that the data on the device will be permanently deleted after a certain number of failed attempts to log in.[62] This has led to numerous high profile legal fights between law enforcement and technology companies like Google and Apple.[63] Law enforcement agencies point out that encrypted hard drives contain crucial evidence in thousands of cases, ranging from terrorist attacks to child sex abuse to drug conspiracies to murder. In a 2016 op-ed, the district attorneys of Manhattan, Los Angeles, and San Diego noted that their offices alone had over 500 smartphones that they have the legal right to open pursuant to a court order, but which were inaccessible due to encryption.

Law enforcement officials have sought to compel private companies to hack into their own products to produce information that was relevant to a criminal investigation. The companies supporting encryption have argued that they should not be forced to make their own encryption methods less secure, since that would make their products less valuable to their consumers. Two Senators from the Intelligence Committee proposed legislation that would require every company that produced an encrypted product to ensure that a "back door" existed in case the government needed access to the encrypted information.[64] This is similar to the "escrow" requirement, which would force everyone who produces a complex encryption device to deposit the key to the encryption in escrow.[65] Law enforcement agents could gain access to the key if, and only if, they made a sufficient showing to a court, and the legal standard they would be required to meet would depend on the level of privacy that the encrypted information deserved.

The cost–benefit analysis provides a clear answer to this dispute. The benefit of creating a backdoor requirement would be very high – without it, a significant amount of evidence would be permanently inaccessible to law enforcement officers.[66] And the privacy cost of such a requirement would be very small as long as the legal standard was high. If the encrypted information were particularly sensitive, courts could require the government to demonstrate that there was an 80 percent likelihood that the decryption process would yield evidence of criminal activity. This would keep the vast majority of encrypted information secret, but still allow the government access to information when the information was nearly certain to assist in its investigations.

Another way of approaching this problem is to ask what institutions are best able to determine the appropriate balance between privacy and security. Traditionally, we have relied on both courts and legislatures to set rules to strike this balance. As we have already seen, neither of these institutions is perfect, but they both have some legitimacy in setting these rules and some level of expertise in knowing how to set the balance. But if encrypted products continue to be produced without a backdoor or escrow requirement, the appropriate balance between privacy and security will be set by private technology companies, with no regard to Fourth Amendment doctrine and no consideration of the needs of society or the will of the majority.

In short, unregulated encryption creates 100 percent privacy with no regard for security. This is a level of privacy that we would never create by law if we had a choice.[67] As we will see in Chapter 8, the government has access to many types of hyper-intrusive surveillance technologies. The proper way to protect privacy is not to abolish the ability to engage in that surveillance, but instead to set proper legal standards to ensure they cannot use those hyper-intrusive tools, whether they are wiretaps or decryption codes in escrow, unless they meet the appropriate legal standard.

NEW TECHNOLOGY AND THE SEVERITY OF THE CRIME

In one sense, new technology has unambiguously caused a loss of privacy, but not in the way that most people realize. Simply put, technology has exponentially increased the damage done by certain crimes. A child pornographer who wants to distribute his goods in the past was limited by very real practical constraints as to the number of pictures he could distribute and the number of people to whom he could distribute them. Today, computers and e-mail make these limits obsolete. A teenage vandal in past eras might break store windows or spray-paint graffiti on walls. Today, that same teenager might write a computer virus and cause thousands or millions of dollars' worth of damage.[68] An anarchist in the nineteenth century might seek to assassinate a President or plant dynamite in an opera house[69] – his twenty-first century counterpart has the ability to destroy cities with a nuclear weapon or poison an entire society with chemical or biological agents.

The reaction has been predictable, and perfectly consistent with the cost–benefit analysis theory: the increased potential for damage caused by these new technologies has led policymakers to conclude that the government should be given more power to investigate suspected criminals. The result is a significant shift in the balance between individual privacy rights and law enforcement's power to investigate crime. For example, the threat of international terrorism was deemed to be so dangerous that the federal government began tracing all of our outgoing international tele-phone calls without court approval.[70] In a recent pair of cases, the threat of terrorism on public transportation has led the Second Circuit to broaden the "special needs" exception to the probable cause and warrant requirement of the Fourth Amend-ment, allowing suspicionless searches and seizures of all riders on subways and ferries.[71] Of course, this shift toward increased government power is evident every-where, not just in the realm of the Fourth Amendment – the threat of terrorism has led the federal government to begin holding suspects in detention without a charge, denying them access to lawyers, and trying them in special tribunals with different rules of evidence in order to protect "national security."[72]

The cost–benefit analysis theory supports this shift from privacy to security, since our formula takes into account the severity of the crime which is being investigated.

A certain type of surveillance might be deemed to be too intrusive if used to catch a drug dealer or a shoplifter, but if it may be appropriate if used to gather evidence against someone who is planning on detonating a nuclear weapon or disabling millions of computers. More precisely, the government should be require to meet a very high standard – an 80 percent likelihood of success, for example – if it wants to use an extremely intrusive method of surveillance to investigate a traditional crime, but should only be required to meet a moderate standard, such as a 50 percent likelihood of success, if it is investigating a crime that could cause massive levels of death or property damage. This is another example of reactive surveillance: because criminals can more easily cause massive amounts of damage, courts and legislatures must respond by adjusting the legal standard when police are investigating these crimes

WATCHING THE WATCHERS

On October 2, 2016, police officers in New York City investigating a shooting incident recovered a gun from an apartment building. They arrested one of the residents of the apartment, a woman named Kimberly Thomas, and charged her with possession of a firearm. At a proceeding months later, the police officer who recovered the gun testified about the incident. He explained that the officers encountered Thomas in the doorway of the apartment and that she was carrying a large laundry bag. She set the bag down in front of the police officer such that it blocked his way, so the officer picked up the bag, noted it felt heavy, and then heard a "clunk" sound when he put it back down on the ground. He kicked the bag and felt something hard, and then searched the bag, finding a firearm.

The search and recovery of the gun was completely legal given these facts. There was one problem: almost none of the facts were true. Thomas' defense attorney obtained the surveillance camera from the hallway of the apartment, which showed the officers confronting Thomas in her doorway. Thomas is not carrying a laundry bag; in fact, no laundry bag is visible anywhere. The police officers briefly speak to Thomas and then enter the apartment. When confronted with the surveillance footage, the prosecutor dropped the charges against Thomas and the case was dismissed.[73]

This episode illustrates yet another way in which new technology can increase privacy: when it is used to monitor the activities of law enforcement. A recurring problem in regulating the practice of law enforcement agents in the criminal procedure context is determining exactly what happened during the investigation. Most disputes about appropriate police conduct involve two witnesses – the police officer and the suspect – and in most cases the judge will give far less weight to the suspect's version of the story. This has led to at least the potential (and in some situations the reality) of abuse on the part of law enforcement officers.[74] If a police officer testifies that he read the *Miranda* rights to the defendant before the interrogation began, or that the defendant failed to ask for a lawyer before confessing to the crime, there is generally little that a defendant can do to persuade the judge otherwise. This is not to say that most police officers lie about their actions during an interrogation, only that the lack of effective monitoring inevitably leads to suboptimal conduct on the part of the at least some police officers.

Nowhere in criminal procedure is this potential for abuse greater than in the search and seizure context, because officer discretion is greatest at that stage of the investigatory process. Police officers pull over cars after allegedly observing erratic driving; they arrest suspects after allegedly seeing the suspect drop a bag of drugs onto the sidewalk; they conduct a *Terry* stop on the basis of alleged suspicious activity. Many of the most scathing critiques of how law enforcement conduct have nothing to do with the legal standards themselves; rather, they center on the serious potential for violation of these standards and subsequent perjury on the part of the law enforcement officer.[75] Unmonitored police conduct in this area poses a significant threat to individual privacy, especially among the poor and minority groups, since they tend to live in high crime areas where police are more likely to bend the law in order to further their investigation.

New technologies offer great promise in this area. In the context of interrogations, introducing a tape recorder or video camera into the interrogation room can serve as an effective way of monitoring police conduct by deterring most abuses and detecting those that do occur. In the search and seizure context, police body cameras can record everything a police officer sees, hears, and does, whether in a squad car, walking a beat, or responding to a call inside a home or a store.[76] This technology prevents abuses on the part of law enforcement by providing judges at the suppression hearing a clear, neutral factual record of how the investigation was conducted.[77]

Body cameras are only one example of new technology that allows courts to monitor and fact-check police officers. Nearly every private individual now wields cameras in their smart phone, and their videos of police/citizen encounters not only end up in the hands of defense attorneys, but they are also posted on the internet for millions to watch, thus further increasing the incentive for police officers to act lawfully. And the statistical tools of big data are available to defense attorneys and civil rights lawyers as well as to police and prosecutors, so it is easier than ever to prove systemic problems in police departments.[78]

CONCLUSION

Modern technology has given law enforcement officers powerful new surveillance tools. Invariably, these tools raise concerns about an Orwellian state in which the government sees and hears all of our private information. The truth is somewhat more complicated: some of these new tools do indeed represent a net loss of privacy, but others are merely a response to the privacy-enhancing technology that individuals are using to make formerly public information private.

The challenge in determining the proper legal standard for these new surveillance tools is to distinguish between reactive surveillance and other types of surveillance. What at first seem to be insidious methods of eavesdropping and snooping – monitoring e-mail addresses or using thermal imagers – are actually remedial measures on the part of the government in an attempt to overcome these privacy-enhancing technologies. As we will see in Chapter 8, there can be a very narrow distinction between reactive surveillance and hyper-intrusive surveillance: some surveillance that is technically responsive to privacy-enhancing technology, like wiretapping phones, goes further than merely responding the enhanced privacy and provides law enforcement agents with for more information than they could have received before the privacy-enhancing technology was employed.

The cost–benefit analysis theory can help us make these distinctions. Most types of reactive surveillance involve a relatively low cost to privacy when compared to the truly hyper-intrusive surveillance. For example, the privacy cost of tracking telephone numbers is far less than that involved in wiretapping telephones; likewise, giving law enforcement agents the ability to decrypt coded information which they have lawfully obtained does not infringe on our privacy to the same degree as allowing them to use backscatter devices to see through our clothing. In the end, calculating the correct privacy cost should be an empirical question: what level of privacy do people now expect in their dialed telephone numbers and the names of the people they are e-mailing? It could be that the privacy-enhancing technologies have increased our reasonable expectation of privacy in some of this information: perhaps in the early twentieth century, everyone accepted the fact that the government could know the name of the person to whom you were sending a letter, and today in the early twenty-first century, we believe that the name of the person to whom you are sending an e-mail should be kept private. But it is also possible that much of what at first appears to be Big Brother surveillance is merely a return to the traditional balance between privacy and security.

Commentators who worry about how new surveillance technology is eroding our privacy should keep in mind that by almost any measure we have more privacy today than at any other time in history. Technology has changed not just the way that the government can spy on our behavior, but also the way we communicate and store information. In some areas, such as encryption technology, anonymous e-mail accounts, and the use of disposable cell phones, current technologies create much greater levels of privacy than we have seen in the past, allowing individuals to keep communications and data hidden from the government to an unprecedented degree and perhaps requiring government intervention to reduce the amount of privacy provided.

In the end, reactive surveillance technology does not represent an increase in efficiency of criminal investigations; it is merely a return to the initial balance between privacy and security. In other words, reactive surveillance is still part of a zero-sum game in which the individuals and law enforcement officials are opposed to each other; a gain for one side always represents a loss for the other. In the next chapter, we will consider newer generations of surveillance technology that are far more discriminating in what they are searching for, thus allowing for narrower and less intrusive searches. We have already discussed metal detectors and body scanners at airports as examples of surveillance technology that searches more quickly and with less invasion of privacy than traditional methods. We will now consider surveillance tools that can be so narrowly targeted that they only alert their human user if they sense illegal activity, much like how a drug-sniffing dog only reacts when contraband is present. These "binary" surveillance methods are the strongest example of positive sum technologies: many of them can increase security while also increasing our privacy.

5

Binary Searches and the Potential for 100 Percent Enforcement

"Then, what clue could you have as to his identity?"
"Only as much as we can deduce."
"From his hat?"
"Precisely."
"But you are joking. What can you gather from this old battered felt?" . . .
"That the man was highly intellectual is of course obvious upon the face of it, and also that he was fairly well-to-do within the last three years, although now he has fallen upon evil days. He had foresight, but has less now than formerly, pointing to a moral retrogression, which, when taken with the decline of his fortunes, seems to indicate some evil influence, probably drink, at work upon him. This may account for the obvious fact that his wife has ceased to love him . . . He has, however, retained some degree of self-respect . . . He is a man who leads a sedentary life, goes out little, is out of training entirely, is middle-aged, has grizzled hair which he has had cut within the last few days, and which he anoints with lime-cream . . . Also . . . it is extremely improbable that he has gas laid on his house."

Arthur Conan Doyle, *The Blue Carbuncle*[1]

In this passage, Detective Sherlock Holmes engages in a very inefficient investigation: using his unmatched powers of deduction, he learns many intimate details about the suspect, but is unable to determine whether the owner of the hat had been involved in criminal activity. Holmes serves as a useful symbol for modern law enforcement agents, who, lacking his superhuman powers of observation and deduction, rely instead upon modern technologies and vast computer databases to conduct surveillance and analyze data. Using these new advances, today's law enforcement officials can deduce the most intimate details of our lives, from the contents of our private phone conversations[2] to the files we store on our computers.[3] Like Holmes, these agents must then sift through these details to detect whether criminal activity is afoot. The need to investigate potential criminal conduct through the distasteful but seemingly unavoidable invasion of privacy creates the constant tension that underpins most of our Fourth Amendment jurisprudence.[4]

But what if the invasion of privacy were avoidable? What if Sherlock Holmes could look at a hat and learn nothing at all about its owner except that for the fact that the owner recently committed a crime? Or, even better, what if Watson could bring Holmes fifty hats from fifty different suspects and Holmes could look at them all and then point at one of them and say, "I can say with certainty that the owner of this hat stole the diamond. The owners of the other hats are all innocent of this crime. I can tell you no other information about any of the owners of these hats." Under our cost–benefit analysis theory, we would be willing to invest a significant amount of resources to engage in this search, since the cost to privacy is nearly zero and the benefit to security is so high.

This chapter discusses a category of surveillance that attempts to meet this ideal: the binary search. Binary searches allow law enforcement agents to bypass the unpalatable prying into individuals' private lives and instead obtain a direct answer to the only question the agent truly cares about: whether or not the individual under surveillance has committed a crime. The term "binary" search is used because the surveillance gives the law enforcement only one of two possible results: that a specific type of illegal activity is present, or that it is not present. The binary search reveals nothing else about the individual under surveillance.[5]

The most widespread example of a binary search today is the use of drug-detection dogs that alert only if they smell illegal substances. However, law enforcement agencies are adopting many other types of binary searches, such as handheld gun detectors, software protocols that sift through e-mails searching for illegal material, or facial recognition technology. These emerging technologies represent the ultimate in positive-sum surveillance, and they will revolutionize the way law enforcement agents investigate crime. This chapter will examine the possible ramifications of this revolution, as well as what limits (if any) the law should impose on binary searches.

THE BIRTH OF THE BINARY SEARCHES

The Supreme Court of the United States first recognized binary searches in the 1983 case of *United States* v. *Place*, which held that a canine sniff of a suitcase by a trained narcotics dog did not constitute a "search" under the Fourth Amendment.[6] The Court offered two rationales for this conclusion: first, a canine sniff is "much less intrusive" (at least when compared to an officer "rummaging through the contents of the luggage"), and second, the sniff could only detect evidence of a contraband item, leaving any private noncontraband items hidden from public view.[7] The Court myopically termed the canine sniff *sui generis*, since it was "aware of no other investigative procedure that is so limited both in the manner in which the information is obtained and in the content of the information revealed by the procedure."[8]

The Court addressed the use of a similar procedure less than six months later when it analyzed the use of a chemical test to determine the presence of narcotics in the case of *United States* v. *Jacobsen*.[9] Fortunately, *Jacobsen* gave the Court an opportunity to refine its *Place* analysis and focus only on the content of information revealed by the procedure, ignoring the "much less intrusive" language in *Place*.[10] The *Jacobsen* Court further refined the concept of a binary search[11] – a search that can only reveal evidence of illegal activity and no other fact – and declared that such a search does not implicate the Fourth Amendment.[12] The Court affirmed the principle of the binary search twenty-one years later in *Illinois* v. *Caballes*, which held that law enforcement officers do not need to show any individualized suspicion before using a drug detection dog during a traffic stop.[13]

In developing the binary search doctrine, the Court in *Place*, *Jacobsen*, and *Caballes* did not break new ground. Rather, it arrived at the logical destination of a journey that began with the seminal case of *Katz* v. *United States*.[14] *Katz* stated that government surveillance implicates the Fourth Amendment if and only if it infringes on an individual's "reasonable expectation of privacy."[15] Justice Harlan's famous concurrence further defined a "reasonable" expectation as one that society recognizes as legitimate, not merely a subjective expectation of not being discovered.[16] An individual has no legitimate privacy interest in purely illegal activity.[17] The *Katz* Court noted that "[a] burglar plying his trade in a summer cabin during the off season may have a thoroughly justified subjective expectation of privacy, but it is not one which the law recognizes as 'legitimate'." By focusing on the legitimacy requirement of the *Katz* test, the Court concluded that if a certain type of investigation (such as a chemical drug test or a canine sniff) can *only* reveal evidence of illegitimate activity, it is not a search.[18]

Before we discuss the benefits of binary searches, we need to answer two questions. The first is definitional: What, exactly, is a "binary search"? An easy definition is that it is a surveillance method that only reveals the presence or absence of illegal activity, and nothing more. But that definition is insufficient, because it does not help law enforcement officers and judges in the real world decide if a given surveillance method is accurate enough to qualify as a binary search. Imagine a device that accurately detects the presence or absence of illegal activity 99 percent of the time, but which mistakenly alerts 1 percent of the time, thereby triggering a full-scale search of an individual who is not involved in any sort of illegal activity? Would such a device still be considered a binary search? This question deals with the *accuracy* of the surveillance.

The second question involves physical intrusiveness. Law enforcement agents may develop a binary search technique that is perfectly accurate but requires the subject to submit to a five-minute wait, or involves entry onto the subject's private party, or involves a humiliating or intimidating procedure. This question deals with the *limitations* on binary searches.

DEFINING A BINARY SEARCH: HOW MUCH ACCURACY IS REQUIRED?

Assume the police owned a small handheld device that detected the presence of narcotics in any passing car with absolute certainty. They could use the device in the same manner as a radar detector, pointing it at the highway and getting a reading from every car within range. To some people, this device would seem extraordinarily intrusive, since it would allow the police to learn information about the contents of every car on the road. Under the binary search doctrine, however, widespread use of this device would be legal, since the owners of the cars have no right to privacy in the information the police are learning. The cost–benefit analysis theory would also approve this device because it would make many other, more intrusive and invidious forms of surveillance obsolete: pulling over cars that fit a certain "profile," pretextual stops based on minor traffic or safety violations, intimidating drivers into consenting to a search during a stop, and even roadblocks set up ostensibly to check for drunk drivers, but which are really set up for officers to look for evidence of narcotics and other contraband.[19]

Of course, this hypothetical presents the "perfect" binary search scenario, in which the binary search is a 100 percent accurate and produces no false positives. In reality, no type of surveillance will reach this standard, which raises our first question: How accurate must a surveillance method be before it is a binary search? The cost–benefit analysis theory can adapt to any level of accuracy: the more accurate the search, the lower the level of suspicion the police must demonstrate before conducting the search. But the tantalizing promise of binary searches is that they can be permissibly used at times when police do not possess *any* level of suspicion. To reach this level of constitutional comfort with binary searches, we must demonstrate that the binary search in question is *so* accurate that it does not implicate the Fourth Amendment at all.[20] This showing would allow widespread and indiscriminate use of the search method in question.

Our first step is to determine whether binary searches must be 100 percent accurate in order to not be considered a search under the Fourth Amendment. The *Caballes* Court explicitly held that the answer was no, but its two-sentence explanation is not particularly illuminating.[21] After raising the question of false positives, the Court first noted that nothing in the record of the specific case before it supported the argument that "false positives[] call into question the premise that drug-detection dogs alert only to contraband."[22] Although technically true, the Court dodged an uncontroverted issue of fact: that drug-detection dogs occasionally alert even though no narcotics are present.[23] Then the Court attempted a doctrinal justification for sidestepping the issue: "Moreover, respondent does not suggest that an erroneous alert, in and of itself, reveals any legitimate private information, and, in this case, the trial judge found that the dog sniff was sufficiently reliable to establish probable cause to conduct a full-blown search."[24]

The *Caballes* Court's logic is as follows: first, a canine sniff does not implicate the Fourth Amendment because it is a binary search – that is, it cannot possibly provide law enforcement with any information in which the subject of the search has a legitimate expectation of privacy.[25] Second, assuming there could be some false positives in this particular method of search, the false positive itself does not reveal any information in which the subject of the search has a legitimate expectation of privacy.[26] Finally, although a false positive will lead to a search that *does* reveal information in which the subject has a legitimate expectation of privacy, the question of whether the alert following a canine sniff provides probable cause is separate and distinct from whether the sniff is a "search" in the first place.[27] The probable cause question is a much easier standard to meet than the binary search standard.

This legalistic sleight of hand is not sustainable. The *Cabelles* Court's logic would allow the use of any binary searches that was accurate enough to create probable cause. For example, if an automatic gun detector were developed that could be pointed at an individual to determine with 60 percent accuracy whether or not the person was carrying an illegal firearm, the Court's argument would allow law enforcement officers to use the device arbitrarily on individuals walking down the street or driving in their cars. The Court would be unconcerned about the 40 percent false positive rate because the police do not invade an individual's legitimate privacy expectations when the machine mistakenly alerts in their case.[28] Then, once the device alerted, the 60 percent chance that the individual was carrying an illegal item would be more than enough to provide probable cause to search the individual.[29] The result would be that 40 percent of the time, the police would be conducting an unjustified search of an individual who had a protected interest in all the items he or she was carrying. In short, by separating the binary search question from the probable cause question, the Court is opening the door to any investigative procedure which is reliable enough to provide probable cause, as long as the procedure itself does not provide law enforcement any privileged information.[30]

Justice Souter's dissent in *Caballes* addressed the issue of false positives, rejecting the majority's creative logic which separated the binary search question from the probable cause question.[31] Because the dog sniffs "reveal undisclosed facts about private enclosures [which are] used to justify a further and complete search of the enclosed area," the sniff is not simply a binary search that can only reveal information about the existence of contraband.[32] Rather, it is "the first step in a process that [given the possibility of false positives] may disclose 'intimate details' without revealing contraband."[33] The possibility of a false positive, therefore, distinguished the dog sniff from the chemical test in *Jacobsen*, because the chemical test "would either show with certainty that a known substance was contraband or would reveal nothing more," while the dog sniff lacks both the "certainty and the limit on disclosure that may follow."[34]

Unlike the majority's treatment of the issue, Justice Souter's dissent is intellectually honest, and it at least suggests an answer to the critical question of how accurate a procedure has to be in order to be considered a binary search. Unfortunately, his proposed requirement of 100 percent accuracy is not likely to be met by any real-life surveillance method. Indeed, even the chemical field test in *Jacobsen* could not provide absolute certainty, since there is always the possibility of human error in administering the test. Thus, Justice Souter's certainty requirement is either an indirect rejection of the binary search doctrine or it simply begs the question of how reliable a binary search must be before it is held to provide the "certainty" that he requires.

In order to properly define the level of certainty required for binary searches, we need to find some middle ground between the low probable cause standard of the *Caballes* majority and the impossibly high "certainty" standard of the dissent. The first step is to establish some basic principles in measuring the error rates of binary searches. When courts evaluate the level of accuracy attained by drug-detection dogs, they tend to conflate different concepts, such as success rates, error rates, and false positive rates.[35] Even worse, some courts look to absolute numbers of errors, which is a meaningless indicator of accuracy.[36] Other courts do not look to any quantitative measure and instead rely on testimony from the dog's handler that the dog has been "trained" or that there have been "few complaints" of false positives.[37] If binary searches are to become widespread, it is imperative that courts develop a consistent and thorough procedure for evaluating their accuracy.

As a starting point, the relevant measure of a binary search's accuracy is the rate at which it returns an incorrect positive response, known as the false positive rate.[38] Of course, an inaccurate binary search might also produce false *negatives*, but this would not be of constitutional concern and would simply make the search method less efficient.[39] A false negative means that the binary search has failed to detect the presence of illegal activity, but a false positive means that an innocent subject will be subjected to a search even though he was not involved in any illegal activity.

There are two important points to consider in calculating the false positive rate generated by a binary search. The first is the difference between the false positive rate and the positive predictive value. A false positive rate is calculated by dividing the number of false positives by the total number of searches conducted by the device. The positive predictive value is calculated by dividing the total number of true positives by the total number of positive responses returned by the device. For example, let us assume that in the course of one year, a drug dog conducts 1,000 sniffs for narcotics, and alerts 100 times out of the 1,000. Of those 100 positive alerts, 90 are accurate and 10 are false positives. This translates into a 1 percent false positive rate (10 false positives out of 1,000 attempts, meaning that only 1 percent of subjects are falsely implicated by the dog), but a 90 percent positive predictive value (90 true positives out of 100 positive responses, meaning that once the dog returns a positive response, the law enforcement agent can only be 90 percent sure that contraband is present).

The two different measurements are significant because although the false positive rate is constant for any given device or search, the positive predictive value will vary widely depending on the actual frequency of the illegal activity that is being investigated. In our example, 9 out of every 100 subjects carried narcotics, but if the dog were randomly sampling the general population, the number might be closer to 9 out of 100,000. Assuming the dog still falsely alerts 1 percent of the time (a consistent 1 percent false positive rate), he will now falsely implicate 1,000 individuals (and correctly alert to the 9 carrying narcotics), but because there are fewer true positives, the positive predictive rate would be dramatically lower than in the previous example: 9 out of 1,009, or 0.9 percent. In other words, if the search is for a type of illegal activity that is very rare (or at least very rare among the pool of subjects being searched), the vast number of innocent subjects will inflate the absolute number of false positives and make the binary search much less accurate. Thus, when courts begin to set guidelines for how reliable a surveillance technique must be before it can be classified as a binary search, they should be suspicious of low false positive rates.

As an example, consider a software program that searches for child pornography by reading through e-mails passing across an Internet service provider or by invading the hard drives of home computers. When it detects an e-mail or a file that appears to contain child pornography, the software would alert a human operator with only the name of the individual who sent or owned the file. The human operator would then use this positive alert to acquire a warrant to seize and search the subject's computer files. Under the *Caballes* doctrine, this procedure would be a binary search, since it provides the user with no information beyond whether or not an individual is engaged in illegal activity. Since the software is a binary device, law enforcement agents could use the software to search through e-mails and personal hard disks without limitation.

But how accurate is this hypothetical piece of software? Law enforcement agents might boast that it has an impressively low 0.01 percent false positive rate, but if it reads through 1 million e-mails and files over the course of a year, and only 10 of those 1 million contain child pornography, the software will alert to 110 subjects over the course of the year, and only 9 percent of those alerts will be accurate. In the other 91 percent of cases, law enforcement officers will be granted a warrant to read through an e-mail or computer file that contains nothing but innocent material in which the owner has a reasonable and legitimate expectation of privacy.

The second, related point is how these numbers would be affected if law enforcement officers began using binary searches indiscriminately. Today, even though law enforcement officers have the right to use canine sniffs without any level of suspicion, the expense and scarcity of drug-detection dogs mean that an officer is unlikely to call in a canine unit unless she already has some suspicion that the subject is carrying narcotics.[40] This resource limitation increases the proportion of individuals in the pool who are carrying narcotics, thus increasing the positive predictive rate (assuming a consistent false positive rate).

In other words, if law enforcement officers use binary searches indiscriminately, without relying on reasonable suspicion or any other indicators that illegal activity may be present, they will decrease the positive predictive value of their binary device.[41] Thus, although *Caballes* gives law enforcement agents the right to use binary searches with impunity, in practice such indiscriminate use will gratuitously increase the rate at which the binary search infringes on individuals' Fourth Amendment rights. Until the technologies begin to approach 100 percent certainty, law enforcement agents could still boost the accuracy rates – and make binary searches more palatable – by using the devices only in situations where there is a high chance of detecting illegal activity.

Given the likelihood that binary searches will inevitably gain widespread use, affecting millions of people every day, courts should impose an extremely high standard of accuracy to ensure that law enforcement officers do not abuse this legal doctrine. This would have two requirements: one procedural, the other substantive.

The procedural step would be to require trial judges to conduct an independent evaluation of any method or technique which the prosecutor claims to be a binary search. In other words, whenever law enforcement conducts binary searches without reasonable suspicion and seeks to admit that evidence under the binary search doctrine, the prosecutor must prove to the court that the surveillance method was sufficiently accurate to be a binary search.[42] This evaluation would be analogous to the *Daubert* hearings in evaluating expert evidence, in which the trial judge acts as the "gatekeeper" in determining if a particular field or discipline is reliable enough to admit.[43] Unlike the *Daubert* context, however, where a judge must simply determine whether a particular science or methodology is "scientifically valid,"[44] a judge evaluating a binary search would impose a much stricter standard. The point of the procedural requirement is to ensure that the judge has enough information to make an accurate evaluation as to the level of accuracy of the search. Of course, if the law enforcement officer had probable cause to carry out the search, no such hearing would be needed. Similarly, if the law enforcement agent had some degree of reasonable suspicion, the court would first conduct a *Terry* inquiry to see if the agent had sufficient facts to justify the search.[45] If so, the search would pass constitutional muster without the need to resort to the *Caballes* doctrine; if not, the court would proceed with a hearing to determine if the search was a binary search and, therefore, fell outside the reach of the Fourth Amendment.

Although conducting this evaluation will be time-consuming at first, courts will quickly begin to establish precedents as to the acceptability or fallibility of certain techniques. Thus, once a device's accuracy rate has been established by precedent, there will be no reason why courts in the same jurisdiction should need to decide *de novo* whether, say, a drug dog or a specific type of gun detector qualified as a binary search. In these cases, all a court would have to determine would be whether the specific use of the binary search was proper (e.g., whether the drug-detection dog was properly trained, or whether the gun detector was properly calibrated). The reliance on precedent to certify or reject certain forms of surveillance will also provide helpful guidance to law enforcement agents as to what devices and procedures they are allowed to use without reasonable suspicion.[46]

The substantive standard itself must be high enough to ensure that the binary search doctrine's inevitable widespread indiscriminate application does not result in too many unjustified searches of innocent subjects. Justice Souter's "certainty" requirement is unworkable in the real world, but given the enormous number of binary searches which might be conducted on innocent individuals, courts should adopt a standard that adapts the desire for "certainty" to the imperfections of the real world. For example, a standard analogous to the "beyond a reasonable doubt" standard in the criminal jury instructions context might be appropriate. As in the probable cause context, courts will probably resist an exact quantification of the standard, but setting a specific number – such as 95 percent – will enhance the transparency and the consistency of the doctrine.

In conducting this analysis, courts should be careful to focus on the positive predictive value of the method – the percentage chance that a positive alert will indicate the existence of contraband. This will require not just evidence of the false positive rate during training or testing (although this could help the judge to determine the positive predictive value), but actual numbers from the field work by law enforcement officers using the device or procedure. As noted in this chapter, using a binary device or procedure indiscriminately will tend to decrease the positive predictive value due to the high volume of innocent individuals that will be targeted.[47] This will not necessarily lead to an unacceptably low level of accuracy; if the device or procedure has an extremely low false positive rate, the positive predictive value could remain quite high, even if the binary search is used randomly on the general population.[48] However, if the binary search in has a lower false positive rate (for newer technology still in development, for example), law enforcement officers could bolster the positive predictive value and perhaps meet a "beyond a reasonable doubt" standard by only using the device or procedure in settings or on individuals with a higher-than-average likelihood of being guilty.[49] By exercising discretion in the use of these less accurate binary searches, and thereby reducing the proportion of innocent individuals subject to the search, law enforcement could dramatically increase the positive predictive value of the search in practice and thus potentially meet the "beyond a reasonable doubt" standard imposed by the courts.

There is one further complication in determining the accuracy of binary searches. Even if these surveillance techniques are honed to the point where they are nearly 100 percent accurate in their factual determinations, there is still a problem of false positives in the legal sense. To be a true binary search, the item being detected must be a clear indicator of criminal activity. For example, a device may detect the presence of a concealed firearm with 100 percent accuracy, but it would only be considered a binary search if it were used in a jurisdiction or under circumstances in which it was illegal to carry a firearm. In the case of an Internet sniffer that detects child pornography, the problem stems from the "knowing" mens rea requirement for possession crimes:[50] Frequently, an individual may unknowingly download child pornography. Perhaps the suspect believed he was downloading adult pornography, or perhaps the images were downloaded by a hidden piece of malware on his computer.[51]

LIMITS ON BINARY SEARCHES: HOW MUCH INTRUSIVENESS IS PERMISSIBLE?

Even if a surveillance method reveals nothing but the presence of illegal activity, it could still carry a privacy cost if the police conduct or extend a seizure while engaging in the surveillance. Under *Terry* v. *Ohio*, a coerced stop, even for a brief period of time, is considered a seizure and therefore is regulated by the Fourth Amendment. Even if there is no seizure or a person or her belongings, the binary search may be intrusive in other ways: it may involve trespassing onto the suspect's private property, or it may be physically intrusive or humiliating.

The easiest cases are those in which the binary search does not involve any kind of seizure and is not physically invasive. These cases could conceivably cover the vast majority of binary searches – a portable gun detector scanning passing pedestrians and automobiles; a drug dog walking around a parked car; a video camera recording images in public and sending them to a computer running facial recognition software; or a computer program screening e-mails being sent through the Internet. These seizure-free binary searches involve no costs to privacy interests, and often carry low administrative costs, and thus under the cost-benefit analysis theory they are an extraordinarily efficient form of surveillance. They are so low in cost, in fact, that law enforcement has an incentive to engage in this form of surveillance on a widespread, indiscriminate scale (assuming, as noted in the previous section, that the positive predictive value of the surveillance remains high enough to ensure it meets the definitions of a binary search). We will discuss the potential ramifications of this development in a later section.

However, some binary searches will be more invasive and obtrusive. Perhaps a binary search causes some minor amount of delay – for example, the subject might have to stand still for a moment while the dog sniffs her or while the gun detector gets an accurate reading; or a mechanical narcotics detector may only work if it is physically touching the subject. As soon as we add some level of delay or physical invasiveness, two questions arise: does the individual feel free to "disregard the police and go about his business," and if not, can the seizure be justified under *Terry* principles?[52]

If the police have no independent basis for the seizure, the question becomes simple to resolve, since it does not require the courts to do anything they are not already doing in other contexts. Courts have a substantial body of case law to guide then in determining what actions on the part of law enforcement constitute a seizure, and how to determine whether the scope of the seizure is valid.[53] Generally, two different factors come into play: the length of the search[54] and the physical invasiveness of the search.[55] In determining whether a certain delay or level of invasiveness is reasonable, courts will look to the specific facts of each case: for example, whether the item being seized is an individual, a piece of luggage, or a piece of mail.[56]

The Court applied this doctrine in its very first binary search case. In *Place*, law enforcement agents suspected that the defendant was carrying narcotics in his luggage, but they lacked probable cause to arrest him or to obtain a warrant. After the defendant refused to give consent to search the suitcase when he landed at LaGuardia airport, the agents seized the luggage and took it to John F. Kennedy International Airport, where a trained narcotics dog sniffed the bags and indicated that one of them contained drugs.[57] By that time, ninety minutes had elapsed since the agents first took the luggage from the defendant.

The Court reviewed both the surveillance by the dog sniff and the seizure of the luggage. As noted above, the Court held that the drug sniffing dog was not a search under the Fourth Amendment because it only revealed the presence or absence of contraband. But this holding turned out to be dicta, since the Court held that the seizure of the bags was unconstitutional. The Court applied the *Terry* standard, balancing "the nature and quality of the intrusion on the individual's Fourth Amendment interests against the importance of the governmental interests alleged to justify the intrusion."[58] The Court agreed with the government that the state had a substantial interest in identifying individuals who traffic in illegal drugs, and implied that the agents possessed specific and articulable facts to support their belief that the defendant trafficked illegal drugs.[59] However, the Court held that the duration of the seizure was unreasonable under the *Terry* rationale, since it had never approved of a ninety-minute seizure under the *Terry* doctrine.[60]

Under the cost-benefit analysis theory, this all-or-nothing analysis will have to be adjusted. In the same way that we needed to refine the test for searches, we will need to refine the test for seizures, by measuring the productivity of each seizure and then setting a precise legal standard for the government to meet in order to legally conduct the seizure. The cost of the seizure will include the length of the seizure and the degree of intrusiveness, as well as the financial cost to the law enforcement agency. The benefit of the seizure will be the chance of the seizure leading to the discovery of evidence, multiplied by the severity of the crime being investigated.

Given how productive binary searches are, courts should allow for more intrusive seizures when they are used to conduct a binary search rather than a traditional search. In mathematical terms, a search-and-seizure scenario would require courts to add the search and seizure costs together, and then balance those against the total benefits of the action. Thus, if the privacy cost of the search is low (or zero, as in the case of a binary search), a court should be willing to tolerate higher seizure costs for the same level of benefit. For example, a *Terry* stop in order to conduct a physical pat-down might require a 30 percent chance of success to be constitutional, while a *Terry* stop in order to conduct a scan with a gun detector may only require a 10 percent chance of success, even though they both have an identical chance of detecting contraband.

Frequently, the binary search requires a seizure, but the justification for the seizure is independent of the binary search itself. This most often occurs when drug detection dogs are used during traffic stops: the police have an independent reason for stopping the car, and while the car is stopped, the police walk the dog around the car to check for drugs. This scenario was addressed by two Supreme Court cases, *Illinois v. Caballes*[61] and *Rodriquez v. United States*.[62]

In *Caballes*, police pulled over defendant for a traffic violation, and then a police officer walked the drug detection dog around the car while another officer conducted the tasks associated with a routine traffic stop. The use of the drug detection dog did not increase the length of the seizure, but the defendant still argued that the dog made the seizure more intrusive and thus required an independent justification under *Terry*. Justice Ginsburg echoed this point in her dissent, arguing that *Terry* does not only require justification for the initial seizure, but also requires that the police officer's actions during the seizure must be "reasonably related in *scope* to the circumstances which justified the interference in the first place."[63] Thus, although the original traffic stop in *Caballes* was valid, Justice Ginsburg argued that the canine drug search would still be unconstitutional if it impermissibly expanded the "scope" of the seizure.[64] She then argued that even if, as was the case in *Caballes*, the use of the drug detection dog does not extend the length of the seizure, the dog can make the stop "broader" and "more adversarial," exposing the subject to "the embarrassment and intimidation of being investigated, on a public thoroughfare, for drugs."[65]

Under Justice Ginsburg's argument, the very use of a drug detection dog in any context constituted some level of seizure, even if the police did not stop the subject. She warned that the result of not applying *Terry* in this way would be "suspicionless, dog-accompanied drug sweeps of parked cars along sidewalks and in parking lots," and "police with dogs, stationed at long traffic lights, circl[ing] cars waiting for the red signal to turn green."[66] Other courts have also held that merely being subjected to a drug dog sniff is intrusive enough to constitute a seizure. When reviewing the use of a drug detection dog on the front porch of a home, the Florida Supreme Court noted:

> Such a public spectacle unfolding in a residential neighborhood will invariably entail a degree of public opprobrium, humiliation and embarrassment for the resident, whether or not he or she is present at the time of the search, for such dramatic government activity in the eyes of many – neighbors, passers-by, and some in the public at large – will be viewed as an official accusation of crime. And if the resident happens to be present at the time of the "sniff test," such an intrusion into the sanctity of his or her home will generally be a frightening and harrowing experience that could prompt a reflexive or unpredictable response.[67]

The *Caballes* Court rejected this broad definition of "seizure" and ruled that the mere use of a drug detection dog on its own does not make the seizure any more intrusive. This ruling paved the way for even more opportunities for widespread use of binary searches: in any situation in which a suspect has already been legitimately seized, a binary search can constitutionally be used during the course of that seizure. For example, if law enforcement agents set up a roadblock for a permissible purpose (such as checking for drunk drivers[68] or illegal immigrants[69]), the agents are allowed to conduct binary searches during that roadblock as long as the searches do not increase the amount of time required for the stop.[70] Under the cost-benefit analysis theory, this is a question that should be solved empirically: do individuals believe the use of a drug detection dog is "intrusive"? If so, under what circumstances? When it circles your car at a red light? When it circles your car during a traffic stop? When it walks by you while you are waiting in line?

It is undisputed, however, that if the drug detection dog increases the *length* of the seizure, it requires its own independent justification. This rule was affirmed in *Rodriguez*, in which the officer completed all the tasks necessary for the traffic stop, and then detained the defendant until backup arrived, at which point the officer deployed his dog and found narcotics. Approximately seven or eight minutes had passed from the time the traffic stop was completed to the time the dog alerted to the drugs. The Court held that even the shortest amount of extra delay was enough to trigger the *Terry* requirements.

Other types of police conduct while conducting a binary search could alter the nature of the interaction enough to require an independent justification. For example, if the binary search required police officers to physically touch suspects, the extra intrusiveness could trigger an independent *Terry* analysis for the binary search. Similarly, if the police officers intrude onto a constitutionally protected area to conduct the binary search, the initial intrusion could be considered an independent search that requires its own justification. This was the case in *Florida v. Jardines*[71],hen the Supreme Court held it was unconstitutional for the police to take a drug-detection dog onto the defendant's front porch to check for marijuana.

POTENTIAL TYPES OF BINARY SEARCHES

Although drug detection dogs are by far the most common type of binary search today, law enforcement agencies are developing and deploying other forms of binary searches. Most of these searches rely on sophisticated software to transform a traditional search into a binary search. These searches use a device that gathers information but then shields the raw data results from human beings and instead route it through a computer program. The program then analyzes the results and determine whether they provided unequivocal evidence of criminal activity.

For example, there are handheld gun detectors that use passive millimeter wave imagery to display an outline of metal objects carried by an individual.[72] The use of these devices is plainly a "search." Even though the device does not physically interfere with the individual, it provides the law enforcement officer with information about the individual that is covered by a reasonable expectation of privacy: a visual outline of all of the metal objects carried in his or her clothing. However, in jurisdictions or circumstances in which it is illegal to carry a concealed firearm, police officers could turn this tool into a binary search device. The first step would be to remove the graphic display from the device and instead installing software that could "view" the image seen by the device. The software would have the ability to analyze the image to determine whether the object being viewed was a firearm. If so, the device would alert the user; if not, the device would do nothing. This "smart" gun detector would pass the binary search test, since it would only tell the law enforcement officer one thing about the individual under surveillance: whether that person was carrying a concealed firearm.

Similarly, law enforcement could conduct binary searches on our digital transmissions. In the "traditional" method of monitoring these communications, a law enforcement officer would gather this data and then study the e-mails and uploaded images – including vast amounts of innocent, private information – to see if the suspect was distributing child pornography. In the act of studying these images or transmissions, the law enforcement officer is conducting a search.[73] In the binary version of these searches, the software is designed not just to collect the e-mails and uploads, but also to analyze them and determine whether they contain any images of child pornography. The officer is notified only if a contraband image is detected. [74] This can be done through what is known as a "hash value" search. Every computer file has a unique identifier known as its "hash value," which is as individualized as a fingerprint. The Federal Bureau of Investigation (FBI) maintains a database containing the hash value of every known computer file containing child pornography. Thus, a computer program could sift through every digital file it obtains, looking for a match with any of the thousands of known contraband hash values. If no match were found, the program would return no results, and the law enforcement officer monitoring the program would learn nothing about the suspect's data other than the fact that it did not contain any known files of child pornography. If a match were found, the law enforcement officer would know with near certainty that the suspect's computer did contain at least one such file.[75]

Law enforcement officials could attach the software searching for these files to an Internet service provider (ISP) to monitor all Internet traffic to and from the suspect's computer. More controversially, they could secretly download the software onto a suspect's computer as an attachment to an e-mail. This type of binary search could also easily be conducted on a massive scale at a relatively low administrative cost: the government could install this binary "sniffer" software on all the major ISPs and monitor virtually all e-mail and Internet traffic in the country. Or, if the government wanted to search hard drives indiscriminately for contraband files, it could send out e-mails with "Trojan Horse" viruses that search through hard drives and send a report back to the government.[76]

There are many other examples of binary searches. Thermal imagers could be designed so that they only alert if the heat patterns show a near certainty of an indoor marijuana farm. Public surveillance cameras can be hooked up to facial recognition software and cross-referenced with photos of individuals with outstanding bench warrants. Smart phones could be designed to include a "textalyzer" – a device which would detect whether someone was sending texts while driving a car – and report all offenders to the police. Dozens of cities are installing gunfire detection systems, which can identify the distinctive noise and/or infrared signature of a firearm being discharged and immediately report the location of the gunfire to the police. In all of these cases, machines and computers are the only ones who learn the information about what we are carrying, what we are writing, or where we are going. These machines will quickly and mindlessly examine and discard any innocent information they discover and then report to the police any illegal activity – indoor unlicensed marijuana farms, individuals with outstanding arrest warrants, the use of texting software while a car is in motion, or the discharge of a firearm within city limits.

These examples of binary searches have something else in common: they are relatively inexpensive. Although each device may be expensive to design and manufacture, once a law enforcement agency purchases the device, it could conduct surveillance on massive numbers of people with little additional cost. The low administrative cost combined with the negligible privacy cost means that law enforcement officers face no significant practical or legal obstacles to engaging in these searches indiscriminately. Thus, we could soon see binary search devices everywhere; we will be scanned by gun detectors and facial recognition software everywhere we go; all of our Internet communications will be filtered through a child pornography detector; all of our cell phones will be hooked up to a texting-while-driving algorithm; all neighborhoods of our cities would be constantly monitored by gunshot detectors. This constant surveillance by sophisticated machines could result in a dramatic drop in criminal activity. Thus, it is worth considering what such a world would look like.

A WORLD OF 100 PERCENT ENFORCEMENT

For some people, the idea of constant surveillance – even by binary search devices – is deeply troubling. Dissenting in *Jacobsen*, Justice Brennan wrote that the binary search doctrine would allow police to release trained narcotics dogs into public areas "to roam the streets at random, alerting the officers to people carrying cocaine."[77] More ominous, at least to Justice Brennan, was the idea that someday law enforcement would develop a device that could instantaneously detect whether someone was carrying cocaine and then "set[] up such a device on a street corner and scan[] all passersby" or "cruis[e] through a residential neighborhood and us[e] the device to identify all homes in which the drug is present."[78]

These concerns resonated with two of the Justices in *Caballes*. Justice Souter dissented from the decision, pointing out that "[A]n uncritical adherence to *Place* would render the Fourth Amendment indifferent to suspicionless and indiscriminate sweeps of cars in parking garages and pedestrians on sidewalks …..").[79] Justice Ginsburg echoed that concern in her dissent, writing that "[t]oday's decision … clears the way for suspicionless, dog-accompanied drug sweeps of parked cars along sidewalks and in parking lots. Nor would motorists have constitutional grounds for complaint should police with dogs, stationed at long traffic lights, circle cars waiting for the red signal to turn green."[80]

The dissenting Justices are all correct about the implications of the binary search doctrine. If anything, they underestimate the degree to which police will develop and deploy binary search devices. But under the cost-benefit analysis theory, these extreme scenarios are more of a utopia than a dystopia. Widespread use of binary searches should be encouraged if it leads to greater security. Justice Brennan's fear of a cocaine detector on a street corner is particularly puzzling: assuming the cocaine detector met our requirements for a binary search, what would be the objection to learning the identity of everyone in the city who possesses cocaine?

Part of the resistance to the idea of a binary search panopticon is that we may not be ready for a world of 100 percent enforcement. At least in the context of minor crimes, there has been significant resistance to automated technology that can perfectly detect criminal activity. Consider the fate of red-light cameras, which automatically photograph the license plate of any car that runs a red light, thus catching everyone who commits this offense. Since running a red light is a crime, and these devices accurately detect everyone who commits this crime, we might expect these devices to be both ubiquitous and uniformly popular – we now have the ability to nearly eliminate this very dangerous traffic offense. But the opposite is true: red light cameras face opposition in almost every jurisdiction where they are used, and some legislators have passed statutes that outlaw their use in the state.[81]

Those who oppose widespread use of binary searches usually use binary drug detectors as their example. This may be because drug detection dogs are currently the most prominent example of binary searches. But it is also because drug possession is a relatively minor offense, and drug laws are unpopular when compared to other crimes.[82] Thus, in criticizing binary drug detectors, many judges and scholars are implicitly arguing that the cost to privacy of ubiquitous monitoring, even of the binary search variety, is not worth increased enforcement of drug laws. This argument is a version of the cost-benefit analysis theory, a version that assumes an unspecified cost to these binary searches and a low benefit to detecting those who are "merely" committing low-level drug crimes. Certainly, this argument loses a lot of persuasive power if police possessed, say, a binary search device to detect rapes or other crimes of violence. If police could drive down a residential street with a device that infallibly detected whether a crime of domestic violence was occurring in any house that they passed, there would be little opposition to its widespread use.

Thus, the objection to the 100 percent enforcement offered by widespread binary searches may be an indirect objection to the substantive law that creates the crime, not to the method of criminal investigation being used. For example, in 2015 there were over 7.8 million outstanding arrest warrants in this country.[83] Instituting a nationwide system of public surveillance cameras connected to facial recognition software could result in the detection and arrest of a large proportion of individuals with these warrants. Yet the vast majority of these arrest warrants are for minor offenses, often issued by jurisdictions in a discriminatory fashion for "crimes" that were primarily designed to raise revenue for the municipality.[84]

The prospect of achieving nearly 100 percent enforcement could and should cause us to reconsider the substantive crimes themselves. More effective enforcement could accelerate criminal justice reform by forcing us to see the true extent – and cost – of certain criminal prohibitions. If we are uncomfortable with a device that allows us to arrest everyone who possesses cocaine, perhaps we are actually uncomfortable with criminalizing cocaine. If we reject a system that would automatically enforce 7.8 million outstanding warrants, perhaps we should devise a system that does not produce so many warrants, or at least does not produce them in such a disproportionate way.

CONCLUSION

Although surveillance techniques and data analysis methods have improved dramatically over the last hundred years, law enforcement agents for the most part must still search for evidence of illegal activity the same way they did in the eighteenth century: by spying, snooping, and eavesdropping on our lives. These agents invariably recover large amounts of private information about suspects (as well as information about those who are not even suspected) and then sift through that information to determine whether the suspect is guilty of a crime.

Binary searches could revolutionize the way in which law enforcement agents conduct surveillance. Modern technologies are quickly evolving to the point where machines and computers can supplant humans as the agents who sift through the private, protected data in order to determine whether criminal activity is present. This represents an improvement on both sides of the cost-benefit equation: the surveillance has a lower privacy cost, low administrative cost, and can be much more effective in detecting illegal activity.

Of course, most new surveillance technology is not designed to conduct binary searches. Implementing a cost-benefit analysis theory will certainly encourage police to adopt binary devices whenever possible, but they will not be available for all crimes. The most prevalent change in surveillance in the next decade will instead come from the field of big data – the massive collection and processing of millions of data points to learn otherwise hidden (and occasionally intimate) information about us. The next two chapters discuss how the cost-benefit analysis theory applies to these powerful new investigatory tools.

6

Public Surveillance, Big Data, and Mosaic Searches

What may seem trivial to the uninformed, may appear of great moment to one who has a broad view of the scene.

C.I.A. v. Sims (1985)[1]

INTRODUCTION

In 2004, Antoine Jones and Lawrence Maynard ran a nightclub in the District of Columbia. The FBI believed that the two men also ran a cocaine trafficking ring. FBI agents tried multiple surveillance methods to gather evidence: they staked out the nightclub; they installed a secret camera that constantly monitored the front door of the club; and they wiretapped Jones' cellphone. After a number of months, the FBI agents finally tried one more technique: they installed a GPS device to the undercarriage of the jeep owned by Jones' wife. For the next twenty-eight days, law enforcement tracked the movements of the jeep, and they were able to notice a pattern in his behavior: Jones was consistently engaging in multiple short meetings at certain locations. These meetings were strong evidence of drug dealing, and they were an integral piece of evidence in the eventual case against Jones and Maynard.[2]

Jones and Maynard ultimately challenged the GPS surveillance, arguing that the use of the device was a "search" under the Fourth Amendment. The government argued that their agents did not need a warrant, because individuals do not have any Fourth Amendment rights in activities that they conduct in public.[3] The defendant responded that continuous GPS monitoring for an entire month was something entirely different, both in degree and in kind. Tracking someone continuously for twenty-eight days, even on public roads, could be seen as an invasion of privacy. And by processing the data from twenty-eight days of continuous monitoring, the government would be able to detect specific patterns of activity and thereby learn private details about the defendant's life, such as a person's religion, medical condition, or drinking habits.

Seven years later, it became evident that the police need not attach GPSs devices to our cars in order to track our locations; helpfully, we all carry GPS devices with us at all times. After the police made some arrests in a series of electronic store robberies in Ohio and Michigan, one of the suspects they arrested identified a man named Timothy Carpenter as an accomplice. The police wanted to know if Carpenter had been at or near the site of the robberies, and so they obtained Carpenter's cell site information records from MetroPCS and Sprint.[4] The private companies provided the government with records for 129 days, comprising nearly 13,000 separate location points – an average of 101 location points per day. The location information proved that Carpenter was indeed near four of the robbery sites at the time the crimes were committed. Prosecutors used this information against Carpenter at trial, and he was convicted of eleven counts of robbery and firearm possession, he was sentenced to over a hundred years in prison.

Like Jones, Carpenter challenged the government's use of electronic location tracking devices, arguing that when the prosecutors obtained Carpenter's cell phone records from MetroPCS and Sprint, they conducted a Fourth Amendment search, which should have required a warrant.[5] The *Carpenter* case thus went beyond the massive data gathering of the *Jones* case and added in an extra element: this data was not actually gathered by the government at all, but instead gathered by a private company, who then handed the information over to the prosecutors. As the *Carpenter* Court noted:

> [S]eismic shifts in digital technology [have] made possible the tracking of not only Carpenter's location but also everyone else's, not for a short period but for years and years. Sprint Corporation and its competitors are not your typical witnesses. Unlike the nosy neighbor who keeps an eye on comings and goings, they are ever alert, and their memory is nearly infallible.[6]

The *Jones* and *Carpenter* cases addressed two new law enforcement techniques. *Jones* involved the police using technology to gather massive amounts of public data about a suspect, while *Carpenter* involved the police obtaining the massive amounts of data that have already been gathered by private entities. In the age of cell phone tracking, public surveillance cameras, and drone reconnaissance, the implications of these decisions were immense even in the narrow context of location tracking. But with the proliferation of public surveillance tools and private data gathering throughout society, combined with the emergence of big data algorithms to process this massive amount of data, the legal status of these methods of surveillance has become perhaps the most important Fourth Amendment question in the past fifty years. The use of this data to detect useful patterns is known as conducting a "mosaic search,"[7] since each individual piece of information on its own is meaningless, but when hundreds or thousands or even millions of these data points are combined together, a meaningful picture emerges.

The past two chapters have discussed reactive surveillance and binary searches, and in each of those cases, the cost–benefit analysis theory has shown that those types of surveillance are not nearly as intrusive as they first appear. In the case of reactive surveillance, the government is merely responding to privacy-enhancing technologies which have made traditional methods of surveillance ineffective. And binary searches which reach a high enough level of accuracy are in fact extremely productive methods of surveillance.

Mosaic searches follow a similar pattern: they may at first seem to be overly intrusive, but once we apply the cost–benefit analysis doctrine, the surveillance ends up being far more reasonable. They are extremely inexpensive, they only reveal information that has already been exposed to the public, and they can very powerful in investigating criminal activity. Unfortunately, in *Jones* and *Carpenter* the Supreme Court has begun to limit these searches, and ironically the primary rationale behind these limits is that these searches are so inexpensive that police can engage in them very easily. As the Court noted in *Carpenter*:

> Cell phone tracking is remarkably easy, cheap, and efficient compared to traditional investigative tools. With just the click of a button, the Government can access each carrier's deep repository of historical location information at practically no expense.[8]

This counter-intuitive argument turns the cost–benefit analysis on its head by seeking to deter some of the most productive searches available to law enforcement.

This chapter and the next chapter use the cost–benefit analysis theory to argue that the growing movement to limit mosaic searches is misguided. This chapter will discuss the question of public mosaic searches such as the one conducted in *Jones*: when police gather public data on their own from sources such as public surveillance cameras, drones, satellites, GPS trackers, and other surveillance devices. Chapter 7 will discuss private mosaic searches like the one conducted in *Carpenter*: when police obtain data from third parties such as internet service providers, telecommunication companies, and manufacturers of smart devices.

Before we turn to the arguments regarding the legal status of mosaic searches, we will return briefly to a discussion of big data surveillance, in order to understand how the government obtains and processes the massive amounts of information required to conduct a mosaic search.

BIG DATA AND CRIMINAL INVESTIGATIONS

We already saw in Chapter 2 how police are using big data tools to help decide where to deploy resources, whether individuals at a location may be dangerous, and identify suspects. We also discussed how law enforcement and courts can use big data's predictive algorithms to provide empirical evidence for the benefits side of the cost–benefit analysis, including whether there is reasonable suspicion or probable cause to believe a crime has been committed. This chapter and the next chapter discuss what limits (if any) the Fourth Amendment should place on the gathering and processing of this data.

New technologies have exponentially increased the amount of public data that police can collect. Cameras in public spaces allow one officer to monitor many different locations at once. Software can mine public information from the internet. Soon drones will be able to track our movements in public every minute of every day. The last chapter described how some of these surveillance technologies can be combined with filtering software to create binary searches that only respond to illegal activity. For example, police can install numerous cameras in public spaces and take thousands of pictures of all the individuals who pass by.[9] The pictures can then be passed through a computer which compares the facial features of each individual to pictures of known fugitives, using standard biometric measurements (size of mouth, distance between the eyes, angle of nose, etc.).[10] In theory, this technology would alert officers on the ground to the presence of any known fugitives that might be present.[11]

But big data surveillance is not usually combined with filtering software to create a binary search. Instead, as in the *Jones* and *Carpenter* cases, it is often used as a mosaic search, to detect patterns which indicate an increased likelihood of criminal activity. Unlike binary searches, these mosaic searches reveal patterns which indicate not only criminal activity but also private innocent activity; thus, they carry some privacy cost. The current legal debate over mosaic searches involves whether this privacy cost makes them so intrusive that they constitute a Fourth Amendment search and thus require a warrant. As we will see, the best way to resolve this dispute is once again to move away from the all-or-nothing zero sum game imposed by the current legal rules and instead apply the flexible, scalable cost–benefit analysis theory.

DUELING ARGUMENTS FOR MOSAIC SEARCHES

The government argued that the GPS tracking in *Jones* was legally indistinguishable from the 1983 case of *United States* v. *Knotts*. In *Knotts*, law enforcement officers put a tracking device inside a container that the suspect then placed in his car. The Supreme Court ruled that law enforcement officers were permitted to use the device to track the suspect as he drove along the public roads. [12] The *Knotts* decision was consistent with a long line of precedent which held that surveillance does not implicate the Fourth Amendment if it only collects information that has been exposed to the public. Garbage that has been left on the street is fair game;[13] as is anything that police officers may see inside a home when they look through a window from a public street.[14] Even if the police use technology in order to help them collect the information, the surveillance is still not considered a Fourth Amendment search if all the police collect is public information. Police routinely use binoculars to observe suspects on public sidewalks; they can also use flashlights to help look for evidence in the dark. In *California* v. *Ciraolo*, the Supreme Court ruled that the police were permitted to use airplanes to fly over the defendant's property and observe the marijuana plants that grew there, since the defendant knowingly exposed his backyard to airplane passengers.[15] On the other hand, if the technology reveals information that the police could *not* obtain by conventional means, its use constitutes a search under the Fourth Amendment. The Court confirmed this distinction in *Kyllo* v. *United States*, in which the government used a thermal imager to detect heat patterns emerging from the defendant's home. Since the surveillance technology revealed private information that the government could only have otherwise obtained by entering the home, its use was the equivalent of a search of the home, and thus was illegal without a warrant.[16]

In other words, the method of collecting data does not matter to the courts; all that matters is whether the data that is collected is information that the suspect has knowingly shared with the public. Thus, it was irrelevant that the police in *Knotts* were using a new piece of technology to track the defendant's movements, since the technology was doing no more than what police officers were permitted to do without a warrant before they had the technology. By this argument, any search that relies solely on public data raises no constitutional issues, regardless of how much public data is collected. Ubiquitous surveillance cameras in public spaces are permissible because they are legally no different from multiple police officers fanning out through a public area and monitoring everyone's activity. Software that can instantly mine all of an individual's public records are permissible, since before computers and the internet, law enforcement officers could gather the same information by traveling to all the appropriate government offices and copying down a suspect's court records, property records, incorporation records, permit applications, and so on. The fact that it can now be done more cheaply (and quickly) should not affect its legality.

Opponents of warrantless mosaic searches see them quite differently.[17] In their minds, at some point the sheer amount of public data that can be gathered by law enforcement officials crosses a line and triggers Fourth Amendment protection. Furthermore, these mosaic searches are not just a more efficient way of conducting a conventional search of public information; they are a qualitatively different type of search because by definition they reveal something more than what the suspect has revealed to the public. The circuit court in the *Jones* case stated that "the difference is not one of degree but of kind, for no single journey reveals the habits and patterns that mark the distinction between a day in the life and a way of life, nor the departure from a routine, that, like the dog that did not bark in the Sherlock Holmes story, may reveal even more."[18]

The circuit court gave some specific examples of inferences that could be derived from these patterns:

> Repeated visits to a church, a gym, a bar, or a bookie tell a story not told by any single visit, as does one's not visiting any of these places over the course of a month. The sequence of a person's movements can reveal still more; a single trip to a

gynecologist's office tells little about a woman, but that trip followed a few weeks later by a visit to a baby supply store tells a different story. A person who knows all of another's travels can deduce whether he is a weekly church goer, a heavy drinker, a regular at the gym, an unfaithful husband, an outpatient receiving medical treatment, an associate of particular individuals or political groups – and not just one such fact about a person, but all such facts.[19]

The ability to deduce facts about a person based on patterns of data is not confined merely to location tracking information; indeed, this technique is the fundamental basis of big data analysis. Law enforcement agencies are using this technique with increasing frequency in many different contexts. After the September 11th terrorist attacks, the National Security Agency engaged in a bulk metadata collection program in which it indiscriminately collected massive amounts of noncontent data, such as the phone numbers dialed and e-mail addresses sent by of millions of Americans. The NSA presumably had software that could process these billions of pieces of data and search for patterns that would indicate a high likelihood of criminal activity. As with location tracking, law enforcement officers gain almost no private information when they obtain one outgoing phone number dialed by an individual on one occasion. But if the government obtains the thousands of phone numbers a person dials over the course of a year, it can learn quite a bit of private information from the pattern: how often the person calls her spouse; the usual times that she is awake or asleep; the number of personal calls she makes while at work; the identities of her close friends; and her hobbies and other interests. Similar information can be learned by examining a year's worth of credit card receipts, or a month's worth of internet searches.[20]

As we saw in Chapter 1, the Supreme Court decided the *Jones* case using the curious theory that the FBI agents conducted a Fourth amendment search when they committed the physical trespass of placing the GPS device on the car constituted a search.[21] But four Justices wrote a concurrence that addressed the location tracking itself and concluded that the twenty-eight days of continuous monitoring was a Fourth Amendment search under the *Katz* test. The Supreme Court concurrence, however, did not rely on the mosaic theory that the circuit court had invoked. Instead, the concurring Justices focused on the extremely low cost of the surveillance. In the pretechnological age, the concurrence argued, continuous twenty-four hour surveillance of a person's public movements was possible, but it was "difficult and costly and therefore rarely undertaken."[22] Because of this practical difficulty, law enforcement officers were usually discouraged from engaging in dragnet-style public surveillance. Now that GPS technology had made this type of surveillance possible, it would be feasible for law enforcement agencies to observe and record nearly every action that we take in public, which would violate our reasonable expectation of privacy.

Thus, the government was already fighting an uphill battle when the *Carpenter* case arrived at the Supreme Court. But in spite of the *Jones* concurrence, the government continued to argue that a person's location in a public place is not private information, relying on *Knotts* for the proposition that when the defendant "traveled over the public streets he voluntarily conveyed to anyone who wanted to look the fact that he was traveling over particular roads in a particular direction, the fact of whatever stops he made, and the fact of his final destination."[23] In fact, as the *Carpenter* dissent pointed out, a person's location is even less private today than it was in the predigital *Knotts* era, since "[m]illions of Americans [today] choose to share their location on a daily basis, whether by using a variety of location-based services on their phones, or by sharing their location with friends and the public at large via social media."[24]

The *Carpenter* majority soundly rejected this argument and finally embraced the mosaic theory wholeheartedly:

> Mapping a cell phone's location over the course of 127 days provides an all-encompassing record of the holder's whereabouts. As with GPS information, the time-stamped data provides an intimate window into a person's life, revealing not only his particular movements, but through them his familial, political, professional, religious, and sexual associations. These location records hold for many Americans the "privacies of life."[25]

The Court also posited that tracking people through their cell phones is worse than tracking them with a GPS device on their cars:

> In the past, attempts to reconstruct a person's movements were limited by a dearth of records and the frailties of recollection. With access to CSLI, the Government can now travel back in time to retrace a person's whereabouts, subject only to the retention polices of the wireless carriers, which currently maintain records for up to five years.[26]

This is perhaps one of the most curious passages in the entire opinion, since it implies that the "dearth of records" and the "frailties of recollection" which prevented the detection and prosecution of countless crimes in the past were somehow superior to the permanent, comprehensive, and accurate records that are available today.

COST–BENEFIT ANALYSIS AND MOSAIC SEARCHES

Jones and *Carpenter* offer two distinct arguments in favor of creating legal barriers to continuous public surveillance. The *Jones* concurrence argues that the low cost of these searches allows law enforcement to watch our public movements at all times, and this constant surveillance violates our reasonable expectation of privacy; thus, the concurring Justices are objecting to the large-scale *gathering* of public data. *Carpenter* invokes the mosaic theory and argues that there is a distinctive, more intimate privacy cost to these searches, because law enforcement officers can deduce information about us above and beyond the information that we have knowingly exposed to the public. Thus, the *Carpenter* Court is objecting to the *processing* of this massive amount of public data. In a sense, the *Jones* concurrence is referring to the massive quantity of data that is now available, while the *Carpenter* Court argues that the police can turn this immense amount of public data into a qualitatively different type of private information. Neither of these arguments carry much weight under the cost–benefit analysis theory. The *Jones* concurrence's reasoning completely ignores any cost–benefit analysis, and although *Carpenter* correctly identifies an extra privacy cost associated with mosaic searches, it neglects to account for their increased benefit.

We will start with the *Jones* concurrence. First, it is important to note that the concurring decision misapplies the *Katz* test. The Justices state that "society's expectation has been that law enforcement agents and others would not – and usually could not – secretly monitor and catalogue every single movement of an individual's car for a very long period."[27] This either assumes that our reasonable expectations of privacy are static – that because individuals believed that continuous location surveillance infringed on our privacy fifty years ago, they still believe this is the case – or it assumes that the *Katz* test refers to our reasonable expectation of privacy at the time of *Katz* rather than our current reasonable expectation of privacy. When nearly every American carries a device that constantly broadcasts its location to multiple entities, it is hard to imagine that many Americans think it is infeasible to monitor our movements over the course of a month. It makes far more sense to interpret the *Katz* test flexibly, to acknowledge that our reasonable expectations of privacy evolve with time, and to use empirical data to determine the actual expectation of privacy that society holds as opposed to the expectation of privacy that the Supreme Court believes that society has.

Furthermore, the *Jones* concurrence creates more doctrinal problems than it solves. As noted above, courts applying the *Katz* test have always held that individuals have no reasonable expectation of privacy in the information they reveal to the public. Abandoning this principle requires one of two options, both of which require abrogating the *Katz* test. Courts could apply the Fourth Amendment's warrant requirements to *all* public surveillance – even to a police officer observing illegal activity firsthand on a public street – but this would be an absurd rule. The only other option would be for courts to distinguish between different kinds of technology that are used during the surveillance, and it is difficult to find a principled reason for any such distinction.

Under this theory, courts would need to decide on a case-by-case basis which technologies cross the line into a Fourth Amendment search. Presumably a law enforcement agent could still use a flashlight or a set of binoculars without needing a warrant. And probably it would be constitutional to use one video camera to monitor a public place. But what if the police installed two cameras and had one officer watching both monitors, in order to double her efficiency? Courts will have to decide what number of video cameras violates our reasonable expectation of privacy. In the context of location tracking, courts will also need to determine how long the tracking can take place before it becomes a "search." Perhaps two days of tracking is too invasive, or perhaps ten. Given the all-or-nothing paradigm of the *Katz* test, strict lines would have to be drawn for each type of technology, and for different types of public spaces, and all of these lines would be arbitrary. The *Jones* concurrence acknowledged this line-drawing problem, but merely stated that it "need not identify with precision the point at which the tracking of this vehicle became a search . . ."[28]

No matter what line is drawn, the result would lead to irrational results, since the *Katz* test would allow police to gather the same information with more costly and intrusive conventional methods. For example, instead of installing one hundred video cameras throughout a public park, the police could hire one hundred extra police officers and station them in exactly the same locations as the cameras would be. These hundred offices would gather the same information as the video cameras, and they would arguably be more intrusive than the cameras (and certainly more expensive for taxpayers), yet their presence would be permissible under the Fourth Amendment.

But most importantly for our purposes, the *Jones* concurrence is a classic application of the equilibrium adjustment theory. The concurrence argues that continuous twenty-four-hour surveillance was so costly in the "pre-computer age" that it was "rarely undertaken." "The surveillance at issue in this case – constant monitoring of the location of a vehicle for four weeks – would have required a large team of agents, multiple vehicles, and perhaps aerial assistance."[29] In other words, because this type of surveillance was infeasible at time zero – whenever that might be – the Justices see the new surveillance technology as disrupting the original balance between privacy and security. Thus, the Justices see their job as restoring the balance back to where it was at time zero. This successfully ensures that privacy protections never diminish, but it also ensures that law enforcement surveillance never becomes more efficient. The concurrence's logic makes sense from a certain point of view: in the past, there were no legal restrictions on surveillance of public places, but there were practical and financial barriers which served as a *de facto* regulation that discouraged or even prevented law enforcement officers from engaging in widespread public surveillance. Once technological advances removed the *de facto* regulation, some courts believed it was necessary to intervene and create *de jure* regulation in order to maintain the balance.

This argument completely inverts the cost–benefit analysis theory. Low-cost public surveillance devices have the potential to dramatically leverage law enforcement resources and thereby provide an enormous increase in security. Technology makes these formerly labor-intensive searches feasible for a much broader category of crimes; the surveillance becomes much more efficient, allowing this type of investigation to occur with a much smaller outlay of human resources.

But under the concurrence's logic, the cheaper and easier the method of surveillance becomes, the higher the legal barriers should be. This logic would significantly impede many types of innovation in criminal investigations, since it would lead courts to add greater restrictions every time the police became more efficient in their surveillance. Police officers have become more efficient in many ways over past decade: they use computers in their squad cars to look up information while in the field; they use GPS systems in their cars to navigate more quickly to crime scenes; and they employ more advanced forensic technology such as DNA sequencing to identify criminals. Past innovations such as the 911 response system, intoxilyzers, radar detectors, and even the two-way radio have all made their investigations cheaper and easier. It would be nonsensical to increase the legal regulations on police officers every time they developed a newer, more efficient method of investigating crime.

Other judges who have advocated for a warrant requirement for mosaic searches have been even more explicit in their equilibrium adjustment arguments by noting how effective GPS tracking can be when compared to conventional surveillance. Judge Alex Kozinski of the Ninth Circuit dissented from a denial of an *en banc* petition in a case very similar to *Jones*, and he argued that GPS tracking represents a greater infringement on privacy because of the difficulty of employing countermeasures against it:

> You can preserve your anonymity from prying eyes, even in public, by traveling at night, through heavy traffic, in crowds, by using a circuitous route, disguising your appearance, passing in and out of buildings and being careful not to be followed. But there's no hiding from the all-seeing network of GPS satellites that hover overhead, which never sleep, never blink, never get confused and never lose attention. [30]

These judges seem determined to keep the rules fair, to make sure neither side gets an unfair advantage in the "competitive enterprise" between the police and the criminals. But as we discussed in Chapter 1, this is the wrong way to look at the question. Our goal is to create the most productive searches by maximizing output and minimizing input, not to ensure an even playing field for all the participants. Judge Kozinski's argument seems to imply that GPS surveillance would be preferable if it were designed to fail at random moments during the day, or if some individuals were able to purchase countermeasures that would scramble their GPS signal. The entire purpose of deploying this technology is to track the suspect's movements in public; it seems odd to critique the technology for providing this information too well.

The best course of action for courts is to use empirical evidence to determine the perceived intrusiveness of constant, long-term surveillance. Although the *Knotts* Court held that surveillance of a single trip on a public road did not implicate the Fourth Amendment because it only recorded public information, this does not mean that the privacy cost of public surveillance is necessarily zero. Indeed, some of the results from Professor Slobogin's intrusiveness surveys indicate that the public does believe that public surveillance carries a privacy cost – and the longer the surveillance, the greater the cost.[31] These results are now over ten years old, and societal attitudes surrounding public surveillance may have changed in the interim, but future empirical work may confirm that society does have some expectation of privacy in their public movements. Calculating the actual privacy costs and assigning a proportional legal standard would be preferable to the current state of the law, which is to assume that intermittent public surveillance is unregulated by the Fourth Amendment, while at some arbitrary point continuous, long-term public surveillance requires probable cause and a warrant.

The Court's reasoning in *Carpenter* moves beyond the gathering of public data and instead considers the privacy cost of the processing of that data as mosaic search. Essentially the circuit court is arguing that mosaic searches reveal private information and therefore carry an additional privacy cost beyond the sum of each individual data point. This privacy cost can be plugged into our equation when determining the productivity of the mosaic search.

Thus, when the police only gather one piece of publicly available information, the privacy cost is near zero, so the productivity of the surveillance is equivalent to its benefit divided by its financial cost. Since the police already internalize the financial cost of the surveillance, there is no reason to add in any legal regulation in order to ensure the optimum level of surveillance. When the police gather thousands of pieces of publicly available information, the privacy cost of each of those individual pieces of information may increase based on the length of the surveillance, but the overall privacy cost of the raw data itself is still just a matter of degree. However, under the mosaic theory, a different kind of privacy cost is created once law enforcement officers process this data and see patterns of behavior. Since this privacy cost is not internalized by law enforcement, there may be a need to add some level of legal regulation before conducting the surveillance.

In order to determine the appropriate level of regulation, we also need to fill in the equation on the benefits side. As it turns out, the same data processing that leads to an additional privacy cost also leads to an increase in the benefits of the surveillance. In other words, although *Carpenter* is correct in pointing out the increased privacy cost to the mosaic searches, it also should have acknowledged the increased benefits that they provide. These benefits could be considerable in many cases, especially when no other method of surveillance is able to provide useful information. As with calculating benefits for other types of surveillance, empirical evidence would be needed to determine how often different types of mosaic searches yield useful information about criminal activity, as well as how accurate the predictions can be once the information is obtained. Using empirical data in setting the legal standard will also encourage the police to only engage in mosaic searches when there is a higher probability of learning useful information.

Two other factors will also be significant in calculating the benefits of the surveillance. The first is the severity of the crime being investigated; thus, using continuous GPS monitoring or obtaining thousands of pieces of telephone metadata should face a lower legal standard if the surveillance if being done pursuant to an investigation for terrorism or kidnapping as opposed to an investigation for a minor-level drug crime. The second relevant factor in calculating benefits will be the higher level of effectiveness that mosaic searches typically offer. As Judge Kozinski noted, GPS tracking is far less susceptible to counter-measures than conventional physical surveillance; also, the suspect is far less likely to detect the surveillance than if an officer were actually following him around.

Thus, although *Carpenter* is correct in identifying the added privacy cost of mosaic searches, the cost–benefit analysis theory must consider the added benefits of these searches as well. It is also critical to point out what values should *not* be part of the formula. Specifically, the extremely low financial cost of mosaic searches should not be a factor to consider. The low financial cost does mean that these searches tend to be far more productive than conventional searches; it is much cheaper to continuously track an individual through his cell phone than with a team of round-the-clock surveillance offices. However, as discussed earlier, the financial cost of the surveillance is already internalized by the police officers, and so it need not be taken into account when deciding what level of legal restrictions the search requires. By the same reasoning, the low financial cost of these searches should also not be a reason to *discourage* these searches, as the *Jones* concurrence argues. If the police have the option of conducting a surveillance at a cost of $1,000 or conducting the same surveillance for $10, the police should be allowed to freely choose the less expensive option.

In many cases, applying a cost–benefit analysis to mosaic searches based on public information will reveal that these searches are extremely productive. Although courts and commentators have created hypotheticals in which very personal information could result from binary searches – regular trips to motels that are frequented by prostitutes, or a distinctive pattern of visits to different medical specialists – it is likely that in many cases, there will be nothing particularly distinctive or deeply personal about the patterns, and thus the average privacy costs of these searches will be relatively low. It is also possible that with the proper legal incentives, law enforcement officers will be able to refine their processing algorithms to be moderately accurate in detecting criminal behavior – perhaps not to the extent that they will qualify as binary searches, but almost certainly to the extent that they flag truly suspicious behavior and ignore most innocent behavior. If so these searches could end up generating a high level of benefit with a very low level of privacy cost. This would result in a very low level of legal restriction – perhaps courts would allow these mosaic searches if law enforcement could identify merely a five or ten percent likelihood of finding useful information, equivalent to the "reason to believe" or "certified relevance" standards that now exist for certain types of surveillance. Add in the fact that the financial cost of these searches is usually very low, and it is quite likely that these searches will become more and more widespread. The next section will consider some examples of how mosaic searches may be used in the near future if they are only lightly regulated.

THE FUTURE OF LOW-COST PUBLIC SURVEILLANCE: BODY CAMERAS, ROBOT POLICE OFFICERS, AND PANOPTIC SURVEILLANCE

The law regarding low-cost public surveillance and mosaic searches is now at a crossroads. Courts have three choices moving forward. First, they could revert to classic Fourth Amendment doctrine and treat these searches as free from any Fourth Amendment restrictions, as long as they only gather information from public sources. Second, they could adopt the reasoning of the *Jones* concurrence or the *Carpenter* Court and hold that these searches – once they pass some arbitrary line – are a full-fledged "search" that require a warrant or that must fit into an exception to the warrant requirement. Third, courts could conduct a cost–benefit analysis by evaluating these searches on a sliding scale, and then require a level of certainty that is appropriate given the privacy cost and the law enforcement benefit of the surveillance.

Of all of these possibilities, the second choice is the worst: requiring probable cause and a warrant for any mosaic search will substantially limit the development and adoption of big data tools for law enforcement purposes. As we have already seen, these tools can be extremely efficient and productive surveillance techniques, and the predictive algorithms they employ are necessary if courts are going to shift to a more quantified cost–benefit analysis method of applying the Fourth Amendment. Police are already deploying technologies such as public surveillance cameras, body cameras, drones, and even robots to observe and record larger and larger amounts of data. These technologies have enormous potential benefits for law enforcement efforts as long as courts allow mosaic searches to continue.

Law enforcement agencies have been using public surveillance cameras since 1968, although they did not become widespread until a few decades later.[32] Today, most American cities have thousands of cameras in public places, with law enforcement agencies monitoring the feeds and/or hard drives recording all of the images. Currently local, state, and federal government agencies operate millions of video cameras, monitoring sidewalks, streets, parks, museums, parking lots, government offices, and dozens of other locations. And this number is a small fraction of the surveillance cameras owned and operated by private parties, such as private homeowners, neighborhood associations, and companies. Unlike police-operated cameras, private cameras can record activities in private spaces as well as public spaces. In the next chapter we will examine the ability of law enforcement to gain access to these private video feeds, but even excluding the private cameras, the large number of public surveillance cameras is still sufficient to fundamentally affect the nature of criminal investigations.

The number of publicly operated public surveillance cameras is about to increase dramatically due to another new type of surveillance technology: police body cameras. There are currently just over one million public police officers in the country.[33] In a 2015 survey, 95 percent of large police departments reported that they were already using or would soon be using body cameras;[34] it is likely that in the near future nearly every police officer will be equipped with a recording device. As of now, the financial cost of using the cameras is high – particularly the cost of storing all of the data they record, which could run into the millions of dollars for larger cities[35] – but as with all forms of digital technology, the cost is expected to shrink substantially in the future.

Up until now, most of the focus on police body cameras has been on whether they are able to deter or detect police misconduct,[36] but their true impact will be on police surveillance, since they provide a permanent, nondegradable record not just of everything an officer sees, but also of everything that is in her field of vision as she goes about her duties. Footage from police body cameras also goes beyond what is exposed to the public, since police officers enter homes and other private spaces as part of their regular jobs. If the police are illegally in a private space, the footage from their cameras will be suppressed, as would their testimony about what they observed. But the vast majority of time, when police enter private homes, it is pursuant to a warrant, consent, emergency response, or some other exception to the warrant requirement; thus, the body camera footage from these areas would be admissible.

Police are also mounting cameras on unmanned aerial vehicles, popularly known as drones. Law enforcement agencies routinely use these devices for search and rescue operations, to investigate active shooters, analyze crime scenes, and conduct basic surveillance.[37] Like many other types of surveillance technology, drones allow police to leverage their resources; one police chief said that a drone is "like having 20 police officers on patrol or more."[38] A CEO of a company that provides drones to police describes his product as "a live version of Google Earth, only with full TiVo capability. It allows us to rewind time and go back and see events that we didn't know occurred at the time they occurred."[39]

In addition to the use of unmanned aerial vehicles, police departments are also turning to robots to carry out duties that are too difficult or dangerous for human police officers. Many police forces use robots to go places where police cannot reach to look for evidence or find explosives.[40] For now, most of these devices are merely remote-controlled machines, but companies are rapidly developing autonomous machines that move on their own and report suspicious or unusual activity. Private security agencies are using these autonomous robots, such as the 5-foot tall wheeled "K-5" machine manufactured by Knightscope. K-5 robots record video, conduct thermal imaging, read license plates, and detect the presence of humans; they rent out for between $7 and $10 per hour, far below the cost of a human security guard.[41] Cobalt Industries created a similar security robot outfitted with a high-definition camera, a directional microphone, and an infrared sensor. The Cobalt robot can navigate through office buildings autonomously, reporting any anomalies to humans that are monitoring its feeds.[42] Meanwhile, other countries have become much more ambitious in developing police robots. Dubai has deployed a "Robo-cop" that can patrol the city; it uses facial recognition technology to look for known criminals and can also collect evidence, receive criminal complaints from civilians, and act as a roving surveillance camera. Dubai says it plans on replacing 25 percent of its police force with robots by 2030.[43]

The extensive law enforcement deployment of public surveillance cameras, body cameras, drones, and robots will revolutionize the investigation of crimes in at least two significant ways. First, these new tools will provide police with a massive increase in the amount of video and other information that can be used not just as data for mosaic searches but will also as act as a permanent record of everything that happened in the past. Second, the new panopticon of inexpensive, roving surveillance will be more evenly spread among the entire population, resulting in what has been termed a "redistribution of privacy."[44]

The first and most obvious ramification of a more mechanized police force is the proliferation of video data that these devices will provide. Nearly all of these devices have video cameras, and almost all of the information that these devices will record is open to the public, and thus unregulated by the Fourth Amendment. We have already seen the beginning of this massive influx of data as public surveillance cameras become more prevalent and as more police officers wear body cameras which record everything that the officer sees. Since drones and robots are far cheaper than human police officers, police departments will be able to deploy them (and their constantly recording cameras) in vastly greater numbers, bringing in even more data than ever before. The collective video feed of surveillance cameras, police body cameras, drone cameras, and ultimately robot police officers on patrol, when combined with the growing ability to store and search through huge amounts of data, will provide police with the ability to go back to any past moment and view what was happening in any public place at that time. This will fulfill the drone producer's promise of a "Google Earth with full TiVo capability."

Professor Stephen Henderson likens this new trove of mosaic evidence to a "time machine" accessible to law enforcement.[45] He points out that the growing amount of video evidence only adds to the vast amount of information already available to law enforcement, such as telephony metadata and cell cite location data. But the video evidence is particularly useful to law enforcement, since video cameras can obtain evidence without requiring its physical removal (and thus without the need to legally justify a seizure); they can preserve evidence that would be destroyed or damaged with the passage of time (and degradation of human memory); and they can present evidence to the fact-finder in a perfectly preserved form, giving the judge or jury a "pristine" view of what happened.[46] As noted in Chapter 4, this video evidence can also be used to detect and deter police abuses,[47] thus protecting the public from police overreach while at the same time gathering powerful evidence of any criminal activity. Professor Henderson concludes that "at least in the limited context of body cameras, the benefits of complete recording seem to outweigh the costs," and advocates only for "meaningful access, use, and dissemination controls."[48] The use restrictions would primarily be for unmistakably private information that the police legally obtained and then want to use at a later date. For example, he argues that re-watching video of the search of a home is a new Fourth Amendment search, equivalent to re-entering the home, and therefore requires another warrant. Under Professor Henderson's argument, these recordings preserve "immense amounts of otherwise ephemeral irrelevant information," and thus "the mere preservation of that information is a meaningful harm, if nothing else because the relevant parties know there is always a risk of its further consumption and dissemination."[49]

This argument is similar to Judge Kozinski's argument against the use of GPS devices to track individuals in public places, and it suffers from the same weaknesses. Essentially Professor Henderson is arguing that because the technology records the evidence so well, it needs to be restricted in ways that conventional evidence gathering does not. But this rule merely serves to make police investigations less efficient. If a police officer is legally inside a home, either pursuant to a warrant, through consent of the owner, in response to an emergency, or any other valid reason, she is allowed to see anything in plain view and commit it to memory, and even take notes as to what she sees. The Fourth Amendment does not place any restrictions on what she can do with that information afterwards: if she has an excellent memory, she can describe every detail of the contents of the home to other police officers in order to further the investigation. A video recording should legally be no different from an officer's memory or contemporaneous notes – it is likely more accurate, and it will last longer, but placing greater legal restrictions on its use only lowers the productivity of the original search by making the surveillance tool less useful to the government. As a matter of policy, communities may want to create their own legal barriers against *public dissemination* of any private information the police have retained. Just as it would be sanctionable if a police officer went on YouTube and described all the intimate details that she observed when she executed a search warrant in a private home, it would also make sense to create rules about publicizing or publicly disseminating police video of private information. But as we have seen in other contexts, the relevant factor is not the technology that was used to conduct the surveillance, but the level of privacy that the information deserves based on its level of intrusiveness.[50]

Thus, in the case of any type of video record, whether made by a human-carried body camera or a camera mounted on a machine, the primary question is the level of privacy intrusion of the initial observation. Recording information of the inside of a person's home would involve a substantial privacy cost, requiring the equivalent of probable cause (perhaps a 50 percent likelihood that evidence will be found) and usually judicial preclearance in the form of a warrant or similar order. Recording the inside of a person's office or car would involve a lower privacy cost, requiring police to meet a lower legal standard, while recording public information would involve no privacy cost, and therefore not be restricted in any way.

As Professor Henderson notes, the time machine analogy works in both directions, since not only will the video feed from surveillance provide a record of what has happened in the past, but the predictive algorithms that use the data will be able to foresee, with greater and greater accuracy, what people are likely to do in the future. (For example, Professor Henderson cites a study that shows that mobile phone data can be used to predict future location 93 percent of the time.[51]) As argued earlier in this chapter, the predictive power of mosaic searches represents a nonnegligible privacy cost that needs to be factored into the cost–benefit analysis, along with the benefits of the mosaic search (which include the likelihood of uncovering evidence of a crime and the severity of the crime being investigated).

Thus, when using data collected by human police or robot police as a time machine to travel into the past, there is no need to impose any extra legal restrictions as long as the original information was open to the public. When using data collected as a time machine to predict the future, or to learn what would otherwise be secret information about the suspect, courts should treat the processing of the collected data as a mosaic search and calculate the likely privacy cost of the extra information that will be obtained by the search.

The second significant way in which the proliferation of public surveillance will impact criminal investigations is through the redistribution – or near-equalization – of privacy. It is no secret that traditional surveillance has focused disproportionally on the poor and nonwhite population of this country.[52] Police tend to patrol poor neighborhoods more heavily than other areas, and the tens of thousands of public surveillance cameras operated by police are overwhelmingly concentrated in less affluent neighborhoods. Privacy automatically increases with wealth in countless other ways: individuals can move out of the cities into the relative isolation of the suburbs; they can stop riding buses and subways and drive in their own private cars; they can purchase privacy-enhancing devices such as encryption programs and document shredders. Similarly, privacy decreases with poverty: public housing units are monitored by surveillance cameras and regularly patrolled by police officers; some families are often visited by government social workers; other families receive public assistance, and the government keeps records of these public assistance programs. A hugely disproportionate percentage of the surveillance state is focused on the lowest income classes of the country.

The conventional wisdom is that the dramatic increase in police surveillance of the past decades have only been politically viable because it is concentrated on the most economically and politically vulnerable members of society. The rise of mosaic searches could change this calculus. In a now-famous exchange in the oral argument in *United States* v. *Jones,* Chief Justice Roberts began quizzing Micheal Dreeben, the Deputy Solicitor General who was arguing that a month of GPS tracking was not a search:

ROBERTS: You think there would also not be a search if you put a GPS device on
             all of our cars, monitored our movements for a month? You think
             you're entitled to do that under your theory?

DREEBEN: The Justices of this Court?

ROBERTS: Yes.

DREEBEN: Under our theory and under this Court's cases, the justices of this
             Court when driving on public roadways have no greater expectation
             of –

ROBERTS: So your answer is yes, you could tomorrow decide that you put a GPS
             device on every one of our cars, follow us for a month; no problem
             under the Constitution?

DREEBEN: Well, equally, Mr. Chief Justice, if the FBI wanted to it could put its
             team of surveillance agents around the clock on any individual and
             follow that individual's movements as they went around on the
             public streets, and they would thereby gather –[53]

But as every Justice knew, the FBI would never commit the resources of a team of surveillance agents around the clock for surveillance unless they had very good reason to believe the target was involved in criminal activity – in which case they would easily be able to obtain a warrant. The extremely low financial cost of this surveillance means that police are able to track anyone with GPS devices. And as long as the courts follow the cost–benefit analysis theory and impose only minor legal restrictions on public surveillance technology, the same economic factors will mean that police will track citizens of all economic classes with drones and GPS devices, and will install more cameras in all public places, not just the economically underprivileged locations. The result will be an equalization of privacy – or perhaps better described as a more equal distribution of privacy intrusions.

Of course, the next generation of public surveillance will not necessarily be evenly distributed. In particular, the uniform adoption of police body cameras may only exacerbate the current inequities of privacy. As noted above, police tend to patrol far more often in lower-income neighborhoods; they are also more likely to engage in encounters with lower-income individuals and enter the private homes of lower-income individuals. But lower financial costs for public surveillance cameras and drones will almost certainly cause those types of surveillance to spread to more affluent neighborhoods, if only because many of the poorer areas are already saturated with public surveillance. And if we include the data collected by private companies that is requisitioned by law enforcement officers, and the mosaic searches which that data makes possible, the increased surveillance on wealthier and more privileged Americans becomes even more obvious. The result is that everybody will soon be experiencing the heightened level of police surveillance that up until now has been borne by only a few.

Professor Bennett Capers has written extensively about this phenomenon; in a 2017 article, he argues that black and Latino Americans are subject to "unequal public privacy":

> Quite simply, black and brown folk are more likely to be watched by the police, stopped by the police, and frisked by the police. In the everyday world of policing, we are treated as the "panoptic sort," and as "always already suspect."[54]

As Professor Capers acknowledges, this "hypervisibility" has multiple causes, many of them insidious, and new surveillance technologies alone are not going to cure this problems.[55] But the more widespread public surveillance becomes, the more equally it will be distributed among all residents of our country. This may lead to calls for greater privacy protections, since those who have economic and political power will experience at least a portion of the privacy intrusions that have been felt by lower economic classes for generations. After Edward Snowden revealed the NSA's program of collecting millions of pieces of information from telephony metadata, the strong public reaction resulted in new legislation to limit the practice.[56] And as we have seen, all nine Justices ruled against the government's long-term use of a GPS tracker in *Jones*. In cost–benefit terms, this means that the privacy cost of this type of surveillance may increase as more individuals (and more individuals from enfranchised groups) are subjected to twenty-four-hour public surveillance. As a result, courts may then begin to impose stronger legal restrictions on mosaic searches or even revisit the doctrine of public surveillance. But whatever the reaction may be, a more equitable distribution of privacy intrusions would be a normative improvement on the current surveillance practices.

This redistribution of privacy intrusions could lead to one other benefit under the cost–benefit analysis theory. Given the current disparity of privacy in this country, many groups of people who are subject to unequal levels of privacy intrusions may experience an extra cost in lost dignity when they are disproportionately the subjects of government surveillance. Poorer Americans and people of color who routinely live with surveillance cameras on their street corners or constant police patrols through their neighborhoods are aware that as a general rule, whiter, richer Americans are usually not subject to the same level of surveillance. This imposes an additional cost to such surveillance by increasing the perceived level of privacy intrusion. If drones and robot police cars patrolled the suburban neighborhoods with the same frequency as public surveillance cameras monitored poorer neighborhoods, the dignity cost of being subjected to such continuous monitoring would be lowered, leading to a lower cost for courts to consider in evaluating this type of surveillance.

AUTOMATED SURVEILLANCE AND DIMINISHING
POLICE DISCRETION

Surveillance cameras, whether mounted on poles, worn by police officers, or embedded into drones, are part of a broader trend of automated, low-cost public data collection used by law enforcement. Many of these new public surveillance tools will monitor public activities automatically, which means that their detection and reporting of crimes will be free of both implicit bias and human discretion. This will result in more evenhanded and fair enforcement of the laws, but perhaps also over-enforcement of many crimes. Human police officers exercise a large amount of discretion in the individuals they arrest and the cases they pursue. Some police discretion is beneficial, even necessary: the penal code contains so many potential crimes that there is no way police officers could arrest everyone that they observe committing a crime.[57] And many police officers may be good judges of character and show appropriate mercy to certain first-time offenders who do not deserve an arrest or a criminal prosecution. But not all police discretion is wisely exercised; as Professor Melanie Reid noted when discussing the difference between human police officers and robot police officers:

> A human police officer may have an axe to grind with his neighbor and may keep monitoring the source of his displeasure until he finds a particular violation he can use against the neighbor. A human officer might stop someone suspected of driving drunk, but might let the driver go because she is attractive and sympathetic. A human police officer might decide to make a pretext traffic stop solely based on the color of the driver's skin or the type of car.[58]

Police discretion may be based on many different factors, from the officer's own personal opinion about which crimes deserve punishment to the officer's implicit bias against certain groups of people. Abuse of police discretion can have a strong impact on minority communities through such practices as racial profiling. Studies have shown that police officers are more likely to stop and frisk black and Latino individuals than white individuals,[59] and to pull over minority drivers at higher rates than white drivers.[60]

Automated policing technology could reduce this discretion, or at the very least bump the discretion further up the chain of command. Crimes detected through public surveillance cameras or through the algorithms of a mosaic search are more likely to be reviewed by higher-level police officers in the department than the more junior officers who patrol the street; also, these devices will record the crimes they detect, creating more official records of criminal activity which will be harder for police to ignore. And if robot police officers detect criminal activity, they will be unable to exercise any discretion at all; although a robot police officer is unlikely to be given the authority to unilaterally make an arrest, it will automatically report the crime (and likely make a record of it), ignoring any legally irrelevant factors that may have influenced their human counterparts.

In Chapter 5, we discussed how binary searches, once they have been perfected and then applied to the general population, could result in 100 percent enforcement of certain crimes. Widespread mechanized public surveillance, along with the mosaic searches it makes possible, could have a similar if less dramatic effect. The result may be a sharp increase in arrests for minor crimes, which could lead to a public outcry that results in legislatures abolishing certain crimes. More likely, it will lead to more institutionalized forms of discretion, in which police departments adopt formal policies of which crimes they will pursue, as opposed to leaving these decisions to individual police officers.[61]

Professor Elizabeth Joh has taken this argument one step further into the future and considered the effect of "automated traffic stops" that could become the norm if cars are equipped with smart boxes that record the vehicle's location, speed, and driving patterns.[62] Software could be designed that would automatically detect nearly every traffic infraction that the driver committed. There would be no Fourth Amendment issue with the police obtaining this information – not only is the information exposed to the public, the software could easily be designed to be a binary search, so that the police would learn nothing about the individual's driving unless she was committing a traffic infraction. This technology would substantially reduce the level of discretion that police exercised in two ways. First, if every car were equipped with such a device, the police would lose any reason to pull over cars in the first place; and second, drivers could be ticketed without even being pulled over, so there would be no opportunity for police to selectively extend the traffic stop by asking for consent to search or questioning the driver to develop probable cause.

It does not take much imagination to move a little further into the future, when self-driving cars replace human-driven cars on the road. Self-driving cars (in theory) will not commit any traffic violations and will never drive drunk. They have the potential to eliminate traffic stops altogether – eliminating both the abuses that occur through racially biased abuse of discretion and the benefits that accrue to society when police are able to use a traffic stop to detect a much more severe crime, such as gun possession or narcotics trafficking. On the other hand, self-driving cars will provide a treasure trove of low-cost public surveillance and mosaic searches, since every car on the road will be broadcasting its location at all times. If police get access to this data, it will make *Jones'* 28-day GPS tracking seem trivial.

CONCLUSION

The vast amount of data that is and will soon become available to law enforcement officers through their own surveillance technologies will revolutionize criminal investigations and has the potential to dramatically increase the productivity of surveillance as long as courts do not overreact by classifying all public data collection and mosaic searches as full-blown Fourth Amendment searches that require probable cause and a warrant. Instead, courts should apply a cost–benefit analysis and determine the level of intrusiveness of the long-term surveillance and of the mosaic aspect of the search, and then balance those costs against the effectiveness of the surveillance and the severity of the crime being investigated.

Regardless of how much data police can obtain from public sources, the total amount of information is tiny when compared to the information they can obtain from private third parties. From phone companies and internet service providers to manufactures of in-home smart devices, third party companies have billions of pieces of data that could be processed and turned into a mosaic search. Although the same cost–benefit analysis that we discussed in this chapter should apply to mosaic searches once police obtain the third party data, one important question needs to be resolved: what type of showing – if any – should law enforcement have to make in order to obtain the information from the third parties in the first place? The next chapter addresses this question.

7

The Third-Party Doctrine Dilemma and the Outsourcing of Our Fourth Amendment Rights

This case should not turn on "whether" a search occurred. It should turn, instead, on whose property was searched.

Carpenter v. *United States* (2018) (Thomas, J., dissenting)[1]

INTRODUCTION

In the course of our everyday lives, we share enormous amounts of information about ourselves. We send e-mail messages that are stored on remote servers, type search terms into Google, tell Alexa what music to play and products to buy, and save our documents, photos, and videos on Dropbox. These companies mine this shared information and process it in order to learn information about us. And increasingly, law enforcement officials are obtaining this shared data when conducting criminal investigations, which allows them to detect and solve crimes far more efficiently and quickly than if they used traditional investigative techniques. Up until recently, law enforcement officers faced virtually no Fourth Amendment obstacles in obtaining this information from third parties, since the infamous "third-party doctrine" held that a person forfeits all constitutional rights in any information that she shares with any other person or company.

The third-party doctrine has always been controversial, and recently the Supreme Court has limited its application in certain circumstances.[2] This chapter argues that the attempts to limit the third-party doctrine are only marginally helpful at best and misguided at worst. Instead, the solution to the third-party data problem is to enhance and enforce the Fourth Amendment rights of the third parties themselves – to ensure that the individuals and corporations who hold the data have the right to object on their own behalf when law enforcement officers seek to obtain the information. This solution is consistent with Fourth Amendment principles and would allow individuals as consumers to choose their preferred level of privacy for their information.

Courts have already begun to recognize the Fourth Amendment rights that third parties might have in their data they collect from others. By buttressing these rights and allowing third parties to challenge attempts by law enforcement to obtain the shared information, courts can create an elegant solution to the third-party doctrine dilemma. Third parties who choose to cooperate fully with law enforcement can still do so, while those who want to assert their Fourth Amendment rights can still fight to protect their data. The original owners of the information – usually the consumers and clients of the third parties – will quickly learn which third parties protect the information and which do not, and will adjust their information-sharing patterns accordingly.

Although the third-party doctrine is easy to criticize – indeed, it is perhaps the most criticized rule in all of criminal procedure – the issues surrounding the doctrine are far more complicated than they appear. The third-party doctrine is somewhat of a paradox. It is based on an anachronistic conception of privacy and can lead to absurd results, but its underlying premise – that third parties should have the ability to choose whether they want to freely share information with law enforcement – is fundamental to our criminal justice system. Thus, most proposals to limit or abolish the doctrine require drawing impossible or unprincipled distinctions between different types of information or different types of third parties. By bolstering the Fourth Amendment rights of the third parties themselves, we can enhance our privacy rights, while still allowing third parties to cooperate with the authorities when they choose to do so.

This chapter will first trace the legal history of the third-party doctrine, and then evaluate proposals to limit or abolish the doctrine. It will then apply the cost–benefit analysis theory to the third-party doctrine and examine how both the law and the practice of third parties is evolving to enhance the privacy protections that third parties can and do give to the shared information that they obtain.

THE RISE AND (PARTIAL) FALL OF THE THIRD-PARTY DOCTRINE

The first step is to define what we mean by "third parties" in the Fourth Amendment context. There are always at least two parties involved in any criminal investigation: law enforcement and the target of the investigation. A "third-party" in this context is a nonlaw enforcement individual or entity that has obtained information from the target. Thus, a third-party could be an individual with whom the target knowingly confides incriminating information, a roommate who accidentally discovers papers in the target's desk, or a corporation who collects data from the target. When law enforcement officers seek to obtain this information from the third-party to use in an investigation against the target, there are two distinct sets of rights in play – the rights of the target, and the rights of the third-party.

For example, assume Sally writes Jim a letter that includes information which incriminates Sally in a crime. Jim reads the letter and then places it in a file cabinet in his home. The police then enter Jim's home without a warrant, search through his file cabinet, and find the letter. They then use the letter in a criminal case against Sally. Under the third-party doctrine, Sally has no Fourth Amendment rights in the letter; thus, her rights have not been violated. Not only does she lose all Fourth Amendment protection in the information when she shared it with Jim, but she also has no standing to challenge a search of someone else's property. Thus, she has no valid objection when the government introduces the letter as evidence against her in a criminal trial.

Of course, there is no question that *Jim's* rights have been violated in this scenario. However, under current law, this violation is unlikely to ever be adjudicated. Jim has no standing to object to the admission of the letter in the criminal case against Sally, so there will be no way for him to assert those rights in Sally's criminal trial. His only recourse is to bring a civil suit against the government for violating his Fourth Amendment rights, but this is unlikely to happen – even in an egregious case like this, the damages for such a violation are likely to be nominal, and he cannot get injunctive relief unless he can establish a likelihood of future violations against him.[3] And if the violation is not so egregious (perhaps the law enforcement agents allege they had implied consent from a co-tenant), the doctrine of qualified immunity would prevent the third-party from even bringing the case.[4] As a result, even when the government violates the rights of the third-party in obtaining the information, third parties rarely challenge the government action.

The foundations of the third-party doctrine originated with a pair of cases from the late 1970s. In *United States* v. *Miller*, the Supreme Court held that an individual lost all Fourth Amendment rights in the financial records that he shared with his bank.[5] In *Smith* v. *Maryland*, the Supreme Court held that an individual lost all Fourth Amendment rights in the outgoing phone numbers that he shared with his telephone company.[6] The Court based this doctrine on two propositions. First, the Court stated that an individual knowingly assumes the risk that the third party will give the shared information with the police, and thus any expectation of privacy she may have in the information is not reasonable. Second, the Court followed an "all or nothing" paradigm of privacy: either a person refuses to share a piece of information with anyone, in which case it should remain secret; or she shares it with someone else, in which case she forfeits all privacy rights with respect to the entire world, including the government. Even at the time of the doctrine's origins in the 1970s, these were dubious propositions. Justice Marshall's dissent in *Smith* attacked the "assumption of risk" argument with respect to outgoing telephone numbers:

> unless a person is prepared to forgo use of what for many has become a personal or professional necessity, he cannot help but accept the risk of surveillance. It is idle to speak of "assuming" risks in contexts where, as a practical matter, individuals have no realistic alternative.[7]

Justice Stewart also dissented, attacking the very premise of the doctrine itself. He argued that individuals maintained some privacy interest in shared information such as outgoing telephone numbers, since they "easily could reveal the identities of the persons and the places called, and thus reveal the most intimate details of a person's life."[8]

These critiques are even more powerful today, making the third-party doctrine appear severely anachronistic. The amount of information that we casually, almost unknowingly, share with third parties is immense. Not only do we share our e-mails and Internet searches with digital providers, but we are also purchasing web-connected items that automatically upload our information to the cloud. The new "Internet of Things" includes thermometers that know the time you leave your home, online book readers that know what you are reading, and GPS trackers built into your car that know where you are and how fast you are going.[9] It is unreasonable to argue that by using e-mail, searching the Internet, or driving a car, a person assumes the risk that the government will obtain her e-mails, Internet search terms, or the location of her car. Furthermore, this information is more private than outgoing telephone numbers, and the rise of big data analytics that we discussed in the last chapter increases the amount of intimate information that the government can learn from a year's worth of otherwise innocuous information.

These critiques led a number of lower courts to push back on the third-party doctrine in the early 2000s. In 2008, the Ninth Circuit held that the Fourth Amendment protected the content of texts that were sent or received from a pager, and stated that the fact that the third-party servicer could access this content was "irrelevant."[10] Two years later, the Sixth Circuit held in *Warhsak* v. *United States* that a defendant had Fourth Amendment rights in e-mails stored on the server of his Internet service provider.[11] Echoing Justice Stewart's dissent from over thirty years before, the Sixth Circuit noted:

> Since the advent of email, the telephone call and the letter have waned in importance, and an explosion of internet-based communication has taken place. People are now able to send sensitive and intimate information, instantaneously, to friends, family, and colleagues half a world away. Lovers exchange sweet nothings, and businessmen swap ambitious plans, all with the click of a mouse button. Commerce has also taken hold in email. Online purchases are often documented in email accounts, and email is frequently used to remind patients and clients of imminent appointments. In short, "account" is an apt word for the conglomeration of stored messages that comprises an email account, as it provides an account of its owner's life. By obtaining access to someone's email, government agents gain the ability to peer deeply into his activities.[12]

A few years later, Justice Sotomayor explicitly called for the abolition of the third-party doctrine in a concurring opinion:

> This approach is ill suited to the digital age, in which people reveal a great deal of information about themselves to third parties in the course of carrying out mundane tasks. People disclose the phone numbers that they dial or text to their cellular

providers; the URLs that they visit and the e-mail addresses with which they correspond to their Internet service providers; and the books, groceries, and medications they purchase to online retailers. . . I for one doubt that people would accept without complaint the warrantless disclosure to the Government of a list of every Web site they had visited in the last week, or month, or year. . . .. I would not assume that all information voluntarily disclosed to some member of the public for a limited purpose is, for that reason alone, disentitled to Fourth Amendment protection.[13]

Some lower courts even reexamined the status of outgoing phone numbers, the subject of one of the original third-party doctrine cases. In 2013, a district court judge held that the NSA program, which collected massive amounts of telephony metadata (essentially, incoming and outgoing phone numbers), violated the Fourth Amendment. In so doing, the judge explicitly rejected the (presumably binding) Supreme Court precedent of *Smith*:

The Government, in its understandable zeal to protect our homeland, has crafted a counterterrorism program with respect to telephone metadata that strikes the balance based in large part on a thirty-four year old Supreme Court precedent, the relevance of which has been eclipsed by technological advances and a cell phone-centric lifestyle heretofore inconceivable.[14]

Meanwhile, a number of states created their own protections for third-party data.[15] For example, only three years after *Smith*, New Jersey's Supreme Court recognized a state constitutional right in outgoing telephone records;[16] the court has since extended that protection to bank records and Internet service provider's subscriber records.[17]

The third-party doctrine received its strongest repudiation in 2018, when the United States Supreme Court decided the case of *Carpenter* v. *United States*.[18] We discussed *Carpenter* briefly in Chapter 6 with respect to its affirmation of the mosaic doctrine, but its impact on the third-party doctrine was even more profound. The police in *Carpenter* contacted the defendant's cell phone companies and requested the cell site location information for the suspected numbers for the four-month period in which certain robberies took place.[19] The police made this request under the Stored Communications Act, which requires a much lesser showing than probable cause; thus, they did not have a warrant when they obtained this information.

The cell site location information incriminated the defendant, and the police used this information against him at trial. After his conviction, Carpenter appealed, arguing that the police conducted a Fourth Amendment search when they looked at his cell site location information.

Under the traditional third-party doctrine, *Carpenter* was an easy case: the defendant had shared his location information with his cell phone providers, and in so doing he had lost all Fourth Amendment rights in that information. But the

Court had already signaled its displeasure with the third-party doctrine in earlier cases, and it used *Carpenter* as an opportunity to limit the doctrine. First, the Court followed the *Warshak* court's reasoning and held that "[t]here is a world of difference between the limited types of personal information addressed in *Smith* and *Miller* and the exhaustive chronicle of location information casually collected by wireless carriers today."[20] In other words, the Court rejected the third-party doctrine's implication that any data that a person turns over to a third party is by definition not especially private. Some information, such as outgoing phone numbers, may be relatively mundane, but others, such as continuous location information, reveal a significant amount of information about a person. Unfortunately, as with its earlier *Jones* decision regarding GPS data, the Court provided no useful clues as to when third-party information crossed the line from nonprivate to private.

Second, the Court held that the concept of "voluntary exposure" of the information does not really apply in the cell phone location context. Just as Justice Marshall argued with respect to telephones in his *Smith* dissent, the Court noted that in modern life, one does not really "choose" to own a cell phone – and once a person owns a cell phone, she automatically broadcasts her location to her cell phone provider without taking any affirmative actions. Thus, "in no meaningful sense does the user voluntarily assume the risk" of turning over the information.[21]

Even before *Carpenter*, many scholars were calling for the abolition of the third-party doctrine,[22] and the *Carpenter* case has only accelerated the trend. Indeed, the third-party doctrine may be the most critiqued aspect of Fourth Amendment jurisprudence. Professor Orin Kerr – one of the doctrine's few defenders – notes that

> It is the *Lochner* of search and seizure law, widely criticized as profoundly misguided. Decisions applying the doctrine "top [] the chart of [the] most-criticized fourth amendment cases." Wayne LaFave asserts in his influential treatise that the Court's decisions applying it are "dead wrong" and "make[] a mockery of the Fourth Amendment." The verdict among commentators has been frequent and apparently unanimous: The third-party doctrine is not only wrong, but horribly wrong.[23]

But things are not as simple as the doctrine's detractors claim. The third-party doctrine performs a number of critical functions in Fourth Amendment jurisprudence, and proposals to limit or abolish the third-party doctrine fail to find a way to substitute for these functions. This means that some version of the third-party doctrine will always be with us, and so we need to come up with a new paradigm for dealing with shared information.

CAN WE ABOLISH OR LIMIT THE THIRD-PARTY DOCTRINE?

As Professor Kerr has noted, the third-party doctrine is necessary to prevent criminals from shielding evidence of their wrongdoing from law enforcement. As Kerr notes:

If a wrongdoer can use third parties as remote agents, he can reduce his exposure to public surveillance. Instead of going out into the world and subjecting himself to exposure, a wrongdoer can bring third-party agents inside and share plans or delegate tasks to them. He can use the third-party services to commit his crimes without exposing himself to spaces open to government surveillance.[24]

In addition to using "remote agents" and keeping their own interactions with those agents secret, criminals could store incriminating information with third-party companies all over the country, thus making it very difficult for law enforcement agencies to track down the information.

Furthermore, the third-party doctrine allows police to use informants to gather information; if the doctrine were abolished, police could not use an informant unless they first obtained a warrant (that is, unless they already had probable cause), or unless the informant gets consent from the target to reveal the information to the police (which would rarely happen).

More fundamentally, the doctrine ensures that third parties who wish to cooperate with the police can do so by ensuring that searches by private individuals are not subject to the same rules as searches by state actors. Abolishing the doctrine would lead to some absurd results. In our prior example, when Sally writes Jim a letter detailing her criminal activities, Jim may choose to bring the letter to the police and show them the incriminating information. Without the third-party doctrine, the Fourth Amendment would bar the police from using this information at trial. Similarly, if a third-party inadvertently discovered evidence of criminal activity on a friend's computer or in a friend's house, and called the police to report the evidence, the Fourth Amendment would also bar the police from using that evidence at trial. In other words, the third-party doctrine allows individuals to share incriminating information – even confidential information – with the police if they choose to do so.

There seems to be no principled reason why this should not apply to corporations as well. Third-party corporations discover evidence of criminal activity all the time: private police and security guards find incriminating information; credit card companies, insurance companies, and financial companies see evidence of fraud; common carries discover that their customers are shipping drugs or other contraband; telecommunication companies and Internet providers notice patterns of usage that reveal criminality. If all of these private individuals and companies had to comply with the Fourth Amendment before informing law enforcement of the illegal activity, a vast amount of criminal conduct would go unpunished.

Another obstacle in limiting or abolishing the third-party doctrine is apparent from the *Carpenter*'s decision itself: where do we draw the line between shared information that is protected and shared information that is not protected? One possibility is to consider the act of sharing itself – is it willful and intentional, as when a person sends a letter to a friend, or is it passive and unavoidable, as when a person uses a cell phone and thereby shares her location with a company? Perhaps the line is somewhere in between, such as the sharing of purchase information with a credit card company – certainly a knowing and voluntary action, but also something that is hard to avoid. The *Carpenter* decision acknowledged but sidestepped this problem. The Court implied that a line could be drawn somewhere: it confirmed that *Smith* and *Miller* were correct to conclude that a person "assumes the risk" of sharing outgoing phone numbers and financial records, but then held that a person does not assume the risk when she shares location data with a telephone company. However, the Supreme Court refused to draw that line with any specificity, nor did it provide any principled guidelines to assist lower courts in drawing the line.

Another possible way to limit the third-party doctrine is to consider the specific information being shared and consider how private the information actually is. *Carpenter* also gave us some hints in this direction: it directed lower courts to consider "the nature of the particular documents sought to determine whether there is a legitimate expectation of privacy concerning their contents."[25] This language sounds like courts should simply apply the *Katz* test to third-party information, just as they do for information held by the suspect. This could mean that the third-party doctrine has been abolished, since the same test would apply to information whether or not it had been handed over to a third-party. More likely, however, courts will adopt a modified reasonable expectation of privacy test, with perhaps a higher standard for information being turned over to third parties. In other words, the fact that a person shared a piece of information with a third party will be a factor in determining whether or not the person has a reasonable expectation of privacy in the information.

Thus, a person has a reasonable expectation of privacy in his financial records when he keeps them in his own home, but according to *United States* v. *Miller*, when he shares those records with a bank, the act of sharing tips the balance and means that he no longer has a reasonable expectation of privacy in the same information. In contrast, a person has a reasonable expectation of privacy in her location over an extended period (according to the concurrence in *United States* v. *Jones*),[26] and retains that reasonable expectation of privacy in the same information even when she shares it with others (as confirmed by *Carpenter*).

This interpretation of *Carpenter.* makes the "reasonable expectation of privacy" determination even more complicated than before. As with any application of the *Katz* test, this evaluation would be more accurate if courts relied on empirical evidence to determine the level of privacy that each type of information deserves; as noted in Chapter 1, courts tend to make arbitrary and often counter-intuitive decisions about what does and does not deserve protection. For now, the *Carpenter* decision merely adds one more subjective factor for courts to consider when applying the already vague *Katz* test.

In 2013, the American Bar Association's Criminal Justice Standards Committee proposed a similar but more nuanced suggestion for limiting the third-party

doctrine. The Committee recommended that courts (or legislatures, or administrative bodies) categorize third-party information based on the level of confidentiality
they deserve; thus all third-party information would be categorized as "highly
private, moderately private, minimally private, or not private."[27] Courts would then
set a corresponding level of protection based on the categorization: the most private
records would receive the highest level of protection, such as a court order that can
only be obtained if law enforcement demonstrates probable cause, while less private
information can be obtained through a court order or subpoena that requires a lesser
showing.[28]

This proposed regime is certainly consistent with the cost–benefit theory, but it
also means that individuals will in many cases retain a certain level of privacy rights
in information that they share with a third-party. As noted above, allowing individuals to retain privacy rights in information they have shared with others leads to
some counter-intuitive results: police would need warrants before using informants,
and friends and acquaintances who learned private, incriminating information
about others would not be allowed to share the information with the police unless
they obtained the consent of the suspect. The ABA Committee avoids these counter-
intuitive results by limiting its findings to records held by a business entity rather
than an individual, since individuals have an "autonomy interest in choosing
[whether] to share information with law enforcement."[29] As will be argued below,
however, there is no reason why corporations should not have the same autonomy to
choose whether to share incriminating information. In fact, since corporations are
repeat actors that can develop well-known reputation for how they handle consumer
information, people who are deciding whether to share information can make a
more informed choice when dealing with corporations than with individuals.

In a recent article, Kiel Brennan-Marquez proposed a different type of limitation
which focuses on the nature of the relationship between the defendant and the third
party with whom the information is shared.[30] Under this theory, if an individual
gives information or data to a third party, the third party cannot share the information with the government if the third party is merely acting as a "fiduciary" of the
information.[31] Thus, if we share information either with an individual or company
with whom we have no relationship, the third-party doctrine applies, and the third
party is free to do anything he or she wants with the information.[32] However, if we
share information with an individual or a company who owes us some kind of duty
of care (i.e., doctor, or a bank, or even an Internet service provider), then the third
party holds the information as a "fiduciary" and is not free to direct the subsequent
flow of the information.[33]

Brennan-Marquez crafts this argument very cleverly, by drawing on the seemingly
unrelated cases of *Ferguson* v. *City of Charleston*,[34] which held that doctors at public
hospitals cannot be required to share the results of urine tests of their patients with
law enforcement, and *Stoner* v. *California*,[35] which held that a hotel manager could
not give consent to the police to search the defendant's hotel room. In both of these

cases, the defendants gave up information or access to a third party, and the Supreme Court held that the third party could not be forced (in the *Ferguson* case) or could not even voluntarily (in the *Stoner* case) give the information or access to the police.[36] Brennan-Marquez argues that these cases are outliers, not just to the third-party doctrine in general but also in their specific fact patterns. *Ferguson* was, in essence, a state-sponsored drug test, and the Court has routinely found that the results of such tests – whether at school[37] or on the job[38] – can legally be shared with law enforcement under the special needs doctrine. And *Stoner* was a "shared property" case, in which both the defendant and others had legal access to an otherwise private location – and in other contexts, the Court has ruled that anyone with a legal right to be present on the property has the right to consent to a law enforcement search.[39]

Brennan-Marquez explains these anomalous cases by focusing on the relationship between the defendant and the third party. In each case, the third party acted as a "fiduciary" of the information or the access – the third party owed the defendant a duty of care with regard to the information. Thus, the third party could not freely give the information or access to others, including law enforcement. According to Brennan-Marquez, this fiduciary doctrine would protect much of our data in the commercial setting, including information shared with email providers, GPS navigation companies, data storage companies, and "optimization companies" like FitBit and Nest Labs, which record and store our personal information.[40]

One problem with the fiduciary doctrine is that, although this carefully crafted explanation certainly *could* explain the Supreme Court's anomalous decisions in *Ferguson* and *Stoner*, this is not the way the Supreme Court *actually* explained the decisions. The law compelling the doctors in *Ferguson* to share information was invalid because it did not require any particularized suspicion and the search was primarily for law enforcement purposes, so it did not fit into the special needs category.[41] And the *Stoner* Court actually fits perfectly into the Court's shared property jurisprudence – the hotel manager did not have the authority to let strangers (or law enforcement) into the hotel room, and no reasonable person would believe he had that authority, so even under the generous "apparent authority" doctrine, his consent was not sufficient to allow the police to search the room.[42]

Another problem with the fiduciary doctrine is the one which Professor Kerr raises in his defense of the third-party doctrine: it provides very little *ex ante* guidance to law enforcement officers who are investigating a case and come upon a third party who possesses useful information. Especially at the early stages of the investigation, law enforcement officers may not know who gave the information to the third party, much less the duty of care that the third party owes to the original owner of the information.

But a more serious critique of the fiduciary doctrine is the radical breadth of its scope. Brennan-Marquez offers his fiduciary doctrine as a supplement to the third-party doctrine – an exception to the default rule that the Fourth Amendment does not protect information which is handed over to third parties. But it is more revolutionary than he lets on. It is one thing to require the government to meet a certain standard of suspicion before it can require the third party to hand over information, but it is quite another to prohibit third parties from *voluntarily* handing over the information to the government if the third party chooses to do so – and to enshrine this ban in the Constitution. True, there are several statutory regimes that regulate the voluntary transfer of information, but the Court has almost never interpreted the Fourth Amendment to prevent individuals from voluntarily coming forward with information. Indeed, the closest the Court has come is in the cases like *Stoner*, in which a landlord or a hotel manager could not consent to a search of property that the defendant had legally leased or rented. But as much as Brennan-Marquez tries to link the shared property cases to the information transfer cases, there is an important distinction. When information is given to a third party absent an express nondisclosure agreement, the third party is generally under no legal or moral obligation to keep that information private. Indeed, companies routinely sell our information to other individuals.[43] When a person rents an apartment or stays in a hotel room, however, the presumption is that the third party will not allow anyone access to the property during the lease or reservation. In other words, the property cases involve a presumption of exclusivity which simply does not exist with most cases of shared information.

Moving beyond the legal arguments, the fiduciary doctrine is also problematic on a policy level. To put it simply: the fiduciary doctrine would frequently prevent a third party from sharing information with law enforcement that could assist in an investigation – even though that third party could legally share the information with anyone else. This would give law enforcement agents who are investigating a crime *less* rights to the information than a company who wants to purchase the information for marketing purposes. More importantly, it would mean that the law is *implying* a duty to keep information confidential, regardless of the actual explicit arrangement between the defendant and the third party. And it would essentially limit the autonomy and freedom of those third parties: regardless of what they wanted to do, they could not pass the information on to law enforcement. As this chapter argues, it is far better to encourage individuals and third parties to come to their own *explicit* agreements about what to do with shared information, and then to give the third parties the legal rights to fulfill those agreements.

On the most fundamental level, those who propose abolishing or limiting the third-party doctrine are guilty of the same fallacy that we have seen elsewhere in this book: focusing only on the privacy side of the equation and ignoring or downplaying the dramatic increase in security that has resulted from the huge amount of information that is now available to law enforcement at almost no cost. The conventional wisdom is that allowing law enforcement access to this enormous amount of digital information is bad for privacy, and therefore the law needs to change to ensure that privacy protections are reset to where they were in some earlier, simpler age. Once again, this perspective probably overstates the privacy cost and ignores the security benefit provided by the existing third-party doctrine.

COST–BENEFIT ANALYSIS OF THIRD-PARTY DOCTRINE

From a cost–benefit analysis perspective, the vast amount of information now held by third parties is a positive-sum shift in the privacy/security balance. Law enforcement agencies now have the ability to access billions of pieces of data at a very low financial cost. This access provides an extraordinary benefit to law enforcement. The ABA Committee noted this benefit when they set out their own moderate limitations to the third-party doctrine:

> Access to such records deters and detects crimes as diverse as kidnapping (phone records), public corruption and organized crime (bank records), and child sexual assault (Internet records). Even a seemingly "routine" street crime might depend upon records access for resolution, as when hospital admission records allow police to discover who might have been involved in a recent shooting, or when toll tag records allow police to learn the culprit in a fatal hit-and-run. Moreover, records access permits law enforcement to deter or punish private access that is itself harmful and criminal, such as identity theft and computer hacking. To paraphrase Judge Richard Posner, secrecy is the criminal's best friend.
>
> When evidence is available via third-party records, records access has the additional benefit of not risking a physical confrontation with the target. When police enter a home or otherwise seek to forcibly obtain information directly from a suspect, there is always a threat of violence and therefore of harm either to the police, to bystanders, or to the suspect him- or herself. The ability to obtain evidence from a neutral third party eliminates this risk. Similarly, while a prosecutor might subpoena records from a suspect, that risks their destruction despite the threat of criminal liability for obstruction. Once again, third party records access largely eliminates that risk.[44]

Examples of law enforcement officers using third-party data to solve crime are now so commonplace that they have become unremarkable, but a brief overview of their benefits would be useful. We have already seen how cell phone providers can provide invaluable location information to law enforcement officers. These providers are, in effect, witnesses to the crime. If a criminal chooses to commit a crime in broad daylight on a crowded street, he knows that there are witnesses to the event, and he knows that the police will likely interview all of the witnesses who saw the criminal at the scene. Similarly, if a criminal chooses to carry (and presumably use) a cell phone while committing a crime, he surely knows that he is sharing his location with his cell phone company, and therefore the police should have the right to contact the cell phone provider to request information. (As argued below, the cell phone provider, like the individual witness, should have the right to not cooperate with the police, forcing the police to obtain a subpoena or a warrant if they can meet the required legal standard). Furthermore, the cell phone makes it easier for the defendant to commit the crime: he can contact his accomplices from any location at any time, track his own location as well as that of his accomplices, and access the Internet before, during, and immediately after the crime. Thus, contacting the third-party service provider to obtain his location, the contact information of his accomplices, and his Internet search history is a form of reactive surveillance, as argued in Chapter 4.

But often the third party is not assisting the defendant in committing a crime; it is merely recording evidence of the crime. Bank statements and credit card statements that indicate fraudulent activity or an unusual spike in income or expenditures can lead law enforcement to investigate crimes. Purchase records from online retailers or from credit card companies can reveal patterns of activity that indicate criminal behavior. As we share more and more information with third parties, the information becomes even more useful to law enforcement officers. Amazon, Google, and Apple have all introduced virtual assistants, which are in millions of American households, listening to our demands. Ordinary appliances are joining the Internet of Things, which can tell law enforcement whether a person's lights were on at a certain time or how much electricity or water is being used at a given time.[45] Wearable technology, such as Apple Watches and FitBits, can also prove crucial in solving crimes. In one Connecticut case, a man claimed his wife was killed while fending off intruders to their home, but her FitBit showed that she was walking around far more than what was consistent with the husband's story.[46] The husband was subsequently charged with the murder. In another case, a woman claimed to be sexually assaulted during a break-in, but her FitBit data was inconsistent with her account, and she was prosecuted for making false statements. In both cases, the FitBit company provided the information to law enforcement only after receiving a warrant. Thus, the devices provided a significant increase to security without any decrease in privacy.[47]

Of course, cases in which the police develop probable cause before accessing the third-party data pose no doctrinal challenge at all. If the law enforcement agency is able to obtain a warrant, the third-party doctrine is immaterial, since the government would get access to the information regardless of whether the suspect retained any privacy rights in the shared information. Nevertheless, it is worth pointing out that the exponential increase in shared information – whether through normal commercial transactions or through new digital devices – has already increased our security immeasurably by giving the police access to evidence that never would have existed before.

The challenging legal question arises when the police want to access this information without a warrant. In those situations, we need to determine what legal standard (if any) the police will have to meet before they can access the information. Under the cost–benefit analysis doctrine, the answer to this question requires us to weigh the security benefits and efficiencies of allowing access to the information against the privacy cost of revealing the information. The privacy cost will need to be empirically determined, but at this point it appears to not be as high as many third-party doctrine defenders claim. After all, millions of individuals already knowingly – and at times, willingly – share this information with third-party companies, from credit card companies to Internet service providers to retail stores. Most of these individuals are also aware of the ubiquitous amount of sharing of third-party information that occurs in the private sector. In other words, the evidence tends to show that the underlying rationale of the third-party doctrine is normatively correct: people abandon their expectation of privacy when they share information with third parties. The data that individuals give to third-party companies is packaged, transferred, and sold to dozens of other companies, who use it for their own marketing campaigns.[48] Data brokers scoop up information, package it into dossiers, and sell it to other companies.[49]

Given this reality, the burden of proof should rest with those who claim that individuals *retain* privacy rights in shared information; as of now, there is not much evidence to that effect. Although some privacy groups protest this widespread dissemination of shared information,[50] there has been no widespread movement to legislate or restrict the practice. It would be inconsistent to allow private companies to purchase this "private" information in order to allow them to market their products more efficiently, but then bar law enforcement officials access to the information when they want to use it to investigate criminal activity.

Nevertheless, it is clear that at least some individuals believe that the information-sharing age has gone too far in giving law enforcement access to this information. And under the cost–benefit analysis theory, we need to calculate the privacy cost in order to craft the appropriate legal rules for this type of information. Fortunately, the nature of third-party information provides us with an elegant way of not only calculating the privacy cost, but also of allowing individuals to choose the level of privacy they want to have for information they share. By enhancing the Fourth Amendment rights of the third parties themselves, courts can allow third parties to determine the degree to which they want to protect their customers' information. Individuals would then be able to share information with the third parties who provide them with the desired level of data protection. But before we can rely on the market to determine individual privacy limits, we must first ensure that the third parties have the legal rights to protect the information on behalf of their consumers.

THIRD-PARTY RIGHTS

As noted above, third-party information presents a paradox. The third-party doctrine plays an important role in Fourth Amendment jurisprudence, and proposals to limit the doctrine face problems of how to draw principles distinctions in crafting those limits. However, there is no question that the doctrine has become more problematic in today's digital age because it fails to recognize that the information being shared with third parties has both a privacy value and a commercial value. The solution to this dilemma is to keep the third-party doctrine intact while increasing the Fourth Amendment rights of the individuals and companies who hold the information.

For all of the scholarly attention paid to the third-party doctrine, there has been very little focus on the rights of the third parties themselves.[51] The paradigm for courts, legislators, and commentators who examine the government acquisition of information from third parties has always been centered on the rights of the *target* in the information, with almost no attention paid to the rights that the third parties themselves might have in keeping the information confidential.

There are a number of sensible reasons for this paradigm. First, the targets are the ones who are in danger of being prosecuted, so it makes sense to focus on the target's rights. And from a legal standpoint, the strict standing requirement for Fourth Amendment challenges often precludes a target from raising any issue regarding the constitutionality of a search of a third party.[52] The only time that third parties can assert their Fourth Amendment rights is in a civil case when the third party refuses to comply with a demand for information, or when the third party sues the government in a later civil action. Furthermore, the third parties who possess this information frequently hand it over to law enforcement voluntarily, without invoking any of their own rights to keep the information public, which leads to a dearth of case law and analysis of this question. Finally, when the third parties do object, courts tend to give them only tepid Fourth Amendment protection, partly because most of these third parties were corporations, who have weaker constitutional rights than individuals.[53]

But the case law that originally denied broad Fourth Amendment protections to third parties now seems outdated to the point of being quaint. These early cases, almost all of which are over fifty years old, tend to focus on subpoenaing bank records or other corporate documents, rather than the type of more personal information held by third parties in today's society.[54] In the modern economy, this personal information has real value to the third parties, and in the current political and economic climate, the third parties have significant interests in protecting it from the government. As noted in the next section, we are beginning to see third parties, particularly corporations, refuse to cooperate voluntarily with law enforcement[55] and even resist subpoenas or other court orders for the information.[56] Courts are now starting to also take notice of the value this information has to third parties, and there are signs that they are beginning to provide broader Fourth Amendment rights to corporations that hold this information. What follows is a brief history of the law of third-party rights from the initial cases in the early twentieth century right up to the 2015 case of *City of Los Angeles* v. *Patel*.

The law regarding third-party rights is complicated by the fact that most third parties are corporations. Granted, this is not always the case; a target may entrust (or hide) information or documents with a friend, family member, or colleague. However, the vast amount of information being recorded and stored by corporations – and the growing usefulness of that information to law enforcement – has made their unique Fourth Amendment status a critical aspect of third-party rights.

The Supreme Court's first significant case regarding corporate Fourth Amendment rights was the 1906 case of *Hale* v. *Henkel*.[57] In *Hale*, the government was investigating the MacAndrews & Forbes Company, and it subpoenaed the company's secretary and treasurer, Edwin Hale, to bring numerous corporate documents to the grand jury. Hale refused, citing the Fourth and Fifth Amendment. The Court dismissed these claims, holding that corporations did not have any Fourth or Fifth Amendment rights:

> If, whenever an officer or employee of a corporation were summoned before a grand jury as a witness he could refuse to produce the books and documents of such corporation, upon the ground that they would incriminate the corporation itself, it would result in the failure of a large number of cases where the illegal combination was determinable only upon the examination of such papers. Conceding that the witness was an officer of the corporation under investigation, and that he was entitled to assert the rights of corporation with respect to the production of its books and papers, we are of the opinion that there is a clear distinction in this particular instance between an individual and a corporation, and that the latter has no right to refuse to submit its books and papers for an examination at the suit of the state.[58]

The Supreme Court has reiterated this principle multiple times since *Hale*, holding that although corporations have limited Fourth Amendment rights, corporate officers cannot refuse to produce records pursuant to a valid subpoena.[59]

As the twentieth century progressed, the Court weakened corporate Fourth Amendment rights even further by creating a new kind of warrant known as the "administrative warrant." This warrant allowed government officials to enter corporate premises and conduct a search for regulatory purposes, such as building code violations. Unlike traditional law enforcement warrants, which required probable cause, administrative warrants would be issued under "a flexible standard of reasonableness that takes into account the public need for effective enforcement of the particular regulation involved."[60] A few years later, the Court all but abolished Fourth Amendment rights for many corporations when the it held that *warrantless* administrative searches of corporations were reasonable, as long as they were statutorily authorized and were directed at a heavily regulated industry, such as liquor distributors or firearms dealers.[61] In one case, the Gun Control Act of 1968 authorized official entry into "the premises ... of any firearms or ammunition ... dealer ... for the purpose of inspecting or examining ... any records or documents required to be kept." The Court argued that the business owners implicitly consented to these searches: "When a dealer chooses to engage in this pervasively regulated business and accept a federal license, he does so with the knowledge that his business records, firearms, and ammunition will be subject to effective inspection."[62] The Court held that a statute authorizing an administrative search was a constitutional substitute for an actual warrant, as long as the statute provided notice to the corporate owner that the search is being made pursuant to the law and limited the scope and discretion of the inspectors.[63]

In theory, the Court only permitted these warrantless searches for "heavily regulated industries," but in practice, the Court seemed willing to call nearly any industry "heavily regulated," including running an automobile junkyard.[64] Thus, by the early twenty-first century, there appeared to be few practical limits to the government's ability to search and obtain information from corporations, as long as the statute authorized the search regime. But everything changed with the 2015 case of *City of Los Angeles v. Patel*.

Patel centered on a Los Angeles municipal code provision that required all hotels to keep a registry with information about their guests and to turn the information over to law enforcement upon request. Under the statute, law enforcement officers did not need to make any kind of showing of need before making the request, nor did the officers need to get judicial approval. A group of hotel owners challenged the ordinance, arguing that it violated their Fourth Amendment rights.[65] Significantly, the information at issue here was third-party shared data: information that guests provided to the hotel when they checked in. Thus, the hotel owners were fighting to keep their customer's information private.

The *Patel* case seemed to be an easy case for the government. By almost any measure, the hotel industry is "heavily regulated," both historically and under then-existing Los Angeles regulations. As Justice Scalia noted in his dissent, the regulatory regime for hotels is "substantially more comprehensive than the regulations governing junkyards … where licensing, inventory-recording, and permit-posting requirements were found sufficient to qualify the industry as closely regulated."[66] But nevertheless the majority struck down the statute, holding that hotel owners cannot be required to turn over their registries to law enforcement without the opportunity for some type of prior judicial review.

The Court emphasized that it was imposing a relatively minor burden on the government. The target corporation need only have the *opportunity* for prior judicial review; thus, the government could still attempt to obtain the records with a subpoena. Only if the target corporation chose to challenge the subpoena would a neutral judicial officer, such as an administrative magistrate, review the government request.[67]

Third party subpoenas are a common method used by investigators to obtain information about a target corporation. As third parties have taken possession of a larger number and a greater diversity of records, government investigators have relied on third-party subpoenas more often, and have used them to investigate many different types of crime, including white collar crime, child pornography, and possession of controlled substances.[68] In some jurisdictions, prosecutors can issue subpoenas directly, while in others, the prosecutors use the grand jury's authority to issue them.[69]

The standards for obtaining subpoenas are low: the government must demonstrate a "reasonable probability" that the requested material will "produce information relevant to the general subject of the . . . investigation."[70] This "relevance" requirement is easily met: when a subpoena is challenged on relevancy grounds, "the motion to quash must be denied unless the district court determines that there is no reasonable possibility that the category of materials the Government seeks will produce information relevant to the general subject of the grand jury's investigation."[71]

Thus, third parties are unlikely to succeed when they challenge subpoenas on relevance grounds. Instead, the most common method of challenging a subpoena is to argue that the subpoena is overly broad or burdensome, and therefore it would require the third party to spend an undue amount of time and resources responding to it.[72] Although this right is derived from the Fourth Amendment,[73] none of the familiar Fourth Amendment tests apply when courts review this challenge. Instead, courts will apply a very practical balancing test, balancing the scope of the investigation and the likelihood that the records will provide material information against the burden that the subpoena places on the recipient of the subpoena.[74] As the *Patel* Court pointed out, this is not a particularly robust standard, but it does prevent widespread fishing expeditions by law enforcement, and as we will see in the next section, more and more companies are seeking to quash subpoenas on these grounds. The hotel owners in *Patel* probably could not prove that handing over the information on their registry is unduly burdensome, but the success rate may be higher for technology companies or telecommunications firms that receive subpoenas demanding a large number of documents or cover a long time period.

The true significance of *Patel*, however, is that it represents a dramatic shift in the trajectory of third-party rights. Before the Court decided *Patel*, courts seemed unwilling to give third-party corporations any right to object to even warrantless searches of their property and records. In finding that the hotel industry is not "heavily regulated," the Court limited the warrantless search doctrine to a small handful of industries, opening the door to greater third-party rights in the future. As courts begin to recognize the value of these records to third parties, they are likely to broaden these rights, providing third parties even stronger tools to fight to protect the shared data that they hold. In an *en banc* decision that preceded the government's appeal to the Supreme Court in the *Patel* case, the Ninth Circuit explicitly recognized that corporations have a privacy right in this third-party data:

> The business records covered by [the challenged ordinance] are the hotel's private property, and the hotel therefore has both a possessory and an ownership interest in the records. By virtue of those property-based interests, the hotel has the right to exclude others from prying into the contents of its records, which is also the source of its expectation of privacy in the records.[75]

The *Patel* case provides companies with a valuable legal tool to resist government rules that mandate turning over shared third-party data. In early 2019, for example, two home-sharing companies, AirBnb and HomeAway, successfully used *Patel* to obtain a preliminary injunction against a New York City Ordinance that required the companies to turn over customer information.[76]

Of course, this legal shift would be immaterial if third parties continued their historic role of nearly automatic cooperation and compliance with law enforcement requests – even the most robust Fourth Amendment protections are irrelevant if the corporation simply waives them and consents to turn over the records. But here, too, a shift is occurring: third parties are responding to the desires of their customers and asserting their Fourth Amendment rights with greater frequency.

THE ROLE OF THIRD PARTIES

As the law of third-party rights shift, the behavior of third parties is also evolving. For most of the history of government investigations, third-party corporations have willingly consented to provide information to law enforcement officers. This cooperation has historically taken one of two forms: volunteered consent and compliance with requests. Volunteered consent occurs when the third party decides on its own initiative to share the information with law enforcement. This is the scenario in which Jim takes Sally's letter to the police; or FedEx notices white powder leaking from a package and calls the Drug Enforcement Agency; or a bank or insurance company detects fraudulent activity in an account and reports it to law enforcement. Because the third parties voluntarily turn over the information, the consent exception to the warrant requirement applies and there are no Fourth Amendment issues involved,[77] regardless of how robust the third party's Fourth Amendment rights might be.

Compliance with requests was perhaps the most common method used by law enforcement when seeking information from third parties: the law enforcement officers asked for the information, and the third party willingly handed it over.[78] Law enforcement officers used this method in a number of the seminal third-party doctrine cases: for example, in *Smith* v. *Maryland*, the police asked the phone company to install a pen register, and the phone company complied.[79] Throughout the 1990s and well into the 2000s, companies not only freely shared information with law enforcement, but also made good money by selling this information, leading some commentators to describe private companies as "Big Brother's little helpers."[80] For most the first decade of the twenty-first century, this cooperation continued, and perhaps even accelerated. In the wake of the 2001 terrorist attacks, the National Security Agency (NSA) began collecting data from telecommunications and Internet companies, first under the Terrorist Surveillance Program, and later under the PRISM program. These companies routinely cooperated with the NSA, providing the law enforcement agency with millions of pieces of telephone and digital metadata upon request.[81]

As it turned out, the NSA program was a turning point for this type of law enforcement/corporate cooperation. Once the cooperation became public in 2013, the massive public outcry led technology companies to change their policies, thus ending the routine compliance with law enforcement requests. Companies that record and store consumer data are now safeguarding their data from government requests, both because they believe it will be better for business if their customers believe the data will be kept private, and because improved methods of metadata analysis makes the data more valuable in a commercial sense. In the wake of the Snowden revelations and the public outcry that followed, companies are beginning to assert their rights to keep this information from the government – both because the information has intrinsic value to them and because their customers are demanding more privacy. Almost all of the major technology companies, including Google, Amazon, and Apple, no longer routinely cooperate with law enforcement requests and are even fighting court orders that demand information. Most famously, in 2016 Apple refused to assist federal law enforcement officials who were investigating a terrorist incident in San Bernardino, even after law enforcement obtained a warrant for the information.[82] Amazon, Google, Microsoft, and a dozen other prominent technology firms filed a brief supporting Apple's position.[83] Similarly, when law enforcement officers believed that evidence of a murder might be found on a suspect's Alexa device, they obtained a warrant and served it on Amazon. Amazon refused to comply with the warrant, stating that it objected to "overbroad and otherwise inappropriate [law enforcement] demands as a matter of course."[84] For its part, Google now routinely challenges subpoenas from law enforcement seeking its customer's data.[85] The company described its rationale in an amicus brief that it filed in support of the hotel in the *Patel* case:

> Customer personal information is a valuable, competitively sensitive resource that can help a business understand its customers and tailor services to their needs. Making that information available to the public would diminish its value and allow competitors to entice customers away from a business.
>
> More importantly, the privacy of such information is important to a business's customers, and a business has an interest in protecting that information in order to retain the trust of its customers. That interest is "one that society is prepared to recognize as 'reasonable.'" *Katz*, 389 U.S. at 361 (Harlan, J., concurring). Many commercial entities promise to limit disclosures of their customers' private information. Indeed, in many circumstances, the law *requires* that a business safeguard customer information from disclosure and that it comply with representations it has made about the purposes for which such information will be collected, used, stored, or shared.[86]

Thus, third parties are willing to fight to protect the third-party information that is entrusted to them, provided they are given the legal tools to do so.

Some scholars object to this "outsourcing" of our Fourth Amendment rights. As Professor Kiel Brennan-Marquez argues:

In today's world, we constantly disclose vast amounts of information to digital intermediaries: email providers, social media sites, and the like. A rote application of the misplaced trust rule would leave these intermediaries categorically free to take up the mantle of law enforcement: to serve as "Big Brother's little helpers," as long as the decision to do so is neither instigated nor remunerated by the state. This status quo is intolerable, and it will only become more intolerable as time goes on.[87]

The concern is understandable, especially given the history of compliance that third-party companies gave to law enforcement requests. But the era of automatic compliance is at an end: third-party corporations realize the value of this information, both to their customers and to themselves. Companies now compete with each other to provide more protection from law enforcement requests, and consumer watchdog websites track and compare these protections.[88] Allowing companies to safeguard this shared information is an elegant solution to the third-party dilemma: the vast majority of information that third parties hold on our behalf will be safeguarded, but third parties who uncover clear evidence of wrongdoing and want to alert the authorities can still do so.

CONCLUSION

Third-party information has created a doctrinal puzzle for over forty years. The Supreme Court initially provided a poor rationalization for the doctrine, and the doctrine has been heavily critiqued by commentators and some lower courts ever since. Even the Supreme Court began to back away from the doctrine in *Carpenter v. United States*, leading many critics to gleefully predict its ultimate demise.

But abolishing the doctrine would be a mistake. Although we may want to keep information that we share with others confidential, it makes little sense to limit the ability of third parties who may want to cooperate with the police, or to allow criminals to purposely use third parties to hide their activity from law enforcement. Instead, courts should strengthen the legal ability of the third parties to exercise their own rights to protect this information. This would preserve the autonomy of the third parties, allowing them to set their own standards regarding when they want to report crimes and when they want to fight to protect their costumer's privacy. It would also allow consumers to examine these standards and then choose which companies they want to trust with their information, just as they now do with individuals. All signs are that most corporations will be very protective of their consumer's data and will fight to protect it from subpoenas and even from warrants, which will protect the consumer's privacy interests. But when they uncover strong evidence of criminal activity, they can still report that to the authorities, thus maintaining most of the significant increase in security and efficiency that the third-party sharing society has given us.

8

Hyper-Intrusive Searches

[I]n the application of a Constitution, our contemplation cannot be only of what has been but of what might be. The progress of science in furnishing the government with means of espionage is not likely to stop with wiretapping. Ways may someday be developed by which the government, without removing papers from secret drawers, can reproduce them in court, and by which it will be enabled to expose to a jury the most intimate occurrences of the home. Advances in the psychic and related sciences may bring means of exploring unexpressed beliefs, thoughts and emotions.

Olmstead v. United States (1928)[1]

INTRODUCTION

Previous chapters have discussed different types of technology-enhanced surveil-lance: reactive surveillance, in which law enforcement uses new tools to combat the privacy-enhancing technology used by criminals; binary searches, which use refined surveillance tools that only report the presence or absence of criminal activity; and mosaic searches, which gather and process vast amounts of data – often from third parties – to learn private information about an individual. We have seen that under the cost–benefit analysis theory, many of these searches do not necessarily need the high levels of restrictions that many commentators (and courts) seek to place on them. Reactive surveillance is a necessary evil, as it represents a zero-sum return to the original equilibrium between privacy and security; while binary searches and mosaic searches can represent an increase in productivity by providing much greater levels of security, often at relatively small costs to privacy.

But some new types of surveillance technology are not reactive nor binary in nature and involve a significantly greater intrusion of privacy than traditional searches. We will call these surveillance methods hyper-intrusive searches. They include electronic eavesdropping devices and hidden cameras installed in homes or offices to see and hear what people are doing in their most private places;[2] parabolic microphones that can listen to conversations through a window from a significant distance;[3] hand-held (nonbinary) detectors that can "see" through clothing and provide an outline of every item the subject is carrying;[4] radar devices that can penetrate the walls of a building and determine the location and movements of individuals inside;[5] and vast and growing DNA databases, which allow law enforcement not only to determine if a certain individual was present at a certain crime scene, but which also contain sensitive and personal health information about the individuals who are catalogued in the database.[6] Not all hyper-intrusive searches involve sophisticated surveillance technology. No-knock search warrants are hyper-intrusive because of the lack of notice to the target of the search. Surgery to remove a bullet from the target is hyper-intrusive because of the extreme level of physical intrusion involved. And searches of cell phones are hyper-intrusive because of the enormous amount of data that individuals carry on their phones.

This type of surveillance has an extreme effect on our personal privacy – government agents see and hear things that were formerly impossible to see and hear; they invade our bodily integrity in ways that go beyond a physical search; and/or they take place under circumstances in which we are unaware of the surveillance. The increased intrusiveness of these surveillance methods has fueled much of the concern over the effect of technology on privacy, and has justifiably led to tight legal restrictions in many cases.

On one level, these searches are the easiest category to deal with under the cost–benefit analysis theory; by definition, their privacy cost is so high that we need to create extremely strict legal rules for law enforcement officers seeking to engage in these activities. So far, this book has discussed on legal rules that are based on the degree of certainty that law enforcement officers must demonstrate before they are able to engage in the surveillance: a very productive search may only require a 20 percent certainty, while a less productive search would require a 60 percent certainty. This chapter expands the type of legal rules that could be imposed on surveillance techniques to include specific requirements that law enforcement officers must meet before they are allowed to engage in the search. The chapter first examines the various restrictions which courts have placed on hyper-intrusive searches, and then considers how each of these restrictions could be used by the cost–benefit analysis theory to discourage less productive searches. In some cases, special restrictions on these searches could increase the productivity of the search, by ensuring that they are only conducted under conditions which minimize the privacy intrusion or maximizing the potential benefit of the search.

DEFINING HYPER-INTRUSIVE SEARCHES

As their name implies, hyper-intrusive searches involve a high level of privacy cost. Unlike reactive searches, these searches do more than merely counteract privacy-enhancing technology. Although many of them also provide a high level of security as well, if left unregulated, they are likely to provide very low levels of useful information compared to the privacy costs they impose. Generally, hyper-intrusive searches share some or all of the following characteristics: they are overbroad (in that they retrieve far more information than is necessary for the investigation); they occur without notice to the individual being searched; they are ongoing; and/or they pose an unusually high threat to human dignity. This chapter focuses on six different types of hyper-intrusive searches: real-time interception of oral, telephonic, or digital communication; covert video surveillance of private places; no-knock execution of search warrants; searches that intrude into the suspect's body; searches of cell phones; and collection and analysis of DNA information.

The Supreme Court missed its first opportunity to identify hyper-intrusive searches as its own category of surveillance when it infamously concluded in 1928 that wiretapping was not a search, which lead to the prescient dissent by Justice Brandeis that opens this chapter. It was not until nearly forty years later, in 1967, that the Supreme Court finally ruled that electronic eavesdropping of a home or a telephone implicated the Fourth Amendment.[7] Around the same time, the Court was setting out guidelines for other kinds of hyper-intrusive searches, such as "no-knock" search warrants that are exercised without notice[8] and invasions of bodily integrity in order to extract fluid or other evidence.[9] Unfortunately these different doctrines evolved independently, and sometimes subversively, since the Court was initially unwilling to explicitly acknowledge that it was dealing with qualitatively different kinds of searches. As a result, the Supreme Court – and lower courts – have been inconsistent in their analyses of hyper-intrusive searches and have wavered between attempting to adapt traditional Fourth Amendment jurisprudence, following the lead of Congressional legislation, or crafting entirely new constitutional standards.

The lack of a coherent constitutional framework for analyzing hyper-intrusive searches is all the more startling and problematic in the modern area. As we have seen throughout this book, new technologies and shifting political attitudes are generating new opportunities for the government to conduct ever more intrusive searches. In some of these cases, such as with binary searches, the courts have acknowledged the unique nature of the surveillance and have designed and applied a consistent doctrine. In other cases, such as with mosaic searches, the courts are only now beginning to identify the nature of the surveillance and are still in the process of developing a consistent approach. Hyper-intrusive searches have been around for over fifty years, but because they appear in different forms, courts have been unable to respond to them in a consistent fashion. This inconsistency will become ever more problematic as hyper-intrusive searches become even more varied. Companies are already developing detectors that can effectively see through walls or clothing.[10] The big data tools that the government uses to analyze publicly available data can also be used to analyze private data, such as intercepted e-mails or text messages. Even the "psychic advances" that Justice Brandeis warned us about –

such as people or machines that can probe into our minds and detect our thoughts, feelings, or intentions – are not entirely inconceivable.[11]

Of course, in addition to being unusually invasive, hyper-intrusive searches are powerful and valuable tools for law enforcement. Wiretapping and audio surveillance, for example, have been essential in investigations and prosecutions of organized crime over the decades.[12] Because of their effectiveness, the government will seek to use these techniques at an ever-increasing rate; thus, the need for consistent and coherent constitutional rules to govern their use is imperative.

In order to arrive at a consistent set of rules, we will first examine the case law and doctrine involving real-time communication surveillance and covert video surveillance, and then compare that to doctrine that courts have applied to other types of hyper-intrusive searches.

INTERCEPTING COMMUNICATIONS: BERGER AND THE RISE OF THE PARTICULARITY REQUIREMENTS

In the 1967 case of *Berger* v. *New York*,[13] the Supreme Court reviewed a New York State statute which regulated electronic eavesdropping by government agents. The statute set out a legal standard for an order authorizing the surveillance which in some ways mirrored the warrant requirement of the Fourth Amendment: the police would have to show "reasonable ground to believe that evidence of crime may be thus obtained, and particularly describing the person or persons whose communications, conversations or discussions are to be overheard or recorded and the purpose thereof."[14] But the statute also recognized that real-time electronic surveillance required a higher standard than traditional surveillance methods; thus, it stated that the order permitting such monitoring could only be issued by a state judge (not merely a magistrate) and that the application had to be made by the attorney general, a district attorney or a police officer above the rank of sergeant.[15] The law also stated that any such order would automatically expire after two months; an extension was possible if the judge found it to be "in the public interest."[16]

Even with these extra requirements, the Supreme Court held that the statute violated the Fourth Amendment. First, the Court held that orders issued under the statute would not conform to the particularity requirement, since the order need only describe "the person or persons whose communications ... are to be overheard."[17] The Court stated that a constitutionally valid order must also state that a specific offense has been or is being committed, and particularly describe the "property" – meaning the conversations – being sought.[18] Second, the Court held that allowing the monitoring to continue for two months "is the equivalent of a series of intrusions, searches, and seizures pursuant to a single showing of probable cause."[19] Third, the Court was troubled by the fact that there was no mandatory termination of the order "once the conversation sought is seized."[20] And finally, the Court noted that the statute "has no requirement for notice as do conventional warrants" and required no "showing of exigent circumstances" in order to justify the lack of notice.[21]

The holding of *Berger* can be understood in two different ways. On the surface, the Court seemed to be saying that the same constitutional standard applies to every search, regardless of whether it is a traditional one-time physical search or an ongoing electronic intangible search. Under this interpretation, the Court held that an ongoing electronic intangible search should be treated as many individual one-time physical searches, and that the standard Fourth Amendment warrant require-ment applies to each of these searches; which would mean that each instance of a search must be particularized and supported by probable cause. This explains the requirement that the specific conversations being sought must be described and the requirement that the eavesdropping cease once the conversation is completed (which treats the ongoing search like a number of individual "searches" for the offending conversation) and also explains the time limit requirements (since every time the government agents hear a new conversation, it should be treated as a new "search").

But an alternate – and ultimately more plausible – reading of *Berger* is that the Court was evaluating a qualitatively different type of search, and creating a new, higher Fourth Amendment standard to apply to the new type of search. This was the same court that, one year later, would decide *Terry* v. *Ohio*, the case which broke with centuries of precedent and created a new, low-intrusion category of search and a lower legal standard to accompany it. But in 1967, the Court was not quite yet willing to officially break with the one-size-fits-all definition of a "search," so the *Berger* Court never explicitly stated that it was creating a new standard for a new kind of search. Indeed, it took pains to stay in the traditional paradigm and apply the same constitutional standard to electronic eavesdropping by simply analogizing ongoing electronic monitoring as "a series of intrusions, searches, and seizures" during which the government agents were seeking to seize "specific conversations."[22] But the effort seemed strained at best, and upon close examination the analogy breaks down completely. Electronic eavesdropping (and any other ongoing electronic intangible search) is fundamentally different from traditional searches in a number of ways. First, maintaining a wiretap or electronic bug is a *continuous* search, not a series of searches – more analogous to a law enforcement official being constantly present and constantly searching a house, which would never be permitted in the context of a traditional search. Second, while it is relatively easy to describe physical items with particularity – financial documents, blunt instruments, narcotics paraphernalia – it is more difficult to describe exactly what kinds of conversations are to be "seized." It is even more difficult – if not impossible – to know if any one conversation might be incriminating until it has already been seized (i.e., listened to and/or recorded).[23] Third, the notice requirements for electronic eavesdropping are necessarily more secretive – unlike many traditional searches, prior notice can *never* be given, and in fact the targets of the search will (hopefully) be unaware of the search while it is occurring. In short, electronic monitoring gave birth to a new kind of search which, in contrast to traditional searches, is ongoing, overbroad, and secretive.

Even after *Berger*, the question remained open as to exactly what kind of showing the Fourth Amendment required before the government would be allowed to engage in this new kind of search. Two of the dissenting Justices believed that given the majority's language, it seemed likely that no warrant for electronic eavesdropping would ever be constitutional.[24] The majority did very little to disabuse this notion: "It is said that neither a warrant nor a statute authorizing eavesdropping can be drawn so as to meet the Fourth Amendment's requirements. If that be true then the 'fruits' of eavesdropping devices are barred under the Amendment."[25]

Congress responded to this challenge by passing Title III the Omnibus Crime Control and Safe Streets Act Wiretap Act of 1968, ubiquitously known as "Title III."[26] Title III regulates interception of all oral and wire communications: before the government can use a bug or wiretap a phone, it has to acquire a court order (a "Title III order"). [27] The requirements for such an order are predictably higher than what had been required under the New York statute struck down in *Berger* and substantially more onerous than what would be required under the Fourth Amendment for a more traditional search.

Title III represents a significant shift in the methods of regulating surveillance. Before Title III, there were essentially only two ways in which courts regulated surveillance: by requiring a certain degree of certainty (such as probable cause) and by requiring courts to preapprove certain types of searches by issuing a search warrant. Title III created a number of new types of restrictions by requiring the government to demonstrate that (1) "normal investigative procedures" have been tried and failed, are unlikely to succeed, or are dangerous (known as the "least intrusive means" requirement);[28] (2) the surveillance will be conducted in a way that minimizes the interception of irrelevant information (known as the "minimization" requirement);[29] and (3) there is probable cause to believe that the interception will reveal evidence of one of a limited list of predicate crimes, with the suspected crime named in the application.[30] In addition, the original legislation required the application to be signed by a federal judge and authorized by a high-level Department of Justice official even before it was submitted to a court.[31] Finally, any Title III order is time-limited to thirty days, so the government must request an extension for any surveillance that extends for a longer period of time.[32]

Although the Supreme Court has never ruled on the constitutionality of the procedures in Title III, the lower appellate courts have embraced it unanimously. Thus, as long as government agents comply with Title III when conducting oral, wire, or electronic surveillance (which they must do to avoid contravening federal law), they can feel secure in knowing that their actions do not violate the Fourth Amendment, even in the post-*Katz* world. In this way the statutory provisions of Title III have effectively preempted Fourth Amendment analysis for oral, wire, and electronic searches, and courts have done little since *Berger* to clarify the scope of

Fourth Amendment protections for electronic eavesdropping. Thus, the development of Fourth Amendment doctrine in this area left to other types of hyper-intrusive searches, as we will see below. However, as we will see below, the statutory framework of Title III has had an outsized influence on one significant type of hyper-intrusive search: covert video surveillance.

COVERT VIDEO SURVEILLANCE: OUTSOURCING
THE FOURTH AMENDMENT

In the late 1970s and early 1980s, a radical Puerto Rican terrorist group known as the FALN[33] orchestrated dozens of bombings in numerous American cities, killing six people and wounding scores of others.[34] Acting on information from an informant, the FBI began following suspected FALN members, who led the agents to an apartment in Chicago that the FALN was using as a safe house.[35] On January 18, 1983, the United States Attorney sought and received permission from a federal judge to install electronic bugs and hidden video cameras in every room of the apartment.[36] For the next six months the FBI maintained the devices, recording the residents as they assembled bombs in the apartment and had telephone conversations with imprisoned FALN members.[37] The investigation culminated on June 29, 1983, when the FBI arrested four defendants and ultimately charged them with conspiracy to construct and plant explosives throughout the city of Chicago.[38]

Unsurprisingly, the videotape of the defendant's activities was the primary evidence in the case against the accused FALN members. Just before the trial, the district court judge granted the defendants' motion to suppress this videotape evidence,[39] and the government appealed the decision. And thus, in the eerily appropriate year of 1984, the Seventh Circuit became the first federal appellate court to rule on the constitutionality of covert video surveillance.[40]

Writing for the court in *United States* v. *Torres*,[41] Judge Richard Posner began his constitutional analysis by applying a type of cost–benefit analysis to the "reasonableness" language of the Fourth Amendment:

> But we do not think there can never be a case where secretly televising people in private places is reasonable. ... We do not think the Fourth Amendment prevents the government from coping with the menace of this organization by installing and operating secret television cameras in the organization's safe houses. The benefits to the public safety are great, and the costs to personal privacy are modest. A safe house is not a home. No one lives in these apartments, amidst the bombs and other paraphernalia of terrorism. They are places dedicated exclusively to illicit business; and though the Fourth Amendment protects business premises as well as homes, the invasion of privacy caused by secretly televising the interior of business premises is less than that caused by secretly televising the interior of a home, while the social benefit of the invasion is greater when the organization under investigation runs a bomb factory than it would be if it ran a chop shop or a numbers parlor.[42]

Not only did the *Torres* court attempt to balance the privacy intrusion with the benefits to public safety, it also included the severity of the crime as a factor in calculating the benefits.

The court then turned to the next question: given the high privacy costs and significant benefits of covert video surveillance, what requirements should the government need to fulfill before engaging in it? The Seventh Circuit noted that the government had established probable cause in this case, but held that probable cause alone was not sufficient. In addition, the government needed to satisfy the particularity requirement of the Fourth Amendment, which the court held are more exacting for video surveillance cases.

The *Torres* court then did a remarkable thing. It noted that the government had also intercepted oral and wire communications in the case, and thus had been required to meet the Title III requirements.[43] Thus, although Title III explicitly does not cover video surveillance, the government in the *Torres* case had complied with the statute when conducting the surveillance. The *Torres* court then held that Title III's requirements "implement the constitutional requirement of particularity" – in other words, that the statutory requirements set out by Congress were identical to the particularity requirements under the Fourth Amendment. Thus,

> [a] warrant for video surveillance that complies with those provisions that Congress put into Title III in order to implement the Fourth Amendment ought to satisfy the Fourth Amendment's requirement of particularity as applied to such surveillance,"[44] and Title III therefore "provides the measure of the government's constitutional obligation of particular description in using television to investigate crime.[45]

The route from *Berger* to *Torres* was a little convoluted, but the courts ended up with the correct doctrine in the end. The *Berger* Court was unwilling to explicitly state that there should be a higher burden for hyper-intrusive searches, though that was the inevitable result of its holding.[46] Congress then had to step in where the *Berger* Court refused to go: to create specific extra requirements for the law enforcement agents to meet when they sought to engage in a certain type of hyper-intrusive search. *Torres* then completed the path, adopting the statutory requirements as constitutional requirements and broadening them to include another type of hyper-intrusive search. Unlike *Berger*, *Torres* explicitly held that a completely new constitutional standard was required for hyper-intrusive searches, and it did so using explicitly cost–benefit language:

> [W]e do not suggest that the Constitution must be interpreted to allow [television surveillance] to be used as generally as less intrusive techniques can be used. The first clause of the Fourth Amendment guarantees the right of the American people to be free from unreasonable searches by federal . . . officers; and a search could be unreasonable, though conducted pursuant to an otherwise valid warrant, by intruding on personal privacy to an extent disproportionate to the likely benefits from obtaining fuller compliance with the law.[47]

Since *Torres*, federal courts have approved the use of covert video surveillance for a myriad of crimes, including loan sharking,[48] marijuana dealing,[49] counterfeiting,[50] money laundering,[51] and illegal gambling.[52] Six other federal circuits have used the Title III safeguards to define the scope of the Fourth Amendment warrant requirement in the context of video surveillance.[53] State courts have used the same analysis in cases of sexual assault[54] and narcotics trafficking.[55]

Torres' adoption of the Title III requirements complies with the cost–benefit analysis theory. Two of the requirements ensure that the benefit to the government is great enough to justify such an intrusive search: the least-intrusive means requirement means that the surveillance will be especially useful to law enforcement, since it has no other way of obtaining the information; and the list of predicate crimes ensures that law enforcement is investigating an especially severe crime. Two other requirements help to lower the cost of the surveillance: the minimization requirement makes the surveillance somewhat less intrusive, while the time limit ensures that the government cannot conduct the surveillance indefinitely. The final requirement – approval of a high-ranking prosecutor – effectively erects another legal obstacle that law enforcement officers must meet before engaging in this hyper-intrusive search. Thus, *Torres* and its progeny borrowed the tools provided by Congress and used them to make hyper-intrusive searches more palatable from a cost–benefit perspective.

NO-KNOCK WARRANTS: THE ORIGINAL HYPER-INTRUSIVE SEARCH

Even before the Supreme Court considered the new technology of electronic monitoring, it addressed the issue of hyper-intrusive searches in a much more mundane context: whether the Constitution permitted government agents to enter a residence without first knocking on the door of the target location and announcing their presence. The Court first addressed this issue in 1963 in the case of *Ker* v. *California*, in a divided opinion that allowed the practice given the circumstances of the case but failed to set out specific rules or set out a sophisticated constitutional analysis.[56] It was not until 1995 that the Court finally resolved the issue, firmly pronouncing in the unanimous opinion of *Wilson* v. *Arkansas*[57] that the "common law 'knock and announce' principle forms a part of the reasonableness inquiry under the Fourth Amendment."[58] Although the Court did not explicitly set out a balancing test, it implied that courts were to compare the heightened intrusion of such a search with the "countervailing law enforcement interests" which might be so great as to render the search reasonable.[59]

To assist courts in applying the balancing test, *Wilson* proposed certain requirements that law enforcement must meet before being authorized to conduct such a search. Citing Justice Brennan's dissent from the earlier *Ker* case, the Court held that a silent entry is reasonable if necessary to prevent violence, or if the occupant already knows the officer's identity and purpose (for example, in the case of escape).[60] The *Wilson* Court added a third factor: if the police "have reason to believe that evidence would likely by destroyed if advance notice were given."[61]

Unlike the *Torres* rationale, which was based in large part on the Fourth Amendment's particularity requirements,[62] *Wilson* relies on the reasonableness language of the Fourth Amendment. This opens the door to a flexible case-by-case balancing test, allowing courts to consider many different factors before deciding whether the proposed hyper-intrusive search was "reasonable" and thus constitutional. The *Wilson* Court was careful to note that it was not setting out strict rules for the lower courts to follow; instead, it explicitly stated it was leaving to the lower courts "the task of determining the circumstances under which an unannounced entry is reasonable under the Fourth Amendment."[63]

Less than two years later, in *Richards* v. *Wisconsin*,[64] the Supreme Court found itself responding to a lower court that had disregarded this message of flexibility and case-by-case balancing. The Wisconsin Supreme Court had concluded that even in the wake of *Wilson*, there was no need to reconsider the state's earlier rule automatically authorizing no-knock warrants for felony drug cases,[65] since exigent circumstances justifying a no-knock entry are always present in felony drug cases. The Supreme Court rejected the use of such a blanket rule, calling it an "overgeneralization" which ignored the need for a court to critically examine the facts and circumstances of each case. The *Richards* Court, like *Torres*, used cost–benefit language, noting that there could be situations in which "the asserted governmental interests in preserving evidence and maintaining safety may not outweigh the individual privacy interests intruded upon by a no-knock entry,"[66] and emphasizing the need to "strike[] the appropriate balance between the legitimate law enforcement concerns at issue in the execution of search warrants and the individual privacy interests affected by no-knock entries."[67] We see this approach in one other area of hyper-intrusive searches: bodily intrusions.

BODILY INTRUSIONS: SLIDING SCALE OF PRIVACY COSTS

Another area of hyper-intrusive searches involves cases in which the government conducts an investigation which infringes on the bodily integrity of the defendant. As with audio and video surveillance, the first inquiry a court must make is whether or not the government action is considered a "search" – that is, whether it intrudes onto a constitutionally protected area. Consistent with the spirit of *Katz*, courts have concluded that examining any part of a defendant's body which is voluntarily exposed to the public – such as fingerprints or hair samples – does not constitute a search.[68]

However, as the state seeks to intrude further into a person's body, the privacy interests of the defendant become stronger and stronger. In such cases, the Supreme Court has measured the security benefits of the search and the privacy and dignity costs to the defendant. Testing the breath of a person who has been arrested for drunk driving does not require a warrant because of the minimal intrusion involved.[69] In contrast, collecting urine for testing in a criminal investigation usually requires probable cause and a warrant, since the privacy intrusion is greater for two reasons. First, the government can learn private information from the person's urine, such as "whether he or she is epileptic, pregnant, or diabetic."[70] And second, collecting the urine for testing sometimes involves "visual or aural monitoring of the act of urination," which is traditionally a very private act.[71]

When the government seeks to invade a person's body and remove something more substantial – such as blood, or a bullet which has become lodged in the body – the courts have classified the action as a hyper-intrusive search, requiring more than a mere showing of probable cause.[72] As with the case of no-knock warrants, the courts have dealt with these types of searches by applying a case-by-case balancing test based on the reasonableness language in the Fourth Amendment.

The Supreme Court first grappled with this issue in the 1966 case of *Schmerber* v. *California*, in which the government removed blood from the defendant's body without his consent. Schmerber was driving home from a bowling alley when his car crashed into a tree, sending both him and his passenger to the hospital.[73] At the hospital, a police officer directed a doctor to withdraw blood from Schmerber's body to determine whether or not he had been intoxicated at the time of the accident.[74] The Supreme Court granted certiorari to determine whether or not this forced extraction of blood violated the defendant's Fourth Amendment rights.[75]

The Court noted that the constitutionality of "intrusions into the human body" was a case of first impression.[76] The Court then reasoned that the Fourth Amendment prohibited all such intrusions "which are not justified in the circumstances, or which are made in an improper manner."[77] The Court was not entirely clear what it meant by "justified in the circumstances." Certainly it meant there must have been probable cause to conduct the search – which the Court concluded existed.[78] It also obviously meant that the officer must have had a warrant or that one of the exceptions to the warrant requirement must have applied – which it did in this case. [79] But after disposing of these standard warrant requirements, the Court went on to look at the benefits and the costs of the procedure. First the Court noted that the benefits of the blood extraction were substantial, noting that the blood test was a "highly effective means of determining the degree to which a person is under the influence of alcohol."[80] The Court then estimated the privacy and dignity costs of the procedure:

> Extraction of blood samples for testing is a highly effective means of determining the degree to which a person is under the influence of alcohol. Such tests are a commonplace in these days of periodic physical examinations and experience with them teaches that the quantity of blood extracted is minimal, and that for most people the procedure involves virtually no risk, trauma, or pain.[81]

The Court further suggested in dictum that if the blood test were administered by someone other than a medical professional, the added "risk of infection and pain" might tip the balance against the government[82] – perhaps a precursor to the "least intrusive means" requirement that would later be applied to other types of hyper-intrusive searches.

Schmerber was decided two years before *Terry*, and so, just as in *Berger*, the Court was unwilling to explicitly state that bodily invasiveness was a qualitatively different kind of search. Therefore the Court was somewhat vague when it discussed the extra requirements of these searches – merely saying that such a search must be "justified in the circumstances" and then applying a common-sense balancing test. Fortunately, *Schmerber* provided the foundation for *Winston v. Lee*,[83] perhaps the clearest and most explicit Fourth Amendment case dealing with hyper-intrusive searches.

Winston involved an attempted robbery in which the victim shot the assailant on left side of his chest during the course of the crime. The assailant fled the scene, and twenty minutes later, the defendant turned up at a hospital with a gunshot wound to his left chest area. After the victim identified the defendant, the defendant was charged with the crime. The government then moved for an order compelling surgery on the defendant in order to remove the bullet from his body to test whether the bullet came from the victim's gun.[84] The defendant claimed that even with a court order, such a procedure would violate his Fourth Amendment rights.

In analyzing the defendant's claim, the Supreme Court stated explicitly that it was dealing with a qualitatively different kind of search:

> [T]he Fourth Amendment generally protects the "security" of "persons, houses, papers, and effects" against official intrusions up to the point where the community's need for evidence surmounts a specified standard, ordinarily "probable cause." Beyond this point, it is ordinarily justifiable for the community to demand that the individual give up some part of his interest in privacy and security to advance the community's vital interests in law enforcement; such a search is generally deemed "reasonable" in the Amendment's terms. A compelled surgical intrusion into an individual's body for evidence, however, implicates expectations of privacy and security of such magnitude that the intrusion may be "unreasonable" even if likely to produce evidence of a crime.[85]

The *Winston* Court went on to list the costs and benefits that should be considered for "surgical search and seizure:" the extent to which the procedure may threaten the safety or health of the individual; the extent of intrusion upon the individual's dignitary interests in personal privacy and bodily integrity; and the community's interest in fairly and accurately determining guilt or innocence.[86] In calculating benefits, *Winston* also considered the other evidence that the government could use against the defendant, including the victim's identification and the timing of the defendant's arrival in the hospital.[87]

The *Winston* Court's rationale has influenced the development of the doctrine for bodily intrusive searches of all kinds. Most recently, it has led a number of lower courts to develop and apply a "continuum" of bodily intrusion jurisprudence, using "reasonableness" as a guide to determine what level of showing is required to justify a search at any point along the spectrum. These courts employ a cost–benefit test similar to the one in *Winston*, estimating the privacy/dignity interests, the invasiveness of the procedure, and the level of information it provides to law enforcement in order to determine whether or not the search is permissible.[88] For example, in *United States* v. *Nicolosi*, the district court judge set out a spectrum of invasive procedures, with voice, hair, and handwriting analysis on one end, moving to breath, saliva, and urine, and finally to blood as the most intrusive.[89]

SEARCHING CELL PHONES: TIGHTENING UP THE WARRANT REQUIREMENT

Recently the courts have begun ruling on a new type of search: searches of the contents of a person's cell phone. Arguably these searches are reactive searches, since individuals are able to increase their privacy significantly by storing information on their (usually encrypted) phones and thus not having to keep paper records in their home or other less secure locations. Under this argument, police who search cell phones are merely reacting to the increased privacy that cell phones have given to their owners, in a very zero-sum, equilibrium-adjustment analysis. However, most courts – including the United States Supreme Court – have treated smart phone searches as hyper-intrusive searches. In the 2014 decision *Riley* v. *California*, the Court held that cell phone searches "implicate privacy concerns far beyond those implicated by the search of a cigarette pack, a wallet or a purse; and said that comparing the searches of physical items to searches of cell phones was like comparing "a ride on horseback" to "a flight to the moon."[90] The Court further noted that searching through cell phone data was both quantitatively and qualitatively more intrusive than a traditional search. Quantitatively, cell phones can store "millions of pages of text, thousands of pictures, or hundreds of videos."[91] Qualitatively, they include Internet search history that could "reveal an individual's private interests or concerns – perhaps a search for certain symptoms of disease, coupled with frequent visits to WebMD"[92] as well as apps that could reflect private information, such as a person's dating life, political affiliation, or religious beliefs.[93]

After having established cell phone searches as being hyper-intrusive, the Court took yet another path in restricting these searches. Generally, law enforcement officers must obtain a warrant to conduct a search, but the warrant requirement has a number of exceptions – so many exceptions that many courts and commentators now refer to the warrant requirement as a warrant "presumption" that can be rebutted. One of these exceptions is a search incident to a lawful arrest, which allows law enforcement officers to search an individual and any container within his wingspan. In the *Riley* case, police officers had relied on this exception to search the defendant after he had been arrested, under the theory (well-supported at the time) that a cell phone was nothing more than a "container," like a briefcase or a backpack. The Supreme Court acknowledged that personal computers had been treated like "containers" for the purposes of this exception but held that searching a cell phone was different from any other type of search, and so refused to apply the search-incident-to-an-arrest exception to cell phones. However, the Court did not create any higher standard for obtaining a warrant to search a cell phone, nor did it add any extra restrictions on how that warrant should be executed (for example, a minimization requirement to lessen the probability of law enforcement officers seeing information that is irrelevant to the crime being charged).

Other courts have expanded on this method of regulating cell phone searches. For example, another warrant exception allows law enforcement the power to search individuals and their belongings at the nation's border without any showing of individualized suspicion.[94] The Supreme Court has long recognized this exception as necessary to protect the "right of the sovereign to control ... who and what may enter the country."[95] However, a few circuit courts have used the broad language in *Riley* to impose a reasonable suspicion requirement for searches of cell phones and other personal electronic devices at the border.[96] Unlike *Riley*, these courts do not require the government to obtain a warrant before engaging in these searches, nor even to prove that probable cause exists – but like *Riley*, they weaken a warrant exception based on the unusually intrusive nature of a cell phone search.

LEGAL TOOLS FOR REGULATING HYPER-INTRUSIVE SEARCHES

It is in the area of hyper-intrusive searches that courts have been most willing to embrace the principles of the cost–benefit analysis theory. These searches are so intrusive that courts are forced out of the all-or-nothing model that defined early Fourth Amendment jurisprudence; instead, courts are required to create and apply greater restrictions on law enforcement agents, above and beyond the probable cause and warrant requirements that apply to traditional searches. The need to place these searches on a spectrum of intrusiveness also leads courts to perform rough calculations of costs and benefits in order to determine the degree of restrictions that are necessary to discourage the surveillance. For example, the *Winston* Court reviewed the facts of the proposed medical procedure in detail in order to evaluate the level of the intrusion which would be caused by the search, noting that a general anesthetic would be used and that there was a slight risk of nerve damage or death.[97] In the future, it would be better to see courts apply more empirical studies to their estimates of costs and benefits: how intrusive is a no-knock search warrant when compared to a traditional search warrant? How often do wiretaps in this type of case lead to useful information for a criminal case? How much personal, innocent information do wiretaps usually reveal? Many of these questions can actually be measured and recorded, rather than simply estimated by the judge.

Furthermore, some of the tools used by courts in responding to these searches show a desire to increase the productivity of the search by decreasing the privacy cost (such as by imposing minimization requirements or time limits) or increasing the benefit (such as by only allowing the surveillance for certain extremely serious crimes). Other requirements that are imposed by the courts are meant to create very high standards for law enforcement agents to reach before being able to engage in these searches, such as proving that the surveillance is the least intrusive means (which also provides evidence of the benefit that the search provides), or obtaining the approval of a high-ranking prosecutor, or approval of a judge rather than merely a magistrate. In other contexts, courts merely require law enforcement to demonstrate a very high standard of certainty before allowing them to engage in the search. Or, as in the case of cell phone searches, courts will maintain the same standard of certainty but will tighten up the warrant requirement by limiting the number of warrant exceptions that apply.

It takes little imagination to foresee that the near future will provide technologies that allow for even more types of hyper-intrusive searches. For example, many new technologies – searches of houses and persons with thermal detectors, detectors that use X-rays to see inside a person's clothing, government interception of e-mail – occur without notice to the person under surveillance. Many of these searches are also likely to be overbroad or pose an extraordinary threat to human dignity, by seeing inside people's homes[98] (or through their clothes) without their knowledge. In short, the issue of regulating hyper-intrusive searches will likely become more and more pertinent as time goes on.

Moving forward, courts will have to choose the best tools for regulating hyper-intrusive searches for each context. In order to do this effectively, the court will need to identify the aspect of the search which makes it hyper-intrusive. If overbreadth is a problem, as in the case of wiretapping and covert video surveillance, then minimization requirements may be an appropriate restriction to impose. If the search carries a high cost to dignity, as in the case of searches which violate bodily integrity, courts should look to ensuring that the benefits are worthwhile by imposing a least intrusive means requirement and only allowing the search if the potential crime is severe enough. And for searches that carry a high privacy costs, such as devices that can see through walls or secretly record the inside of a home, courts could impose a very high standard of certainty to deter law enforcement officers from engaging in these searches unless they can demonstrate a very high chance of success.

An important step is for courts to formally acknowledge when they are dealing with a hyper-intrusive search and then consider all of the potential regulatory tools that are available. Unfortunately, many courts do not yet see the common threads between different types of hyper-intrusive searches, which limits their arsenal in crafting the appropriate response.

For example, in the 1990 case of *United States* v. *Villegas*,[99] the Second Circuit reviewed a warrant which allowed agents to covertly enter the defendant's property and take pictures of various areas and items.[100] The court categorized such a procedure as a "seizure of intangible evidence," which had been "explored principally in the context of the interception of conversations."[101] The Second Circuit relied primarily on the audio and video eavesdropping cases to demonstrate that such a search was permissible under the Fourth Amendment.[102] Thus, when the court turned to the aspect of the search which made it hyper-intrusive – the covert entry – it turned to the wiretapping line of cases, noting that in electronic bugging cases prior courts had authorized covert entry to install the necessary equipment.[103] In devising a "safeguard" for such searches, the Second Circuit first discussed Title III, and then – citing *Torres* – noted that certain Title III requirements had been adopted "by analogy" into the Fourth Amendment for video cases.[104]

The *Villegas* court ended up rejecting the strict particularity requirements of Title III, holding that a covert search to take photographs was "less intrusive than a wiretap or video camera surveillance."[105] Having rejected the *Torres* approach, but without any alternate paradigm with which to analyze this kind of search, the court created a new rule that the officers must make "a showing of reasonable necessity" for the delay of notification.[106] The court, overly focused on the audio and video surveillance cases, failed to consider other types of hyper-intrusive searches, such as no-knock warrants, which have already analyzed no-notice searches and created the extra requirements that law enforcement officers must meet to engage in those searches. Because the *Villegas* court did not consider the broader category of hyper-intrusive searches, it was unable to use the precedents that already existed for no-notice searches.

In another example, a district court in the Southern District of New York reviewed a warrant which authorized the government to intercept, open, and photocopy the mail of a prisoner who was awaiting trial.[107] The court was concerned with the breadth of the warrant, and thus turned to *Berger* to see how the Supreme Court had applied the particularity requirement of the Fourth Amendment in the analogous case of electronic surveillance.[108] The court then noted that *Berger's* analysis "does not appear to turn on the particular technology involved,"[109] and then cited the Title III requirements. The court then explained that "[t]hese four safeguards have been imported from Title III into other contexts as Fourth Amendment requirements,"[110] citing three video surveillance cases.[111] The court stated that it had "serious concerns" about the constitutionality of the search of mail if Title III safeguards were not followed, noting that both the mail search and electronic eavesdropping are continuous, overbroad, and secretive,[112] and it requested further briefing on the subject.[113] As with *Villegas*, the court did not look to other types of hyper-intrusive search cases, such as *Winston* and other bodily intrusion cases, and thus did not consider applying the explicit cost–benefit analysis that courts routinely apply in those contexts.

CASE STUDY: DNA EVIDENCE

One of the most urgent questions involving hyper-intrusive searches is the collection, preservation, and processing of DNA evidence. Up until now, DNA evidence has primarily been used as a means to identify perpetrators (or to exclude individuals who are proven to not be the perpetrator). But as DNA sequencing technology gets more sophisticated, law enforcement agents will be able to learn more and more private information about individuals based on their DNA.

Current law is relatively permissive about the collection of DNA evidence. Although the Supreme Court has held, consistent with *Schmerber* and *Winston*, that collecting a DNA sample from someone's body is a "search,"[114] law enforcement officers are allowed to collect "abandoned" DNA samples from anywhere in public that a suspect may have left them, such as in saliva from used napkins, coffee cups, or envelopes.[115] Furthermore, in *Maryland* v. *King*, the Court permitted warrantless DNA collection for the purposes of identification from individuals who have been arrested.[116] In reaching this lenient rule, the *King* Court applied the "reasonableness" doctrine of the bodily intrusion cases, which incorporated some cost–benefit analysis principles: the Court "weigh[ed] the promotion of legitimate governmental interests against the degree to which [the search] intrudes upon an individual's privacy."[117] The Court estimated that the cost to privacy was low, since the bodily intrusion involved only a "gentle rub along the inside of the cheek;" the genetic material that was processed was junk DNA that did not reveal any of the suspect's genetic traits;[118] and the individuals being subjected to the test were already under arrest and therefore had diminished privacy rights.[119] On the benefits side, the state has a substantial interest in determining the identity and criminal history of an arrestee.[120]

King's holding has been controversial: the case itself included a vehement four-justice dissent, and many commentators have disagreed with its reasoning.[121] The most common critique, when translated into cost–benefit terms, is that the *King* Court undercounts the true privacy cost of the search. Justice Scalia's dissent argues that an intrusion into the body, however gentle, represents a "weighty" privacy intrusion;[122] others have argued that although the state in *King* only tests DNA for identification purposes, any DNA sampling procedure carries a significant privacy cost because future testing could reveal intimate medical facts about the subject.[123]

As *King* implies, it is not only the *collection* of DNA that raises Fourth Amendment concerns; the retention and processing of DNA also carries privacy costs. When DNA samples are only used to identify suspects, they carry no greater privacy costs than fingerprints, but if they are later used to learn intimate medical information about the individual, their privacy costs can be much higher. Thus, the privacy costs of DNA evidence is dependent upon what type of tests the government applies to the DNA after it has been collected. As genetic technology has advanced over the past few decades, the potential privacy cost of DNA sampling has become quite significant.

Blood testing cases provide a useful analogy to DNA searches. In *Schmerber*, decided in 1966, the Supreme Court held that the warrantless extracting of blood to test a driver for intoxication was permissible as long as the police officer had probable cause to believe the suspect was intoxicated. The *Schemerber* Court calculated a relatively low value for the privacy cost of the search: blood tests are "commonplace" in modern society, and the procedure involves "virtually no risk, trauma, or pain."[124] Twenty-three years later, in 1989, the Court again reviewed the constitutionality of drawing blood in *Skinner* v. *Railway Labor Association*, and found a somewhat greater privacy cost, noting that beyond the physical intrusion, the "ensuing chemical analysis of the sample to obtain physiological data is a further invasion of the [suspect's] privacy interests," because it "can reveal a host of private medical facts about an individual, including whether he or she is epileptic, pregnant, or diabetic."[125] And twenty-seven years after that, in the 2016 case of *Birchfield* v. *North Dakota*, the Court added yet another privacy cost to blood tests: "In addition, a blood test ... places in the hands of law enforcement authorities a sample that can be preserved and from which it is possible to extract information beyond a simple BAC reading. Even if the law enforcement agency is precluded from testing the blood for any purpose other than to measure BAC, the potential remains and may result in anxiety for the person tested."[126] In other words, as biological technology progressed, the privacy cost of blood tests increased, from the mere physical intrusion, to the intimate medical information that blood tests could reveal, to the indefinite preservation of that information and the anxiety that preservation may create. As these privacy costs grew, the court reversed its position, from allowing warrantless blood testing in *Schmerber* to forbidding it in *Birchfield*.

DNA sampling can carry an even higher privacy cost than blood tests. DNA analysis can reveal a person's genetic diseases, ethnic background, and even certain traits, such as tendency towards addictive behavior or obesity.[127] This is as true for abandoned DNA that is obtained from public places as it is for DNA that is forcibly taken from someone's body. Although we saw in Chapter 6 that individuals have no reasonable expectation of privacy in any information they reveal to the public, there is a good argument that this principle should not apply to abandoned DNA. Under the holding of *Kyllo* v. *United States*, government agents cannot use a "sense-enhancing" device to learn private information that they could otherwise not learn from standard observation.[128] In *Kyllo*, law enforcement officers violated the Fourth Amendment when they examined heat waves that were emanating into the outside world using a thermal imager, which provided the officers with extremely detailed and precise information about the location and intensity of the heat patterns. Similarly, when police use sophisticated DNA analysis techniques to sequence a person's DNA and learn information about them, they have moved beyond information that was knowingly exposed to the public. Thus, collection of DNA samples represents a hyper-intrusive search, since it reveals intimate information beyond what a traditional search would allow, and it is not in any way reacting to privacy-enhancing technologies used by the public.

However, under the cost–benefit analysis theory, the total privacy cost depends on exactly what the DNA sample is used for. If the police only use the DNA to learn a person's identity, it carries no privacy cost, since a person's identity when they are in public is generally not secret. There may be some exceptions in which a person desires to remain anonymous in public and so wears a mask or stays hidden, but generally a person does not have a reasonable expectation of privacy in their identity.[129] This was a key aspect if the *King* decision; the Court noted that the Maryland statute that authorized the DNA collection only permitted it to be stored and used for identification purposes.

Once we recognize the nature of the hyper-intrusive search, we can determine what extra rules are necessary to regulate it. One possibility is to increase the degree of certainty that police must demonstrate before engaging in DNA collection, but that does little to increase the productivity of the search. Instead, courts should impose minimization requirements, as they do in the wiretapping and covert video surveillance context. This minimization requirement is already implied in *King*: the government can only use the DNA to identify the suspect or link him to previous unsolved crimes, and may not use it to learn any other intimate information about him.[130]

When looked at in this context, Justice Scalia's dissent is somewhat curious. He and the other four dissenting Justices point out that the DNA collection in *King* was not actually used to identify the suspects, but rather to enter into a nationwide database to see if the suspect had committed other crimes.[131] Under Justice Scalia's argument, this transformed the DNA collection from a routine "police booking procedure" into a criminal investigation.[132] But this fact does not change the privacy cost of the procedure. The DNA in the national database consisted of samples of DNA from unsolved crimes; in other words, if the suspect's sample matched with a sample from the database, the police would have nearly conclusive proof that the suspect had been involved in an earlier unsolved case. Significantly, the police could not get any *other* information about the suspect by submitting the sample to the database: the only thing they could learn was whether or not the suspect was implicated in an earlier crime. This is a classic example of a binary search, as discussed in Chapter 5. Therefore, the collection of DNA and submission of the DNA to an unsolved crime database poses no legitimate privacy costs, and police should be allowed to conduct this type of search without implicating the Fourth Amendment.

The implications of this analysis are significant. If police are permitted to indiscriminately collect DNA and use the samples to identify individuals and link them to unsolved crimes, there is nothing in the constitution to stop them from creating a DNA database for every American citizen – as long as they only use the collected DNA for one of those two purposes. Although this result sounds dystopian, it is in reality not very different from the world we already live in. As of 2018, the FBI's Combined DNA Index System (CODIS), which combines all states' DNA databases, contained 13.3 million profiles from convicted criminals and 3 million profiles of arrestees.[133] And as always, the government databases are just the tip of the iceberg: as of 2018, over twelve million Americans have submitted their DNA to a commercial testing company like 23andme or ancestry.com.[134] As we saw in Chapter 7, if these private companies wish to assert their own Fourth Amendment rights, the government would have to go to court to get access to the privately owned genetic information, but if the government's use was limited to identification purposes alone, the showing would be minimal. Furthermore, some of the genetic testing sites are open source for identification purposes, to allow individuals to identify as many distant relatives as possible. Finally, the potential for familial genetic searches leverages the size of these DNA databases by a large factor. Thus, even if a perpetrator's genetic code is not in any DNA database, the police may find a partial match with the DNA of the perpetrator's father or cousin. The police can then investigate the relative until he leads them to the actual perpetrator. In 2018, police used this technique to track down Joseph James DeAngelo, whom they suspect is the Golden State Killer, a man who committed over twelve murders and fifty rapes over a twelve-year period. The police took a sample of DNA from one of the crime scenes and sent it to a public genetic matching website, which identified over ten possible relatives of the perpetrator out of the 650,000 individuals on the site. Police then used this information to identify DeAngelo as the likely suspect, and they confirmed this after obtaining samples of DeAngelo's DNA that he had left outside his home.[135] In short, we already live in a world where the identifying genetic information for nearly every American is available to law enforcement.

Even with this minimization requirement on the legitimate use of the DNA, the costs of DNA searches are not negligible. There is a risk that individual state officials will violate the law and test the DNA in unauthorized ways, thereby learning our intimate medical secrets. There is also a risk that the law might change, and the government could legally learn very private information from the DNA database that it already amassed under the identification-only law. And there is the anxiety felt by most Americans that is associated with that risk. These risks can be minimized by only permitting the government to store the information from the junk strands of the DNA and destroy the original DNA, thus preserving only the "public" part of the data.[136] As Professor Tracey Maclin has pointed out, although most of the laws that permit collection of DNA from arrestees and convicted criminals limit the use of the DNA to identification purposes, there is currently no legal limitation on what law enforcement agents can do when they find abandoned DNA.[137] *King* implied that the DNA analysis in question was only permissible because of its limited purpose by emphasizing that the genetic data that was tested under the Maryland statute did not reveal any genetic traits,[138] but a stronger statement of the law is necessary in order to ensure the costs are minimized.

On the other side of the equation, the benefits of unfettered DNA collection for identification purposes cannot be ignored. Not only will a comprehensive DNA database help to solve the millions of cold cases that remain unsolved, it will also deter and help solve future crimes. The knowledge that a person's DNA is easily traced will deter many would-be criminals, and the difficulty of committing a crime, especially a violent crime, without leaving any DNA residue will lead to a higher number of convictions. One recent study found that the requirement that each additional DNA sample added to the CODIS database decreased violent crime by .051 offenses per 100,000 residents and property crime by .323 offenses per 100,000 residents.[139] The aggregate effects are large: from 2000 to 2010, the growth of state and national DNA databases caused a decrease of violent crime between 7 percent and 45 percent and a decrease in property crime between 5 percent and 35 percent.[140]

In summary, the cost–benefit analysis theory leads to a minimization rule that allows the government unfettered access to DNA samples but restricts their use only to identification and links to unsolved crime databases. Professor David H. Kaye has proposed a similar rule and called it the "biometric exception" to the Fourth Amendment.[141] In reality, permitting the government to collect and analyze DNA samples in this way is not really an "exception" to the Fourth Amendment, even under current doctrine, since this investigative technique reveals nothing private about the person other than the fact that he was involved in a previous crime, which is a fact in which the suspect has no legitimate expectation of privacy.

CONCLUSION

The frequency and variety of hyper-intrusive surveillance methods is likely to increase dramatically over the next few decades. In responding to these searches, courts need to be open to applying all of the potential tools in their arsenal, from requiring higher standards of certainty to imposing specific requirements like minimization, least intrusive means tests, time limitations, or limiting the surveillance to certain severe crimes. Depending on the context, many of these tools can increase the productivity of the search by lowering the privacy costs of what would otherwise be a very intrusive search.

Courts also need to keep in mind the vast benefits offered by many of these surveillance methods. As we have seen throughout this book, technological innovations have been very useful to law enforcement agencies in detecting crime and identifying criminals. Law enforcement officials should be required to empirically demonstrate these benefits and may (if the courts impose a least intrusive means requirement) need to demonstrate that the benefits are significantly greater than those offered by less intrusive surveillance method. Only once the costs have been minimized and the benefits have been demonstrated should courts allow the government to engage in these searches.

Conclusion

Implementing the Change

Insofar as the respondent's complaint appears to be simply that scientific devices ... enabled the police to be more effective in detecting crime, it simply has no constitutional foundation. We have never equated police efficiency with unconstitutionality, and we decline to do so now.

United States v. Knotts (1983) [1]

THE PROBLEM OF UNDERENFORCEMENT

Under our current criminal justice system, the vast majority of crimes go unpunished. According to victim surveys, there were approximately 5.7 million violent felonies and nearly 16 million felonious property crimes committed in this country.[2] Most of these crimes are never reported to the police;[3] most of the crimes known to the police never result in an arrest;[4] and only about half of those whom the police arrest are convicted.[5] As a result, today's criminal justice system obtains convictions for only about one million of the twenty-one million felonies estimated to be committed each year. [6] These statistics do not include the vast numbers of so-called "victimless" felonies, such as drug sales, drug possession, firearms possession, child pornography possession, drunk driving, or other criminal activity that are not captured by victim surveys.[7] While the true extent of those crimes cannot be precisely measured, including them in the calculation would significantly increase the ratio of unpunished to punished crime.

Given the fact that the United States has the highest incarceration rate in the Western industrialized world,[8] many individuals may feel that the last thing we need to do is to catch and punish more criminals. There is little doubt among criminal law scholars that we already criminalize too much conduct and that our punishments are too severe.[9] But the solution is not to maintain a criminal justice system that is so inefficient that it randomly allows the vast majority of crimes to go undetected and the majority of crimes that are detected to go unsolved.[10] The low rate of detection and apprehension undermines respect for the law and delegitimizes the criminal justice system. Ironically, this widespread and arbitrary underenforcement of crime probably serves to exacerbate the overcriminalization crisis by masking the true extent of the problem. As noted in Chapter 5, one benefit of near-perfect crime enforcement would be forcing individuals and politicians to address the full societal impact of criminalizing large swaths of human activity.

THE PROMISE OF NEW SURVEILLANCE TECHNOLOGY

New surveillance technologies have the potential to exponentially increase our ability to detect, investigate, and prosecute criminal activity. The danger is that these new technologies will also erode our privacy until we are left with a dystopian, all-knowing surveillance state. But as this book has tried to demonstrate, there does not always need to be a trade-off between privacy and security. With the proper legal framework, we can design and utilize this technology in ways that maximize the effectiveness and minimize the level of intrusiveness of the surveillance.

In short, we need to stop seeing new surveillance technology as a problem and start seeing it as a solution. Much of the supposedly intrusive new surveillance technology is merely reactive – law enforcement responses to the widespread availability of powerful privacy-enhancing technologies. Advances in cryptography, communication, and data storage now enable individuals to achieve nearly complete secrecy for many of their activities, rendering traditional investigative techniques useless, and preventing law enforcement officers from investigating criminal activity even when they have a legitimate and court-approved reason to conduct the investigation.

In order to reach the optimum level of privacy and security, we must reject the standard paradigm that views criminal procedure as either a competition between law enforcement and criminals or as a balance between privacy and security. Instead, we must approach these issues as economic problems and seek to maximize the output of security while minimizing the input of privacy. The first step on this path is to ensure that decision-makers understand the true costs and benefits of different types of surveillance.

For a number of reasons, the courts, upon which we rely to establish proper boundaries for government surveillance, are imperfect institutions for measuring and accommodating the privacy and security interests at stake.[11] First, courts exist to resolve a particular case and controversy set before them. Their job is not to determine the *best* kind of search to employ, but only whether a particular search was appropriate and excessive in a particular case. Thus, they can only set outer limits as to what searches are permissible or impermissible. Second, courts have devised tests that ignore or downplay a number of important factors in determining whether surveillance is permissible. For the most part, courts ignore the severity of the crime being investigated when evaluating a surveillance technique,[12] as well as the financial outlay required to conduct the surveillance.[13] Courts also occasionally display a lack of awareness of the practical realities of law enforcement, misperceiving both the challenges that police face in investigating crime and the abusive practices that some police engage in during those investigations.

Most importantly, courts are not are not structurally designed to accurately measure the costs and benefits of new surveillance technologies. They lack the investigative infrastructure required to fully understand how these technologies function in practice and how successful different surveillance techniques might be in detecting criminal activity. Even when measuring intrusiveness – the one factor that courts have focused on through decades of case law – courts do not have the necessary resources to measure society's norms, nor monitor how those norms change over time. Thus, courts tend to rely on their own idea of what should or should not be private instead if actually examining data regarding what degree of privacy society is prepared to accept.[14] Like all human institutions, courts sometimes err when they rely on their intuition or personal experience to determine what society thinks is reasonable – such as when the Supreme Court held in *Olmstead* that a person who uses a telephone "intends to project his voice to those quite outside" and therefore does not deserve the protection of the Fourth Amendment.[15]

Even when the Supreme Court is not as dramatically wrong as it was in *Olmstead*, its judgments are sometimes incongruous with what a majority of society *actually* believes ought to be private. As we saw in Chapter 1, surveys have shown a significant disconnect between the conduct that the Supreme Court believes violates a reasonable expectation of privacy and what individuals believe violates a reasonable expectation of privacy.[16] And as some scholars have noted, the Court appears disinterested in empirical evidence on this issue.[17]

Fortunately, courts are not the only institutions in charge of regulating surveillance; over the past few decades, legislatures have adopted a much more active role in this area. Today there are dozens of federal provisions that limit the use of technology by law enforcement, such as Title III of the Omnibus Crime Control and Safe Streets Act of 1968 (Title III),[18] which regulates oral and wire communications; the 1986 Electronic Communications Privacy Act (ECPA),[19] which extends Title III to electronic communications; the Stored Communications Act (SCA),[20] which was part of ECPA and regulates government access to stored wire and electronic communications held by third-party ISPs; the Foreign Intelligence Surveillance Act of 1978 (FISA),[21] which sets out rules for electronic surveillance of agents of foreign powers; and the Uniting and Strengthening America by Providing Appropriate Tools Required to Intercept and Obstruct Terrorism Act of 2001 (USA PATRIOT Act), which, among other effects, broadens the type of surveillance allowed under FISA and the ECPA.[22] All of these statues create a complex regime of surveillance regulation, so that when a court evaluates the legality a surveillance method, especially a method involving a relatively new technology, the court will frequently apply statutory rules rather than the Fourth Amendment.[23] Many scholars view this growing Congressional involvement as a positive development because a legislature is better equipped to determine the optimal balance between the needs of law enforcement and the privacy rights of individuals.[24] Legislative bodies can act more quickly in response to changes in technologies and law enforcement needs, and they have the resources to learn what changes are occurring and how those changes affect surveillance methods.[25] A legislature has the ability to hear from different experts and gather information about the administrative costs of different methods of surveillance, the public's perception of the intrusiveness of the surveillance, and the likelihood of achieving the surveillance successfully detecting criminal activity. Furthermore, because a legislature is the very body that decides the severity of every crime, it is uniquely positioned to measure the potential benefit of different types of surveillance.

Legislatures are of course, constrained by the courts' interpretation of the Fourth Amendment. If the Supreme Court decides that a particularly productive surveillance method requires law enforcement officers to obtain a warrant or demonstrate a similarly high standard of suspicion, Congress' ability to encourage that surveillance method is constrained. But the Supreme Court has shown some willingness to defer to Congress on standards for surveillance methods, especially where Congress has been willing to step in and take the lead.[26] This should give Congress the confidence to redefine the way we approach surveillance regulation and move us away from an intrusion-only analysis to a holistic review of all of the relevant factors of when evaluating the desirability of a particular surveillance method.

This shift of regulatory power over surveillance methods from courts to legislatures must only be an intermediate step. Although legislatures are better equipped than courts to make the appropriate calculations, they are still not the ideal institution for the task. As noted in Chapter 1, new surveillance tools and new types of privacy-enhancing devices are being developed at a rapid pace. Society's expectations of privacy are also rapidly shifting in response to these technologies and other social and cultural phenomena. Finally, there are a multitude of surveillance forms that can be applied in a wide variety of contexts, so that even if legislatures provide broad outlines of the appropriate cost/benefit analysis, these outlines can do little more than provide rough guidelines to courts and law enforcement officers. Thus, the ideal institution for making identifying and maintaining appropriate surveillance standards would an administrative agency which would provide courts with classifications for different types of surveillance.

FOUR GUIDING PRINCIPLES

Most of the work required to measure both the intrusiveness and the potential benefit of different types of surveillance is just beginning. This book proposes four fundamental principles to guide us as we build a new paradigm of Fourth Amendment jurisprudence:

1 *Develop New Binary Surveillance Tools*

We should design surveillance technologies to be binary searches whenever possible. If a surveillance method can only detect illegal activity, it cannot infringe on any legitimate expectation of privacy. Currently, the most significant obstacle to widespread use of binary searches is their current lack of accuracy, since a false positive result will lead to a potentially intrusive search of an innocent individual. As surveillance technology gets smarter – that is, as the tools used to investigate crime become better able to sift through innocent activity and identify only the illegal activity – binary searches will become more accurate. Once a binary search becomes sufficiently accurate, law enforcement officers can use it with impunity, effectively achieving perfect enforcement of certain categories of crime. These technologies could include Internet sniffers that monitor e-mail to detect child pornography; gun detectors located everywhere where guns are prohibited (such as airport concourses or public courthouses); and gunshot detection systems in cities.

2 *Encourage Low-Cost Surveillance Methods*

All other things being equal, a lower cost surveillance method is preferable to a higher cost surveillance method. Criminal investigations are not a game in which courts must strive to keep the playing field level. Modern day law enforcement officers should be permitted to exploit the advantages of extremely low-cost surveillance methods, such as surveillance cameras (including body cameras on police officers), cell phone location tracking, and inexpensive access to massive amounts of data collected by other government agents and private parties. Most of these surveillance methods merely collect data that is already exposed to the public; they are revolutionary because they gather it more cheaply, process it more effectively, and preserve it more accurately than traditional modes of surveillance. Many commentators and courts have treated the low cost of these surveillance methods as a negative development, since it removes the natural economic barriers that used to limit the amount of information police could collect. These critics have called for enhancing legal restrictions on lower cost surveillance methods in order to level the playing field and eliminate the efficiency gains that police have been able to achieve. Under the cost-benefit analysis theory, however, that analysis has it exactly backward – or, more accurately, the analysis ignores the substantial benefit that these surveillance techniques offer the criminal justice system.

The proper response is to embrace these cheaper, more efficient methods of surveillance. Ideally, we could reduce the privacy cost of these low-cost collection techniques by combining them with algorithms that analyze patterns of behavior and detect those patterns that indicate a high likelihood of criminal behavior. Such algorithms may not be able to transform these big data searches into purely binary searches, since they would likely only be able to indicate a high probability of illegality, not the near-certainty required under the binary search doctrine. But the algorithms should be able to calculate the likelihood of criminal activity given a certain pattern of movement, series of credit card purchases, collection of outgoing phone calls, and other types of data. Law enforcement officers could be prohibited from accessing these large caches of data unless the algorithm indicated that the likelihood of criminal activity rose above a certain threshold.

Using these algorithms would lower the privacy cost of these panoptic low-cost surveillance methods, since machines and not individual law enforcement officers would be the ones combing through these massive amounts of data. The greater efficiency of these algorithms would also reduce the administrative cost of the surveillance, giving law enforcement officers more time to focus on the patterns flagged as likely to indicate criminal activity. Unfortunately, none of these advances will be possible if the courts pre-empt the use of this information by bluntly imposing a warrant requirement when the police are able to use low-cost technology to investigate cases more efficiently.

3 Enhance Third-Party Rights

Courts should resist the calls to abolish or substantially weaken the third party doctrine. The doctrine is critical to ensuring that criminals cannot hide evidence by transferring it to third parties in order to hide it from law enforcement. It also enables third parties to cooperate with law enforcement officers if they who wish to do so. Instead, courts should bolster the Fourth Amendment rights for individual and corporate third parties who hold our data. Strengthening these rights would acknowledge that the shared information has value to these third parties. It would also increase the autonomy of third parties, allowing them to decide whether to share information or fight to protect it. This, in turn, will allow consumers to review the standards and practices of the third parties and then decide for themselves what level of privacy they want from the companies that hold their data.

4 Properly Limit Hyper-Intrusive Searches

Video cameras hidden in private homes, machines that can see through walls, and devices that allow real time interception of cell phone communication are all examples of surveillance methods that carry an extremely high cost to privacy. Although today we focus on the hyper-intrusive searches made possible by modern surveillance technologies, it is important to recognize that this category of surveillance has been around for a long time. For most of the twentieth century, courts and legislatures have addressed hyper-intrusive searches such as no-knock search warrants, telephone wiretaps, and invasive surgery. Thus, the criminal justice system has already developed numerous tools to lower the privacy cost of such searches and restrict law enforcement's access to them to situations in which the security benefit is significant enough to justify the cost to privacy. Courts need to be more effective in seeing the links between these different types of hyper-intrusive searches so that they are aware of the full range of options they can use to limit and regulate the government when it wants to engage in these searches. Courts can then apply the appropriate restrictions to new hyper-intrusive searches to ensure that they are properly regulated.

*　*　*

Our country maintains a healthy skepticism of police power. That skepticism originated at the time of our nation's founding, when British soldiers conducted broad, warrantless searches against us. It has only intensified in recent years as new surveillance technologies and dystopian visions of the future fuel fears of an omniscient police state that gathers, stores, and processes our most intimate information. But the truth is more complex. For the most part, technological advances have increased our privacy, allowing us to shield most of our activities from public view and making criminal investigations nearly impossible to carry out without utilizing the newest surveillance tools. The equilibrium adjustment theory captures this complexity relatively well, by pointing out that many of the seemingly intrusive investigative methods are in fact merely reactive surveillance, and their use does nothing more than restore the pre-existing balance between law enforcement and criminal suspects.

But the equilibrium adjustment theory is incomplete, because it still works within the conventional paradigm of surveillance regulation. It assumes a zero-sum game in which the goal is to keep the playing field level, maintaining a consistent balance between our privacy and our security. Modern surveillance technology has the potential to radically increase the ability of law enforcement to detect crime and collect evidence, often with little or no effects on our privacy. Instead of categorizing every type of surveillance into either a search or not a search based on a perceived level of intrusion, we must look at the *productivity* of the surveillance, by weighing the costs of the search against its benefits. This will require us to calculate the intrusiveness of law enforcement actions as well as the likelihood of success of the actions.

Admittedly, courts will resist this new paradigm. But the current model of surveillance law is broken. Judges use personal experience, intuition, and imperfect analogies to decide for themselves what types of police behaviors infringe on society's reasonable expectation of privacy, and are often unaware of how society's expectations have changed. Perhaps even worse, courts routinely defer to police regarding the likelihood of success of their searches, allowing police to use their own intuition when conducting frisks and searches, while citing factors such as "high crime neighborhood" with little or no evidence to connect these factors to the necessary legal standard of suspicion. These calculations are based on anecdotal evidence at best, and can be subject to the worst kinds of unconscious and explicit bias. In the past, this inaccuracy was unavoidable; today, it is indefensible. We now have the tools to accurately calculate and quantify the costs and benefits of different types of surveillance and unlock the full potential of the modern surveillance state.

Notes

1 GEORGE ORWELL, 1984 158 (Bernard Crick ed., Oxford University Press 1984) (1949).
2 *Id.*
3 Television use did not become widespread until the postwar era; in 1945, it is estimated that there were only 7,000 working television sets in the entire country. "Brief History of Television," https://guides.library.duke.edu/c.php?g=480747&p=3321107 (last visited Jan. 21, 2019). Also in the postwar era, one of the first "high-speed" electrical computers began operation. It was called ENIAC ("Electrical Number Integrator and Calculator") and it used 18,000 vacuum tubes and took up 1,800 square feet of floor space. Jeremy Myers, *A Short History of the Computer*, www.softlord.com/comp/ (last visited Jan. 21, 2019).
4 This view is also held by many leading scholars and judges. *See, e.g.,* Lopez v. United States, 373 U.S. 427, 466 (1963) (Brennan, J., dissenting) ("Electronic surveillance ... makes the police omniscient; and police omniscience is one of the most effective tools of tyranny.")
5 Jennifer Lee, *Police Seek to Increase Surveillance*, N.Y. TIMES, May 31, 2005, at B3 (noting that after police announced installation of four hundred surveillance cameras in high-crime, high-traffic areas in New York City, some people feared the cameras would compromise their privacy). One Councilman in Loma Linda, California equated the installation of surveillance cameras in public areas with "Cuba or communist Russia." Jacob Ogles, *Privacy Experts Worry about Public Cameras*, INLAND VALLEY DAILY BULLETIN (Ontario, CA), Nov. 20, 2005.
6 *See* Olmstead v. United States, 277 U.S. 438, 466 (1928).
7 *See, e.g.,* United States v. Torres, 751 F.2d 875, 885 (7th Cir, 1984).
8 *See, e.g.,* United States v. Jones, 364 F.Supp. 1303, 1304–5 (D. Utah 2005).
9 *See infra* Chapter 5, notes 39–42 and accompanying text.
10 *See, e.g.,* United States v. Kennedy, 81 F.Supp. 2d 1103 (D. Kan. 2000).
11 *See, e.g.,* United States v. Gray, 78 F.Supp. 2d 524, 526 (E.D. Va. 1999).
12 *See* Kyllo v. United States, 533 U.S. 27, 29–30 (2001).

13 *See, e.g., Stringray Tracking Devices: Who's Got Them?*, ACLU, www.aclu.org/issues/priv
    acy-technology/surveillance-technologies/stingray-tracking-devices-whos-got-them.   (last
    updated Nov. 2018) (last visited Jan. 21, 2019); Tom Jackman, *Police Use of "StingRay"
    Cellphone Tracker Requires Search Warrant, Appeals Court Rules*, WASH. POST, Sept. 21,
    2017,   www.washingtonpost.com/news/true-crime/wp/2017/09/21/police-use-of-stingray-cell
    phone-tracker-requires-search-warrant-appeals-court-rules/?noredirect=on&utm_term=
    .26012166aa0a (last visited Jan. 21, 2019); Brad Heath, *Police Secretly Track Cellphones to Solve
    Routine Crimes*, USA TODAY, Aug. 23, 2015, www.usatoday.com/story/news/2015/08/23/
    baltimore-police-stingray-cell-surveillance/31994181/ (last visited Jan. 21, 2019).

14 *See, e.g.*, 165 Cong. Rec. H8277 – H8278 (daily ed. Oct. 31, 2017) (statement of Rep. Poe);
    F.A.I.R. Surveillance Act of 2017, H.R. 957, 115th Cong. (2017).

15 *See, e.g.*, Arizona v. Evans, 514 U.S. 1, 17–18 (1995) (O'Connor, J., concurring) ("With the
    benefits of more efficient law enforcement mechanisms comes the burden of correspond-
    ing constitutional responsibilities"); Kyllo v. United States, 533 U.S. 27, 34 (2001) ("As
    technology has enhanced the Government's capacity to encroach upon areas normally
    guarded from inquisitive eyes, this Court has sought to "assure [] preservation of that
    degree of privacy against government that existed when the Fourth Amendment was
    adopted.");
    Robert Barnes, *Justices Appear to Favor More Restraints on Government Access to Digital Infor-
    mation*, WASH. POST, Nov. 29, 2017, www.washingtonpost.com/politics/courts_law/justices-
    appear-to-favor-more-restraints-on-access-to-digital-information/2017/11/29/5f7aaae2-d499-11e7-
    b62d-d9345ced896d_story.html?noredirect=on&utm_term=.5be1b4ae606d   (last   visited
    Jan. 21, 2019).

16 *See, e.g.*, Robert M. Bloom & William T. Clark, *Small Cells, Big Problems: The Increasing
    Precision of Cell Site Location Information and the Need for Fourth Amendment Protec-
    tions*, 106 J. CRIM. L. & CRIMINOLOGY, 167, 201 (2016); Julie E. Cohen, *What Privacy Is
    For*, 126 HARV. L. REV. 1904, 1933 (2013).

17 *See, e.g.*, Jim Steyer, *Europeans Win Data Privacy Right – What About Us?*, SAN FRANCISCO
    CHRONICLE, May 30, 2018, www.sfchronicle.com/opinion/openforum/article/Europeans-
    win-data-privacy-rights-what-about-12955091.php. (CEO and founder of Common Sense
    Media calls for the California legislature to pass privacy reforms); Tom Simonite, *Few
    Rules Govern Police Use of Facial-Recognition Technology*, WIRED, (May 22, 2018, 09:35
    PM),   www.wired.com/story/few-rules-govern-police-use-of-facial-recognition-technology/
    (describing the current lack of regulations for facial recognition technology, while examin-
    ing how this technology could be regulated by companies and the government); Tim Wu,
    An American Alternative to Europe's Privacy Law, N.Y. TIMES, May 30, 2018, www.nytimes
    .com/2018/05/30/opinion/europe-america-privacy-gdpr.html (arguing for a common law,
    case by case approach to regulating privacy issues with the way technology companies use
    personal data in the United States); *Editorial: Searching Your Smartphone at the Border*,
    CHICAGO TRIBUNE (May 22, 2018, 2:40 PM), www.chicagotribune.com/news/opinion/
    editorials/ct-edit-smartphone-border-court-privacy-20180521-story.html (claiming that fed-
    eral courts have understood that advances in technology require updating the law and
    expressing optimism that the Supreme Court will follow the lower federal courts' lead in
    protecting privacy rights); Leroy Pernell, *Commentary: OPD-Amazon Facial Recognition:
    A Right to Privacy?*, ORLANDO SENTINEL (May 23, 2018, 1:30 PM), www.orlandosentinel

.com/opinion/os-ed-opd-facial-recognition-us-constitution-20180523-story.html (arguing that given the news that the Orlando Police Department is testing facial recognition software by Amazon, it is time to consider the questions that these technology applications raise regarding due process and the Fourth Amendment).

18 See U.S. CONST. AMEND. IV ("The right of the people to be secure in their persons, houses, papers, and effects, against unreasonable searches and seizures, shall not be violated, and no Warrants shall issue, but upon probable cause, supported by Oath or affirmation, and particularly describing the place to be searched, and the persons or things to be seized.").

19 See Wilkes v. Wood, 19 Howell's State Trials 1153 (C.P.1763) and Entick v. Carrington, 19 Howell's State Trials 1029 (C.P. 1765). These two cases, in which British citizens challenged the king's agents and won, became well known in the colonies.

20 See Paxton's case, 1761, in which sixty-three merchants in Boston challenged the British customs agents, and the Malcolm Affair of 1766, in which customs officials attempted to search the cellar of the merchant Daniel Malcom.

21 "Early Police in the United States," ENCYCLOPEDIA BRITANNICA, www.britannica.com/topic/police/Early-police-in-the-United-States (last visited Jan. 21, 2019).

22 Tim Weiner, ENEMIES: A HISTORY OF THE FBI 12 (1st ed. 2012).

23 See Carrol v. United States, 267 U.S. 132, 149 (1925). A later case emphasized that probable cause "deal[s] with probabilities," but "[t]hese are not technical; they are the factual and practical considerations of everyday life on which reasonable and prudent men, not legal technicians, act." Brinegar v. United States, 338 U.S. 160, 175 (1949).

24 Olmstead v. United States, 277 U.S. 438 (1928).

25 Id. at 466. Ultimately Congress had to step in and create statutory protections against wiretapping. See Wiretapping Act of 1934.

26 See, e.g., Carroll v. United States, 267 U.S. 132 (1925); Duke v. Taylor Implement Mfg. Co., 391 U.S. 216 (1968); United States v. Chadwick, 433 U.S. 1 (1977); Rakas v. Illinois, 439 U.S. 1287 (1978); Arkansas v. Sanders, 442 U.S. 753 (1979); California v. Acevedo, 500 U.S. 565 (1991).

27 For example, Acevedo ruled that police officers can search containers inside vehicles, overruling Chadwick and Sanders, which ruled that police could not do so.

28 United States v. Knotts, 460 U.S. 276 (1983) (beeper to track movements); United States v. Place, 462 U.S. 696 (1983) (drug-sniffing dog); United States v. White, 401 U.S. 745 (1971) (informant with listening device); Smith v. Maryland, 442 U.S. 735 (1979) (outgoing phone numbers); Dow Chemical Co. v. United States, 476 U.S. 227 (1986) (telescopic photography from an airplane); Florida v. Riley, 488 U.S. 445 (1989) (visual observation from a helicopter); Skinner v. Railway Labor Executives' Ass'n, 489 U.S. 602 (1989) (urine test of federal railroad employees);

29 Katz v. United States, 389 U.S. 347 (1967).

30 Terry v. Ohio, 392 U.S. 1 (1968).

31 In game theory, a "zero-sum game" is a situation in which a participant's gain (or loss) of utility is exactly balanced by the losses (or gains) of the utility of the other participant. Merriam-Webster Dictionary, "Zero-sum game," www.merriam-webster.com/dictionary/zero-sum%20game (last visited Jan. 21, 2019).

32 Orin S. Kerr, An Equilibrium-Adjustment Theory of the Fourth Amendment, 125 HARV. L. REV. 476 (2011).

33 1 BENJAMIN FRANKLIN, MEMOIRS OF THE LIFE AND THE WRITINGS OF BENJAMIN FRANKLIN 270 (London, Henry Colburn 1818).

34 Lo-Ji Sales, Inc. v. New York, 442 U.S. 319, 326 (1979) (quoting Johnson v. United States, 333 U.S. 10, 14 (1948)); United States v. Chadwick, 433 U.S. 1, 9 (1977) (quoting Johnson, 333 U.S. at 14).

35 *See* Kerr, *supra* note 32.

36 *Id.* at 543.

37 *Id.*

38 *Id.* at 482–85. Professor Kerr suggests using the "timeless rules of Fourth Amendment law" as the starting point of the law for Year Zero.

39 *See id.* at 502–8.

40 Carroll v. United States, 267 U.S. 132 (1925).

41 Kerr, *supra* note 32. at 513–17.

42 *Id.* at 496–99.

43 In rejecting the constitutionality of warrantless use of thermal imagers, Justice Scalia famously noted that a thermal imager would allow the government agent to learn "at what hour each night the lady of the house takes her daily sauna and bath." Kyllo v. United States, 533 U.S. 27, 38 (2001).

44 See United States v. Jones, 565 U.S. 400, 406 (2012) (internal quotations and citations omitted).

45 One argument in favor of using "Year Zero" is based on the originalist theory of constitutional interpretation; that is, we should interpret the "reasonableness" clause of the constitution as the drafters of the Fourth Amendment would have interpreted it. But in this context originalism cannot be taken literally – there is no way to know how the drafters of the Fourth Amendment would analyze thermal imagers or searches of cell phones. And since there is so little case law involving the Fourth Amendment in the first century of its existence, it is nearly impossible to tell what the drafters thought the optimal balance would be between liberty and privacy. At any rate, if new technologies can provide increased security with the same level of privacy, or increased privacy with the same level of security, it would be overly formalist to reject the new technology merely because it provided society with a better situation than existed at the time of the Amendment's drafting. *See, e.g.,* Christopher Slobogin, "An Original Take on Originalism," 125 HARV. L. REV. F. 84, 84–90 (2011–2012).

46 *See* Ric Simmons, *Searching for Terrorists: Why Public Safety is Not a Special Need,* 59 DUKE L.J. 843, 851 (2010).

47 Katz v. United States, 389 U.S. 347 (1967); Terry v. Ohio, 392 U.S. 1 (1968).

48 *See, e.g., FCC v. AT&T,* 131 S. Ct. 1177, 1184 (2011); Cyrus Farivar, *Tech Companies, Law Profs Agree: The Fourth Amendment Should Protect Data,* ARS TECHNICA (Aug. 15, 2017, 2:51 PM), https://arstechnica.com/tech-policy/2017/08/tech-companies-law-profs-agree-the-fourth-amendment-should-protect-data/ (last visited Jan. 21, 2019); Lily Hay Newman, *Verizon – Yes, Verizon – Just Stood Up for Your Privacy,* WIRED (Aug. 16, 2017, 10:00 AM), www.wired.com/story/verizon-privacy-location-data-fourth-amendment/ (last visited Jan. 21, 2019).

CHAPTER 1

1 Epigraph source: Oliver Wendell Holmes, *The Path of the Law,* 10 HARV. L. REV. 457, 469 (1897). The Law and Economics movement is generally thought to have begun with the

publication of two groundbreaking articles in the early 1960s: Ronald Coase, *The Problem of Social Cost*, 3 J.L & ECON. 1 (1960) and Guido Calabresi, *Some Thoughts on Risk Distribution and the Law of Torts*, 70 YALE L.J. 499 (1961).

2 *Cf.* Orin S. Kerr, *An Economic Understanding of Search and Seizure Law*, 146 U. PENN. L. REV. 591 (2016); Craig S. Lerner, *The Reasonableness of Probable Cause*, 81 TEX. L. REV. 951 (2003); Steven Penney, *Reasonable Expectations of Privacy and Novel Search Technologies: An Economic Approach*, 97 J. CRIM L. & CRIMINOLOGY 477 (2007); HUGO M. MIALON & SUE H. MIALON, THE EFFECTS OF THE FOURTH AMENDMENT: AN ECONOMIC ANALYSIS, (Emory Law Sch. Pub. Law & Legal Theory Research Paper Series, Paper No. 06-3, 2006), *available at* http://papers.ssrn.com/abstract=755035 (last visited Jan. 21, 2019); ANDREW SONG, TECHNOLOGY, TERRORISM, AND THE FISHBOWL EFFECT: AN ECONOMIC ANALYSIS OF SURVEILLANCE AND SEARCHES, (Berkman Ctr. For Internet & Soc'y, Working Paper No. 73, 2003), *available at* http://papers.ssrn.com/abstract= 422220 (last visited Jan. 21, 2019). *See generally* Frank H. Easterbrook, *Criminal Procedure as a Market System*, 12 J. LEGAL STUD. 289 (1983) (discussing law and economics with regard to the trial aspects of criminal procedure, such as prosecutorial discretion, plea bargaining, and sentencing). There have also been a number of articles using economic principles to determine the effect of the exclusionary rule. For an example, see Myron W. Orfield, Jr., *The Exclusionary Rule and Deterrence: An Empirical Study of Chicago Narcotics Officers*, 54 U. CHI. L. REV. 1016 (1987).

3 RICHARD A. POSNER, ECONOMIC ANALYSIS OF LAW (6th ed. 2003). Posner briefly discusses plea bargaining, *Terry* stops, the exclusionary rule, and coerced confessions. *Id.* at 577–80, 712–16.

4 Penney, *supra* note 2, at 478–79.

5 Some may argue that the goal of the Fourth Amendment is to protect fundamental privacy rights, rather than to find the "appropriate balance" between privacy and security. This is something of an oversimplification, however. Every constitutional provision that protects fundamental rights involves a determination of the scope of those rights against conflicting societal values. For example, the First Amendment protects the right to freedom of expression, but the Court has never held that that right is absolute; instead, First Amendment jurisprudence involves determining how to balance that right against other societal needs that may come into conflict with it: the need for national security, the need to protect copyrighted work; the need to protect against defamatory statements, and so on. Konigsberg v. State Bar of Cal., 366 U.S. 36, 50–51 (1961) (explaining that the protections of the First Amendment are not absolute). Likewise, the privacy right protected by the Fourth Amendment cannot be absolute; it must be balanced against the needs of law enforcement to provide security. Furthermore, the Fourth Amendment explicitly uses the word "reasonable," meaning that courts must engage in some kind of balancing in determining whether a given type of surveillance is constitutional. US. Const. Amend. IV.

6 Throughout this Article, I will use the word "surveillance" to cover any method of investigation carried out by law enforcement officials, from accessing a Department of Motor Vehicles database, to wiretapping a telephone, to strip-searching a suspect. This awkward terminology is required because the term "search" has a very particular meaning in Fourth Amendment jurisprudence as a method of surveillance that implicates the Fourth

Amendment to the degree that it requires probable cause or a warrant. *See* Katz v. United States, 389 U.S. 347, 350–53 (1967).

7 Of course, more efficient crime control is not just about identifying the guilty; it is also about collecting evidence that can exonerate the innocent.

8 *See* United States v. Knotts, 460 U.S. 276, 284 (1983) ("Insofar as respondent's complaint appears to be simply that scientific devices such as the beeper enabled the police to be more effective in detecting crime, it simply has no constitutional foundation. We have never equated police efficiency with unconstitutionality, and we decline to do so now.")

9 Professor Christopher Slobogin describes this type of sliding scale as the "proportionality principle." *See* CHRISTOPHER SLOBOGIN, *Privacy at Risk*, 23–47 (2007).

10 There has been a substantial amount of law and economics work in the substantive criminal law area – for example, using economic tools to determine the proper sanction for certain crimes. *See, e.g.*, Gary S. Becker, *Crime and Punishment: An Economic Approach*, 76 J. POL. ECON. 169 (1968); Richard A. Posner, *Optimal Sentences for White-Collar Criminals*, 17 AM. CRIM. L. REV. 409 (1980). Other scholars have argued for privatization of the criminal justice system. *See, e.g.*, BRUCE L. BENSON, TO SERVE AND PROTECT: PRIVATIZATION AND COMMUNITY IN CRIMINAL JUSTICE (1998). Some scholars have applied econometric principles to determine the effects of certain criminal procedure doctrines such as the exclusionary rule. *See, e.g.*, Raymond A. Atkins & Paul H. Rubin, *Effects of Criminal Procedure on Crime Rates: Mapping Out the Consequences of the Exclusionary Rule*, 46 J.L. & ECON. 157 (2003).

11 *See, e.g.*, Easterbrook, *supra* note 2.

12 Lerner, *supra* note 2, at 1019–22.

13 *See* United States v. Carroll Towing Co., 159 F.2d 169, 173 (2d Cir. 1947).

14 Lerner, *supra* note 2, at 1019–20.

15 *Id.*

16 Professor Lerner would reduce the social cost (C) by the factor "(1-P)," because he argues that the Supreme Court has determined there is no constitutionally recognized privacy intrusion if the search is successful. *Id.* at 1020. However, he seems to misinterpret the Supreme Court doctrine in this area. The Supreme Court has held that if the surveillance can detect *only* information about illegal activity, then the surveillance does not infringe on any constitutionally protected rights – for example, a drug sniffing dog that tells the police nothing about the object of the search other than the fact that contraband is or is not present. *See, e.g.*, Illinois v. Caballes, 543 U.S. 405, 408–9 (2005). But this doctrine does not mean that a certain type of surveillance does not infringe on any constitutionally protected rights in every case in which the police find contraband. If the police search a suspect's house and find narcotics, the search still infringed on the suspect's rights – and definitely impacted the Fourth Amendment – because the police saw a lot of other private information while looking for the narcotics. Under Professor Lerner's revised formula, there would be no privacy intrusion and the social cost of this search would be zero.

Professor Lerner would also increase the social cost (C) by the factor "m," which he calls a "privacy multiplier," in order to "reflect the fact that not all seemingly identical searches are in fact identical, at least in the subjectively experienced intrusion on one's privacy." *Id.* at 1021. For example, Professor Lerner argues that an African-American person who is pulled over for the tenth time that year may subjectively feel a greater infringement than a white person who is pulled over for the first time. *Id.* As I note below, I am in favor of a using a more generalized "cost to society" rather than trying to calculate a specific subjective cost for each individual.

17 Lerner, *supra* note 10, at 1015.

18 *Id.* at 1020 ("[t]he expected social benefit of a successful search increases if the crime under investigation is, say, aircraft privacy rather than tax fraud.").

19 *Id.* at 1019–20.

20 *See, e.g.,* Akhil Amar, *Fourth Amendment First Principles*, 107 HARV. L. REV. 757, 801–2 (1994).

21 *See, e.g.,* Dunaway v. New York, 442 U.S. 200, 207–12 (1979).

22 Lerner, *supra* note 10, at 1019–20.

23 Essentially Professor Lerner is engaged in the process of calculating productivity as well, although his ultimate goal is to determine a minimum level of productivity at which a surveillance method will be permitted. This minimum level will be termed "probable cause." Under Professor Lerner's theory, the minimum level is a productivity of "1" which occurs when the costs of the search equal the expected benefits of the search. Thus, this is the level at which he argues that judges should find probable cause.

24 The output of a system is defined as "[t]he various useful goods or services that are either consumed or used in further production." PAUL A. SAMUELSON & WILLIAM D. NORDHAUS, ECONOMICS 747 (18th ed. 2004). In our case, the output of the system is the identification of criminals and the collection of evidence.

25 I am using the term "productivity" in the most basic sense: as a simple ratio of output to input. For example, assume a factory produces $10,000 worth of widgets in an hour, using one hundred workers being paid $20 per hour, raw supplies at the rate of $2,000 per hour, and equipment and capital which depreciates at $1,000 per hour. Thus, the factory spends $5,000 each hour and produces $10,000 worth of products, and has a productivity ratio of 10/5, or 2. There are a number of ways to increase the productivity of the factory: If the workers can be trained at negligible cost to produce $15,000 worth of widgets per hour using the same equipment, the productivity would increase to a ratio of 15/5 or 3. Or, if cheaper raw materials were used, salaries could be cut (without sacrificing output), or new, cheaper equipment could be installed, the same $10,000 of output could be produced at a cost of $4,000, for a productivity ratio of 10/4, or 2.5.

26 Song, *supra* note 2, at 16–17.

27 The Supreme Court, of course, originally did *not* believe that surveillance of telephone communications required a warrant. *See* Olmstead v. United States, 277 U.S. 438, 466 (1928). This was before the "reasonable expectations" test of Katz v. United States, but the Court did note in *Olmstead* that it if an individual "project[s] his voice to those quite outside" his house, it is not "reasonable" to conclude that the Fourth Amendment protects his communication. *Id.* Congress disagreed, however, issuing a blanket protection for all telephone communications with the Federal Communications Act of 1934. When the Court finally revisited the issue of protection for telephone communications in *Katz*, it held that individuals did indeed have a reasonable expectation of privacy in those communications, even if they were made from a public phone booth. *Katz*, 389 U.S. 347, 351 (1967).

28 *See, e.g.,* United States v. Heckenkamp, 482 F. 3d 1142, 1146 (9th Cir. 2007) (holding that an individual has a "reasonable expectation of privacy in his computer"). *But see* United

States v. Lifshitz, 369 F.3d 173, 190 (2d Cir. 2004) (holding that there was no reasonable expectation of privacy in "transmissions over the Internet or e-mail that have already arrived at the recipient").

29 *See* Declan McCullagh, *Police Blotter: When Can Cops Run License-Plate Searches?*, CNET NEWS, Sept. 15, 2006, http://news.cnet.com/police-blotter-when-can-cops-run-license-plate-searches/2100-1030_3-6116296.html (last visited Jan. 21, 2019).

30 For more serious crimes, DNA evidence can be gathered from crime scenes and compared against DNA of known suspects – provided the police are able to acquire DNA from those suspects. National Institute of Justice, "DNA Evidence: Basics of Analyzing," https://nij.gov/topics/forensics/evidence/dna/basics/pages/analyzing.aspx (last visited Jan. 21, 2019). But the acquisition, storage, and potential misuse of DNA evidence could be seen as an increase in privacy cost – perhaps an unacceptable increase.

Some of these new technologies provide an identical benefit at a lower administrative cost and a lower privacy cost, which results in an unambiguous increase in Fourth Amendment productivity. Others, however, are more challenging to evaluate because they are less costly in a monetary sense but more costly in terms of their effect on our privacy. For example, law enforcement officers can gather DNA evidence from crime scenes and compare it against the DNA of known suspects from around the country, creating an enormous benefit at a relatively low cost compared to more traditional methods of investigation. However, the acquisition, storage, and potential misuse of that evidence comes at a significant cost to our privacy. Similarly, police can use our own telephones to track our location at all times, or install cameras in public places and watch all of our public movements. All of these types of surveillance provide increased security at a lower administrative cost, but they represent an increased privacy cost; thus, courts need to create legal barriers to discourage these searches even though they are cheaper. We will explore how our formula evaluates this category of surveillance in Chapter 6.

31 Note that throughout this book, when we refer to privacy, we are discussing privacy with regard to the government. Certainly private actors, such as corporations, can also intrude on our privacy, and in some ways, these private actors are a greater threat to our privacy than the government. In Chapter 7, this book will examine some of the ways in which corporations intrude on our privacy, but only in the context of how the government may gain access to the data collected by corporations.

32 Penney, *supra* note 2, at 492–94; Song, *supra* note 2, at 11–16.

33 Penney, *supra* note 2, at 492–93; Song, *supra* note 2, at 11–14.

34 Penney, *supra* note 2, at 493–94; Song, *supra* note 2, at 14–16.

35 United States v. Jones, 565 U.S. 400, 404–06 (2012).

36 Katz v. United States, 389 U.S. 347, 360 (1967) (Harlan, J., concurring).

37 Admittedly, this analysis depends upon a certain definition of "reasonable expectation of privacy" – specifically, that "reasonable expectation of privacy" is equivalent to the information that society as a whole legitimately expects should be kept private. In other words, "reasonable expectation of privacy" is a description (or approximation) of society's shared beliefs about privacy. Although this is the most commonly held view of what the Court means when it uses this term, others have proposed different possible definitions. *See, e.g.*, Orin Kerr, *Four Models of Fourth Amendment Protection*, 60 STAN. L. REV. 503, 507–22

(discussing four different possible definitions: the "probabilistic" model, the "private facts" model, the "positive law" model, and the "policy" model).

38 We discuss these changes in more detail in Chapter 4.

39 For a more detailed discussion of how technology has increased our privacy, see Simmons, *supra* note 37, at 536–40.

40 476 U.S. 207, 215 (1986); *see also* Kyllo v. United States, 533 U.S. 27, 33–34 (2001) ("It would be foolish to contend that the degree of privacy secured to citizens by the Fourth Amendment has been entirely unaffected by the advance of technology. For example, as the cases discussed above make clear, the technology enabling human flight has exposed to public view (and hence, we have said, to official observation) uncovered portions of the house and its curtilage that once were private.").

41 533 U.S. at 40.

42 *Id.* at 33–34.

43 *See* 18 U.S.C. § 2515 (2006).

44 *See* Michael S. Leib, *E-mail and the Wiretap Laws: Why Congress Should Add Electronic Communication to Title III's Statutory Exclusionary Rule and Expressly Reject a "Good Faith" Exception*," 34 HARV. J. LEGIS. 393, 406–9 (1997) (detailing the numerous ways in which electronic communication receives less protection under the ECPA).

45 *Id.*

46 *Id.* at 408–9.

47 *Id.* at 410.

48 *Id.* at 409–10.

49 *See* Kristen Purcell, *Search and email still top the list of most popular online activities*, PEW RES. CTR., INTERNET & AM. LIFE PROJECT (Aug. 9, 2011), http://pewinternet .org/Reports/2011/Search-and-email.aspx (last visited Jan. 21, 2019) (noting growth in e-mail usage among Americans).

50 *Id.* at 285.

51 The terms "digital natives" and "digital immigrants" were coined by John Palfrey, Jr., *Case Commentary: We Googled You*, HARV. BUS. REV., June 2007, at 5.

52 *See* William McGeveran, *Disclosure, Endorsement, and Identity in Social Marketing*, 2009 U. ILL. L. REV. 1105, 1126 (2009); Kim Bartel Sheehan, *Toward a Typology of Internet Users and Online Privacy Concerns*, 18 INFO. SOC'Y 21, 30 (2002).

53 *See generally* Mary G. Leary, *Reasonable Expectations of Privacy for Youth in a Digital Age*, 80 MISS. L.J. 1033, 1044–48 (2011); Sonia Livingstone, *Taking Risky Opportunities in Youthful Content Creation: Teenagers' Use of Social Networking Sites for Intimacy, Privacy, and Self-Expression*, 10 NEW MEDIA & SOC'Y 393 (2008).

54 Mary G. Leary, *The Missed Opportunity of United States v. Jones: Commercial Erosion of Fourth Amendment Protection in a Post-Google Earth World*, 15 U. PA. J. CONST. L. 331 (2012).

55 Teri Dobbins Baxter, *Low Expectations: How Changing Expectations of Privacy Can Erode Fourth Amendment Protection and a Proposed Solution*, 84 TEMP. L. REV. 599, 613 (2012).

56 *Id.* at 622 ("As [younger people] age, their privacy expectations may become the norm and reflect the views of an increasing share of the population. As discussed above, subjective privacy expectations among youth are diminishing even outside of regulated spaces such

as schools. If these attitudes persist into adulthood, the expectations of society as a whole may shift and diminish over time. Consequently, 'society' may be less willing to accept that certain subjective expectations are reasonable. As youth continue to influence society, courts must be aware of the changes and make decisions regarding the reasonableness of privacy expectations accordingly. Even if judges – particularly older judges – maintain heightened expectations of privacy, if the government can establish that large segments of society do not support those expectations, the judges will have to choose between their own beliefs and those of other, potentially larger, segments of society.").

57 *Id.* at 600.

58 *Id.* at 622–36.

59 130 S. Ct. 2619 (2010).

60 *Id.* at 2625.

61 *Id.* at 2625–26.

62 *Id.* at 2626.

63 .*Id* at 2626–27. The courts differed, however, as to whether the city's search was reasonable. The lower court found that the reasonableness of the search depended upon the city's purpose in carrying out the search, and sent that question to the jury; the Ninth Circuit held that the search was unreasonable, regardless of the purpose. *Id.*

64 480 U.S. 709, 710–13 (1987).

65 *Quon*, 130 S. Ct. at 2629–30 (citations omitted).

66 United States v. Jones, 565 U.S. 400, 427 (2012).

67 Baxter, *supra* note 55, at 616.

68 *Id.* at 622–36.

69 To be sure, the Supreme Court occasionally uses language that appears to reject the idea that society's reasonable expectation of privacy is evolving. For example, in United States v. Kyllo, the Court sought to "assure[] preservation of that degree of privacy against government that existed when the Fourth Amendment was adopted." 533 U.S. 27, 34 (2001). The cost–benefit analysis theory does need to be adapted to ensure there is some floor to privacy rights, regardless of how productive a certain method of surveillance may be.

70 We will discuss hyper-intrusive searches and the higher standards they require in Chapter 8.

71 Often the Court is ruling on whether an action which is obviously a search (such as searching a house or car) is permissible under one of the Fourth Amendment's warrant exceptions.

72 Katz v. United States, 389 U.S. 347 (1967); Terry v. Ohio, 392 U.S. 1 (1968); United States v. Karo, 468 U.S. 705 (1984); New York v. Class, 475 U.S. 106 (1986); Arizona v. Hicks, 480 U.S. 321 (1987); O'Connor v. Ortega, 480 U.S. 709 (1987); Skinner v. Railway Labor Executives' Ass'n, 489 U.S. 602 (1989); Vernonia School Dist. 47J v. Acton, 515 U.S. 646 (1995); Ferguson v. City of Charleston, 532 U.S. 67 (2001); Kyllo v. United States, 533 U.S. 27 (2001); Maryland v. King, 569 U.S. 435 (2013); Birchfield v. North Dakota, 136 S. Ct. 2160 (2016). The Court has also ruled that three other types of surveillance are a "search" under the Jones "physical trespass" test: placing a GPS device on a car, United States v. Jones, 565 U.S. 400 (2012); bringing a drug-sniffing dog onto the porch, Florida v. Jardines 569 U.S. 1 (2013); and forcing a released felon to wear a GPS monitoring bracelet, Grady v. North Carolina, 135 S. Ct. 1368 (2015).

73 United States v. White, 401 U.S. 745 (1971); Coolidge v. New Hampshire, 403 U.S. 443 (1971); Cardwell v. Lewis, 417 U.S. 583 (1974); California Bankers Ass'n v. Shultz, 461 U.S. 21 (1974); Rakas v. Illinois, 439 U.S. 128 (1978); Smith v. Maryland, 442 U.S. 735 (1979); United States v. Knotts, 460 U.S. 276 (1983); Texas v. Brown, 460 U.S. 730 (1983); United States v. Place, 462 U.S. 696 (1983); Illinois v. Andreas, 463 U.S. 765 (1983); United States v. Jacobsen, 466 U.S. 109 (1984); Oliver v. United States, 466 U.S. 170 (1984); Hudson v. Palmer, 468 U.S. 517 (1984); Dow Chemical Co. v. United States, 476 U.S. 227 (1986); California v. Greenwood, 486 U.S. 35 (1988); Florida v. Riley, 488 U.S. 445 (1989); Minnesota v. Dickerson, 508 U.S. 366 (1993); Illinois v. Caballes, 543 U.S. 405 (2005).

74 The cases that hold these actions to be a "search" state that the action of the police officer to reveal the information – moving the stereo equipment or moving papers to reveal the VIN – are what make the action a "search." *See* New York v. Class, 475 U.S. 106 (1986); Arizona v. Hicks, 480 U.S. 321 (1987).

75 Minnesota v. Carter, 525 U.S. 83, 97 (1998).

76 565 U.S. 400 (2012).

77 *Id.* at 404–5.

78 *Id.* at 404–5. The Court justifies its adoption of the trespass doctrine primarily on the grounds that a physical intrusion "would have been considered a 'search' within the meaning of the Fourth Amendment when it was adopted." *Id.* (citations omitted).

79 *See id.* at 424–25 (Alito., J., concurring).

80 569 U.S. 1, 5–6 (2013).

81 135 S.Ct. 1368, 1369 (2015). The Court applied the trespass doctrine and held that the ankle monitor was a "search" under the Fourth Amendment, and then remanded for the lower court to determine whether the search was reasonable.

82 *See Jones*, 565 U.S. at 424–25 (Alito., J., concurring).("[T]he Court's reasoning largely disregards what is really important (the *use* of a GPS for the purpose of long-term tracking) and instead attaches great significance to something that most would view as relatively minor (attaching to the bottom of a car a small, light object that does not interfere in any way with the car's operation. Attaching such an object is generally regarded as so trivial that it does not provide a basis for recovery under modern tort law.")

83 Christopher Slobogin & Joseph E. Schumacher, *Reasonable Expectations of Privacy and Autonomy in Fourth Amendment Cases: An Empirical Look at "Understandings Recognized and Permitted by Society,"* 42 DUKE L.J. 727, 733–37 (1993).

84 For example, surgery received an average score of 74.7, searching a bedroom received an average score of 85.23, and monitoring a phone for thirty days received an average score of 85.86. The Supreme Court has ruled that all of these surveillance techniques are a "search." *Id.* at 739. In contrast, searches of public areas like parks and alleys resulted in very low averages (6.48 and 18.33 respectively), and the Court has ruled that surveillance of public places are not Fourth Amendment "searches." *Id.*

85 *See* United States v. Oliver, 466 U.S. 170 (1984) (holding that trespassing in open fields is not a search); Illinois v. Caballes (stating in dicta that dog sniffs are not a searcg); Terry v. Ohio, 392 U.S. 1 (1968) (holding that a pat down is a search). A search of a public field received a score of 56.58; a dog sniff received a score of 58.33, and a frisk received a score of 54.76. *See* Slobogin & Schumacher, *supra* note 83, at 740–41.

86 *See, e.g.,* Chistopher Slobogin, *Privacy at Risk,* 110–14, 183–86; Christopher Slobogin, *Government Data Mining and the Fourth Amendment,* 75 U NIVERSITY OF C HICAGO L AW R EVIEW 317 (2008).

87 *See* Slobogin & Schumacher, *supra* note 83, at 742–51.

88 *See* Christine S. Scott-Hayward, Henry F. Fradella, & Ryan G. Fischer, *Does Privacy Require Secrecy? Societal Expectations of Privacy in the Digital Age,* 43 A M . J. C RIM . L. 19. 42–56 (2015). *See also* Jeremy A. Blumenthal, Meera Adya, & Jacqueline Mogle, *The Multiple Dimensions of Privacy: Testing Lay "Expectations of Privacy,* 11 U. P A . J. C ONST . L. 331 (2009) (expanding on Slobogin & Schumaker's work).

89 *Id.* at 341 (summarizing the various Fourth Amendment privacy surveys and noting that "they seem to indicate a gap in the Court's assumptions about the way real people think and act in the real world." The authors note that there may not be a consensus about what is meant by "privacy," which muddles the results.) *Id.*

90 Matthew Kugler and Lior Jacob Stahilevitz argue that in determining what privacy expectations society is prepared to recognize as reasonable under the Katz test, courts should ask "whether people in general expect privacy in a given situation." Matthew Kugler and Lior Jacob Strahilevitz, *Actual Expectations of: Privacy, Fourth Amendment Doctrine, and Mosaic Theory,* 2015 S. C T . R EV . 205, 223 (2015). *But see* Jeffrey J. Rachlinski, *Evidence-Based Law,* 96 C ORNELL L. R EV . 901 (2011) (arguing in favor of more evidence-based law but acknowledging that the political nature of law complicates the attempts of applying empirical work to legal decisions).

91 *See* Santa Clara, Cal., Ordinance NS.300.897, § A40–7(D) (May 24, 2016), https://assets .documentcloud.org/documents/2854213/Attachment-149330.pdf (last visited Jan. 21, 2019); *see also* Andrew Selbst, *Disparate Impact in Big Data Policing,* 52 G A . L. R EV . 109, 185 (2017) (advocating the adoption of impact statements for new surveillance technology, including an estimate of the disparate impact of the new technology).

92 Michael Gentithes, *The End of Miller's Time: Adjusting the Third-Party Doctrine for Sensitive Information,* 52 G a . L. R ev . (forthcoming). Professor Gentithes only proposes using a sensitivity index for information that has been shared with third parties; he rejects using it as part of a "broader Fourth Amendment jurisprudence." *Id.*

93 Miriam H. Baer, *Pricing the Fourth Amendment,* 58 W ILLIAM AND M ARY L AW R EVIEW 1103, 1133–42 (2017).

94 *Id.* at 1139–42.

95 *Id.* at 1154–59.

96 *Id.* at 1163–65.

97 The Anticipated Surveillance Impact Reports from Santa Clara County require the agency to estimate both the impact on privacy and civil liberties and the fiscal costs of the new technology. *Id.*

98 There is another potential benefit of some kinds of surveillance: they can *deter* crime from happening in the first place. Certain types of surveillance – what we could call proactive surveillance – can prevent a potential crime entirely or halt a crime in progress. In contrast, reactive surveillance, even when successful, will serve only to apprehend or convict a criminal who has already committed a crime. Some types are primarily pro-active. For example, plainly visible video cameras in public parks or in private stores can deter potential criminals from committing the crime in the first place, because the

potential criminals realize their chances of apprehension and conviction are prohibitively high. *See* Steve Chapman, *Do Cameras Stop Crime? What Has Been Learned in Chicago*, CHICAGO TRIBUNE, Feb. 20, 2011, http://articles.chicagotribune.com/2011-02-20/news/ct-oped-0220-chapman-20110220_1_cameras-crime-justice-policy-center. Other types of surveillance are both proactive and reactive in that they both deter future crimes and gather evidence of current crimes. For example, wiretaps on telephones and street-level *Terry* stops are proactive surveillance techniques, which are more likely to identify potential criminals before they have committed a more severe crime. (They are still caught committing a lesser crime – conspiracy instead of murder, or possession of a firearm instead of armed robbery.) There are also purely reactive surveillance techniques which do not provide any significant deterrent value. Searches of a home after an arrest are likely to only find evidence of a crime that has already been committed – that is, the crime for which the suspect was originally arrested. For that matter, surveillance for most low-level drug crimes does nothing to prevent more serious crimes from occurring – the drugs have already been sold or possessed, and the successful surveillance after the crime has been committed can lead only to an arrest of the perpetrators after the crime has already occurred. (Of course, basic deterrence doctrine leads us to expect that any successful surveillance that leads to the conviction of a criminal will deter that criminal and others from committing the crime in the future, but that type of indirect crime prevention is true for every type of surveillance.) Proactive crime surveillance is a more direct method of deterring crime altogether or preventing a more serious crime from occurring. When I originally proposed this formula, I added on the expected deterrence value of surveillance as one of the benefits to take into account. *See* Ric Simmons, *Ending the Zero-Sum Game: How to Increase the Productivity of the Fourth Amendment*, 36 JOURNAL OF LAW & PUBLIC POLICY 549 (2013). However, I have removed it from this model for a number of reasons: first, courts have never accepted this as a legal justification for surveillance; second, although proactive surveillance provides an extra benefit, it frequently comes at such a high cost – the surveillance may affect larger numbers of innocent people (as with Terry stops) or the surveillance may be more intrusive (as with video surveillance – that it will never be able to justify a search; and third, it overcomplicates the analysis we are trying to conduct.

99 *See Raw Video: Phil Bonus Arrested on Suspicion of DUI*, ORLANDO TRIBUNE, Oct. 8, 2012, www.wesh.com/article/raw-video-phil-bonus-arrested-on-suspicion-of-dui/3776365 (last visited Jan. 21, 2019).

100 Professor Lerner adopts this method in his original formula. *See supra* note 10, 23–25 and accompanying text. Other scholars have argued that the "reasonableness" standard in the Fourth Amendment ought to take the severity of crime into account. *See supra* note 20 and accompanying text.

101 *See, e.g.*, Dunaway v. New York, 442 U.S. 200, 208 (1979).

102 *See, e.g.*, Craig S. Lerner, *The Reasonableness of Probable Cause*, 81 TEX. L. REV. 951, 1014–22 (2003); Joseph D. Grano, *Probable Cause and Common Sense: A Reply to the Critics of Illinois v. Gates*, 17 U. MICH. J.L. REFORM 465, 504–5 (1984); Albert W. Alschuler, *Bright Line Fever and the Fourth Amendment*, 45 U. PITT. L. REV. 227, 229–31 (1984).

103 Lerner, *supra* note 102, at 1015–17.

104 Llaguno v. Mingey, 763 F.2d 1560, 1566 (7th Cir. 1985) (en banc). Other Justices and judges have also hinted at the need for a sliding scale, though the hints are usually made in dissents. *See, e.g.,* Brinegar v. United States, 338 U.S. 160, 183 (1949) (Jackson, J., dissenting) (arguing that the societal interest in searching a car trunk for a kidnapped child was greater than the societal interest in searching a car trunk for bootlegged alcohol, and thus he would be tempted to make an "exception" to the Fourth Amendment in the former case); United States v. Soyka, 394 F.2d 443, 452 (2d Cir. 1968) (en banc) (Friendly, J., dissenting) ("[T]he gravity of the suspected crime and the utility of the police action [should be] factors bearing on the validity of the search or arrest decision.").

105 *See* Timothy C. MacDonnell, *Orwellian Ramifications: The Contraband Exception to the Fourth Amendment*, 41 U. MEM. L. REV. 299, 302 & n.15 (2010) (using the term "contraband exception," rather than "binary search," because a binary search may not involve contraband and therefore would be covered by the Fourth Amendment); Ric Simmons, *The Two Unanswered Questions of Illinois v. Caballes: How to Make the World Safe for Binary Searches*, 80 TUL. L. REV. 411, 424 (2005).

106 *See, e.g.,* Illinois v. Caballes, 543 U.S. 405, 409 (2005) (finding that conducting a drug sniff during a lawful traffic stop was not unreasonable search and seizure); United States v. Jacobsen, 466 U.S. 109, 123 (1984) (noting that "Congress has decided . . . to treat the interest in privately possessing cocaine as illegitimate"); United States v. Place, 462 U.S. 696, 707 (1983) (holding that subjecting luggage to a canine "sniff test" does not constitute a search under the Fourth Amendment).

107 *See* United States v. Jacobsen, 566 U.S. 109, 111–12, 117–18 (1984).

108 *Jacobsen*, 466 U.S. at 126.

109 *See* Bart Jansen, *TSA Defends Full-Body Scanners Are Airport Checkpoints*, USA TODAY, Mar. 2, 2016 at www.usatoday.com/story/news/2016/03/02/tsa-defends-full-body-scanners-airport-checkpoints/81203030/ (explaining that the average amount of time for a frisk at the airport was 80 seconds, though with extra waiting time for a same-sex officer, the average waiting time increased to 150 seconds).

110 *See* Slobogan and Schumacher, *supra* note 83, at 738.
Although our equation intentionally omits administrative costs, it is worth acknowledging that the administrative costs of frisks are relatively high. Although frisks do not require any special equipment, individual frisks take longer to conduct than walking through a metal detector; therefore, more officers are required to conduct the same amount of surveillance in the same amount of time.

111 *Id.*

112 The administrative cost of magnetometers is somewhat higher: the machines cost between $10,000 and $15,000 and require multiple personnel to operate. *Magnetometers, X-Rays, and More: Airport Security Technology*, FoxNews.com, Dec. 29, 2009, *available at* www.foxnews.com/tech/magnetometers-x-rays-and-more-airport-security-technology (last visited Jan. 21, 2019); Markham Heid, *You Asked: Are Airport Body Scanners Safe?*, TIME Health, Aug. 23, 2017, at http://time.com/4909615/airport-body-scanners-safe/ (last visited Jan. 19, 2019). However, magnetometer surveillance is faster than physical frisks, so more suspects can be processed in the same amount of time.

113 *See Shoe Bomb Suspect 'One of Many'*, BBC News, Dec. 26, 2001, http://news.bbc.co.uk/1/hi/uk/1729614.stm (last visited Jan. 21, 2019).

114 Today, there are many examples of more sophisticated surveillance methods. For example, law enforcement officers can swab the hand of every passenger and then test the swab for explosives to see if the suspect has handled explosives recently. *See Magnetometers, supra* note 112. Different methods (or combination of methods) will have its own distinct levels of administrative cost, privacy cost, and success rate, and thus its own unique level of productivity.

115 *See* Jansen, *supra* note 109. The full body scanners, which use a millimeter wave detection system, have been the standard form of surveillance at American airports since 2013. They replaced a different type of full-body scan, known as "backscatter" machines, that produced "near-naked" images of the subjects. The millimeter wave detectors were an improvement on the backscatter machines because they produced the same level of security but involved a lesser intrusion into privacy, since the image produced in the former did not reveal intimate parts of the subject's body. *Id.* These scanners are more expensive than magnetometers: they cost about $150,000, and the officers who staff them must have even more training, since they must be able to interpret the images to determine whether a weapon is present. *See* Heid, *supra* note 112.

116 *See* Slobogin, *Privacy at Risk*, at 112.

117 *See* Ric Simmons, *Searching for Terrorists: Why Public Safety is Not a Special Need*, 59 DUKE L.J. 843, 851–55 (2010).

CHAPTER 2

1 United States v. Broomfield, 417 F.3d 654, 655 (7th Cir.2005) (Posner, J.)

2 *See* Andrew Guthrie Ferguson, *Predictive Policing and Reasonable Suspicion*, 62 EMORY L.J. 259, 319–20 (2012). Unfortunately, as these algorithms become more accurate, they also become more complicated, and the databases they use become even larger and more detailed, making them less comprehensible to the average police officer or judge.

3 *See* Andrew Guthrie Ferguson, *Big Data and Predictive Reasonable Suspicion*, 163 U. PA. L. REV. 327, 352–53 (2015).

4 A famous Forbes story reported that Target had used big data from seemingly random purchasing to determine that a minor customer was pregnant and then sent the customer coupons for pregnancy and new baby items before the teenager had notified her parents that she was pregnant. *See* Kashmir Hill, *How Target Figured Out a Teen Girl Was Pregnant before Her Father Did*, FORBES (Feb. 16, 2012, 11:02 AM), www.forbes.com/sites/kashmirhill/2012/02/16/how-target-figured-out-a-teen-girl-was-pregnant-before-her-father-did/#3363735834c6 [https://perma.cc/BA2Q-8HK4].

5 *See* Brian Fung, *The Big Data of Bad Driving, and How Insurers Plan to Track Your Every Turn*, WASH. POST (Jan. 4, 2016), www.washingtonpost.com/news/the-switch/wp/2016/01/04/the-big-data-of-bad-driving-and-how-insurers-plan-to-track-your-every-turn/ (last visited Jan. 21, 2019).

6 *See* EVA WOLKOWITZ & SARAH PARKER, BIG DATA, BIG POTENTIAL: HARNESSING DATA TECHNOLOGY FOR THE UNDERSERVED MARKET 11 (2015), https://s3.amazonaws.com/cfsi-innovation-files/wp-content/uploads/2017/02/13062352/Big-Data-Big-Potential-Harnessing-Data-Technology-for-the-Underserved-Market.pdf (last visited Jan. 21, 2019).

7 *See* Meta S. Brown, *When and Where to Buy Consumer Data (and 12 Companies Who Sell It)*, FORBES (Sept. 30, 2015, 9:49 AM), www.forbes.com/sites/metabrown/2015/09/30/when-and-where-to-buy-consumer-data-and-12-companies-who-sell-it/#c8b7ed1711bc (last visited Jan. 21, 2019).

8 *See* Maurice Chammah, *Policing the Future*, VERGE (Feb. 3, 2016), www.theverge.com/2016/2/3/10895804/st-louis-police-hunchlab-predictive-policing-marshall-project (last visited Jan. 21, 2019).

9 *See* Justin Jouvenal, The new way police are surveilling you: Calculating your threat 'score', WASH. POST (Jan. 10, 2016), www.washingtonpost.com/local/public-safety/the-new-way-police-are-surveilling-you-calculating-your-threat-score/2016/01/10/e42bccac-8e15-11e5-baf4-bdf37355daoc_story.html?utm_term=.cfb3030b472e (last visited Jan. 21, 2019).

10 *See* Elizabeth E. Joh, *The New Surveillance Discretion: Automated Suspicion, Big Data, and Policing*, 10 HARV L. & PO'Y REV 15, 24 (2016).

11 *See* Matt Stroud, *The minority report: Chicago's new police computer predicts crimes, but is it racist?*, VERGE (Feb. 19, 2014, 9:31 AM), www.theverge.com/2014/2/19/5419854/the-minority-report-this-computer-predicts-crime-but-is-it-racist.

12 *See* Shaila Dewan, *Judges Replacing Conjecture with Formula for Bail*, N.Y. TIMES (June 26, 2015).

13 *See* Christopher Slobogin, *Risk Assessment*, in THE OXFORD HANDBOOK OF SENTENCING AND CORRECTIONS 196, 203–5 (Joan Petersilia & Kevin R. Reitz eds., 2012).

14 Recently, there have been signs that the Fourth Amendment may be expanded so that the gathering or processing of massive amounts of public data may be considered a search. Although government surveillance of public places, or of publicly available sources, does not implicate the Fourth Amendment, *see, e.g.*, United States v. Knotts, 460 U.S. 276, 281–82 (1983), the Supreme Court has hinted at the possibility that gathering and processing large amounts of information from public sources to learn information about a suspect could implicate the Fourth Amendment through the "mosaic" theory, United States v. Jones, 132 S. Ct. 945, 954–55 (2012) (Sotomayor, J., concurring), but that doctrine has not yet gained widespread acceptance in courts. For an overview and a critique of the mosaic theory, see Orin S. Kerr, *The Mosaic Theory of the Fourth Amendment*, 111 MICH. L. REV. 311 (2012).

15 William M. Grove, David H. Zald, Boyd S. Lebow, Beth E. Snitz, and Chad Nelson, *Clinical Versus Mechanical Prediction: A Meta-Analysis*, 12 *Psychological Assessment* 19 (200) at www.psych.umn.edu/faculty/grove/096clinicalversusmechanicalprediction.pdf.

16 *See infra* notes 18–23 and accompanying text.

17 There is likely to be enormous resistance to adopting a system that is outcome determinative in any of these contexts, though I will argue that such an option is preferable in certain contexts. *See infra* notes 80–117 and accompanying text.

18 For an excellent overview of the use of predictive algorithms by police officers, see Andrew Guthrie Ferguson, *Policing Predictive Policing*, 94 WASH U. L. REV. (forthcoming 2017).

19 *See* Sewell Chan, *Why Did Crime Fall in New York City?*, N.Y. TIMES CITY ROOM (Aug. 13, 2007, 2:10 PM), http://cityroom.blogs.nytimes.com/2007/08/13/why-did-crime-fall-in-new-york-city/?_r=2 (last visited Jan. 21, 2019).

20 In addition to New York, sophisticated crime-mapping software has been used in Los Angeles, St. Louis, Philadelphia, San Francisco, Washington, DC, Oakland, and many other cities.

See Stuart Wolpert, Predictive Policing Substantially Reduces Crime in Los Angeles During Months-Long Test, UCLA NEWSROOM (Oct. 7, 2015), http://newsroom.ucla.edu/releases/ predictive-policing-substantially-reduces-crime-in-los-angeles-during-months-long-test   (last visited Jan. 21, 2019); Maurice Chammah, Policing the Future, VERGE (Feb. 3, 2016), www.theverge.com/2016/2/3/10895804/st-louis-police-hunchlab-predictive-policing-marshall-project (last visited Jan. 21, 2019); Darwin Bond-Graham & Ali Winston, All Tomorrow's Crimes: The Future of Policing Looks a Lot Like Good Branding, SF WEEKLY (Oct. 30, 2013),   www.sfweekly.com/sanfrancisco/all-tomorrows-crimes-the-future-of-policing-looks-a-lot-like-good-branding/Content?oid=2827968 (last visited Jan. 21, 2019); Eugene K. Chow, Is Predictive Policing Making Minority Report a Reality?, WEEK (Oct. 7, 2013), http://theweek .com/articles/459396/predictive-policing-making-minority-report-reality (last visited Jan. 21, 2019); Darwin Bond-Graham, Oakland Mayor Schaaf and Police Seek Unproven 'Predictive Policing' Software, E. BAY EXPRESS (June 24, 2015), www.eastbayexpress.com/oakland/ oakland-mayor-schaaf-and-police-seek-unproven-predictive-policing-software/Content?oid= 4362343 (last visited Jan. 21, 2019).

21 *See* Chammah, *supra* note 20.

22 *Id*; *see* Cameron Albert-Deitch, *Predictive Policing Crime Prevention Software Successful for APD*, ATLANTA MAGAZINE (Nov. 10, 2014), www.atlantamagazine.com/news-culture-articles/predictive-policing-crime-prevention-software-successful-for-apd/   (last   visited Jan. 21, 2019). PredPol is now being used by more than fifty different police agencies in the United States and Britain. *See* Chammah, *supra* note 20.

23 *See* Chammah, *supra* note 20. Other jurisdictions have seen similar improvements in crime rates: Norcross, Georgia saw a 20 percent decrease in crime after adopting PredPol, which led the Atlanta police department to adopt it as well. *See* Albert-Deitch, *supra* note 22.

24 *See* Chammah, *supra* note 20.

25 *Id.*

26 *See* Justin Jouvenal, supra note 9.

27 *Id.*

28 *Id.*

29 *See* Stroud, supra note 11.

30 *Id.*; *see also* ROBERT L. MITCHELL, *Predictive Policing Gets Personal*, COMPUTER-WORLD (Oct. 24, 2013, 7:00 AM), www.computerworld.com/article/2486424/government-it/predictive-policing-gets-personal.html (last visited Jan. 21, 2019) (describing a similar program in North Carolina).

31 Stroud, *supra* note 11.

32 *Id.* Kansas City has been using a similar program, known as KC NoVA, which targets individuals "at risk" of committing violent crimes. The program warns these individuals that they are being watched and that "harsh penalties will be imposed for even petty slights once warnings have been given," but it also provides services such as housing and social services to help the individuals stay out of trouble. *See* John Eligon & Timothy Williams, *Police Program Aims to Pinpoint Those Most Likely to Commit Crimes*, N.Y. TIMES (Sept. 24, 2015), www.nytimes.com/2015/09/25/us/police-program-aims-to-pinpoint-those-most-likely-to-commit-crimes.html?_r=0 (last visited Jan. 21, 2019).

33 *See* SEE BERNARD E. HARCOURT, AGAINST PREDICTION 10 (2007).

34 *Id.*

35 *Id.* ch. 4.

36 *Id.* at 123.

37 Another example of law enforcement using big data to try to detect criminal activity is the National Security Agency's massive metadata collection program. *See* ACLU v. Clapper, 785 F.3d 787, 792, 816–17 (2d Cir. 2015).

38 *See* Ferguson, *supra* note 3, at 368–69.

39 *See, e.g.,* Illinois v. Wardlow, 528 U.S. 119, 124 (2000).

40 *See, e.g.,* State v. Carter, 697 N.W.2d 199, 205 (Minn. 2005).

41 A recent comprehensive report from the RAND Corporation surveyed every known use of predictive algorithms in law enforcement and showed no evidence of such algorithms being used to determine reasonable suspicion or probable cause. *See* WALTER L. PERRY ET AL., RAND CORP., PREDICTIVE POLICING: THE ROLE OF CRIME FORECASTING IN LAW ENFORCEMENT OPERATIONS 107–8 (2013).

42 For example, in the *Wardlow* case, the Court merely accepted the testimony of the officer that the stop occurred in an "area known for heavy narcotics trafficking." 528 U.S. at 119–23. In fact, the actual crime data from the Chicago district where the stop occurred showed that the district ranked just at the median for criminal activity of the twenty-five districts in the city. *See* Amici Curiae Brief of the National Ass'n of Police Organizations et al. in Support of Petitioner at 7, *Wardlow,* 528 U.S. 119 (No. 98–1036), 1999 WL 451226, at *7. For an excellent discussion of how crime mapping has been used (or ignored) by the Supreme Court, see Andrew Guthrie Ferguson, *Crime Mapping and the Fourth Amendment: Redrawing "High-Crime Areas,"* 63 HASTINGS L.J. 179 (2011).

43 Ferguson, *supra* note 42, at 221–22 ("If the officer did not base his decision on specific data about a specific crime problem in a specific area, or if the data relied upon did not demonstrate a specific and relevant crime problem, then reliance on this information should not be considered.").

44 *Id.* at 224–25. Professor Ferguson notes that using actual data about high-crime areas will probably be an improvement. ("While not perfect, a more data-driven approach is an improvement over the police 'war stories' that have essentially served as the basis of prior designations of high-crime areas. In fact, analysis of crime data has shown that subjective opinions about high-crime areas are often erroneous.").

45 Ferguson, *supra* note 42, at 223.

46 In fact, the best numbers to consider would not be based on arrest, but rather on actual criminal activity. Using arrest numbers as a proxy for criminal activity may lead to a number of inaccuracies.

For a good discussion on the difficulty of determining whether a neighborhood is a "high-crime area" in the absence of any evidence from big data, see United States v. Wright, 485 F.3d 45, 49–50 (1st Cir. 2007).

47 *See, e.g., Wardlow,* 528 U.S. at 122 ("[Officer Nolan] immediately conducted a protective patdown search for weapons because in his experience it was common for there to be weapons in the near vicinity of narcotics transactions.").

48 CAROLINE WOLF HARLOW, BUREAU OF JUSTICE STATISTICS, FIREARM USE BY OFFENDERS 3 (2001). The report also found that 2.9 percent of those who committed sexual assault carried a firearm, while 4 percent of those who committed burglary carried a

firearm. *Id.* Of course, the *Terry* standard asks courts to consider the likelihood that the suspect has a weapon, not merely a firearm, but this only emphasizes the need to apply more accurate statistics to the analysis.

49 *Wardlow*, 528 U.S. at 125; United States v. Dykes, 406 F.3d 717, 720 (D.C. Cir. 2005) (suspect was stopped in an area "known for the sales of cocaine and marijuana" and he fled upon seeing the officers exit their cars).

50 Tracey L. Meares & Bernard E. Harcourt, *Foreword: Transparent Adjudication and Social Science Research in Constitutional Criminal Procedure*, 90 J. CRIM. L. & CRIMINOLOGY 733, 792 (2000). Meares and Harcourt use statistics from a 1999 study in New York City which analyzed 175,000 *Terry* stops conducted by police over a one-year period.

51 The *Wardlow* dissent made this point when arguing that flight from the police was not a useful indicator of criminal activity. *See* Wardlow, 528 U.S. at 679–680 (Stevens, J., dissenting).

52 United States v. Sokolow, 490 U.S. 1, 13–14 (1989) (Marshall, J., dissenting). Illegal immigration profiles came under a similar attack in a dissent in United States v. Zapata-Ibarra, 223 F.3d 281, 281–82 (5th Cir. 2000) (Wiener, J., dissenting).

53 Samuel R. Gross & Katherine Y. Barnes, *Road Work: Racial Profiling and Drug Interdiction on the Highway*, 101 MICH. L. REV. 651, 740 (2002); *see also* Charles L. Becton, *The Drug Courier Profile: "All Seems Infected That Th' Infected Spy, As All Looks Yellow to the Jaundic'd Eye,"* 65 N.C. L. REV. 417 (1987); United States v. Broomfield, 417 F.3d 654, 655 (7th Cir. 2005) ("Whether you stand still or move, drive above, below, or at the speed limit, you will be described by the police as acting suspiciously should they wish to stop or arrest you. Such subjective, promiscuous appeals to an ineffable intuition should not be credited."); Utah v. Strieff, 136 S. Ct. 2056, 2069 (2016) (Sotomayor, J., dissenting) ("[An officer's] justification must provide specific reasons why the officer suspected you were breaking the law, but it may factor in your ethnicity, where you live, what you were wearing, and how you behaved. The officer does not even need to know which law you might have broken so long as he can later point to any possible infraction – even one that is minor, unrelated, or ambiguous." (citations omitted)).

54 959 F. Supp. 2d 540 (S.D.N.Y. 2013).

55 *Id.* at 559–60. In the data from New York City reviewed by the court, "furtive movements" was cited as a factor 42 percent of the time; "high crime area" 55 percent of the time, and "suspicious bulge" 10 percent of the time. *Id.* at 559. Sometimes the only factors cited by the officer were two of these three factors. *Id.*

56 *Id.* at 561. The officers in New York are hardly unique in their use of vague factors. In Philadelphia, police were engaging in overly aggressive *Terry* stops using factors such as "loitering" or "acting suspiciously"; after the police were sued over their tactics, they agreed in a consent decree to stop using these factors. *See* Plaintiffs' Fifth Report to Court and Monitor on Stop and Frisk Practices at 2–4, Bailey v. City of Philadelphia (E.D. Pa. 2013) (No. 10-5952).

57 *Floyd*, 959 F. Supp. 2d at 559.

58 In the *Sokolow* case itself, the Ninth Circuit held that there was no reasonable suspicion because the factors used by the agents were "vague and inchoate," "hazy in form, susceptible to great adaptations, and almost entirely speculative," and that "[t]he obvious lack of substantiation [of the government's conclusion] betrays its lack of merit." United

States v. Sokolow, 831 F.2d 1413, 1423–24 (9th Cir. 1987). But seven Supreme Court Justices looked at the same factors and concluded that probable cause did exist. United States v. Sokolow, 490 U.S. 1, 9 (1989).

59 *Floyd*, 959 F. Supp. 2d at 558.

60 *Id.*

61 *See, e.g.*, Terry v. Ohio, 392 U.S. 1, 28 (1968).

62 *See, e.g.*, United States v. $109,179 in U.S. Currency, 228 F.3d 1080, 1086–87 (9th Cir. 2000).

63 *See, e.g.*, United States v. Davis, 530 F.3d 1069, 1082–84 (9th Cir. 2008).

64 *See, e.g.*, People v. Shackelford, 546 P.2d 964, 966–67 (Colo. App. 1976).

65 *See, e.g.*, United States v. Mattarolo, 209 F.3d 1153, 1158 (9th Cir. 2000).

66 As it turns out, the court's assumptions about which crimes carry a high chance of weapons being present is sometimes correct and sometimes not. The Bureau of Justice study revealed that a person committing a robbery does have a high probability of carrying a weapon (34.5 percent), but that burglary (4 percent), sexual assault (2.9 percent) and narcotics trafficking (7.8 percent) do not. Harlow, *supra* note 48, at 3.

67 *Terry*, 392 U.S. at 28.

68 *Id.*

69 *See, e.g.*, United States v. Thomas, 863 F.2d 622, 629 (9th Cir. 1988).

70 *See, e.g.*, Ramirez v. City of Buena Park, 560 F.3d 1012, 1022 (9th Cir. 2009).

71 Thomas v. Dillard, 818 F.3d 864, 878 (9th Cir. 2016).

72 *Id.* at 880–81.

73 *Id.* at 898 (Bea, J., concurring in part and dissenting in part).

74 The regular inability of courts to effectively and accurately use statistics has led some commentators to argue against quantifying legal standards such as probable cause because judges are not generally skilled at mathematics and statistical analysis. *See, e.g.*, Max Minzner, *Putting Probability Back into Probable Cause*, 87 Tex. L. Rev. 913, 951 (2009); Kerr, *supra* note 135, at 132. However, courts already use statistical evidence to some extent in evaluating reliability of different tools used by law enforcement officers. *See infra* notes 75 and accompanying text. Courts also use statistical evidence in evaluating and applying expert testimony. *See* Daubert v. Merrell Dow Pharm., 509 U.S. 579, 597 (1993). Furthermore, since judges are "repeat players" in reviewing reasonable suspicion and probable cause determinations, they will develop an expertise with statistics in the probable cause context as the results of predictive algorithms become more widespread. *See* Minzner, *supra* note 74, at 954–55.

75 *Dillard*, 818 F.3d at 896–97 (Bea, J., concurring in part and dissenting in part) (citing Callie Marie Rennison, Bureau of Justice Statistics, Intimate Partner Violence and Age of Victim, 1993–99 7 (Oct. 2001), www.bjs.gov/content/pub/pdf/ipva99.pdf (last visited Jan. 21, 2019).

76 The Ninth Circuit acknowledged this in its opinion, noting that "domestic violence calls vary widely in the actual threats they pose to officers and others." *Dillard*, 818 F.3d at 881 (majority opinion).

77 Predictive algorithms are already being used by courts in other contexts, such as bail hearings and sentencing hearings. *See* Ric Simmons, *Quantifying Criminal Procedure*, 2016 Mich. St. L. Rev. 947, 965–68 (2016).

78 Bennett Capers, *Policing, Technology, and Doctrinal Assists*, 69 FLA. L. REV. 723, 755–59 (2017); *see also infra* note 129–30 and accompanying text.

79 Some scholars argue that many of the risk prediction factors currently in use in sentencing decisions may be unconstitutional because they rely directly or indirectly on race or other suspect classes. *See, e.g.,* Sonja B. Starr, *Evidence-Based Sentencing and the Scientific Rationalization of Discrimination*, 66 STAN. L. REV. 803, 819 (2014). *But see* Christopher Slobogin, *Risk Assessment and Risk Management in Juvenile Justice*, 27 CRIM. JUST. 10, 13–15 (2013) (use of gender and age in sentencing decisions is permissible because it survives intermediate scrutiny); J.C. Oleson, *Risk in Sentencing: Constitutionally Suspect Variables and Evidence-Based Sentencing*, 64 SMU L. REV. 1329, 1385–88 (2001) (sentencing factors survive a strict scrutiny analysis).

80 *See, e.g.,* Sarah Ludwig, *Credit Scores in America Perpetuate Racial Injustice. Here's How*, GUARDIAN (Oct. 13, 2015, 10:14 AM), www.theguardian.com/commentisfree/2015/oct/13/your-credit-score-is-racist-heres-why (last visited Jan. 21, 2019); 15 U.S.C. § 1691 (2012).

81 *See* Lee Price, *Racial Discrimination Continues to Play a Part in Hiring Decisions*, ECON. POL'Y INST. (Sept. 17, 2003), www.epi.org/publication/webfeatures_snapshots_archive_09172003/ (last visited Jan. 21, 2019); 42 U.S.C. § 2000e-2 (2012).

82 *See, e.g.,* United States v. Brignoni-Ponce, 422 U.S. 873, 886–87 (1975) ("[Mexican ancestry] alone ... does not justify stopping all Mexican-Americans to ask if they are aliens.").

83 *Id.* ("The likelihood that any given person of Mexican ancestry is an alien is high enough to make Mexican appearance a relevant factor ... ."); *see also* United States v. Martinez-Fuerte, 428 U.S. 543, 562–63 (1976).

84 United States v. Montero-Camargo, 208 F.3d 1122, 1135 (9th Cir. 2000).

85 *See, e.g.,* State v. Kuhn, 517 A.2d 162, 165 (N.J. Super. Ct. App. Div. 1986) ("No rational inference may be drawn from the race of [a person] that he may be engaged in criminal activities.").

86 It is harder to come up with an example in the bail context where the defendant's race was actually a relevant factor in determining flight risk or danger to the community. Certain factors that are correlated to race (such as income level or employment status) may be relevant, however.

87 As we will see, one of the objections to using mechanical predictions is that the underlying data may be tainted by preexisting biases in the criminal justice system that overstate the criminal activity of certain ethnic minorities.

88 *See, e.g.,* Whren v. United States, 517 U.S. 806, 813 (1996) ("[T]he constitutional basis for objecting to intentionally discriminatory application of laws is the Equal Protection Clause, not the Fourth Amendment."). *But see* Gross & Barnes, *supra* note 53, at 733–38 (surveying lower court decisions and concluding that "American judges are ambivalent and divided about the use of race as a basis for individualized suspicion under the Fourth Amendment. Lower court cases go both ways, but increasingly the tone is negative").

89 Adarand Constructors, Inc. v. Pena, 515 U.S. 200, 235 (1995).

90 *See, e.g.,* Lowery v. Commonwealth, 388 S.E.2d 265, 267 (Va. Ct. App. 1990).

91 *See, e.g.,* United States v. Taylor, 956 F.2d 572, 578–79 (6th Cir. 1992) (en banc); *see also* Tracey Maclin, *Race and the Fourth Amendment*, 51 VAND. L. REV. 333 (1998) (discussing the legality of racial profiling).

92 *See* Gross & Barnes, *supra* note 53, at 743 (citing settlement agreements with the Maryland State Police and various other Department of Justice racial profiling consent decrees).

93 481 U.S. 279, 291–92 (1987).

94 *Id.* at 293–99 & n.11.

95 *Id.*

96 *Id.* at 292–93.

97 *Id.* at 297.

98 *Id.* at 298 (quoting Pers. Adm'r of Mass. v. Feeney, 442 U.S. 256, 279 (1979)).

99 Batson v. Kentucky, 476 U.S. 79, 97–98 (1986).

100 *Id.* at 97.

101 *See, e.g.,* Conor Friedersdorf, *The NYPD Officers Who See Racial Bias in the NYPD,* Atlantic (Jan. 7, 2015), www.theatlantic.com/national/archive/2015/01/the-nypd-officers-who-see-racial-bias-in-the-nypd/384106/ (last visited Jan. 21, 2019).

102 The term "redlining" came from "residential security maps" that were used by the Federal Home Loan Bank Board ("FHLBB") in the 1930s to describe the quality of real estate investments in different parts of the city. Certain areas, known as "Type D" neighborhoods, were outlined in red on the map to indicate the riskiest areas for mortgages. *See* Kenneth T. Jackson, Crabgrass Frontier: The Suburbanization of the United States (1985).

103 *See* Bruce Schneier, Data and Goliath: The Hidden Battles to Collect Your Data and Control Your World 109 (2015).

104 The problem of indirect discrimination is related to a more sinister problem – that of intentional "masking." Masking occurs when a decision-maker truly wishes to discriminate but knows that doing so explicitly is forbidden. The decision-maker then intentionally chooses factors which are close statistical proxies for race and then uses them as factors. *See, e.g.,* Solon Barocas & Andrew D. Selbst, *Big Data's Disparate Impact,* 104 Cal. L. Rev. 671, 692–93 (2016). Masking can occur when a decision-maker uses traditional clinical judgments as well when she uses mechanical predictions but could be easier to achieve with big data methods. *Id.*

105 *See, e.g.,* Stroud, *supra* note 11; Julia Angwin et al., *Machine Bias,* ProPublica (May 23, 2016), www.propublica.org/article/machine-bias-risk-assessments-in-criminal-sentencing (last visited Jan. 21, 2019).

106 *See, e.g.,* Illinois v. Wardlow, 528 U.S. 119, 124 (2000).

107 *See* Elizabeth Kneebone & Steven Raphael, Metro. Policy Program at Brookings, City and Suburban Crime Trends in Metropolitan America 2–3 (May 2011), https://gspp.berkeley.edu/assets/uploads/research/pdf/p66.pdf (last visited Jan. 21, 2019).

108 Proxies for race are also used at other stages of the criminal justice system. At bail hearings, for example, magistrates will routinely consider the prior criminal history of the defendant in deciding whether the defendant is a flight risk or a danger to others. See DAVID N. ADAIR, JR., FED. JUDICIAL CTR., THE BAIL REFORM ACT OF 1984 6 (3d ed. 2006), www.fjc.gov/sites/default/files/2012/BailAct3.pdf (last visited Jan. 21, 2019). Criminal history is linked to race because certain ethnic groups have higher rates of conviction than others. See George Gao, Chart of the Week: The Black-White Gap in

Incarceration Rates, PEW RES. CTR. (July 18, 2014), www.pewresearch.org/fact-tank/ 2014/07/18/chart-of-the-week-the-black-white-gap-in-incarceration-rates/ (last visited Jan. 21, 2019).Other factors that magistrates use, such as employment or home ownership, are strongly correlated to poverty, which is correlated to race. Adair, supra, at 6.

109 Of course, these biases permeate the rest of the criminal justice system as well, as evidenced by the statistics cited in McCleskey v. Kemp, 481 U.S. 227, 293–99 (1987), and other studies showing biases in prosecutorial charging decisions, jury verdicts, and sentencing. *See, e.g.,* Robert J. Smith & Justin D. Levinson, *The Impact of Implicit Racial Bias on the Exercise of Prosecutorial Discretion,* 35 SEATTLE U. L. REV. 795, 805–22 (2012) (bias in charging decisions); Robert Barnes, *Supreme Court to Hear Case of Alleged Racial Bias by Juror,* WASH. POST (Apr. 4, 2016), www.washingtonpost.com/politics/courts_law/supreme-court-to-hear-case-of-alleged-racial-bias-by-juror/2016/04/04/c9256e9c-fa92-11e5-9140-e61d062438b b_story.html (last visited Jan. 21, 2019) (bias by jurors); Edward Helmore, *Racial Bias Evident in South Carolina Criminal Sentences, Study Reveals,* GUARDIAN (Feb. 29, 2016, 12:01 AM), www.theguardian.com/us-news/2016/feb/29/racial-bias-criminal-sentencing-south-carolina [https://perma.cc/2UFC-BLC2] (last visited Jan. 21, 2019).

110 John Cassidy, *The Statistical Debate behind the Stop-and-Frisk Verdict,* NEW YORKER (Aug. 13, 2013), www.newyorker.com/news/john-cassidy/the-statistical-debate-behind-the-stop-and-frisk-verdict (last visited Jan. 21, 2019).

111 *Floyd v. City of New York,* 959 F. Supp. 2d 540, 556, 573–75 (2013).

112 *Id.* at 574. This disproportionality cannot be explained by a higher rate of criminal activity by black citizens, since the "hit rate" for stopping black citizens was actually lower than that for white citizens – 1.0 percent of the frisks of black citizens resulted in a weapon, and 1.8 percent resulted in contraband, while 1.4 percent of the frisks of whites resulted in a weapon, and 2.3 percent resulted in contraband. *Id.*

113 *See* Plaintiffs' Third Report to Court and Monitor on Stop and Frisk Practices, Bailey v. City of Philadelphia (E.D. Pa. 2013) (No. 10-5952).

114 *See* IAN AYRES & JONATHAN BOROWSKY, A STUDY OF RACIALLY DISPARATE OUT-COMES IN THE LOS ANGELES POLICE DEPARTMENT (Oct. 2008), www.aclusocal.org/ sites/default/files/wp-content/uploads/2015/09/11837125-LAPD-Racial-Profiling-Report-ACLU.pdf (last visited Jan. 21, 2019). The report shows that black residents are three times as likely to the subject of a *Terry* stop as white residents, but that black residents are less likely to receive a citation after the stop, demonstrating that "African Americans are more often subject to stops without justification where no ticket could be issued." ACLU OF S. CAL., RACIAL PROFILING AND THE LAPD: A SUMMARY OF PROFESSOR IAN AYERS' REPORT ON RACIALLY DISPARATE OUTCOMES IN THE LOS ANGELES POLICE DEPARTMENT, www.aclusocal.org/sites/default/files/wp-content/uploads/2015/ 09/99227648-Racial-Profiling-the-LAPD.pdf (last visited Jan. 21, 2019).

115 *See* ACLU FOUND. OF MASS., BLACK, BROWN AND TARGETED: A REPORT ON BOSTON POLICE DEPARTMENT STREET ENCOUNTERS FROM 2007–2010 (Oct. 2014), www.aclum.org/sites/default/files/wp-content/uploads/2015/06/reports-black-brown-and-targeted.pdf (last visited Jan. 21, 2019).

116 *See* John Lamberth, *Driving While Black: A Statistician Proves That Prejudice Still Rules the Road, in* RACE, ETHNICITY, AND POLICING: NEW AND ESSENTIAL READINGS 32, 33 (Stephen K. Rice & Michael D. White eds., 2010).

117 *See, e.g.,* Jerry Kang, *Trojan Horses of Race*, 118 HARV. L. REV. 1489, 1491–528 (2005).

118 *See* Barocas & Selbst, *supra* note at 686.

119 This is, of course, not really a hypothetical case. Studies have shown, for example, that black citizens are nearly four times as likely to be arrested on charges of marijuana possession as white citizens, even though both blacks and whites use the drug at similar rates. In some states, black citizens were eight times as likely to be arrested. Ian Urbina, *Blacks Are Singled out for Marijuana Arrests, Federal Data Suggests*, N.Y. TIMES (June 3, 2013), http://nyti.ms/18KaQO5 (last visited Jan. 21, 2019). One of the reasons for this disparity is that "police departments, partly driven by a desire to increase their drug arrest statistics, can concentrate on minority or poorer neighborhoods to meet numerical goals." *Id.*

120 *See, e.g.,* Suzanne Macartney, Alemayehu Bishaw, and Kayla Fontenot, Poverty Rates for Selected Detailed Race and Hispanic Groups by State and Place: 2007–2011; American Community Survey Briefs, United States Census Bureau (Feb. 2013) (showing black and Latino poverty rates at twice those for white Americans).

121 *Id.* at 10–12; *see also* RAM SUBRAMANIAN ET AL., VERA INST. JUSTICE, INCARCER-ATION'S FRONT DOOR: THE MISUSE OF JAILS IN AMERICA 15 (Feb. 2015), www .safetyandjusticechallenge.org/wp-content/uploads/2015/01/incarcerations-front-door-report .pdf (last visited Jan. 21, 2019).

122 SENTENCING PROJECT, REPORT OF THE SENTENCING PROJECT TO THE UNITED NATIONS HUMAN RIGHTS COMMITTEE: REGARDING RACIAL DISPARITIES IN THE UNITED STATES CRIMINAL JUSTICE SYSTEM 10–12 (AUG. 2013), https://sentencingpro ject.org/wp-content/uploads/2015/12/Race-and-Justice-Shadow-Report-ICCPR.pdf (last visited Jan. 21, 2019).

123 *See* Jane Bambauer, *Hassle*, 113 MICH. L. REV. 461, 464–65 (2015) (arguing that the "hassle rate" – the rate at which individuals are stopped by the police – is at least as important as the "hit rate" – the rate at which these encounters uncover criminal activity – because a low hassle rate will ensure that the police have particularized suspicion when they conduct their stops).

124 *See generally* Wayne A. Logan & Andrew Guthrie Ferguson, *Policing Criminal Justice Data*, 101 MINN. L. REV. 541 (2016).

125 *See* HARCOURT, *supra* note 33 at 145–71.

126 *Id.* at 112.

127 *See* Stroud, *supra* note 11 (discussing Chicago's "heat list" and noting that "[f]rom what the CPD is willing to share, most of the collected information for the heat list is focused on rap sheets – arrest and conviction records. So rather than collecting information on everyone, they're collecting and using information on people who have had interactions with the police").

128 *See* Bambauer, *supra* note 123, at 473–74.

129 *See* Barocas & Selbst, *supra* note 104, at 686 ("Data gathered for routine business purposes tend to lack the rigor of social scientific data collection.").

130 *See id.* at 674.

131 *Id.* at 727.

132 *See Data Collection: National Crime Victimization Survey*, BUREAU JUST. STAT., www .bjs.gov/index.cfm?ty=dcdetail&iid=245 (last visited Jan. 21, 2019).

133 *See, e.g., Uniform Crime Reporting,* FBI, www.fbi.gov/about-us/cjis/ucr/ucr#cius (last visited Jan. 21, 2019).

134 *See, e.g.,* Ybarra v. Illinois, 444 U.S. 85, 91 (1979); Maryland v. Pringle, 540 U.S. 366, 371 (2003); United States v. Cortez, 449 U.S. 411, 418 (1981). The only exception involves special needs searches, when police officers are (at least in theory) acting for a purpose other than crime control and are therefore permitted to conduct reasonable searches on defined groups of people (such as airline travelers, drivers, or students) in order to further that purpose. *See, e.g.,* Mich. Dep't of State Police v. Sitz, 496 U.S. 444, 449–50 (1990).

135 For a detailed discussion of the individualization requirement, see Bambauer, *supra* note 123, at 490–94. Bambauer begins with a variation on this hypothetical, in which the police obtain results of a study that shows that 60 percent of all Harvard dorm rooms contain illegal drugs. *Id.* at 462. This is adopted from a hypothetical proposed by Professor Orin Kerr. *See* Orin Kerr, *Why Courts Should Not Quantify Probable Cause,* in *The Political Heart of Criminal Procedure* 135–37 (Michael Klarman, David Skeel & Carol Steiker eds., 2012).

136 *See* Arnold H. Loewy, *Rethinking Search and Seizure in a Post-9/11 World,* 80 Miss. L.J. 1507, 1518 (2011) (arguing that "demographic probabilities" are insufficient to create probable cause or reasonable suspicion; the police must also notice something "specific to the defendant to create the probability as to him").

137 *See, e.g.,* Barbara J. Underwood, *Law and the Crystal Ball: Predicting Behavior with Statistical Inference and Individualized Judgment,* 88 Yale L. Journal 1408, 1425–29 (1979); Michael L. Rich, *Machine Learning, Automated Suspicion Algorithms, and the Fourth Amendment,* 164 U. Pa. L. Rev. 871, 896–901 (2016). In fact, many of the objections to using statistical information in the criminal investigation process focus only on the requirement for individualized suspicion. *See* Erica Goldberg, *Getting Beyond Intuition in the Probable Cause Inquiry,* 17 Lewis & Clark L. Rev. 789, 806–7 (2013).

138 *See, e.g.,* Harcourt, *supra* note 33 at 173–92.

139 *See* Bambauer, *supra* note 123, at 469. Professor Bambauer examines (and rejects) four different conceptions of individualized suspicion: the need for case-by-case assessment, the need to engage in human intuition, the need to focus on conduct under the control of the suspect, and tracing suspicion from a crime to a suspect instead of from an individual to a crime. *Id.* at 469–82. She then proposes her own definition of individualization, which focuses on the "hassle rate" – that is, the proportion of the innocent population who are searched. *Id.* at 482–94. Using big data algorithms to determine reasonable suspicion or probable cause is not compatible with all of these definitions – for example, it downplays or eliminates the use of human intuition and will frequently start with an analysis of a suspect rather than with a crime. But these algorithms will be particularly useful if one adopts Professor Bambauer's concept of hassle rates, since they focus on specific hit rates and miss rates that can easily be quantified and included in a crime prediction algorithm.

140 That is, it would be inappropriate to do so outside the context of a special needs search. *See supra* note 134.

141 *See* Terry v. Ohio, 392 U.S. 1, 30 (1968).

142 *See* Ferguson, *supra* note 3, at 388. Big Data Professor Ferguson further argues that there needs to be a link between the suspect's suspicious background information and his

current actions: "Courts analyzing big data suspicion should thus be careful to require a direct link between the past data about a suspect and the observed suspicion." *Id.* Otherwise, Professor Ferguson argues that the background information is irrelevant to the reasonable suspicion analysis. *Id.* It is not clear how "direct" the link would have to be; however, many different types of criminal activity may be linked together in an officer's mind (such as prior convictions of illegal weapons possession combined with a current observation indicating possible drug dealing). *Id.* The linkage could be even more indirect – and yet statistically significant – when big data is used. For example, assume that a statistical analysis of thousands of burglars shows that individuals who have prior convictions for child abuse are 35 percent more likely to commit burglary than those without such a conviction. Even though there is no logical link between the two crimes, this fact could be considered as one factor (among many others) by an algorithm determining whether probable cause exists to believe a specific suspect is guilty of burglary.

143 444 U.S. 85, 87–89 (1979).

144 *Id.* at 94; *see also* United States v. Cortez, 449 U.S. 411, 418 (1981) ("[T]he process . . . must raise a suspicion that the particular individual being stopped is engaged in wrongdoing.").

145 *See* Ferguson, *supra* note 3, at 387–88.

146 If the software does not consider individualized suspicion, then police and judges must use it only as a factor in their analysis. *See infra* notes 176–82.

147 *See supra* notes 123–25 and accompanying text.

148 *See* Logan & Ferguson, *supra* note 124, at 13–14.

149 *See supra* notes 134–44 and accompanying text.

150 Jouvenal, *supra* note 9.

151 George Hostetter, *In Wake of Paris, Fresno P.D. Rolls out Big Data to Fight Crime*, CVObserver (Nov. 16, 2015), www.cvobserver.com/crime/in-wake-of-paris-fresno-p-d-rolls-out-big-data-to-fight-crime/4/ (last visited Jan. 21, 2019. For example, the police were asked at a city council meeting whether a misdemeanor conviction alone would be enough for the program to conclude that the suspect was "red," the highest level of danger. *Id.*

152 Matt Cagle, *This Surveillance Software Is Probably Spying on #BlackLivesMatter*, ACLU S. Cal. (Dec. 15, 2015), www.aclunc.org/blog/surveillance-software-probably-spying-blackli vesmatter (last visited Jan. 21, 2019). The result of the public records request was eighty-eight pages of emails that included lists of "high-frequency social media terms" that could be indicative of criminal activity. *Id.* (follow "88 pages of documents" hyperlink; then see E-mail from Media Sonar to Angeline MacIvor (Jan. 27, 2015, 10:43 AM), www.aclunc.org/docs/201512-social_media_monitoring_softare_pra_response.pdf (last visited Jan. 21, 2019).

153 Stroud, *supra* note 11. In fact, the Chicago Police Department refused to even reveal the names of the people on their "heat list," because they argue such disclosure could endanger the safety of law enforcement officers or the general population. *Id.* They have revealed some of the factors that they use, such as criminal records, social circles, gang connections, and whether the suspect has been a victim of an assault or a shooting. *See* Eligon & Williams, *supra* note 32. Unfortunately, a partial release of certain factors does little to address the transparency concerns discussed in this Article.

154 *See* Alexis C. Madrigal, *The Future of Crime-Fighting or the Future of Racial Profiling?: Inside the Effects of Predictive Policing*, Huffington Post (Mar. 28, 2016, 7:54 AM),

www.huffingtonpost.com/entry/predictive-policing-video_us_56f898c9e4b0a372181a42ef (last visited Jan. 21, 2019).

155 Cagle, *supra* note 152 (follow "88 pages of documents" hyperlink; then see e-mail from Media Sonar to Angeline MacIvor (Jan. 27, 2015, 10:43 AM), www.aclunc.org/docs/201512-social_media_monitoring_softare_pra_response.pdf (last visited Jan. 21, 2019).

156 Machine learning is defined as the following process: "A computer program is said to learn from experience E with respect to some class of tasks T and performance measure P, if its performance at tasks in T, as measured by P, improves with experience E." TOM M. MITCHELL, MACHINE LEARNING 2 (1997).

157 *See* RICHARD BERK, CRIMINAL JUSTICE FORECASTS OF RISK: A MACHINE LEARNING APPROACH 110–11 (2012).

158 *Id.* at 111.

159 *See* Rich, *supra* note 137, at 886 ("Absent an intentional decision to the contrary, machine learning tends to create models that are so complex that they become 'black boxes,' where even the original programmers of the algorithm have little idea exactly how or why the generated model creates accurate predictions. On the other hand, when an algorithm is interpretable, an outside observer can understand what factors the algorithm relies on to make its predictions and how much weight it gives to each factor. Interpretability comes at a cost, however, as an interpretable model is necessarily simpler – and thus often less accurate – than a black box model.").

160 Some would argue that the judge would also need to know the weights that the algorithm assigned to each factor, so that the judge would be better able to accurately add in other factors if she was using a "formal factor" model. If so, the program could be designed to provide explicit percentages for each factor every time it produces a result.

161 *See supra* notes 77–78 and accompanying text.

162 Daubert v. Merrell Dow Pharm., 509 U.S. 579, 597 (1993).

163 *See supra* notes 109–10 and accompanying text.

164 *See* Sendhil Mullainathan, *Racial Bias, Even When We Have Good Intentions*, N.Y. TIMES (Jan. 3, 2015), www.nytimes.com/2015/01/04/upshot/the-measuring-sticks-of-racial-bias-.html?abt=0002&abg=1 (last visited Jan. 21, 2019).

165 Ferguson, *supra* note 3, at 377.

166 *Id.* at 378.

167 *See id.* Of course, once predictive algorithms become more sophisticated, we will have a better idea about how high this percentage could be based on only background information. However, because of the particularized suspicion requirement, even if background information alone took us to the required threshold, reasonable suspicion would still not exist.

168 The actual Detective McFadden used these observations alone to arrive at reasonable suspicion. Terry v. Ohio, 392 U.S. 1, 6 (1968).

169 This is the method suggested by Professor Ferguson, who notes that a modern-day Detective McFadden can add the personal observations to the information he gathered from the various police databases to make his finding of reasonable suspicion "easier and, likely, more reliable." Ferguson, *supra* note 3, at 377–78. *Infra* notes 177–80 and accompanying text, this will require Detective McFadden to engage in a Bayesian

analysis, using 5 percent as a prior probability and then adding in his observations to adjust that probability upwards.

170 Reasonable suspicion requires "specific and articulable facts." *Terry*, 392 U.S. at 21. Probable cause requires "facts and circumstances within their [the arresting officers'] knowledge." Draper v. United States, 358 U.S. 307, 313 (1959) (quoting Carroll v. United States, 267 U.S. 132, 162 (1925)).

171 *See* Goldberg, *supra* note 137, at 800.

172 *See supra* notes 55–56 and accompanying text.

173 *See* Ferguson, *supra* note 3, at 392.

174 *Id.* at 406.

175 *See* Goldberg, *supra* note 137, at 833.

176 For an example of Bayes's theorem being applied in a legal context, see Jonathan J. Koehler & Daniel N. Shaviro, *Veridical Verdicts: Increasing Verdict Accuracy through the Use of Overtly Probabilistic Evidence and Methods*, 75 CORNELL L. REV. 247, 255–56 (1990).

177 Bayes' theorem can be expressed mathematically as: $P = xy/[xy + z(1-x)]$. *Id.* P is the number we are trying to calculate, known as the "posterior probability" – that is, the updated probability that a certain fact is true; in this case, it is the odds that criminal activity is occurring or that contraband will be found if the search is conducted. X is the "prior probability" – the probability that a certain fact is true before the extra information is added; in this case, the odds of criminal activity or contraband that are calculated by the predictive algorithm based on all the factors that it takes into consideration. Y is the probability that if the fact is true, then the extra information will be present; in this case, the odds that the independent pieces of information not considered by the algorithm exist because the defendant is engaged in criminal activity or contraband is present. And z is the probability that the fact is not true given the extra information; in this case, the chance that given that all the independent pieces of information are true, there is no criminal activity or contraband (i.e., there is a perfectly innocent explanation for all the independent pieces of information). Obviously, the decision-maker will have to estimate y and z, but this is not too different from what police officers and judges already do – only in this case they will have a much more accurate base rate to start from.

178 *See supra* note 165 and accompanying text; Ferguson, *supra* note 3, at 377–79.

179 Some robbers might simply barge in without investigating the location first, but most robbers would want to take a good look at the location, looking to see how many people are present, where the cash register or other valuables are kept, and (in the modern age) whether there are any security cameras inside. *See* Ferguson, *supra* note 3, at 378.

180 Applying Bayes' theorem: $P = .05^*.9/[.05^*.9 + .1^*(1-.05)] = .321$.

181 Again, applying Bayes' theorem: $P = .01^*.9/[.01^*.9 + .1^*(1-.01)] = .043$.

182 Koehler & Shaviro, *supra* note 176, at 256.

CHAPTER 3

1 United States v. Cortez, 449 U.S. 411, 418 (1981).

2 Here is an example of where Bayesian analysis would be useful – courts would start with a 15 percent baseline and then add in other factors to increase or decrease the likelihood. *See* the discussion in Chapter 2 for more details.

3 Terry v. Ohio, 392 US. 1, 17 (1968).

4 Wilson v. Arkansas, 514 U.S. 927, 934 (1995).

5 Winston v. Lee, 470 U.S. 753, 759 (1985).

6 18 U.S.C. § 3122(b)(2) (2006). This is a provision of the Electronic Communications Privacy Act ("ECPA").

7 18 U.S.C. §§ 2701–2712 (2006). This is a provision of the Stored Communications Act ("SCA").

8 18 U.S.C. § 2518. Title III orders require not just probable cause but also proof that there were no less intrusive means of obtaining the information and proof that minimization procedures are use during the monitoring.

9 Professor Slobogin's proportionality analysis strikes a similar balance, though it focuses almost solely on the privacy intrusion of the surveillance. As he puts it: "[t]he innocent person who is arrested or the target of bedroom surveillance will expect a 'damn good reason' for the inconvenience and intrusion. The innocent person who is stopped on the street for brief investigation or tracked by a public camera s likely to be satisfied with a less extensive explanation for the government attention." CHRISTOPHER SLOBOGIN, PRIV-ACY AT RISK: THE NEW GOVERNMENT SURVEILLANCE AND THE FOURTH AMEND-MENT, 39 (2007).

10 There were certainly scattered examples of statistical prediction instruments before the big data era. Statistical prediction methods were developed as early as 1935 to determine the likelihood of a prisoner's success if paroled; by the late twentieth century similar statistical prediction instruments were being used by dozens of states. *Id.* at 1, 7–9. Likewise, in the 1970s and 1980s federal Drug Enforcement Administration officers used "drug courier profiles" to determine which passengers at airports to investigate. *Id.* at 15–16. But the rise of big data, with its vast amounts of information and vastly powerful methods of processing that data, brings the promise (or the threat) of a true revolution in the sophistication and the proliferation of these tools.

11 The Supreme Court has explained that "probable cause is a fluid concept – turning on the assessment of probabilities in particular factual contexts – not readily, or even usefully, reduced to a neat set of legal rules." Illinois v. Gates, 462 U.S. 213, 232 (1983).

12 For example, a magistrate might reasonably conclude that a defendant who does not have a steady job seems less likely to come back to court on her own; furthermore, last month the magistrate remembers releasing a defendant who did not have a steady job and sure enough, she did not appear for her court date.

13 Some of these requirements are found in the statutory standard for real-time interception of telephone or electronic transmissions. *See* 18 U.S.C. § 2518 (2006).

14 If the surveillance is not a "search" under the Fourth Amendment and is not covered by any statutory restrictions, the government is free to conduct the surveillance with no showing of individualized suspicion. *See, e.g.*, United States v. Place, 463 U.S. 696 (1983).

15 This is the standard under the ECPA for gathering "non-content information" (such as address information) from real-time surveillance. *See* 18 U.S.C. § 3122(b) (2006).

16 This is the standard for a *Terry* stop. Terry v. Ohio, 392 U.S. 1, 30 (1968).

17 In some contexts, police still must show probable cause, but they are allowed to conduct the search without first getting a warrant – for example, searches of automobiles. Chambers v. Maroney, 399 U.S. 42, 48 (1970).

18 Kyllo v. United States, 533 U.S. 27, 40 (2001).

19 *See, e.g.*, Illinois v. Gates, 462 U.S. 213, 232 (1983) (describing probable cause as a "fluid concept ... not readily, or even usefully, reduced to a neat set of legal rules").

20 *See, e.g.*, United States v. Sokolow, 490 U.S. 1, 7–8 (1989) ("We think the Court of Appeals' effort to refine and elaborate the requirements of 'reasonable suspicion' in this case creates unnecessary difficulty in dealing with one of the relatively simple concepts embodied in the Fourth Amendment. In evaluating the validity of a stop such as this, we must consider 'the totality of the circumstances – the whole picture.'" (quoting *Cortez*, 449 U.S. at 417)); *Gates*, 462 U.S. at 232 (describing probable cause as a "fluid concept").

21 Maryland v. Pringle, 540 U.S. 366, 370–71 (2003).

22 *Sokolow*, 490 U.S. at 7.

23 *Gates*, 462 U.S. at 238.

24 Carroll v. United States, 267 U.S. 132, 161 (1925). In another case, the Court noted that probable cause "deal[s] with probabilities. These are not technical; they are the factual and practical considerations of everyday life on which reasonable and prudent men, not legal technicians, act." Brinegar v. United *States*, 338 U.S. 160, 175 (1949).

25 *Sokolow*, 490 U.S. at 7.

26 INS v. Delgado, 466 U.S. 210, 217 (1984).

27 *Sokolow*, 490 U.S. at 8.

28 Rita James Simon, *Judges' Translations of Burdens of Proof into Statements of Probability*, *in* The Trial Lawyer's Guide 113 (John J. Kennelly, James P. Chapman & William J. Harte eds., 1969).

29 *Id.*

30 *See* David Leonhardt, *What I Was Wrong about This Year*, N.Y. Times, Dec. 24, 2017 at www .nytimes.com/2017/12/24/opinion/2017-wrong-numbers.html?_r=0 (last visited Jan. 21, 2019).

31 *See* Orin Kerr, *Why Courts Should Not Quantify Probable Cause*, *in* The Political Heart of Criminal Procedure 132 (Michael Klarman, David Skeel & Carol Steiker eds., 2012).

32 *Id.* at 133–34.

33 *Id.*

34 *Id.* at 137–39.

35 *Id.* at 135–37.

36 *Id.* at 138–39.

37 Professor Kerr's objection to quantification also focuses on the inability of judges to use specific numerical probabilities in their decision-making process and the cognitive biases that would prevent them from using probability numbers appropriately. For example, Professor Kerr discusses the representative heuristic and anchoring effects, both of which tend to make individuals misjudge numerical probabilities, sometimes quite dramatically. This argument has broader implications for adopting big data's mechanical predictions, which will be discussed in *infra*, notes 67–76 and accompanying text.

38 *See* Illinois v. Gates, 462 U.S. 213, 230–31 (1983).

39 *See* Michael L. Rich, *Machine Learning, Automated Suspicion Algorithms, and the Fourth Amendment*, 164 U. Pa. L. Rev. 871, 897–98 (2016).

40 *Id.* at 897.

41 *Id.* Professor Rich gives an example of a predictive algorithm that considers location, time of day, facial recognition technology, prior criminal activity and other background information, and then adds in the specific behavior that a certain suspect is approaching multiple people on the street and briefly engaging in a hand-to-hand transaction with each of them. *Id.* at 898. The algorithm predicts a strong possibility of drug dealing. *Id.* A police officer who investigates notices that (1) the suspect does not change his behavior when he sees the police officer; and (2) a person who just engaged in a hand-to-hand transaction with the subject drops a church flyer on the ground immediately after the encounter. *Id.* The predictive algorithm did not account for these extra observations, which almost certainly obliterate the probable cause conclusion, but any human being would be able to process this new data appropriately. *Id.*

42 *See* Ahlers v. Schebil, 188 F.3d 365, 371 (6th Cir. 1999).

43 *See, e.g.,* Aguilar v. Texas, 378 U.S. 106, 114 (1964).

44 Illinois v. Gates, 462 U.S. 213, 230–33, 238–39 (1983). The Supreme Court noted that a magistrate's job in reviewing a warrant application was "simply to make a practical, commonsense decision whether, given all the circumstances set forth in the affidavit before him, including the 'veracity' and 'basis of knowledge' of persons supplying hearsay information, there is a fair probability that contraband or evidence of a crime will be found in a particular place." *Id.* at 238.

45 *See* Rich, *supra* note 39, at 895–901.

46 *See id.* at 897–900; L. Song Richardson, *Police Efficiency and the Fourth Amendment*, 87 IND. L.J. 1143 (2012).

47 *See, e.g.,* Gardenhire v. Schubert, 205 F.3d 303, 318 (6th Cir. 2000).

48 *See* notes 19–26 and accompanying text.

49 *See, e.g.,* Barry Jeffrey Stern, *Warrants without Probable Cause*, 59 BROOK. L. REV. 1385, 1436–37 n.172 (1994) (noting that the Supreme Court "has not defined [the probable cause] standard in a manner that is particularly illuminating to those charged with enforcing and interpreting the criminal law"); Erica Goldberg, *Getting beyond Intuition in the Probable Cause Inquiry*, 17 LEWIS & CLARK L. REV. 789, 833 (2013) (noting that even in the absence of quantitative evidence, "assigning a numerical value to probable cause can still assist judges in making probable cause determinations, so long as they appreciate that this number serves only as a reference").

50 Mich. Dep't of State Police v. Sitz, 496 U.S. 444, 454–55 (1990).

51 *Id.* at 455.

52 *See supra* note 60 and accompanying text (referencing Florida v. Harris, 133 S. Ct. 1050, 1057–58 (2013)); *see also* Goldberg, *supra* note 49, at 828.

53 *See* Plaintiffs' Fifth Report to Court and Monitor on Stop and Frisk Practices at 3–4, Bailey v. City of Philadelphia (E.D. Pa. 2013) (No. 10-5952). The police conceded that the rate of stops without documented reasonable suspicion was around 35 percent but argued that this high number was due to "incomplete paperwork, improper narratives used by police officers, and an overall lack of credibility in the electronic data base." *Id.* at 4.

54 Floyd v. City of New York, 959 F. Supp. 2d 540, 558–59 (S.D.N.Y. 2013). The *Terry* case also gives police the right to search the suspect only if the police officer has "reason to believe" the suspect was armed. "Reason to believe" is often thought to be similar to the

"reasonable suspicion" standard. In the *Floyd* litigation, police recovered weapons only 1.5 percent of the time; thus, 1.5 percent is not sufficient under a "reason to believe" standard.

55 Jeffrey Goldberg, *The Color of Suspicion*, N.Y. TIMES (June 20, 1999), www.nytimes .com/1999/06/20/magazine/the-color-of-suspicion.html?pagewanted=all   (last   visited Jan. 21, 2019).

56 *See* JOHN C. LAMBERTH, RACIAL PROFILING DATA ANALYSIS STUDY: FINAL REPORT FOR THE SAN ANTONIO POLICE DEPARTMENT 48 tbl.8 (Dec. 2003).

57 *See* Samuel R. Gross & Katherine Y. Barnes, *Road Work: Racial Profiling and Drug Interdiction on the Highway*, 101 MICH. L. REV. 651, 658 (2002).

58 *Id.* at 674 tbl.9.

59 *See* Max Minzner, *Putting Probability Back into Probable Cause*, 87 TEX. L. REV. 913, 925 (2009).

60 Florida v. Harris, 133 S. Ct. 1050, 1057 (2013). Of course, the Harris Court repeated the admonition that the probable cause inquiry in the drug dog context should be a totality of the circumstances test, including not just the drug dog's reliability but also whether the handler gave inappropriate cues or whether the dog was working under unfamiliar conditions. *Id.* at 1057–58. Later in the chapter, we discuss the method for courts to combine the specific quantified numbers from tools (such as drug dogs or predictive algorithms) with other factors.

61 *Harris*, 133 S. Ct. at 1057–58.

62 United States v. Donnelly, 475 F.3d 946, 955 (8th Cir. 2007).

63 United States v. Anderson, 367 F. App'x 30, 33 (11th Cir. 2010).

64 United States v. Ludwig, 641 F.3d 1243, 1252 (10th Cir. 2011).

65 United States v. Koon Chung Wu, 217 F. App'x 240, 246 (4th Cir. 2007).

66 *See also* United States v. Sanchez-Tamayo, No. 1:10-CR-0532-JOF-JFK, 2011 WL 7767740, at *14 (N.D. Ga. Nov. 28, 2011) (noting that courts have approved a drug dog reliability rate of "approximately 50%–60%" as sufficient to establish probable cause). *But see* United States v. Huerta, 247 F. Supp. 2d 902, 910 (S.D. Ohio 2002) (rejecting probable cause finding even though the drug dog had a 65 percent success rate).

67 Minzner, *supra* note 59, at 922–23. These rates may be inflated somewhat because some of the jurisdictions that were studied involved police officers who did not return their warrants after the search, presumably because nothing was received. *Id.* at 923 n.38. Even taking into account this possibility, warrant success rates still ranged between 46 percent and 93 percent. *Id.* This higher number does not necessarily mean that courts are setting a higher bar for probable cause in warrant applications; it could be that probable cause is always set at, say, 40 percent for any kind of search, and that most warrant applications achieve a much higher level of success because law enforcement officers want to ensure they get approved when they take the time and expend the resources to apply for a warrant. *Id.* at 922.

68 C.M.A. McCauliff, *Burdens of Proof: Degrees of Belief, Quanta of Evidence, or Constitutional Guarantees?*, 35 VAND. L. REV. 1293, 1327 (1982).

69 Many judges did not return the survey; some responded in letter form without giving a numerical answer; some responded by criticizing the project, saying that it was inappropriate to attempt to quantify these concepts. *See id.* at 1325, n.184.

70 The study also shows that the definition of probable cause is not just vague but also likely misleading: It purports to require evidence sufficient to support a belief that an offense has

been committed, which would seem to mean that it is more likely than not that an offense has been committed. *Id.* at 1327. However, the average probability from the judges was 44.5 percent – below the "more likely than not" standard. *Id.* at 1332. The First Circuit agreed with this formulation, holding that probable cause was a lower standard than preponderance of the evidence. United States v. Melvin, 596 F.2d 492, 495 (1st Cir. 1979). In other words, "probable cause" does not actually mean "probable"; it means something that is close to probable.

71 *Id.* at 1327–28. Although a few outlying judges (somewhat inexplicably) answered 0 percent or 100 percent, the vast majority of judges were within the 10 percent to 60 percent range: 15 percent answered 10 percent, 20 percent answered 20 percent, 30 percent answered 30 percent, 13 percent answered 40 percent, 14 percent answered 50 percent, and 5 percent answered 60 percent. *Id.*

72 Fifty-eight magistrates were sent the survey by e-mail; the other 561 were sent the survey by regular mail. The magistrates had the option of completing the survey online or by filling out a paper survey. Fifty-two magistrates responded to the survey. A fair number of magistrates indicated discomfort or outright refusal when asked to quantify these legal standards; 12 percent of those who replied to the survey refused to provide a specific number; another 9 percent answered the survey questions but indicated in their comments that it was inappropriate to set a specific percentage. Overall, forty-six magistrates responded with a numerical value.

73 One magistrate called to explain that he could not fill out the survey because he believed the decision could not be reduced to mere numerical probabilities.

74 The survey was administered through the Mechanical Turk marketplace, which provides respondents who are more representative of the population at large than the usual participants on academic surveys, such as college students. Respondents from the Mechanical Turk do tend to skew younger, more female, and more educated than the general population. *See* Danielle N. Shapiro et al., *Using Mechanical Turk to Study Clinical Populations*, 1 CLINICAL PSYCHOLOGY SCIENCE 213, 213 (2012).

75 CHRISTOPHER SLOBOGIN, PRIVACY AT RISK: THE NEW GOVERNMENT SURVEILLANCE AND THE FOURTH AMENDMENT, 184 (2007). An earlier survey, which did not measure the intrusiveness of car searches, rated a frisk at 68 and a bedroom search at 76 *Id.* at 112.

76 Other studies have shown a similar dissonance for the legal concept of "beyond a reasonable doubt." When mock jurors were asked how certain they were of the state's evidence, it turned out that the vast majority of them voted to acquit if they were less than 60 percent certain and voted to convict if they were more than 65 percent certain. Thus, the "actual" level of certainty for beyond a reasonable doubt is between 60 percent and 65 percent – a far cry from the 90–99 percent that lawyers and judges believe it to be. *See* Lawrence T. White and Michael D. Cicchini, *Is Reasonable Doubt Self-Defining?* 64 VILLANOVA L. REV. 1 (2019).

77 Slobogin, Privacy at Risk, at 38–39

78 *Id.*

79 *Id.*

80 *See* Dorothy K. Kagehiro & W. Clark Stanton, *Legal v. Quantified Definitions of Standards of Proof*, 9 LAW HUM BEHAV. 159 (1985).

81 *Id.* at 164. A 2018 study of mock jurors confirmed this finding, determining that giving mock jurors different standards of proof resulted in no statistical difference in conviction rates. *See* Cicchini, *supra* note 76.

82 *Id.* at 163.

83 Kagehiro & Stanton, *supra* note 81, at 159.

84 572 U.S. 393 (2014).

85 *Id.* at 413.

86 529 U.S. 266 (2000).

CHAPTER 4

1 Nancy Gibbs and Lev Grossman, TIME, *Interview with Tim Cook*, Mar. 17, 2016.

2 *See, e.g.*, Patricia L. Bellia, *Surveillance, Records & Computers: Surveillance Law Through Cyberlaw's Lens*, 72 GEO WASH. L. REV. 1375, 1458 (2004)(arguing that government agents should have to obtain a warrant before seizing e-mail messages stored by a third party).

3 As far back as 1991 – eons in the technological age – an amateur video photographer captured the beating of Rodney King by four Los Angeles police officers, who were eventually convicted for violating King's civil rights. United States v. Koon, 833 F.Supp 769 (C.D. Cal. 1993). As *Time* magazine noted in its "Person of the Year" issue for 2006: "Do a YouTube search today on the term police brutality, and you get more than 780 videos, from Houston, Hungary, Egypt, and beyond." James Poniewozik, *The Beast with a Billion Eyes*, TIME, Dec. 25, 2006/Jan. 1, 2007, at 63.

4 *See, e.g.*, Mark O'Keefe, *China Widens Crackdown on the Faithful*, Oregonian, Sept. 18, 1999, at A11 (describing how underground Christian leaders in China communicates with each other via cell phone while traveling around the country to evade the authorities).

5 The ENIAC computer in use in Orwell's day was capable of making 300 calculations per second. Myers, *supra* note 3. A modern laptop computer available for around $1,000 can perform over two billion calculations per second. *See* www.dell.com/en-us/shop/dell-laptops/xps-15/spd/xps-15-9570-laptop (last visited Jan. 21, 2019).

6 There are a few exceptions. Some scholars have looked at the ways in which technology has increased privacy, particularly in the context of encryption. *See generally* Orin S. Kerr, *The Fourth Amendment in Cyberspace: Can Encryption Create a "Reasonable Expectation of Privacy?,"* 33 CONN. L. REV. 503, 530–31 (2001) (noting that "code itself extends far greater privacy protection than the warrant requirement of the Fourth Amendment ever could"). Professor Kerr also noted in another article that in the narrow context of surveillance "[s]ome new technologies make pre-existing forms of surveillance more intrusive; others have the opposite effect." Orin S. Kerr, *The Fourth Amendment and New Technologies: Constitutional Myths and the Case for Caution*, 102 MICH. L. REV. 801, 865 (2004)(giving examples of thermal insulators, soundproofing, and white-noise generators as examples of technological countermeasures which could be employed by individuals to defeat new surveillance technologies). But Kerr also notes that "[m]ost commentators focus on the [intrusive] half of this equation while ignoring the second half," – and even Kerr himself is only talking about counter-surveillance technology, not common, everyday technology

(such as cell phones, computers, and the Internet) which have increased privacy (and secrecy) for nearly every member of society. *Id.* at 865 n.383.

7   *See, e.g.*, Laurie Thomas Lee, *Can Police Track Your Wireless Calls? Call Location Information and Privacy Law*, 21 CARDOZO ARTS & ENT. L.J. 381, 382 (2003)(suggesting that while consumers enjoy new technologies, such as cell phones, such technology has become the consumer's "ankle bracelet," because the government can now monitor citizens' movements more easily).

8   *See, e.g.*, Max Guirguis, *Electronic Mail Surveillance and the Reasonable Expectation of Privacy*, 8 J. TECH L. & POL'Y 135, 153–156 (2003)(arguing that the Fourth Amendment should be interpreted to provide more privacy to e-mail conversations than to phone conversations); Andrew E. Taslitz, *The Fourth Amendment in the Twenty-First Century: Technology, Privacy, and Human Emotions*, 65 LAW & CONTEMP. PROBS. 125, 130 (2002) (arguing that the Supreme Court's approach to Fourth Amendment cases undervalues privacy).

9   In 1900, life expectancy at birth was only forty-seven years. NATIONAL CENTER FOR HEALTH STATISTICS, HEALTH, UNITED STATES, 2005 167 tbl. 27 (2005), available at www.cdc.gov/nchs/data/hus/hus05.pdf#027 (last visited Jan. 21, 2019). Life expectancy in the year 004 was nearly seventy-eight years. *See* ARIALDI M. MINIÑO, MELONIE HERON & BETTY L. SMITH, CTRS. FOR DISEASE CONTROL, DEATHS PRELIMINARY DATA (2004) www.cdc.gov/nchs/products/pubs/pubd/hestats/prelimdeaths04/preliminarydeaths04.htm (last visited Jan. 21, 2019).

10 *See infra* notes 16–17 and accompanying text.

11 Greenwood v. California, 486 U.S. 35, 54 (1988) (Brennan, J., dissenting) (suggesting that an operator can listen in on telephone conversations)

12 *See, e.g.*, N.Y. Times Co. v. Gonzalez, 459 F.3d 160 (2nd Cir. 2006) (discussing the constitutionality of subpoenaing a reporter's phone records from a third party); Olmstead v. United States, 277 U.S. 438 (1928) (discussing the use of wiretaps as early as 1928).

13 For example, one problem police sometimes encounter when intercepting a phone call is converting the communication to a digital signal, which requires the use of sophisticated software. Larry Downes, Electronic *Communications and the Plain View Exception: More "Bad Physics,"* 7 HARV. J. L. & TECH. 239, 241 n.9 (1994). There is obviously no need for such technology when intercepting and reading mail.

14 In response to this practice, federal and state governments have passed laws making it easier for law enforcement to track and wiretap telephone calls from such "disposable" phones. *See generally* Charles H. Kennedy & Peter P. Swire, *State Wiretaps and Electronic Surveillance after September 11*, 54 HASTINGS L.J. 971, 980–82 (2003). In the past, wiretap warrants applied only to a specific phone line. *Id.* at 980. Thus, use of disposable cell phones could render such warrants useless because a criminal could have moved on to another phone before law enforcement obtained a warrant to wiretap the previous phone. However, in 1986, so-called roving wiretaps were authorized for domestic surveillance under the Electronic Communications Privacy Act. *Id.* at 981; *see also* Electronic Communications Privacy Act, Pub. L. No. 99–508, 100 Stat. 1848 (1986); 18 U.S.C. § 2518 (2000). A roving wiretap warrant permits surveillance of "any communications device a target of an investigation is likely to use, without specifying the telephone or other facilities in the orders or applications." Kennedy & Swire, *supra*, at 980–81. Essentially, a roving

wiretap wiretaps the person, rather than the phone. The USA Patriot Act extended such roving wiretap authority to foreign intelligence investigations and now allows such a wiretap order to apply nationwide, rather than simply in the district in which the authorizing judge sits. *Id.* at 981–82; *see also* USA Patriot Act of 2001, Pub. L. No. 107–56, §§ 206, 216(a), 115 Stat. 272, 282, 288 (2001). Although these statutes assist law enforcement in tracking and wiretapping disposable phones, they are not perfect. Law enforcement would still need to discover what disposable phone a terrorist is using or would be likely to use before a roving wiretap would be of any use.

15 *See* Charles Barry Smith, *Current U.S. Encryption Regulations: A Federal Law Enforcement Perspective*, 3 N.Y.U. J. Legis. & Pub. Pol'y 11, 15–16 (2000)(describing encryption technology and criminals' and terrorists' use of such technology to evade law enforcement).

16 Catherine J. Lanctot, *Attorney-Client Relationships in Cyberspace: The Peril and the Promise*, 49 Duke L.J. 147, 162 n.34 (1999)(citing U.S. Patent No. 174,465 (issued Mar. 7, 1876)).

17 In the early part of the twentieth century, only 1.5 million Americans had telephones. *Id.* Even by the beginning of World War II, fewer than half of Americans had telephones. *Id.* Cost may have been part of the cause of the rarity of telephones. *See* Susan W. Brenner, *Law in an Era of Pervasive Technology*, 15 Widener L.J. 667, 714–15, n.289 (2006). Telephone companies attempted to increase the pervasiveness of telephones in the early twentieth century by cutting in half the service cost so more Americans could afford them. *Id.*

18 As late as 1985, there was only one residential phone line for every three citizens, and fewer than one residential phone line per household. United States Census Bureau, Statistical Abstract of the United States, tbls.2, 57, 1131 (2007), www.census .gov/library/publications/2006/compendia/statab/126ed/information-communications.html (last visited Jan. 21, 2019). Census records show that there were 79 million residential phone lines for a population of about 85 million households and 238 million people. *Id.*

19 *See* Pew Research Center: Internet and Technology, October 29, 2015, at www.pewinter net.org/2015/10/29/technology-device-ownership-2015/ (last visited Jan. 21, 2019).

20 In fact, many cell phones themselves are free when the individual purchases a service plan.

21 *See, e.g.,* www.amazon.com/.

22 *See, e.g.,* www.apple.com/itunes/store/.

23 *See, e.g.,* www.apple.com/dotmac/ (describing the software iLife).

24 Kyllo v. United States, 533 U.S. 27, 29–30 (2001).

25 This hypothetical assumes the counterfactual premise that possession of marijuana was illegal one hundred years ago. Possession of marijuana was legal in this country until the first states began to outlaw it in the second decade of the twentieth century. *See generally* Richard J. Bonnie and Charles H. Whitebread, II, *The Forbidden Fruit and the Tree of Knowledge: An Inquiry into the Legal History of American Marijuana Prohibition*, 56 Va. L. Rev. 971, 992–95 (1970). The first federal statute outlawing marijuana was the Marijuana Tax Act of 1937. Marijuana Tax Act of 1937, Pub. L. No. 75–238, 50 Stat. 551 (1937) (repealed 1970).

26 *See* Oliver v. United States, 466 U.S. 170, 179–81 (1984); Hester v. United States, 265 U.S. 57, 59 (1924).

27 It is interesting to note that the thermal imager at issue in *Kyllo* did not actually detect the marijuana itself; merely the technological device that the defendant used in order to grow the marijuana. *See* Kyllo v. United States, 533 U.S. 27, 27 (2001).

28 277 U.S. 438 (1928).

29 The *Olmstead* case itself involved a vast conspiracy of seventy-two individuals who were importing and selling liquor in violation of Prohibition. *Id.* The Supreme Court noted that the conspiracy was of an "amazing magnitude":

> [The conspiracy] involved the employment of not less than 50 persons, of 2 sea-going vessels for the transportation of liquor to British Columbia, of smaller vessels for coastwise transportation to the state of Washington, the purchase and use of a branch beyond the suburban limits of Seattle, with a large underground cache for storage and a number of smaller caches in that city, the maintenance of a central office manned with operators, and the employment of executives, salesmen, deliverymen dispatchers, scouts, bookkeepers, collectors, and an attorney. In a bad month sales amounted to $176,000; the aggregate for a year must have exceeded $2,000,000.

> *Id.* at 456. Olmstead himself was the "leading conspirator and the general manager" of the business. *Id.* Given the geographic scope and the number of personnel involved in the conspiracy, there is no doubt that the telephone assisted Olmstead greatly both in carrying out his criminal actions and in concealing these actions from law enforcement.

30 *See id.* "It is plainly within the words of the [Fourth] [A]mendment to say that the unlawful rifling by a government agent of a sealed letter is a search and seizure of the sender's papers or effects. The letter is a paper, an effect, and in the custody of a government that forbids carriage, except under its protection." The Court also noted that that there was a "constitutional provision for the Postoffice Department," and the government had a relationship with "those who pay to secure protection of their sealed letters." *Id.* at 464.

31 *Id.* at 466. "Neither the cases we have cited nor any of the many federal decisions brought to our attention hold the Fourth Amendment to have been violated as against a defendant, unless there has been an official search and seizure of his person or such a seizure of his papers or his tangible material effects or an actual physical invasion of his house 'or curtilage' for the purpose of making a seizure"

32 *See* Federal Communications Act of 1934, 47 U.S.C. § 605 (2000).

33 *See* Goldman v. United States, 316 U.S. 129, 134 (1942) (holding that placing a Dictaphone against the adjoining wall of defendant's office to eavesdrop on his conversations did not implicate the Fourth Amendment since the law enforcement agents did not violate defendant's property rights in using the Dictaphone).

34 Although *Katz* involved a defendant who was speaking on the phone, the device used by the law enforcement agents did not tap into the phone line but simply attached an electronic listening device to the outside of the phone booth the defendant was using. Katz v. United States, 389 U.S. 347, 362 (1967) (Harlan, J., concurring). Thus, the case did not involve reactive surveillance technology (such as a telephone wiretap) but simply first-category electronic bugging.

35 442 U.S. 735 (1979).

36 *Id.* at 737.

37 *Id.*

38 *Id.*

39 *Id.* at 737.

40 The Court made it clear that although the phone company installed the pen register, it did so at the request of the police, and so was acting as an "agent" of the police for the purposes of the Fourth and Fourteenth Amendment. *Id.* at 740 n.4.

41 The Federal Communications Act of 1934 prohibited intercepting and disclosing any information passing over telephone lines. 47 U.S.C. § 605 (2000).

42 *Id.* at 741. "Indeed, a law enforcement official could not even determine from the use of a pen register whether a communication existed. These devices do not hear sound. They disclose only the telephone numbers that have been dialed – a means of establishing communication. Neither the purport of any communication between the caller and the recipient of the call, their identities, nor whether the call was even completed is disclosed by pen registers. *Id.* (quoting United States v. New York Tel. Co., 434 U.S. 159, 167 (1977)).

43 *Id.* at 743–44.

44 *Id.* at 742.

45 *Id.* at 743–44.

46 *Id.* at 744 (citing United States v. Miller, 425 U.S. 435, 442–444 (1976)).

47 Couch v. United States, 409 U.S. 322, 323 (1973).

48 United States v. White 495 U.S. 745, 746–47 (1971).

49 As was the case with wiretapping fifty years earlier, the United States Congress has stepped in to protect the content of e-mail messages. *See* Electronic Communications Privacy Act, Pub. L. No. 99–508, 100 Stat. 1848 (1986); 18 U.S.C. § 2510(12) (2000) (amending Title III so that the heightened standards apply to electronic messages as well).

50 *See generally* Orin S. Kerr, *Internet Surveillance Law after the USA Patriot Act: The Big Brother That Isn't,* 97 NW. U. L. REV. 607 (2003) (discussing the necessity of transferring information to an organization within three different communications networks: the postal service, the telephone, and the Internet). One example of this is web surfing. *See id.* at 613 n.29. In order to visit a website, a user types the website address into the browser. *Id.* The computer then sends out signals to the remote computer that hosts the website and the website sends a signal back. *Id.* In other words, "[c]ommunications networks require partial (and sometimes total) disclosure to the network provider to help the provider deliver the contents." *Id.* at 628.

51 *Id.*

52 Professor Orin Kerr dealt with these questions in the context of digital technology searches, noting that under current precedent (derived from a pre-digital era), law enforce-ment agents do not commit a search or a seizure if they copy the contents of your hard drive and store the contents on their own computers. Orin S. Kerr, *Searches and Seizures in a Digital World,* 119 HARV. L. REV. 531, 558–60 (2005). Kerr notes that this is a "troublesome result:" *Id.* at 560. "The idea that the government could freely generate copies of our hard drives and indefinitely retain them in government storage seems too Orwellian – and downright creepy – to be embraced as a Fourth Amendment rule." *Id.*

53 Kyllo v. United States, 533 U.S. 27, 40 (2001).

54 For example, in Franklin County, Ohio, an interested neighbor (or any other person in the world) can go to the Franklin County Auditor's website and simply type in his neighbor's name to discover a myriad of information about his neighbor's home, including the price for which his neighbor bought the home and the current appraisal. See http://property.franklincountyauditor.com/_web/search/commonsearch.aspx?mode=owner (last visited Jan. 21, 2019). http://franklin.governmaxa.com/propertymax/rover30.asp. To learn who is contributing to a federal political candidate, one need only visit the Federal Election Commission's website and either type in the candidate's name or type in an individual's name to see to whom that individual is contributing. how much money a friend or co-worker gave to a federal candidate for office, one need only visit the Federal Election Commission's website and type in that friend's or co-worker's name. See www.fec.gov/data/ (last visited Jan. 21, 2019).

55 Federal law requires each state to implement such a sex offender registry and to participate in the national sex offender registry. 42 U.S.C. § 14071 (2006). The national sex offender registry, like most state registries, is available online for public viewing. *See* Dru Sjodin National Sex Offender Public Registry, U.S. Dept. of Justice, www.nsopr.gov (last visited Jan. 21, 2019) (enabling a person to look up sex offenders by zip code or other information and view the offender's name, address, picture, classification, offenses, and even the offender's "victim preferences"). Some states go beyond the minimum federal mandate and require local authorities to actively inform the community of sex offenders living in that community by going door-to-door or mailing information about the offender directly to the affected community. *See, e.g.,* D.C. CODE § 22–4011 (2006) (allowing active notification); N.J. STAT. ANN. § 2C:7–8c (2006) (requiring active notification to the affected community when risk of re-offense is high).

56 Tom Zeller, Jr., Breach Points Up Flaws in Privacy Laws, N.Y. TIMES, Feb. 24, 2005, at C1 (discussing "big data brokers" that collect and sell consumer information).

57 Shaun B. Spencer, *Reasonable Expectations and the Erosion of Privacy*, 39 SAN DIEGO L. REV. 843, 860–61 (2002).

58 *See generally* Note, Kristen M. Jacobsen, *Game of Phones, Data Isn't Coming: Modern Mobile Operating System Encryption and Its Chilling Effect on Law Enforcement*, 85 GEO. WASH. L. REV. 566 (2017).

59 Kerr, *Encryption, supra* note 6, at 530. As Professor Orin Kerr noted, "it becomes clear that the government will be technically unable to decrypt any encrypted communication that is encrypted with anything other than a very short key, and that the decryption of even a short key would consume extraordinary amounts of government resources." *Id.*

60 For example, a code that used a key that was 128 digits long (thus creating 3.4 * 1038 possible keys) would take the fastest computer in the world millions of years to decipher.

61 *Id.*

62 *See* Jacobsen, *supra* note 58, at 573–36 (2017).

63 *See, e.g.,* Thomas Brewster, "Inside Google's Fight to Keep the US Government Out of Gmail Inboxes," FORBES, (May 21, 2017) www.forbes.com/sites/thomasbrewster/2017/05/21/google-epic-court-fight-with-us-government-over-gmail-privacy/#54e8a4030205 (last visited Jan. 22, 2019) (discussing several high-profile cases in which law enforcement has attempted to get information from Google. In many of these cases, Google has agreed to hand over the information stored in America, but has refused to hand over information

stored overseas); Thomas Brewster, "Apple Fights 'Dangerous' FBI Order for Backdoor into San Bernardino Shooter iPhone," FORBES, (Feb. 17, 2016) www.forbes.com/sites/thomasbrewster/2016/02/17/tim-cook-takes-on-fbi-over-encryption-bypass/#422fdc604bc7 (last visited Jan. 22, 2019) (discusses the legal battle between Apple and the FBI over access to the iPhone of one of the San Bernardino shooters).

64 Hosenball, Mark; Volz, Dustin (Apr. 13, 2016). "U.S. Senate panel releases draft of controversial encryption bill." Yahoo! Finance. Reuters, available at https://finance.yahoo.com/news/u-senate-panel-releases-draft-192224282.html (last visited Jan. 21, 2019).

65 D. Forest Wolfe, Comment, *The Government's Right to Read: Maintaining State Access to Digital Data in the Age of Impenetrable Encryption*, 49 EMORY L.J. 711, 719 (2000).

66 Some scholars have argued that it is too early to assess the actual impact of encryption technology, since the police have multiple "workaround" strategies that could be used in many cases to defeat encryption. *See* Orin S. Kerr & Bruce Schneier, *Encryption Workarounds*, 107 GEORGETOWN LAW JOURNAL 989 (2018).

67 In a question and answer session at the 2016 South by Southwest Conference, then-President Obama noted that 100 percent privacy was not the answer. ""If it's technologically possible to make an impenetrable device or system, where encryption is so strong that there's no key – there's no door – then how do we apprehend the child pornographer? How do we solve or disrupt a terrorist plot? What mechanisms do we have to even do things like tax enforcement? If you can't crack that at all, if government can't get in, then everyone's walking around with a Swiss bank account in their pocket, right?" He later noted that: "[y]ou cannot take an absolutist view on this. If your view is strong encryption no matter what, and we can and should create black boxes, that does not strike the balance that we've lived with for 200 or 300 years. And it's fetishizing our phones above every other value. That can't be the right answer." The former President's solution is similar to the one proposed in this book: to provide a key for all all robust encryption that was "accessible by the smallest number of people possible for a subset of issues that we agree are important." Sam Machkovech, "Obama Weighs In on Apple v. FBI," ARSTECHNICA, Mar. 11, 2016 at https://arstechnica.com/tech-policy/2016/03/obama-weighs-in-on-apple-v-fbi-you-cant-take-an-absolutist-view/ (last visited Jan. 21, 2019).

68 One of the most destructive crimes in history was the creation of the "I Love You" virus in 2000, which infected 45 million computers and caused an estimated $10 billion of damage in this country alone. *See* Peter Csonka, "The Council of Europe's Convention on Cyber-Crime and Other European Initiatives," CAIRN, www.cairn.info/revue-internationale-de-droit-penal-2006-3-page-473.htm (last visited Jan. 21, 2019).

69 *See* THE ECONOMIST, *The Anarchists: For Jihadists, Read Anarchist*, Apr. 18, 2005.

70 Eric Lichtblau & James Risen, *Spy Agency Mined Vast Data Trove, Officials Report*, N.Y. TIMES, Dec. 24, 2006, at A1.

71 MacWade v. Kelly, 460 F.3d 260 (2d Cir. 2006) (subways); Cassidy v. Chertoff, 471 F.3d 67 (2d Cir. 2006) (ferries).

72 *See, e.g.*, Linda Greenhouse, *Justices Are Urged to Dismiss Padilla Case*, N.Y. TIMES, Dec. 18, 2005, at A14.

73 Joseph Goldstein, "Testilying by Police: A Stubborn Problem," N.Y. TIMES, Mar. 18, 2018, at www.nytimes.com/2018/03/18/nyregion/testilying-police-perjury-new-york.html (last visited Jan. 21, 2019).

74 *Id.* An investigation by the *New York Times* revealed twenty-five cases in a three year period in which "prosecutors determined that a key aspect of a New York City police officer's testimony was probably untrue." The article estimates that this is "almost certainly only a fraction" of cases in which police officers lie about their investigation, since most cases are resolved by plea deals before the officer takes a witness stand.

75 *See* Christopher Slobogin, *Testilying: Police Perjury and What to do About It*, 67 U. Colo. L. Rev. 1037, 1041–48 (1996) (discussing surveys and other data which support the notion that police, with prosecutors' knowledge, regularly lie in warrant applications and in suppression hearings to cover up lack of probable cause or failure to properly follow *Miranda* rules). One set of commentators, in response to evidence suggesting a high rate of police testilying, suggested liberalizing rules of evidence to allow defendants more ability to impeach police officers' testimony. *See* Gabriel Chin & Scott Wells, *The "Blue Wall of Silence" as Evidence of Bias and Motive to Lie: A New Approach to Police Perjury*, 59 U. Pitt. L. Rev. 233, 272–99 (1998).

76 Some scholars have argued that police body cameras also represent a threat to privacy, since they create a permanent record of everything that police officers see, including private locations. *See, e.g.*, Stephen Henderson, *Fourth Amendment Time Machines (And What They Might Say About Police Body Cameras)*, 18 U. Pa. J. Const. L. 933, 933 (2016). We will discuss this in greater detail in Chapter 6.

77 Not incidentally, they also provide excellent substantive evidence for the actual criminal trial, thus enhancing security as well. We will discuss this further in Chapter 5.

78 As Professor Andrew Ferguson has pointed out, the Supreme Court's cases involving the exclusionary rule such as Herring v. United States, 555 U.S. 135 (2009) and Utah v. Strieff, 136 S.Ct. 2056 (2016) require defendants to establish recurring or systemic police negligence. It is nearly impossible to build this record using traditional tools, but big data analysis can simplify this burden of proof. *See* Andrew Guthrie Ferguson, *The Exclusionary Rule in the Age of Blue Data*, 72 Vand. L. Rev. 101 (2019).

CHAPTER 5

1 Arthur Conan Doyle, The Adventures of Sherlock Holmes 149 (Oxford University Press 1993) (1892).

2 *See, e.g.*, Katz v. United States, 389 U.S. 347, 348 (1967).

3 *See, e.g.*, United States v. Jarrett, 338 F.3d. 339, 340–41 (4th Cir. 2003), *cert. denied*, 540 U.S. 1185 (2004).

4 *See, e.g.*, Terry v. Ohio, 392 U.S. 1, 20–21 (1968) (stating the "reasonableness" of a search under the Fourth Amendment depends on balancing "the need to search" against "the invasion which the search ... entails" (quoting Camara v. Mun. Court, 387 U.S. 523, 534–37 (1967)).

5 *See* United States v. Colyer, 878 F.2d 469, 474 (D.C. Cir. 1989).

6 462 U.S. 696, 707 (1983). Arguably, this conclusion was merely dicta, since the Supreme Court found the government action unconstitutional on other grounds, namely that the length of the seizure was out of proportion to the facts supporting reasonable suspicion. *See id.* at 709–10; David A. Harris, *Superman's X-Ray Vision and the Fourth Amendment: The New Gun Detection Technology*, 69 Temp. L. Rev. 1, 33 (1996).

7 *Place*, 462 U.S. at 707.

8 *Id.*

9 466 U.S. 109, 111 (1984).

10 *Id.* at 122–24. In determining whether the chemical test was a "search," the Court merely asked whether the government activity "infringe[d] an expectation of privacy that society is prepared to consider reasonable." *Id.* at 122. Later, in summarizing *Place*, the Court likewise ignored the "limited matter" aspect of the *Place* analysis, stating that the reason the canine sniff in *Place* was not a search was because "the governmental conduct could reveal nothing about noncontraband items." *Id.* at 124 n.24.

11 Although *Place* and *Jacobsen* created and refined the concept of a binary search, the Court did not use the term in either case. The term was first coined by the United States Court of Appeals for the District of Columbia Circuit in United States v. Colyer, 878 F.2d 469, 474 (D.C. Cir. 1989) ("As in *Place*, the driving force behind *Jacobsen* was the recognition that because of the binary nature of the information disclosed by the sniff, no legitimately private information is revealed.").

12 *Jacobsen*, 466 U.S. at 124.

13 125 S. Ct. 834, 837 (2005).

14 389 U.S. 347 (1967).

15 *Id.* at 360 (Harlan, J., concurring).

16 *Id.* at 361 (Harlan, J., concurring).

17 See *Jacobsen*, 466 U.S. at 123.

18 See *Id.*

19 The incentive for law enforcement officials to set up pretextual roadblocks is quite strong given the recent decision of *City of Indianapolis* v. *Edmond*, in which the Supreme Court held that although it is permissible to set up roadblocks to check for drunk drivers, it is impermissible to set up roadblocks "whose primary purpose [is] to detect evidence of ordinary criminal wrongdoing," such as drug trafficking. 531 U.S. 32, 38 (2000).

20 Assuming, of course that the Court continues to adhere to the current "all-or-nothing" structure of Fourth Amendment jurisprudence for searches: an investigative technique either implicates the Fourth Amendment and thus requires probable cause, or it does not implicate it and requires no showing of suspicion at all. In *Caballes*, the Supreme Court was invited to create a new intermediate *Terry*-like category for searches. See *People* v. *Caballes*, 802 N.E.2d 202, 205 (2003) (holding that a canine sniff was unconstitutional without "specific and articulable facts" to support the sniff), *vacated by Caballes*, 125 S. Ct. 834. However, the Court declined this invitation. See *id.* at 837–38.

21 *Id.* at 838. ("Although respondent argues that the error rates, particularly the existence of false positives, call into question the premise that drug-detection dogs alert only to contraband, the record contains no evidence or findings that support his argument.")

22 *Id.*

23 As Justice Souter noted in his dissent, the case law in the field contains ample evidence of the fallibility of drug-detection dogs. See *id.* at 839–40 (Souter, J., dissenting) (citing six lower court federal cases and the reply brief in the *Caballes* case as evidence that drug-detection dogs have a false positive rate as high as 60 percent); *see also* Robert C. Bird, *An Examination of the Training and Reliability of the Narcotics Detection Dog*, 85 KY L.J. 405, 415 (1997) (noting that Rhode Island police dogs correctly alert 95–98 percent of the

time). How to measure properly the accuracy of drug-detection dogs is yet another issue that was not discussed by the *Caballes* majority, and in many lower courts it is unclear if the "accuracy rate" of the dog in question refers to the false positive rate or the positive predictive value of the alert.

24 *Caballes*, 125 S. Ct. at 838.

25 *Id.*

26 *Id.*

27 *See id.*

28 This might not be true, of course, if there were consistent reasons why the device emitted a false positive, and if the law enforcement officer using the device could then deduce private, legitimate information about the subject of the search from the false positive alone. For example, imagine a mechanical narcotics detector which only gave a false alert when the subject of the search was carrying a certain kind of prescription drug. If this were the case, officers who used the device regularly would learn "protected" information from the false alerts – i.e., they would have used the device without probable cause to discover information about legitimate (and very private) items that the person carried.

29 Although the Supreme Court has refused to assign a "numerically precise degree of certainty" to determine whether or not probable cause exists, it has held that probable cause exists if there is a "substantial basis" for concluding that there is a "probability" of criminal activity. Illinois v. Gates, 462 U.S. 213, 235–36 (1983).

30 The Supreme Court implicitly affirmed this position in Florida v. Harris, in which the defendant challenged the use of a drug detection dog on his truck after he was pulled over. The only question the Court considered was whether the dog's positive alert constituted probable cause, without even considering whether probable cause was sufficient to render the dog sniff a binary search. *See* Florida v. Harris, 568 U.S. 237 (2013).

31 *Id.* at 839–40 (Souter, J., dissenting). Justice Souter first established a fact which the majority was unwilling to acknowledge: that drug dogs do indeed have error rates. Noting that the "infallible dog . . . is a creature of legal fiction," he cites six different cases in which courts have found significant error rates in canine sniffs. *Id.* (Souter, J., dissenting).

32 *Id.* at 840 (Souter, J., dissenting).

33 *Id.* (Souter, J., dissenting) (internal quotations omitted).

34 *Id.* at 842 (Souter, J., dissenting).

35 *See, e.g., United States v. Kennedy*, 131 F.3d 1371, 1378 (10th Cir. 1997) (noting that the dog in question had a "success rate" of 71 percent, and calculating the "success rate" by dividing the total number of alerts by the total number of true positives).

36 *See, e.g., Laime v. State*, 60 S.W.3d 464, 476 (Ark. 2001) (noting that the drug dog "Moose" had been incorrect "at least ten times and possibly as many as fifty times").

37 *See* United States v. Sundby, 186 F.3d 873, 876 (8th Cir. 1999) ("To establish the dog's reliability, the affidavit need only state the dog has been trained and certified to detect drugs. An affidavit need not give a detailed account of the dog's track record or education." [citations omitted]); United States v. Meyer, 536 F.2d 963 (1st Cir. 1976). *See generally* Dave Hunter, *Common Scents: Establishing a Presumption of Reliability for Detector Dog Teams Used in Airports in Light of the Current Terrorist Threat*, 28 U. DAYTON L. REV. 89, 95–96 (2002) (stating that courts usually only require the handler's testimony that the dog is trained and reliable). Ostensibly, these courts are using this low standard simply in order to

determine if the alert is sufficient to establish probable cause, but since many courts simply adopt the *Place* rationale for indiscriminate canine sniffs without any examination of the dog's level of accuracy, the inquiry into reliability for probable cause becomes the de facto inquiry into the level of accuracy necessary to be considered a binary search.

38 An "inaccurate" binary search could also be defined as a binary search that revealed a small amount of legitimate, noncontraband information to the officer. However, the doctrinal underpinnings of *Place, Jacobsen*, and *Caballes* strongly suggest that no room is available for compromise in this dimension of "accuracy." A method that reveals any amount of noncontraband information will violate the binary search doctrine entirely by infringing on the subject's legitimate expectation of privacy.

39 As an extreme example, assume law enforcement develops a computer software program which copies and opens every e-mail that passes across an Internet service provider, looking for illegal images of child pornography. In order to make the software into a pure binary search, the detection algorithm would presumably be set to alert only upon seeing the most extreme and obvious images of child pornography. This would ensure a false positive rate of close to zero, but it would allow many false negatives – cases in which milder, but still illegal, child pornography escaped notice. Numerous false negatives would make the software somewhat less useful, detecting perhaps only one out of every one hundred or thousand images of child pornography that it examined, but the high rate of false negatives would not affect its constitutionality.

40 This is mostly due to a lack of resources: since drug-detection dogs and their handlers are expensive, using them indiscriminately might not make sense, even if law enforcement officers have the right to do so. However, if mechanical devices that can conduct a binary search for narcotics are produced and used analogously to radar detectors, the cost of conducting such a search could become much lower and police would have no economic incentive to conduct a binary search only when suspicious circumstances exist.

41 *See* Bird, *supra* note 23, at 427–32.

42 Some courts have shown resistance to a requirement that the government demonstrate the accuracy rates of their drug-detection dogs. *See* United States v. Dicesare, 765 F.2d 890, 897 (9th Cir. 1985) (upholding the lower court's decision prohibiting disclosure of the United States Customs Service narcotics training manual on the grounds that it would compromise investigative techniques).

43 *See* Daubert v. Merrell Dow Pharms., Inc., 509 U.S. 579, 592–93 (1993) (holding that judges are responsible for determining whether the proffered expert testimony is scientific evidence which would assist the trier of fact).

44 *Id.*

45 *See* Terry v. Ohio, 392 U.S. 1, 20–21 (1968).

46 If the law enforcement agent possessed probable cause or even reasonable suspicion to conduct the search, there might be no need to conduct a hearing to determine whether the surveillance was a binary search; rather, the court could simply conduct a *Terry* inquiry to ensure that the law enforcement agent possessed sufficient "specific and articulable facts to reasonably warrant the intrusion." *Id.* at 20–21. If so, the search would be constitutional regardless of its status as a binary search, if not, the prosecutor could still seek to get the search "certified" as a binary search, in which case it would not need to pass the *Terry* test.

47 *See supra* notes 40–41 and accompanying text.

48 For example, assume that law enforcement used a binary search with a false positive rate of 1 in 10 million to search for contraband (such as possession of computer child porn files) that 1 in 100,000 people possessed. If used randomly on the general population, this search would have a positive predictive value of over 99 percent (for example, if used on 10 million people in 1 year, it would return 101 positive results, 100 of which would be true positives and only 1 of which would be a false positive). This rate could certainly satisfy a "beyond a reasonable doubt" standard for accuracy.

49 This is not to say the law enforcement officers would have to have some level of "reasonable suspicion" before conducting the binary search; such a requirement would obviate the need for the binary search doctrine in the first place. There may be many contexts in which the likelihood of finding illegal activity would be significantly increased even if the law enforcement officer could not articulate specific facts to justify reasonable suspicion: officers acting on an unquantifiable hunch, for example, or only using the binary device in certain locations (such as airports or bus depots) where illegal activity is more likely to be occurring.

50 *See* 18 U.S.C. § 1966A (2006).

51 To some extent, this is true for every type of surveillance. A successful surveillance simply means that evidence is found that could lead to conviction, not that the evidence on its own proves the defendant's guilt beyond a reasonable doubt.

52 *See* Florida v. Bostick, 501 U.S. 429, 434 (1991) (holding that police may approach an individual and ask questions, as long as the individual feels free to disregard the police and terminate the encounter).

53 These determinations are always very fact-specific, but the tests for judges to follow have been set out in numerous cases. *See, e.g.*, Florida v. Royer, 460 U.S. 491, 500 (1983) ("[A]n investigative detention must be temporary and last no longer than is necessary to effectuate the purpose of the stop. Similarly, the investigative methods employed should be the least intrusive means reasonably available to verify or dispel the officer's suspicion in a short period of time. It is the State's burden to demonstrate that the seizure it seeks to justify on the basis of a reasonable suspicion was sufficiently limited in scope and duration to satisfy the conditions of an investigative seizure." (citations omitted)).

54 *Place* itself made clear the importance of the delay caused by the search: although the drug sniff itself was a suitable binary search, the ninety-minute seizure of the bag was such a prolonged delay that the procedure violated the Fourth Amendment. *Place*, 462 U.S. at 709. A lengthy delay can also convert an otherwise permissible "investigative stop" justified under *Terry* into an arrest which must be supported by probable cause. *See, e.g.*, United States v. Sharpe, 470 U.S. 675, 685 (1985) ("Obviously, if an investigative stop continues indefinitely, at some point it can no longer be justified as an investigative stop.").

55 One of the factors in determining the level of "physical invasiveness" is the "intimidating" or "offensive" nature of the conduct by the law enforcement. *See, e.g.*, B.C. v. Plumas Unified Sch. Dist., 192 F.3d 1260, 1266 (9th Cir. 1999) (holding that a dog sniffing students in close proximity violates the Fourth Amendment because "the level of intrusiveness is greater when the dog is permitted to sniff a person than when a dog sniffs unattended luggage"). The *B.C.* case unfortunately applied the "intrusiveness" factor to the *search* question rather than the *seizure* question, holding that the canine sniff infringed on the

students' "reasonable expectation of privacy" because the use of the dog was "offensive." *Id.* The link between the "offensiveness" of the method used by law enforcement and the degree to which someone's reasonable expectation of privacy is infringed is not clear. However, the link between offensiveness and the degree of *seizure* is quite strong.

56 *Compare Place*, 462 U.S. at 709 (holding that a ninety-minute seizure of someone's luggage is unreasonable), *with* United States v. Van Leeuwen, 397 U.S. 249, 252 (1970) (holding that a one-day seizure of a letter that had been sent through the mail is not unreasonable).

57 *Id.* at 699.

58 *Id.* at 703.

59 *Id.* Although the Court never stated directly that the agents had specific and articulable facts, they based their decision on the duration of the seizure, implying that a shorter seizure would have been permissible. *Id.* at 708–10. Thus, the Court implied that the agents did indeed have enough specific and articulable facts to conduct a brief, limited *Terry* seizure. *See id.*

60 *Id.* at 709–10. The Court acknowledged that seizures of property can vary in their degree of intrusiveness, based on the duration of the seizure and the type of property being seized. *Id.* at 705–8.

61 125 S.Ct. 834 (2005)

62 135 S.Ct. 1609 (2015)

63 *Id.* at 845 (Ginsburg, J., dissenting) (quoting Terry v. Ohio, 392 U.S. 1, 20 (1968)).

64 *Id.* at 844–45 (Ginsburg, J., dissenting).

65 *Id.* at 845 (Ginsburg, J., dissenting). She also notes that a "drug-detection dog is an intimidating animal," and that "drug dogs are not lap dogs." *Id.* (Ginsburg, J., dissenting) (quoting United States v. Williams, 356 F.3d 1268, 1276 (10th Cir. 2004) (McKay, J., dissenting)). As it turns out, some drug-detection dogs *could* be lap dogs; in fact, lap dogs (such as beagles and terriers) are in many ways better suited to the job than larger, more intimidating dogs. See, e.g., Sandra Guerra, *Criminal Law: Domestic Drug Interdiction Operations: Finding the Balance*, 82 J. Crim. L. & Criminology 1109 (1992) (arguing that because smaller dogs have "superior sensory abilities," and because larger dogs can be unduly intimidating, police forces should be required to use only smaller, "non-threatening breeds" for canine sniffs); Robert C. Bird, *An Examination of the Training and Reliability of the Narcotics Detection Dog*, 85 KY L.J. 405, footnote 41 (1997) (agreeing that smaller dogs have better olfactory abilities, but noting that law enforcement agents prefer larger breeds because they can traverse obstacles more effectively).

66 *Caballes*, 125 S. Ct. at 845–46 (Ginsburg, J., dissenting). a drug-sniffing dog that approaches an individual's belongings, home, or person represents some level of intrusion, even if there is no chance that the surveillance will reveal any legitimate information about your possessions.

67 Jardines v. State, 73 So. 3d 34, 48–49 (Fla. 2011) (citation omitted).

68 *See, e.g.*, Mich. Dep't of State Police v. Sitz, 496 U.S. 444, 456 (1990) (allowing a delay of twenty-five seconds at a random sobriety checkpoint).

69 *See* United States v. Martinez-Fuerte, 428 U.S. 543, 545–48 (1976) (allowing a delay of up to three to five minutes at random roadblocks meant to check for illegal immigrants).

70 *See, e.g.*, *Moore*, 58 F.3d at 1553; United States v. Jeffus, 22 F.3d 554, 557 (4th Cir. 1994) (holding that a fifteen-minute wait at a routine traffic stop is not unreasonable, and

because the standard aspects of a traffic stop took the entire fifteen minutes, the use of a drug-detection dog during that time did not increase the length of the seizure and was therefore constitutional); Merrett v. Moore, 58 F.3d 1547, 1553 (11th Cir. 1995) (holding that because drug-detection dogs used at an otherwise constitutional roadblock did not increase the amount of delay suffered by motorists, the "state's decision to use dogs at the roadblocks does not make the operation unconstitutional").

71 569 U.S.1 (2013).

72 Alyson L. Rosenberg, Comment, *Passive Millimeter Wave Imaging: A New Weapon in the Fight against Crime or a Fourth Amendment Violation?*, 9 ALB. L.J. SCI. & TECH. 135, 138–40 (1998).

73 *See, e.g., id.* at 40.

74 *See, e.g.,* Ric Simmons, *From* Katz *to* Kyllo: *A Blueprint for Adapting the Fourth Amendment to Twenty-First Century Technologies*, 53 HASTINGS L.J. 1303, 1352 (2002). The federal government currently uses an "Internet-sniffing" protocol known as "DCS1000" (formerly known as "Carnivore") which can be attached to an Internet service provider's site and sift through incoming and outgoing e-mails, looking for and then copying messages to or from the target individual. *See* Dan Eggen, *"Carnivore" Glitches Blamed for FBI Woes*, WASH. POST, May 29, 2002, at A7. Obviously in its current form the protocol is nonbinary and requires not just a warrant but a Title III order before it can be used. However, future versions of the protocol could conceivably be designed to detect only illegal activity simply to alert law enforcement as to the name of the individual sending the offending e-mail.

75 A recent Fifth Circuit case correctly applied the binary search doctrine in a case involving hash values. In United States v. Reddick, 2018 WL 3949510 (Aug. 17, 2018), the defendant uploaded computer files to SkyDrive, a Microsoft cloud hosting service. Microsoft compared the hash values of the uploaded files to hash values of known child pornography and found a some matches. The company sent these files to the police, who opened the files and confirmed that they contained child pornography. The Fifth Circuit concluded that when the police opened the files, they were not conducting a search, because they already knew from the hash values that the files contained contraband. In other words, opening the files did not intrude into the defendant's privacy any more than looking at the hash files did. The police may have obtained more information about the specific nature of the child pornography when they open the files, but that was not a significant expansion of the search. Thus, the hash file comparison is analogous to a gun detector flashing positive on a suspect in a gun-free zone, in that it reveals the existence of illegal activity and nothing more. Opening the file is analogous to searching the suspect and finding the gun – when the police find the gun, they know more information (the type of gun, the size of the gun, etc.) but obtaining that extra information does not constitute a "search."

76 *See* MacDonnell, *supra* note 90, at 345–46.

77 *Id.* at 138 (Brennan, J., dissenting). Many commentators have rejected the binary search doctrine at least in part because of these concerns. *See, e.g.,* Harris, *supra* note 6, at 37–45.

78 *Jacobsen*, 466 U.S. at 138 (Brennan, J., dissenting).

79 125 S. Ct. at 839 (Souter, J., dissenting)

80 *Id.* at 845–46 (Ginsburg, J., dissenting)

81 See, e.g., Charlie Lapastora, *Red-Light Cameras Come under Fire, At Least 7 States Trying to Ban Them*, Fox News, Jan. 31, 2018, at www.foxnews.com/us/2018/01/31/red-light-cameras-come-under-fire-at-least-7-states-trying-to-ban-them.html; see also www.cleve land.com/metro/index.ssf/2018/03/bill_to_punish_cities_with_red.html (Ohio); www.illi noispolicy.org/illinois-moves-to-ban-red-light-cameras-statewide/ (Illinois); www.desmoi nesregister.com/story/news/politics/2018/02/27/traffic-enforcement-cameras-banned-under-bill-passed-iowa-senate/357336002/ (Iowa).

82 *See, e.g.,* Melia Robinson, *Jeff Sessions Is on a Crusade to Stamp Out Legal Marijuana – but Republicans Might Not Be Onboard*, Business Insider, Jan. 4, 2018, at www.businessinsi der.com/jeff-sessions-crack-down-on-legal-marijuana-unpopular-with-republicans-2018-1.

83 *See* Utah v. Streiff, 136 U.S. S.Ct. 2056, 2068 (2016) (Sotomayor, J., dissenting).

84 *See id.* at 2068–69 (Sotomayor, J., dissenting).

CHAPTER 6

1 C.I.A. v. Sims, 471 U.S. 159, 178 (1985) (internal quotations and citations omitted).

2 *See* United States v. Maynard, 615 F.3d 544 (D.C. Cir. 2010). The court stated that these patterns were "central to [the prosecutor's] presentation of the case," and noted that he referred to the GPS evidence in his opening statement.

3 Brief for the United States, United States v. Maynard, 615 F.3d 544 (D.C. Cir. 2010). The FBI had in fact applied for and received a warrant to install the GPS device, but the warrant specified that the device had to be attached within ten days of the date of the warrant. *Id.* The FBI attached the warrant on the eleventh day. Thus, the courts appropriately treated the GPS installation as a warrantless surveillance.

4 As the Supreme Court noted in the *Carpenter* case, this information is constantly being collected by our cell phones, and it is getting more and more accurate:

> Cell phones continuously scan their environment looking for the best signal, which generally comes from the closest cell site. Most modern devices, such as smartphones, tap into the wireless network several times a minute whenever their signal is on, even if the owner is not using one of the phone's features. Each time the phone connects to a cell site, it generates a time-stamped record known as cell-site location information (CSLI). The precision of this information depends on the size of the geographic area covered by the cell site. The greater the concentration of cell sites, the smaller the coverage area. As data usage from cell phones has increased, wireless carriers have installed more cell sites to handle the traffic. That has led to increasingly compact coverage areas, especially in urban areas.

> Carpenter v. United States, 138 S.Ct. 2206, 2211–12 (2018).

5 The government obtained the records pursuant to an order under the low standard required by the Stored Communications Act, which only requires a showing of "specific and articulable facts showing that there are reasonable grounds to believe" that the records sought are "relevant and material to an ongoing criminal investigation." *Id.* at 2212.

6 *Id.* at 2219.

7 Maynard, 615 F.3d at 562.

8 Carpenter, 138 S.Ct. at 2217–18.

9 *See* American Civil Liberties Union: Q&A on Face-Recognition, http://aclu.org/privacy/ spying/14875res20030902.html (last visited on Jan. 21, 2019).

10 *Id.*

11 *See id.* Although in practice, the technology has not been particularly effective so far. Numerous studies have shown that the technology fails to identify target individuals if the camera angle has changed, or if the target has grown or shaved facial hair. *Id.*

12 United States v. Knotts, 460 U.S. 276, 282 (1983).

13 California v. Greenwood, 486 U.S. 35 (1988).

14 *See, e.g.*, Harris v. United States, 390 U.S. 234, 236 (1968).

15 476 U.S. 207.

16 Kyllo v. United States, 533 U.S. 27 (2001).

17 *See, e.g.*, Christopher Slobogin, *Camera Surveillance of Public Places and the Right to Anonymity*, 72 MISS. L.J. 213 (2002)(arguing that courts should interpret the Fourth Amendment to recognize the right to be free from video surveillance in public, and suggesting that courts should set up some guidelines for the use of such surveillance).

18 United States v. Maynard, 615 F.3d 544, 562. The circuit court also argued that Jones' movements in public for twenty-eight days was not in fact public information because "the whole of one's movements over the course of a month is not *actually* exposed to the public because the likelihood anyone will observe all those movements is not just remote, it is effectively nil." *Id.* at 560.

19 *Id.* at 562.

20 Unlike the GPS tracking in the Jones case, most of these examples do not involve collecting public data; rather, law enforcement agencies must obtain the data from third party corporations who have already collected it through their ordinary course of business. We will discuss how the source of the data may matter in the next chapter, when we examine the third-party doctrine.

21 Jones, 565 U.S. at 405–6.

22 *Id.* at 429 (Alito, J., concurring).

23 Knotts, 460 U.S. at 281–282.

24 Carpenter, 138 S.Ct, at 2232 (Kennedy, J., dissenting)

25 *Id.* at 2217 (internal quotations and citations omitted).

26 *Id.* at 2218. The Court also repeated the "potential dragnet" concern from the Jones concurrence, noting that the extremely low cost of these searches now allows police "secretly monitor and catalogue every single movement of an individual's car for a very long period." *Id.* (*quoting* Jones, 465 U.S. at 430 (Alito, J., concurring).

27 *Id.* at 430 (Alito, J., concurring).

28 *Id.* at 430 (Alito, J., concurring).

29 Jones, 565 U.S. at 429 (Alito, J., concurring).

30 United States v. Pineda-Moreno, 617 F.3d 1120, 1126 (9th Cir. 2010) (Kozinski, J., dissenting).

31 *See* Christopher Slobogin, PRIVACY AT RISK 112 (2007). Public surveillance cameras at national monuments, government buildings, airports, and train stations rate an average of 20 on one of his surveys, a relatively low number (inspections of coal mines score a 25, and 15-second roadblock checks rate a 35. But the more widespread the cameras become, and the longer the monitoring lasts, the more intrusive the surveillance becomes: surveillance

cameras on a public street score a 53 (and this rises to 73 if the tapes are preserved, just a few scores below a bedroom search); monitoring a car with a beeper for 3 days scores a 63. Professor Slobogin uses this data as well as arguments that public surveillance could violate the First Amendment, the Due Process Clause, and a general right to privacy in order to argue in favor of a "right to public anonymity." This right would mean, among other things, that the police would need to justify the use and placement of public surveillance cameras and would need to develop policies regulating the storage and dissemination of the information that is recorded. *Id.* at 116–18.

32 Gary C. Robb, *Police Use of CCTV Surveillance: Constitutional Implications and Proposed Regulations*, 13 UNIV. MICH. J. LAW REF. 571, 572 (1979).

33 *See* U.S. Dep't of Just., Bureau of Justice Statistics, National Sources of Law Enforcement Employment Data, Apr., 2016 at www.bjs.gov/content/pub/pdf/nsleed.pdf (last visited Jan. 21 2019).

34 Amanda Ripley, *A Big Test of Police Body Cameras Defies Expectations*, THE UPSHOT, N.Y. TIMES, Oct. 20, 2017, at www.nytimes.com/2017/10/20/upshot/a-big-test-of-police-body-cameras-defies-expectations.html (last visited Jan. 21, 2019).

35 Jennifer L. Doleac, *Do Body-Worn Video Cameras Improve Police Behavior?* BROOKINGS INSTITUTE, Oct. 25, 2017, at www.brookings.edu/blog/up-front/2017/10/25/do-body-worn-cameras-improve-police-behavior/ (last visited Jan. 21, 2019) (reporting that the District of Columbia police department spent $1 million on body cameras and will spend an additional $2 million per year on data storage for the video from those cameras).

36 *See id.*

37 Marco Margaritoff, *Drones in Law Enforcement: How, Where and When They're Used*, THE DRIVE, Oct. 13, 2017 at www.thedrive.com/aerial/15092/drones-in-law-enforcement-how-where-and-when-theyre-used (last visited Jan. 21, 2019).

38 Matt Alderton, *To the Rescue! Why Drones in Police Work Are the Future of Crime Fighting*, REDSHIFT, Apr. 13, 2018, at www.autodesk.com/redshift/drones-in-police-work-future-crime-fighting/ (last visited Jan. 21, 2019).

39 *Id.*

40 April Glaser, *11 Police Robots Patrolling Around the World*, WIRED, July 24, 2016, at www.wired.com/2016/07/11-police-robots-patrolling-around-world/ (last visited Jan. 21, 2019).

41 Shan Li. *Robots are becoming security guards. 'Once it gets arms . . . it'll replace all of us,'* L.A. TIMES, Sept. 6, 2016, at www.latimes.com/business/la-fi-robots-retail-20160823-snap-story.html (last visited Jan. 21, 2019).

42 Robbie Gonzales, *I Spent the Night with Yelp's Robot Security Guard, Cobalt*, WIRED, Aug. 4, 2017, at www.wired.com/story/i-spent-the-night-with-yelps-robot-security-guard-cobalt/ (last visited Jan. 21, 2019).

43 Susannah Breslin, *Meet the Terrifying New Robot Cop That's Patrolling Dubai;* FORBES LIFESTYLE, June 3, 2017 at www.forbes.com/sites/susannahbreslin/2017/06/03/robot-cop-dubai/#5a2688206872 (last visited Jan. 21, 2019).

44 *See* I. Bennett Capers, *Race, Policing, and Technology*, 95 N. C. L. REV. 1241, 1285–92 (2017).

45 Stephen E. Henderson, *Fourth Amendment Time Machines (And What They Might Say about Police Body Cameras)*, 18 U. PA. J. CONST. L. 993 (2016).

46 *Id.* at 966–67.

47 *Id.* at 968–69 (detailing many cases in which body camera evidence has revealed police misconduct).

48 *Id.* at 971.

49 *Id.* at 970.

50 I have elsewhere argued against the adoption of use controls, since they cannot be justified by Fourth Amendment doctrine, they deter the creation of reasonable collection restrictions, and can unduly hinder law enforcement operations. *See* Ric Simmons. *The Mirage of Use Restrictions*, 96 N. C. L. REV. 133 (2017).

51 *Id.* at 936 (*citing Chaoming Song et al., Limits of Predictability in Human Mobility*, 327 SCIENCE 1018, 1021 (2010), http://barabasi.com/f/310.pdf (last visited Jan. 21, 2019).

52 *See, e.g.,* Floyd v. City of New York, 959 F. Supp. 2d 540, 556, 584 (S.D.N.Y. 2013) (citing studies that show that over 83 percent of the *Terry* stops in the city were conducted on black and Latino residents, significantly greater than their proportion of the population).

53 Transcript of Oral Argument at 9–10, *United States v. Jones*, 565 U.S. 400 (2012), No. 10-1259.

54 *See* Capers, *supra* note 44, at 1290 (citations omitted).

55 *Id.* at 1291.

56 *Id.* at 1287; *see* USA FREEDOM ACT, PUB. L. 114–23 (2015).

57 *See* Elizabeth Joh, *Discretionless Policing: Technology and the Fourth Amendment*, 95 CAL. L. REV. 199, 206–7 (2007).

58 Melanie Reid, *Rethinking the Fourth Amendment in the Age of Supercomputers, Artificial Intelligence, and Robots*, 119 W. VA. L. REV. 863, 878–79 (2017).

59 *See supra* note 52.

60 *See, e.g.,* Note, Sean Childers, *Discrimination During Traffic Stops: How and Economic Account Justifying Racial Profiling Falls Short*, 87 N.Y.U. L. REV. 1025 (2012). Police are permitted to make pretextual stops, *see* Whren v. United States, 517 U.S. 806 (1996); Atwater v. City of Lago Vista, 532 U.S 318 (2001), an as many commentators have noted, traffic codes "provide[] an officer with a reason to stop virtually anyone." Joh, *supra* note 57, at 210.

61 *Id.* at 229 (arguing that there will always be some exercise of police discretion on some level).

62 *Id.* at 221–23.

CHAPTER 7

1 Carpenter v. United States, 138 S.Ct. 2206, 2235 (Thomas, J., dissenting) (2018) (internal citation omitted).

2 *See id.* at 2220.

3 *See* City of Los Angeles v. Lyons, 461 U.S. 95, 105 (1983). In order to allege a justiciable case or controversy in such a civil suit, a defendant has to assert "a real or immediate threat that he would again" suffer a Fourth Amendment violation at the hands of the plaintiff.

4 *See, e.g.,* Pearson v. Callahan, 555 U.S. 223, 244 (2009).

5 United States v. Miller, 425 U.S. 435 (1975).

6 Smith v. Maryland, 442 U.S. 735 (1979).

7 Smith, 442 U.S. 735, 750 (1979) (Marshall, J., dissenting).

8 *Id.* at 748 (1979) (Stewart, J., dissenting).

9 *See* Andrew Guthrie Ferguson, *The Internet of Things and the Fourth Amendment of Effects*, 104 Cal. L. Rev. 805, 807–8 (2016).

10 Quon v. Arch Wireless Company, 529 F.3d 892, 905 (9th Cir. 2008).

11 United States v. Warshak, 631 F.3d 266, 274–75 (2010).

12 *Id.* at 284.

13 United States v. Jones, 565 U.S. 400, 417–18 (2012) (Sotomayor, J., concurring) (citations omitted). We will discuss the third-party doctrine at greater length in Chapter 7.

14 Klayman v. Obama, 957 F.Supp. 2d 1, 43 (D.D.C. 2013). The circuit court later vacated the district court judge's ruling, and eventually the district court dismissed the case for lack of standing.

15 *See* Stephen E. Henderson, *Learning from All Fifty States: How to Apply the Fourth Amendment and Its State Analogs to Protect Third Party Information from Unreasonable Search*, 55 Cath. U. L. Rev. 373 (2006).

16 State v. Hunt, 91 N.J. 338 (1982).

17 *See* State v. McAllister, 184 N.J. 17 (2005); State v. Reid, 194 N.J. 386 (2008).

18 138 S.Ct. 2206 (2018).

19 Cell site location information is routinely generated by every cell phone. Even when cell phones are not in use, they are continuously "pinging" nearby cell phone towers so that the wireless network knows which cell tower is best able to make a connection with the phone.

20 *Id.* at 2219.

21 *Id.* at 2220.

22 *See* Orin Kerr, *The Case for the Third-Party Doctrine*, 107 Mich. L. Rev. 561, 563 n.5 (2009) (noting that "[a] list of every article or book that has criticized the doctrine would make this the world's longest law review footnote," and then citing eleven of the most prominent critiques of the doctrine).

23 *Id.* at 563–4 (citations omitted).

24 *Id.* at 575.

25 *Carpenter*, 138 S.Ct. at 2219.

26 565 U.S. 400 (2012).

27 *See Law Enforcement Access to Third Party Records*, in ABA Standards for Criminal Justice (3d Ed.), at 19–20, available at www.americanbar.org/content/dam/aba/publications/crim inal_justice_standards/third_party_access.authcheckdam.pdf (last visited Jan. 21, 2019).

28 *Id.* at 91, 99–100.

29 *Id.* at 6. The report also notes that the large number of records kept by business entities represents a "much more significant threat to privacy" than information held by individuals. While this is certainly true, it is not a principled reason to create one set of rules for individuals and one set of rules for corporations. Although the massive amounts of information held by corporations do, in the aggregate, contain more private information than the information held by individuals, individuals can still obtain extremely private information about others, and it is unclear why, under the ABA Committee's regime, such information should be exempt from Fourth Amendment protection.

30 Kiel Brennan-Marquez, *Fourth Amendment Fiduciaries*, 84 Ford. L. Rev. 611, 616 (2015).

31 *Id.* at 649–55.
32 *Id.*
33 *Id.*
34 532 U.S. 67 (2001).
35 376 U.S. 483 (1964).
36 Brennan-Marquez, *supra* note 30, at 623–33.
37 Vernonia School District 47J v. Acton, 515 U.S. 646 (1995).
38 Skinner v. Railway Labor Executives Association, 489 U.S. 602 (1989).
39 United States v. Matlock, 415 U.S. 164 (1974); Illinois v. Rodriguez, 497 U.S. 177 (1990). Of course, if another co-tenant of the property objects at the same time as the first consents, the consent is invalid unless the objecting co-tenant has been removed from the location. Georgia v. Randolph, 547 U.S. 103 (2006); Fernandez v. California, 134 S.Ct. 1126 (2014).
40 *See, e.g.*, Brennan-Marquez, *supra* note 30 at 644–45.
41 Ferguson v. South Carolina, 532 U.S. 67, 82–85 (2001). Brennan-Marquez acknowledges that his fiduciary doctrine was not the reason the Supreme Court reached its conclusion in *Ferguson*, but he criticizes the decision on the grounds that the transmission of the information from the patient to the doctor was voluntary, so under the Court's doctrines it should not be considered a search. Brennan-Marquez, *supra* note 30 at 624–26. But the South Carolina law in question required doctors to turn over the drug test results to the police, which transformed the fundamental nature of the interaction between the patients, the doctors, and law enforcement. Thus, according to the Supreme Court, the doctors were not acting as private parties, or even as "state actors" because they worked at a public hospital; they were acting as agents of law enforcement and collecting the information for law enforcement purposes. *Ferguson*, 532 U.S. at 80.
42 Stoner v. California, 376 U.S. 483, 488 (1964). Again, Brennan-Marquez acknowledges the Court's reasoning, and concedes that there is no "logical contradiction" between the argument that the hotel manager retains the right to enter the room himself as part of his business duties, but has no right to let others (be they private parties or law enforcement) into the room. Brennan-Marquez, *supra* note 30, at 631–33. But Brennan-Marquez argues that a more "plausible" explanation for the result in *Stoner* is a broader interpretation that hotel managers could *never* turn over information to law enforcement, even if they initially entered the room and found the incriminating evidence independent of any law enforcement interaction. *Id.* This interpretation fits in well with his fiduciary doctrine, but it is a very ambitious reading of the case.
43 There are some exceptions to this general rule, such as confidential information shared with a doctor or a lawyer. This is perhaps what makes *Fernandez* such a compelling case to support the fiduciary doctrine – it seems intuitive that doctors will not voluntarily give your medical information to others and there are even statutory regimes that prevent it. But this type of confidential information is the exception, not the rule; just like it is misleading to extrapolate the shared property cases to all shared information cases, it is also misleading to extrapolate the doctor/patient relationships to *all* commercial relationships.
44 ABA Law Enforcement Access, *supra* note 27, at 3–4.
45 *See* Andrew Guthrie Ferguson, *The Internet of Things and the Fourth Amendment of Effects*, 104 CAL. L. REV. 805 (2016).

46 Christine Hauser, *In Connecticut Murder Case, a Fitbit Is a Silent Witness*, THE N.Y. TIMES, Apr. 27, 2017.

47 *Id.*

48 Jon Mitchell, *Here Are 20 Companies Who Sell Your Data (& How To Stop Them)*, readwrite, Apr. 26, 2012, https://readwrite.com/2012/04/26/here-are-20-companies-who-sell-your-data-how-to-stop-them/. (last visited Jan. 21, 2019) (Acxiom, RapLeaf, Spokeo, PrivateEye, Radaris, Been Verified).

49 *See* Bernard Marr, *Where Can You Buy Big Data? Here Are the Biggest Consumer Data Brokers*, FORBES, Sep. 7, 2017 at www.forbes.com/sites/bernardmarr/2017/09/07/where-can-you-buy-big-data-here-are-the-biggest-consumer-data-brokers/#63118e26c278. (last visited Jan. 21, 2019). The largest data broker, Acxiom, as claims that it has data on "all but a small percentage" of American households. *Id.*

50 Privacy International filed complaints under the GDPR against consumer marketing data brokers Acxiom & Oracle. Privacy International also filed a complaint against Experian and Equifax, and AdTech data brokers Quantcast, Tapad, and Criteo; *see* www.huntonprivacyblog.com/2018/11/13/privacy-advocacy-organization-files-gdpr-complaints-data-brokers/ (last visited Jan. 21, 2019). Meanwhile, privacy advocates like EPIC, the Center for Digital Democracy, Consumer Watchdog, Patient Privacy Rights, U.S. PIRG, and the Privacy Rights Clearinghouse claimed victory after asking the FTC to block Facebook's proposed privacy policy changes in 2013. The advocates claimed that the changes would make it easier to use users' data for advertising.

51 The sole exception appears to be a brief discussion in Orin Kerr's article defending the third-party doctrine, in which he gives a number of examples of companies fighting subpoenas on behalf of their customers. As Professor Kerr notes, "[p]rotecting customer privacy is good for business." Kerr, *supra* note 22, at 598.

52 Alderman v. United States, 394 U. S. 165, 394 U. S. 174 (1969) ("Fourth Amendment rights are personal rights which, like some other constitutional rights, may not be vicariously asserted.")

53 *See, e.g.*, Oklahoma Press v. Walling, 327 U.S. 186 (1946) (holding that corporations have no rights under the Fifth Amendment); United States v. Morton Salt Co., 338 U.S. 632, 652 (1950) (stating that "corporations can claim no equality with individuals in the enjoyment of a right to privacy").

54 *See* Wayne R. LeFave, Search and Seizure: A Treatise on the Fourth Amendment at § 4.13 (d) (5th ed. West 2012) ("In the reported cases, most of the subpoenaed documents are business records or tax-related documents.")

55 Microsoft Corp. v. U.S., 829 F.3d 197 (2nd Cir. 2016) (Microsoft refused to help agents in an investigation of drug traffickers by denying agents access to emails on computer servers in Dublin).

56 In re information associated with one Yahoo email address that is stored at premises controlled by Yahoo, No. 17-M-1234, 1235, 2017 WL 706307 (E.D. Wis. Feb. 21, 2017) (Yahoo did not originally comply with the warrant).

57 201 U.S. 43 (1906).

58 *Id.* at 74.

59 *See, e.g.*, Oklahoma Press v. Walling, 327 U.S. 186 (1946); United States v. Morton Salt, 338 U.S. 632, 652 (stating that "corporations can claim no equality with individuals in the enjoyment of a right to privacy.")

60 See v. City of Seattle, 387 U.S. 541, 545 (1967); *see also* Camara v. Municipal Court, 387 U.S. 523 (1967).

61 Colonnade Catering Corp v. United States, 397 U.S. 72 (1970); United States v. Biswell, 406 U.S. 311 (1972).

62 *Id.* at 316.

63 New York v. Burger, 482 U.S. 691, 702–4 (1987).

64 *Id.*

65 City of Los Angeles v. Patel, 135 S.Ct. 2443 (2015).

66 *Id.* at 2461 (Scalia, J., dissenting).

67 *Id.* at 2453–54.

68 Christopher Slobogin, *Subpoeanas and Privacy*, 54 DePaul L. Rev. 805, 839–40 (2005). In white collar crime cases, law enforcement use of subpoenas against corporate third-party record holders has always been routine. *See, e.g.,* United States v. Miller, 425 U.S. 435 (1976).

69 *See, e.g.,* In re Subpoena Duces Tecum, 228 F.3d 341 (4th Cir. 2000). Administrative agencies, such as the IRS or a state Medicaid Fraud Control Unit, can also issue subpoenas, though frequently the agency must petition a court in order to enforce the subpoena. *See* United States v. Morgan, 761 F.2d 1009 (4th Cir. 1985).

70 United States v. R. Enterprises, Inc., 498 U.S. 292, 301 (1991).

71 *Id.*

72 *See* LeFave, *supra* note 54, at § 4.13(d).

73 F.T.C. v. American Tobacco Co., 264 U.S. 298 (1924).

74 *See, e.g.,* In Re Grand Jury Proceedings: Subpoena Duces Tecum, 827 F.2d 301 (8th Cir. 1987).

75 Patel v. City of Los Angeles, 738 F.3d 1058, 1061 (9th Cir. 2013) (en banc) (Watford, J.) aff'd, 135 S. Ct. 2443.

76 *See* AirBnB v. City of New York, 2019 WWL 91990, 1/3/2019.

77 Certain rules or statutes may prohibit the third party from releasing the information to law enforcement – for example, if the third party has privileged information.

78 When the third party agrees to hand over the information, the third party is effectively waiving any Fourth Amendment rights it has to the information. The only legal difference between volunteering and consenting to a request is that law enforcement must take care to ensure that the third party does not turn into a state actor. If the third party conducts a search after being requested to do so by the government (for example, the government asks a private individual to become an informant), the target will have the same rights to object to the search as he or she would if the government itself conducted the search. Likewise, if the government routinely asks a third party to turn over information to the government, a court might find that the third party was de facto a state actor and allow the target to object to the third party's collection of the information. However, both of these alternatives do not affect the third party's rights to object to the information, only the target's rights to object.

79 442 U.S. 735 (1979).

80 Chris Jay Hoofnagle, *Big Brother's Little Helpers: How Checkpoint and Other Commercial Data Brokers Collect and Package Your Data for Law Enforcement*, 29 N.C. J. Int'l L. & Com. Reg. 595,

81 Barton Gellman & Laura Poitras, *U.S., British Intelligence Mining Data from Nine U.S. Internet Companies in Broad Secret Program*, THE WASH. POST, June 7, 2013. The NSA documents revealed that the PRISM program collected data from multiple corporate partners, including Microsoft, Yahoo, Google, Facebook, PalTalk, AOL, Skype, YouTube, and Apple. *Id.*

82 *See* Katie Benner & Eric Lichtblau, *U.S. Says It Has Unlocked iPhone without Apple*, THE N.Y. TIMES, Mar. 28, 2016.

83 *See* Hayley Tsukayama, *Amazon CEO Jeffrey Bezos: Debate between Privacy and Security Is "Issue of Our Age,"* THE WASH. POST, May 18, 2016.

84 *See* Amy B. Wang, *Can Alexa Help Solve a Murder? Police Think So – But Amazon Won't Give Up Her Data,*

85 *See* Mike Masnick, *Google Files Legal Challenge to Attorney General Jim Hood's Subpoenas*, TECHDIRT, December 19, 2014, at www.techdirt.com/articles/20141219/09440829488/google-files-legal-challenge-to-attorney-general-jim-hoods-subpoenas.shtml (last visited Jan. 21, 2019); Dale R. Kuykendall and Jeannette Youngblood, *Google Loses Bid to Avoid Compliance with Subpoena for User's Gmail Messages*, NATIONAL LAW REVIEW, Oct. 31, 2014, at www.natlawreview.com/article/google-loses-bid-to-avoid-compliance-subpoena-user-s-gmail-messages (last visited Jan. 21, 2019).

86 City of Los Angeles v. Patel, *Brief for Google Inc. as Amicus Curiae Supporting Respondents*, at 13–14 (citations omitted).

87 *See, e.g.*, Brennan-Marquez, *supra* note 30 at 613 (internal footnotes omitted).

88 *See, e.g.*, The Electronic Frontier Foundation, *Who Has Your Back? Government Data Requests 2017*, at www.eff.org/who-has-your-back-2017 (last visited Jan. 21, 2019).

CHAPTER 8

1 Olmstead v. United States, 277 U.S. 438, 474 (1928) (Brandeis, J., dissenting) (internal quotations omitted).

2 *See* Charles B. Craver, *Privacy Issues Affecting Employers, Employees, and Labor Organizations*, 66 LA. L. REV. 1057, 1068–70 (2006)(discussing employees' potential statutory protection from employers' use of hidden cameras in private places, such as lavatories or locker rooms, and hidden microphones that pick-up conversations between co-workers); Daniel R. Dinger, *Should Parents Be Allowed to Record a Child's Telephone Conversations When They Believe the Child Is in Danger?: An Examination of the Federal Wiretap Statute and the Doctrine of Vicarious Consent in the Context of a Criminal Prosecution*, 28 SEATTLE U. L. REV. 955, 968–89 (2005)(discussing the legality of parental electronic recording of children's telephone calls in the home); *see also* Shana K. Rahavy, *The Federal Wiretap Act: The Permissible Scope of Eavesdropping in the Family Home*, 2 J. HIGH TECH. L. 87, 95–98 (2003).

3 *See* United States v. Karo, 468 U.S. 705, 712 (1984) (describing a parabolic microphone as "capable of picking up conversations in nearby homes"); United States v. Infelise, No. 90 CR 87, 1991 U.S. Dist. LEXIS 17174, at *17 n.1 (N.D. Ill. Oct. 18, 1991) ("A parabolic microphone is a portable device that allows the listener to eavesdrop on all conversations that come within the range of the microphone."); Daniel J. Solove, *Reconstructing*

Electronic Surveillance Law, 72 GEO. WASH. L. REV. 1264, 1265 (2004)("parabolic microphones can record conversations at long distances.").

4 *See* David A. Harris, *Superman's X-Ray Vision and the Fourth Amendment: The New Gun Detection Technology,* 69 TEMP. L. REV. 1, 7–13 (1996)(describing the development of portable detectors which can "see" through clothing from a distance to detect guns); *see also* Steven G. Brandl, *Back to the Future: The Implications of September 11, 2001 on Law Enforcement Practice and Policy,* 1 OHIO ST. J. CRIM. L. 133, 149 (2003)(noting the use of low level x-rays that facilitate detection of weapons, explosives, drugs, and contraband under clothing).

5 *See* United States v. Denton, 775 F.3d 1214, 1218–19 (2014); *see also* Brad Heath, *New Police Radars Can "See" Inside Homes,"* USA TODAY, Jan. 19, 2015 at www.usatoday.com/story/news/2015/01/19/police-radar-see-through-walls/22007615/ (last visited Jan. 21, 2019).

6 *See generally* Seth F. Kreimer, *Truth Machines and Consequences: The Light and Dark Sides of "Accuracy" in Criminal Justice,* 60 N.Y.U. ANN. SURV. AM. L. 655 (2005).

7 In the 1960s the Supreme Court established that a "search and seizure" of intangibles (such as an oral conversation or electronic transmissions) implicated the Fourth Amendment to the same extent as a traditional, physical search. *See* United States v. Katz, 389 U.S. 347, 363 (1967) (Harlan, J. concurring) (enunciating the "reasonable expectation of privacy" test); *see also* Osborn v. United States, 385 U.S. 323, 330 (1966) (allowing use of a "wired" informer only if a warrant were first issued by a neutral magistrate); Berger v. New York, 388 U.S. 41, 63–64 (1967) (striking down a New York state law authorizing eavesdropping warrants as overbroad). Of course, exceptions may apply to the warrant requirement in the case of a physical search – such as a search incident to an arrest or hot pursuit – but none of these exceptions apply to the electronic monitoring of a premises.

Before *Katz,* the Court had consistently ruled that wiretapping or electronic eavesdropping in itself did not constitute a search. *See, e.g., Olmstead,* 277 U.S. at 438 (allowing wiretapping of a telephone without a warrant); Goldman v. United States, 316 U.S. 129 (1942) (allowing electronic eavesdropping of an office as long as the eavesdropping device did not infringe on the property rights of the defendant). Of course, the method that the government used in conducting the electronic eavesdropping could violate the Fourth Amendment. *See, e.g.,* Silverman v. United States, 365 U.S. 505 (1961) (prohibiting electronic eavesdropping when the eavesdropping device infringed on the defendant's property interest). It is also worth noting that although wiretapping was not a search under the Fourth Amendment, it was largely prohibited by statute under the Federal Communications Act of 1934. *See* 47 U.S.C. § 605 (1934).

8 *See, e.g.,* Ker v. California, 374 U.S. 23 (1964).

9 *See, e.g.,* Schmerber v. California, 384 U.S. 757 (1966); *see also infra* notes 69–89 and accompanying text.

10 *See* "Vayyar Sensors Can See through Walls and Help Detect Breast Cancer," CNBC, (Jan. 12, 2018) www.cnbc.com/2018/01/12/vayyar-sensors-can-see-through-walls-and-help-detect-breast-cancer.html (last visited Jan. 21, 2019) (describing radio-based surveillance systems in development which will allows the user to see through walls in so much detail that the machine can sense if a person inside has stopped breathing)

11 As of now, psychic investigatory techniques are the realm of science fiction – such as the "precognitives" that foresaw murders in the film MINORITY REPORT (Twentieth Century

Fox & Dreamworks, LLC 2002). But machines which can allegedly determine whether or not someone is lying have been around for a number of decades. And technology evolves quite rapidly. Less than a century ago the concept of placing tiny electronic bugs or undetectable video cameras into a residence to record the inhabitants' every word or action – or even the idea of cutting a person open or withdrawing fluid from their body to gather evidence – was the realm of science fiction, not serious jurisprudence.

12 *See, e.g.*, Benjamin Freed, "FBI Tells Local Reporters It Was Listening in on Phone Calls with Former DC Council Member," Washingtonian, (Aug. 22, 2013), www.washingtonian .com/2013/08/22/fbi-lets-local-reporters-know-it-was-listening-in-on-phone-calls-with-dis graced-dc-council-member/ (last visited Jan. 22, 2019) (discussing the wiretaps used in the bribery case against DC Councilmember Michael Brown); Tyler Lauretta, "Arizona Head Coach Sean Miller Will Not Coach Saturday Amid FBI Probe over Potential Bribe Caught on Wiretap," Business Insider, (Feb. 24, 2018) www.businessinsider.com/arizona-sean-miller-fbi-wiretap-2018-2 (last visited Jan. 22, 2019) (discussing allegations that a college football coach offered a bribe to entice a top recruit to attend his school).

13 388 U.S. 41 (1967).

14 N.Y. CRIM. PROC. § 813-A (1958) (*overturned by* Berger v. New York, 388 U.S. 41 (1967)).

15 *Id.*

16 *Id.*

17 *Berger*, 388 U.S. at 55–56.

18 *Id.* at 58–59.

19 *Id.* at 59.

20 *Id.* at 59–60.

21 *Id.* at 60.

22 *Id.* at 58–60.

23 In a traditional search, many innocent items of tangible property may be viewed or even handled by the government agents carrying out the search, but if they are ultimately left behind they are not seized. In contrast, when government agents listen to and/or record intangible property such as a conversation, the seizure occurs simultaneously with the search.

24 *See Berger* 388 U.S. at 71 (Black, J., dissenting) ("[I]t seems obvious to me that [the majority's] holding, by creating obstacles that cannot be overcome, makes it completely impossible for the State or the Federal Government ever to have a valid eavesdropping statute."); *id.* at 89–90 (Harlan, J., dissenting) ("Despite the fact that the use of electronic eavesdropping devices as instruments of criminal law enforcement is currently being comprehensively addressed by the Congress and various other bodies in the country, the Court has chosen, quite unnecessarily, to decide these cases in a manner which will restrict, if not entirely thwart, such efforts.").

25 *Id.* at 63. The Court softened this statement somewhat by citing four previous decisions had allowed electronic eavesdropping, but one of those cases was soon to be overruled by *Katz. See Goldman*, 316 U.S. at 129 (allowing use of an electronic eavesdropping device that did not penetrate the wall of the defendant). The "property-rights" based doctrine upon which this decision relied was renounced in *Katz*.

   The other three cases dealt with informants wearing wires for specific conversations, and thus had limited applicability to a *Berger*-type situation, where none of those being monitored had consented to the intrusion. *See* On Lee v. United States, 343 U.S. 747 (1952); Lopez v. United States, 373 U.S. 427 (1963); Osborn v. United States, 385 U.S. 323 (1966).

26 *See* 18 U.S.C. § 2510–22 (2000).

27 In 1986, Congress passed the Electronic Communications Privacy Act ("ECPA"), which amended Title III to include protections for electronic communications. The language of the ECPA tracked the "wire communication" provisions, setting the same high requirements for all interceptions of electronic communications.

28 *See* 18 U.S.C. § 2518(3)(c)

29 *See* 18 U.S.C. § 2518(5)

30 *See* 18 U.S.C. § 2518(4)(c).

31 *See* 18 U.S.C. § 2516.

32 *Id.*

33 Fuerzas Armadas de Liberacion Nacional Puertorriquena ("Armed Forces of Puerto Rican National Liberation").

34 *See* United States v. Torres, 583 F. Supp. 86, 91 (E.D. Ill. 1984). Between 1974 and 1983, the FALN carried out 130 bombings, causing extensive property damage as well as 6 deaths and 84 injuries in San Francisco, Chicago, and New York. *Id.*

35 *Torres*, 583 F. Supp. at 91–92.

36 *Id.* at 90.

37 *Id.* at 93. Based in part on information obtained from the monitoring of the first apartment, the government requested an order to monitor a second apartment as well. Over the six-month period, the FBI recorded 130 hours of videotapes. *Id.* at 94.

38 *Id.* at 88–89.

39 *Id.* at 104–5. The defendants had also moved to suppress the oral communications which had been intercepted, but that motion was denied. *Id.* at 105.

40 United States v. Torres, 751 F.2d 875, 885 (7th Cir. 1984). Before confronting the constitutional question, the *Torres* Court first confirmed that video surveillance was neither authorized nor regulated by any existing statute, since Title III and the ECPA only applied to oral, wire, and electronic interception. *Id.* at 877–82. The Court nevertheless held that Rule 41 of the Federal Rules of Criminal Procedure gave judges the power to issue such warrants. Thus, covert video surveillance was broadly authorized by Rule 41 and not regulated by any statute, so only the Fourth Amendment regulated this practice. Although this analysis was challenged by the concurrence in *Torres* and a handful of other courts, *see, e.g.*, United States v. Koyomejian, 946 F.2d 1450 (9th Cir. 1991), *overturned en banc by* United States v. Koyomejian, 970 F.2d 536 (9th Cir. 1992), it has now become the accepted law of every circuit court which has considered the question. *Torres*, 751 F.2d at 887.

41 751 F.2d 875 (1984).

42 *Id.* at 883 (citations omitted).

43 *Id.* at 883–84.

44 *Id.* at 884.

45 *Id.* (citations omitted).

46 *See supra* notes 22–23 and accompanying text.

47 *Torres,* 751 F.2d at 883.
48 United States v. Biasucci, 786 F.2d 504, 506–7 (2d Cir. 1986).
49 United States v. Cuevas-Sanchez, 821 F.2d 248, 249 (5th Cir. 1987).
50 United States v. Mesa-Rincon, 911 F.2d 1433, 1435 (10th Cir. 1990).
51 *Koyomejian,* 970 F.2d at 542.
52 United States v. Williams, 124 F.3d 411, 414 (3d Cir. 1997).
53 *See Williams,* 124 F.3d at 416 (3rd Cir. 1997); United States v. Falls, 34 F.3d 674, 680 (8th
    Cir. 1994); *Koyomejian,* 970 F.2d at 542; *Mesa-Rincon,* 911 F.2d at 1437 (10th Cir. 1990);
    Cuevas-Sanchez, 821 F.2d at 252 (5th Cir. 1987); *Biasucci,* 786 F.2d at 510.
    Only a spirited concurrence by Judge Kozinski of the Ninth Circuit – which has been all
    but ignored by subsequent cases – has questioned *Torres'* holding. *See* Koyomejian, 970
    F.2d 536, 542–51 (1992). Judge Kozinski argued that the "least intrusive means" require-
    ment has consistently been rejected by the Supreme Court in evaluating the constitution-
    ality of a search, since applying such a test "could raise insuperable barriers to the exercise
    of virtually all search-and-seizure powers." United States v. Martinez-Fuerte, 428 U.S. 543,
    557 n.12 (1976). *See also* Nadine Strossen, *The Fourth Amendment in the Balance:
    Accurately Setting the Scales Through the Least Intrusive Alternatice Analysis,* 63
    N.Y.U.L. Rev. 1173, 1176 (1988)("Of particular significance, the Court's [F]ourth
    [A]mendment balancing analyses have neither systematically evaluated the marginal law
    enforcement benefits of challenged searches and seizures, nor regularly incorporated the
    'least intrusive alternative' requirement, which is an integral component of other balan-
    cing tests.") For a discussion of cases which reject a "least intrusive means" analysis, *see*
    Koyomejian, 970 F.2d at 546–48 (Kozinski, J., concurring) (*citing* Cady v. Dombrowski,
    413 U.S. 433, 447 (1973); United States v. Sokolow, 490 U.S. 1 (1989); Colorado v. Bertine,
    479 U.S. 367, 374 (1987); United States v. Montoya de Hernandez, 473 U.S. 531, 542
    (1985); Block v. Rutherford, 468 U.S. 576, 591 n.11 (1984); Michigan v. Long, 463 U.S. 1032
    n.16 (1983)).
    Judge Kozinski also argued that a search need be "minimized" only in the sense that the
    warrant must particularly state the items to be seized and the executing officers may not exceed
    the scope of the warrant in conducting the search – there is no further requirement that the
    executing officer must conduct the search in a way which will avoid seeing items not covered
    by the warrant. *See Koyomejian,* 970 F.2d at 548–49 (Kozinski, J. concurring). He also pointed
    out that the requirement that the warrant specify the "particular offense" that the subject is
    suspected of committing is also unprecedented; neither the language of the Fourth Amend-
    ment nor the case law interpreting it supports such a declaration in the warrant. *Id.* at 548.
    Other elements of the *Torres* test are not unique to video surveillance. For example, the
    requirement that the warrant contain a "particular description of the type of communi-
    cation sought to be intercepted," *Torres,* 751 F.2d at 883, is simply an adaptation of the
    language of the Fourth Amendment itself: that the warrant must "particularly describe the
    place to be searched, and the persons or things to be seized." U.S. Const. amend. IV.
    There is an argument that two of the other Title III factors are based on the Supreme
    Court's *Berger* decision: the description of a "particular offense" and the 30-day time limit.
    See Mesa-Rincon, 911 F.2d at 1439; Kent Greenfield, Comment, *Cameras in Teddy Bears:
    Electronic Video Surveillance and the Fourth Amendment,* 58 U. Chi. L. Rev. 1045,
    1051–52 (1991).

When Torres first adopted the Title III safeguards as a constitutional standard, the court seemed to regard any potential problems with such an action as harmless error. As Judge Posner wrote in Torres: "[w]e doubt the government will resist [our] view, for there will be few if any cases where it does not try anyway to conform its application for a television-surveillance warrant to Title III. It wants the sounds as well as the sights, and it can get a warrant for the former only by complying with Title III." United States v. Torres, 751 F.2d 875, 885 (7th Cir. 1984). Nearly all of the other video surveillance cases which import the Title III requirements agree, essentially arguing that the government will always be forced to meet these standards in situations when they use video surveillance. See, e.g., United States v. Koyomejian, 970 F.2d 536, 551 (9th Cir. 1992) (Kozinski, J., concurring) ("The constraints imposed by the court and other circuits thus not only had no practical effect on the cases at issue, but practically no effect on the world at large.").

This is not necessarily true. In the first place, there are a number of cases in which the government might use video surveillance but not use the audio surveillance. For example, in People v. Teicher, a New York state case, the defendant, who was a dentist, was charged with sexually assaulting his patients while they were under anesthesia. 422 N.E.2d 506 (N.Y. 1981). The government used both video surveillance and audio surveillance, but the only useful evidence came from eyewitness testimony and the videotape, since the audiotape contained "little of an inculpatory nature." Id. at 512. Likewise in many of the federal video surveillance cases, the government argues in its own warrant applications that audio surveillance would not be useful – for example, in Torres the government explained that the defendants, aware that their safe house might be bugged, would build bombs in silence, play music loudly while talking, or speak in code. Torres, 751 F.2d at 877. In Mesa-Rincon, the government did not even apply for an order to intercept oral communication, since the noise of the counterfeiting machines allegedly drowned out all conversation. See Mesa-Rincon, 911 F.2d at 1444. In short, there are many cases in which the government might conceivably apply for video surveillance and not audio surveillance, and thus the courts' importation of Title III into the Fourth Amendment has a very real impact.

54 *Teicher*, 422 N.E.2d 506, 513–515 (N.Y. 1981) (dentist sexually assaulting patients).

55 Ricks v. Maryland, 537 A.2d 612, 620 (Md. 1988).

56 374 U.S. 23 (1963). Five years prior to *Ker*, the Supreme Court held that under 18 U.S.C. § 3109, federal agents were required to knock and announce their intentions before entering an apartment. *See* Miller v. United States, 357 U.S. 301, 313 (1958). However, that case was based only on statutory law which only covered federal agents, and did not address the question of whether the Fourth Amendment regulated "no-knock" entries.

57 514 U.S. 927 (1995).

58 *Id.* at 929.

59 *Id.* at 934; *see also id.* at 936 ("We simply now hold that although a search or seizure of a dwelling might be constitutionally defective if police officers enter without prior announcement, law enforcement interests may also establish the reasonableness of an unannounced entry.")

60 *Id.* at 935–36.

61 *Id.* at 936 (citing *Ker*, 374 U.S. at 40–41). The Court also cites a California Supreme Court case in support of this exception.

62 *See* Torres, 751 F.2d at 884 ("Each of these four requirements is a safeguard against electronic surveillance that picks up more information than is strictly necessary and so violates the Fourth Amendment's requirement of particular description.")

63 *Id.* at 936.

64 Richards v. Wisconsin, 520 U.S. 385, 389–90 (1997).

65 *Id.* at 389–90. The Wisconsin Supreme Court had held in 1994 that as long as the police have a search warrant in a felony drug case, they necessarily have reasonable cause to believe exigent circumstances exist. State v. Stevens, 181 511 N.W.2d 591 (Wis. 1994), *cert. denied,* 515 U.S. 1102 (1995).

66 *Richards,* 520 U.S. at 393.

67 *Id.* at 394 (citations omitted).

68 *See* United States v. Bullock, 71 F.3d 171, 175–76 (5th Cir. 1995) (taking hair samples not a search); Davis v. Mississippi, 394 U.S. 721, 727 (1969) (explaining that detention to collect fingerprints does not necessarily violate the Fourth Amendment). As we will see below, this definition becomes problematic when we move into the area of DNA analysis.

69 Birchfield v. North Dakota, 136 U.S. 2160 (2016).

70 *See, e.g.,* Skinner v. Railway Labor Executives' Assn., 489 U.S. 602, 617 (1989) (noting in dicta that a warrant is usually required in criminal cases before the state can take a urine test).

71 *Id.*

72 *See Schmerber v. California,* 384 U.S. 757 (1966) (extracting blood); Winston v. Lee, 470 U.S. 753 (1985) (government sought to perform surgery to remove a bullet lodged in defendant). *See generally* Rochin v. California, 342 U.S. 165, 172 (1952) (holding that forced stomach pumping "shocks the conscience" and thus violates the Due Process Clause of the 14th Amendment). Recently in County of Sacramento v. Lewis, 523 U.S. 833, 849 n.9, the Supreme Court noted that *Rochin* was decided before the Fourth Amendment had been incorporated into the Fourteenth Amendment, and that today the case would be decided under the Fourth Amendment, albeit with the same result. *See also infra* notes 73–87 and accompanying text.

73 *Schmerber,* 384 U.S. at 759 n.2.

74 *Id.* at 758–59.

75 *Id.* at 759. The Court also considered (and rejected) Schmerber's claim that the forced blood test violated his rights under the Due Process clause, his right against self-incrimination, and his right to counsel. *Id.* at 759–66.

76 *Id.* at 767–68.

77 *Id.* at 768.

78 The Court noted there was probable cause for the arrest because the officer smelled liquor on the defendant's breath and his eyes were bloodshot, watery, and glassy. *Id.* at 768–69. The Court later concluded that these facts also "suggested the required relevance and likely success of a test of petitioner's blood for alcohol" – in other words, probable cause for the search itself. *Id.* at 770.

79 The Court held that an exception to the warrant requirement applied since the evidence would have disappeared during the delay necessary to obtain a warrant. *Id* at 770–71.

80 *Id.* at 771.

81 *Id.* (citation omitted).

82 *Id.* at 771–72. More recent cases involving drawing blood, such as *Missouri v. McNeely*, 569 U.S. 141 (2013) and *Birchfield v. North Dakota* 136 S.Ct. 2160 (2016) have analyzed the search under the exigent circumstances exception doctrine rather than as a hyper-intrusive search. The exigent search doctrine, however, still requires a case-by-case factual assessment and a balancing test between the needs of law enforcement and the privacy rights of the defendant.

83 470 U.S. 753 (1985).

84 *Id.* at 755–56.

85 *Id.* at 759.

86 *Id.* at 760–63.

87 *Id.* at 763.

88 *See, e.g.,* United States v. Nicolosi, 885 F.Supp. 50, 55–56 (1995 E.D.N.Y.); *Vickers*, 38 F. Supp. 2d at 167 (balancing the defendant's right to bodily integrity against numerous other factors, including the probative value of the evidence, the invasiveness of the procedure, and the risk of pain, injury, or embarrassment).

89 Nicolosi, 885 F.Supp. at 55.

90 Riley v. California, 134 S.Ct. 2473, 2488–9 (2014).

91 *Id.* at 2489.

92 *Id.* at 2490.

93 *Id.*

94 Government agents may conduct "routine" searches and seizures of persons and property without a warrant or any individualized suspicion. Almeida-Sanchez v. United States, 413 U.S. 266, 272–73 (1973); United States v. Montoya de Hernandez, 473 U.S. 531, 538 (1985).

95 United States v. Ramsey, 431 U.S. 606, 620 (1977).

96 See, e.g., United States v. Kolsuz 890 F.3d 133 (4th Cir. 2018). Not all circuit courts agree with this broadening of *Riley*. See, e.g., United States v. Touset, 890 F.3d 1227 (11th Cir. 2018);

97 Winston v. Lee, 470 U.S. 753, 764–65 (1985).

98 In 2014, then-Judge Gorsuch of the Tenth Circuit considered the constitutionality of a hand-held radar device that police used when exercising an arrest warrant. The device tells police whether anyone is inside the home, where they are inside the home, and whether or not they are moving. According to Judge Gorsuch's opinion:

> The government brought with it a Doppler radar device capable of detecting from outside the home the presence of "human breathing and movement within." All this packed into a hand-held unit "about 10 inches by 4 inches wide, 10 inches long." The government admits that it used the radar before entering – and that the device registered someone's presence inside. It's obvious to us and everyone else in this case that the government's warrantless use of such a powerful tool to search inside homes poses grave Fourth Amendment questions. New technologies bring with them not only new opportunities for law enforcement to catch criminals but also new risks for abuse and new ways to invade constitutional rights. See, e.g., Kyllo v. United States, 533 U.S. 27, 33–35, 121 S.Ct. 2038, 150 L.Ed.2d 94 (2001) (holding that using warrantless thermal imaging to show activity inside a home violated the Fourth Amendment). Unlawful searches can give rise not only to civil claims but may require the suppression of evidence in criminal proceedings. We have little doubt that the radar device

deployed here will soon generate many questions for this court and others along both of these axes.

　　United States v. Denson, 775 F.3d 1214, 1218 (10th Cir, 2014). In the *Denson* case, the Tenth Circuit held that the use of the device was constitutional because the police had an arrest warrant and other evidence already gave them reason to believe that Denson was inside the home; thus, the device was only used to ensure the safety of the officers. But in most other contexts, the use of this device would violate *Kyllo* and qualify as a hyper-intrusive search.

99　899 F.2d 1324 (2d Cir. 1990).

100　*Id.* at 1330–31.

101　*Id.* at 1335.

102　*Id.*

103　*Id.* at 1336.

104　*Id.* at 1336–37.

105　*Id.* at 1337. In keeping with the standard criteria for hyper-intrusive searches, the *Villegas* court noted that the covert "seizure" of photographs was neither continuous nor indiscriminate, and thus was less intrusive than audio or video surveillance.

106　*Id.*

107　United States v. Heatley, 1998 U.S. Dist. LEXIS 15207 (S.D.N.Y. Sep. 30, 1998).

108　*Id.* at *17.

109　*Id.* at *19.

110　*Id.* at *21.

111　*Id.* Although the court says that Title III was imported into "other contexts" (plural), it only cites cases from a single context.

112　*Id.*

113　*Id.* at *22–*23. The case was later transferred to a different judge, who ruled that the Title III safeguards were inapplicable, because he believed that the mail search was "a conventional rummaging through papers for evidence that is in the mainstream of Fourth Amendment jurisprudence." United States v. Heatley, 41 F. Supp. 2d 284, 290 (S.D.N.Y. 1998).

114　Skinner v. Ry. Labor Execs. Ass'n, 489 U.S. 602, 616–17 (1989); Maryland v. King, 569 U.S. 435, 446 (2013).

115　*See, e.g.,* State v. Athan, 158 P.3d 27.37 (Wash 2007 (en banc); Williamson v. State, 993 A. 2d 626, 641–42 (MD Ct. App. 2010) (finding that DNA testing of the DNA of DNA on a cup the defendant discarded did not violate the Fourth Amendment); People v. Gallego, 190 Cal.App.4th 388, 395 (3d. Dist. CA 2010) (holding that the DNA testing of material on a cigarette butt that the defendant had abandoned was not a "search" under the Fourth Amendment); Raynor v. State, 99 A.3d 753, 759 (MD Ct. App. 2014) (finding that testing of DNA material defendant left on a chair was not a "search" under the Fourth Amendment).

116　King, 569 U.S. at 465–66.

117　*Id.* at 448 (citations and internal quotations omitted).

118　*Id.* at 463–4.

119　*Id.* at 449.

120　*Id.* at 449–61.

121 *See, e.g.*, Tracey Maclin, *Maryland v. King: Terry v. Ohio Redux*, 2013 SUP. CT. REV., 359 (2013).

122 *Id.* at 469 (Scalia, J., dissenting).

123 *See, e.g.*, Tracey Maclin, *Government Analysis of Shed DNA Is a Search Under the Fourth Amendment*, 48 TEX. TECH. L. REV., 287, 304–5 (2015)(hereinafter Maclin, *Government Analysis*).

124 Schmerber, 384 U.S. at 771.

125 Skinner, 489 U.S. at 616–7.

126 Birchfield v. North Dakota, 136 S.Ct. 2160 (2016).

127 *See* James Randerson,*What DNA Can Tell Us*, The Guardian, Apr. 26, 2008, www .theguardian.com/science/2008/apr/27/genetics.cancer (last visited Jan. 21, 2019); Jacque Wilson, 5 *Cool Things DNA Testing Can Do*, CNN, Apr. 25, 2013, www.cnn.com/2013/04/ 25/health/national-dna-day-tests/index.html (last visited Jan. 21, 2019).

128 Kyllo v. United States, 533 U.S. 27 (2001).

129 As with any other privacy cost under the cost–benefit analysis theory, this cost should ultimately be measured empirically.

130 There is also an argument that courts should impose a least intrusive means requirement, and require the government to demonstrate that there is no other way to solve the cold cases contained in the DNA database other than to use the suspect's DNA. In other words, if the unsolved cases have fingerprint evidence, the police should first submit a suspect's fingerprint evidence to see if the suspect's fingerprints match the fingerprints from the unsolved case. However, because this use of DNA evidence is effectively a binary search, as mentioned below, there is no need to use the least intrusive means requirement.

131 *See* King, 569 U.S. at 474–5 (Scalia, J., dissenting).

132 *Id.* at 466.

133 CODIS-NDIS Statistics, FBI, www.fbi.gov/about-us/lab/codis/ndis-statistics (last updated Oct. 2018) (last visited Jan. 21, 2019).

134 Antonio Regalado, 2017 Was the Year Consumer DNA Testing Blew Up, MIT Technology Review, Feb. 12, 2018, www.technologyreview.com/s/610233/2017-was-the-year-con sumer-dna-testing-blew-up/ (last visited Jan. 21, 2019). There are over ninety direct-to-consumer genetic testing companies in the United States. Amy Dockser Marcus, *What Consumers Should Know About Commercial DNA Testing*, THE WALL STREET JOURNAL, Sept. 14, 2018, www.wsj.com/articles/what-consumers-should-know-about-commer cial-dna-testing-1536952428 (last visited Jan. 21, 2019).

135 *See* Tim Arango, Adam Goldman, and Thomas Fuller, *To Catch a Killer: A Fake Profile on a DNA Site and a Pristine Sample*, THE N.Y. TIMES, Apr. 27, 2018 at www .nytimes.com/2018/04/27/us/golden-state-killer-case-joseph-deangelo.html (last visited Jan. 21, 2019).

136 Some commentators have shown understandable concern that even the junk DNA that is stored in the CODIS database could someday be linked to private traits, either because of a discovery that the genes in question caused certain traits or were commonly linked with genes that caused certain traits. *See, e.g*, Elizabeth E. Joh, *Reclaiming "Abandoned" DNA: The Fourth Amendment and Genetic Privacy*, 100 Nw. U. L. REV. 857, 870 (2006). As of now, however, no such links have been found. David H. Kaye, A *Fourth*

Amendment Theory for Arrestee Data DNA and Other Biometric Databases, 15 U. Pa. J. Const. L. 1095, 1145–50 & n. 299 (2013). Future advances in genetic sequencing may necessitate a change in the rules.

137 Maclin, *Government Analysis, supra* note 123 at 304–5.

138 *King*, 569 U.S. at 464–5.

139 Jennifer L. Doleac, *The Effects of DNA Databases on Crime*, 9 AEJ: Applied Economics 165, 167 (2017).

140 *Id.*

141 Kaye, *supra* note 136, at 1139–41. Professor Kaye proposes five conditions for his exception to be met: "1) the person legitimately is detained (or the data are acquired without confining the individual); (2) the process of collecting the data is not physically or mentally invasive; (3) collection proceeds according to rules that prevent arbitrary selection of individuals; (4) the biometric data are used only to establish or authenticate the true identity of a given individual or to link individuals to crime scenes; and (5) the authentication or intelligence-gathering system is valid, reliable, and effective." *Id.*
Professor Mary Leary proposes a similar restriction for DNA evidence: allowing for the warrantless seizure and testing of DNA for identification purposes, but requiring a court order if the government wishes to learn anything further from the DNA sample. *See* Mary Leary, *Touch DNA and Chemical Analysis of Skin Trace Evidence: Protecting Privacy While Advancing Investigations*, 26 Wm & Mary Bill Rts. J. 251, 284–5 (2017).

CONCLUSION

1 United States v. Knotts, 460 U.S. 276, 284 (1983).

2 United States Department of Justice, Bureau of Justice Statistics, Criminal Victimization 2016 (Dec. 2017, NCJ 251150) at www.bjs.gov/content/pub/pdf/cv16_sum.pdf.

3 United States Department of Justice, Federal Bureau of Investigation, 2016 Crime in the United States, Table 17, at https://ucr.fbi.gov/crime-in-the-u.s/2016/crime-in-the-u.s.-2016/tables/table-17 (hereinafter "2016 Crime Report").

4 *Id.*

5 On the federal level, there were 151,460 arrests in 2016 and 69,487 convictions, which means that 46 percent of arrests led to a conviction. *See* United States Department of Justice, Bureau of Justice Statistics, *Federal Justice Statistics, 2015–2016*, at 3, 10, at www.bjs.gov/content/pub/pdf/fjs1516.pdf (last visited Jan. 29, 2019). This ratio has varied between approximately 66 percent in 1994 to approximately 40 percent in 2013. *Id.* at 1.
Conviction rates are difficult to pin down at the state level, but a survey of different states indicates that most states ratio of convictions to arrests is similar to the federal number. For example, in New York State only 57 percent of arrests for violent felonies resulted in a conviction. *See* New York State Division of Criminal Justice Services, Data Source Notes, at www.criminaljustice.ny.gov/crimnet/ojsa/dispos/nys.pdf (last visited Jan. 29, 2019).

6 For 2016, the attrition was as follows: Violent crime: 5.7 million crimes reported by victims; 1.2 million crimes known to law enforcement; 530,000 arrests. Property crime: 16 million crimes reported by victims; 7.3 million crimes known to law enforcement, 1.3 million

arrests. *See* 2016 Crime Report, *supra* note 3. Estimating a generous 60 percent conviction rate for all felony arrests leads approximately 1.1 million felony convictions each year.

7 A famous saying usually attributed to Benjamin Franklin holds that "it is better that a hundred guilty persons should escape than that one innocent person should suffer." Benjamin Franklin, letter to Benjamin Vaughan, Mar. 14, 1785. – The Writings of Benjamin Franklin, ed. Albert H. Smyth, vol. 9, p. 293 (1906). Franklin was paraphrasing the British legal theorist William Blackstone, who said that "For the law holds, that it is better that ten guilty persons escape, than that one innocent suffer." William Blackstone, in his Commentaries on the Laws of England, 9th ed., book 4, chapter 27, p. 358 (1783, 1978). Blackstone himself may have been paraphrasing Voltaire, who stated that "'tis much more Prudence to acquit two Persons, tho' actually guilty, than to pass Sentence of Condemnation on one that is virtuous and innocent." Voltaire, *Zadig*, pg. 53 (1749, 1974). The ratio of guilty escapees to innocent incarcerated has apparently increased over the years. For a lengthy discussion of the many different ways in which this ratio has been used by courts and commentators, *see* Alexander Volokh, n *Guilty Men*, 146 U. PENN. L. REV. 173 (1997). As it turns out, our criminal justice system surpasses this ratio by a large margin. As noted in the text, about twenty million felonies go unpunished each year. On the other side of the equation, it is impossible to know the exact number of innocent persons who are punished by the criminal justice system, but by almost any measure the number is not very high. Most estimates of false convictions estimate a rate of between .5 percent and 1 percent per year. Even taking one of the highest estimates of 4 percent would mean that there are about 40,000 innocent individuals per year who are falsely convicted and punished, compared with the twenty million criminals who commit felonies each year and are not punished, which means that we let five hundred guilty persons escape justice for every one innocent person who suffers.

Of course, it is a terrible moral wrong whenever any individual is falsely accused of a crime. The high number of exonerations – just over two thousand in twenty-seven years – is dramatic and troublesome, but not statistically significant when trying to determine the correlation between conviction and actual guilt, given the fact that there are over one million felony convictions each year. *See Exonerations by Year and Type of Crime*, Nat'l Registry Exonerations, www.law.umich.edu/special/exoneration/Pages/Exoneration-by-Year-Crime-Type.aspx (last visited Jan. 21, 2019).

See Paul G. Cassell, *Overstating America's Wrongful Conviction Rate? Reassessing the Conventional Wisdom About the Prevalence of Wrongful Convictions*, 60 ARIZ. L. REV. 815 (2018) (estimating the wrongful conviction rate at between .016 percent and .062 percent); George Thomas, *Where Have All the Innocents Gone?* 60 ARIZ L. REV. 865 (2018) (estimating the wrongful conviction rate in North Carolina at between .125 percent and .5 percent); C. RONALD HUFF ET AL., CONVICTED BUT INNOCENT: WRONGFUL CONVICTION AND PUBLIC POLICY 55, 81 (1996)(estimating the national wrongful conviction rate at 0.5 percent); Morris B. Hoffman, *The Myth of Factual Innocence*, 82 CHI.-KENT L. REV. 663, 673 (2007)(using Innocence Project Data to estimate the wrongful conviction rate to be between .0016 percent and 1.95 percent); Marvin Zalman, *An Integrated Justice Model of Wrongful Convictions*, 74 ALB. L. REV. 1465, 1473 (2010) (estimating a wrongful conviction rate of felonies between 0.5 percent and 1 percent each year). Some estimates are higher, ranging from 4 percent all the way up to 10 percent.

See, e.g., Keith A. Findley, *Adversarial Inquisitions: Rethinking the Search for the Truth*, 56 N.Y. L. Sch. L. Rev. 911, 918 (2011)(estimating a false conviction rate of at least 0.5 percent and as high as 5 percent or more); D. Michael Risinger, *Innocents Convicted: An Empirically Justified Factual Wrongful Conviction Rate*, 97 J. Crim. L. & Criminology 761, 769–80 (2007)(suggesting that previous studies have over- and under-estimated the error rate, and predicting a "corrected" estimation of between 3.3 percent and 5 percent); Samuel R. Gross & Barbara O' Brien, *Frequency and Predictors of False Conviction: Why We Know So Little, and New Data on Capital Cases*, 5 J. Empirical Legal Stud. 927, 929–30 (2008)(discussing the frequency of false convictions and estimating a false conviction rate of up to ten percent); Virginia Hughes, How Many People Are Wrongly Convicted? Researchers Do the Math, Nat'l Geographic: Only Human (Apr. 28, 2014), http://phenomena.nationalgeographic.com/2014/04/28/how-many-people-are-wrongly-convicted-researchers-do-the-math/ (last visited Jan. 21, 2019) (estimating a 4.1 percent rate of false convictions). The number of false convictions may be higher if one is concerned with legal innocence rather than factual innocence. For example, in some cases the lack of adequate counsel may result in a conviction when a competent or less overworked defense attorney could have successfully made a suppression motion, or convinced the jury that reasonable doubt existed. *See* Roberts, *Unreliable Conviction, supra* note 1, at 580–85 (discussing the disparity of resources between defense counsels and prosecutors and the heavy case-load burden on defense attorneys). These types of false convictions, however, would not affect the actual correlation between the fact of the conviction and the fact of the defendant's guilt.

8 *See* Peter Wagner and Wendy Sawyer, Mass Incarceration: The Whole Pie 2018, Prison Policy Initiative, available at www.prisonpolicy.org/factsheets/pie2018.pdf (last visited Jan. 11, 2019).

9 *See, e.g.*, Mike C. Materni, *The 100-Plus-Year-Old Case for a Minimalist Criminal Law (Sketch of a General Theory of Substantive Criminal Law)*, 18 New Crim. L. Rev. 331 (2015); Darryl K. Brown, *Criminal Law's Unfortunate Triumph over Administrative Law*, 7 J.L. Econ. & Pol'y 657 (2011); Stuart P. Green, *Is There Too Much Criminal Law?*, 6 Ohio St. J. Crim. L. 737 (2009).

10 Scholars have proposed many possible solutions to this problem, such as strategically decriminalizing certain crimes, changing the incentive structure for prosecutors, and imposing less draconian sentences for all criminals. *See, e.g.*, Jerald L. Mosley, Decriminalizing Prostitution in Recognition of Fundamental Rights, Los Angeles Lawyer (2016); Improving the Indigent Defense Crisis Through Decriminalization, 70 Ark. L. Rev. 769 (2017); Barbara O'Brien, *A Recipe for Bias: An Empirical Look at the Interplay Between Institutional Incentives and Bounded Rationality in Prosecutorial Decision Making*, 74 Mo. L. Rev. 999 (2009); Eric S. Fish, *Prosecutorial Constitutionalism*, 90 S. Cal. L. Rev. 237 (2017); Ames Grawert & Priya Raghavan, *Criminal Justice Reform Must Start with Sentence Reform*, 31 Fed. Sent. R. 101 (2018); Jalila Jefferson-Bullock, *How Much Punishment is Enough?: Embracing Uncertainty in Modern Sentencing Reform*, 24 J. L. & Pol'y 345 (2016).

11 Justice Gorsuch described this problem in his *Carpenter* dissent:
    Even taken on its own terms, Katz has never been sufficiently justified. In fact, we still don't even know what its "reasonable expectation of privacy" test is. Is it supposed to pose

an empirical question (what privacy expectations do people actually have) or a normative one (what expectations should they have)? Either way brings problems. If the test is supposed to be an empirical one, it's unclear why judges rather than legislators should conduct it. Legislators are responsive to their constituents and have institutional resources designed to help them discern and enact majoritarian preferences. Politically insulated judges come armed with only the attorneys' briefs, a few law clerks, and their own idiosyncratic experiences. They are hardly the representative group you'd expect (or want) to be making empirical judgments for hundreds of millions of people. Unsurprisingly, too, judicial judgments often fail to reflect public views.

Carpenter v. United States, 138 S.Ct. 2206, 2265 (2018) (Gorsuch, J., dissenting) (citing the Slobogin & Schumacher surveys of reasonable expectation of privacy).

12 This is not true for every type of Fourth Amendment analysis. *See supra* notes 24–27 and accompanying text; Max Minzner, *Putting Probability Back into Probable Cause*, 87 TEX. L. REV. 913, 940 (2009) ("Currently, the Fourth Amendment is blind to the type of crime underlying the search.").

13 Had the caselaw evolved in a different way, courts may have considered these factors in determining whether a surveillance was "reasonable" under the Fourth Amendment. Instead, however, courts have chosen to essentially ignore these factors.

14 *See* Minnesota v. Carter, 525 U.S. 83, 97–98 (1998) (Scalia, J., concurring) ("In my view, the only thing the past three decades have established about the *Katz* test ... is that, unsurprisingly, those 'actual (subjective) expectation[s] of privacy' 'that society is prepared to recognize as "reasonable,"' bear an uncanny resemblance to those expectations of privacy that this Court considers reasonable. . . . [The Fourth Amendment] did not guarantee some generalized 'right of privacy' and leave it to this Court to determine which particular manifestations of the value of privacy 'society is prepared to recognize as "reasonable."' Rather, it enumerated ('persons, houses, papers, and effects') the objects of privacy protection to which the *Constitution* would extend, leaving further expansion to the good judgment, not of this Court, but of the people through their representatives in the legislature.") (citations omitted).

15 Olmstead v. United States, 277 U.S. 438, 466 (1928). Luckily, Congress stepped in to correct this mistake a few years later. *See* Communications Act of 1934, Pub. L. No. 416–73D, § 605, (codified as amended at 47 U.S.C. § 605 (2006)).

16 *See* Slobogin & Schumacher, *supra* note 139. at 738–41. Professors Slobogin and Schumacher's article lists the "average intrusiveness" level for dozens of different types of surveillance based on a survey and then notes "frequent contrasts" between the survey results and the Supreme Court rulings on what constitutes a search. In areas ranging from the use of undercover officers to reviewing of bank records to seizures of luggage on buses, the Court has apparently misjudged the actual level of privacy that society considers to be reasonable.

17 *Id.* at 743.

18 *See* 18 U.S.C. §§ 2516–2518 (2006).

19 *See* Pub. L. No. 99–508, 100 Stat. 1848 (1986).

20 *See* 18 U.S.C. §§ 2701–12 (2006).

21 *See* Pub. L. No. 95–511, 92 Stat. 1783 (1978).

22 *See* Pub. L. No. 107–56, 115 Stat. 272 (2001).

23 Part of the problem with legislation in this area is that there are many different statutes covering many different situations. A broader, more comprehensive piece of privacy legislation would be easier for law enforcement to follow and easier for courts to implement.

24 *See* Orin Kerr, *The Fourth Amendment and New Technologies: Constitutional Myths and the Case for Caution*, 102 MICH. L. REV. 801, 853, 864–77 (2004). *But see* LAWRENCE LESSIG, CODE AND OTHER LAWS OF CYBERSPACE 216 (1999)(arguing that courts must be counted on to apply consistent constitutional values to all types of surveillance).

25 Kerr, *supra* note 24, at 864–77.

26 For example, the Fourth Circuit warned against "wield[ing] the amorphous 'reasonable expectation of privacy' standard in a manner that nullifies the balance . . . struck by Congress in Title III," and affirmed that the "primary job of evaluating [new technologies'] impact on privacy rights and of updating the law must remain with . . . the legislature." United States v. McNulty (*In re* Askin), 47 F.3d 100, 105–6 (4th Cir. 1995). When the courts began looking for rules to regulate covert video surveillance, they showed even greater deference to Congress by adopting the exact standards that Congress set up to regulate wiretapping and holding that those same standards were mandated under the Fourth Amendment – essentially allowing the legislature to define the scope of Fourth Amendment protection in this area. *See, e.g.*, United States v. Torres, 751 F.2d 875, 885 (7th Cir. 1984) (explaining its intent to "borrow the warrant procedure of Title III, a careful legislative attempt to solve a very similar problem, and hold that it provides the measure of the government's constitutional obligation of particular description in using television to investigate crime").

Index